THE DARK SIDE OF FAMILIES

THE DARK SIDE OF FAMILIES

Current Family Violence Research

Edited by

DAVID FINKELHOR

RICHARD J. GELLES

GERALD T. HOTALING

MURRAY A. STRAUS

SAGE PUBLICATIONS
Beverly Hills / London / New Delhi

For information address:

SAGE Publications, Inc.
275 South Beverly Drive
Beverly Hills, California 90212

SAGE Publications India Pvt. Ltd.
C-236 Defence Colony
New Delhi 110 024, India

SAGE Publications Ltd
28 Banner Street
London EC1Y 8QE, England

Printed in the United States of America

Library of Congress Cataloging in Publication Data

Main entry under title:

The dark side of families.

Based on papers presented at the National Conference for Family Violence Researchers, Durham, N.H., 1981.
Bibliography: p.
1. Family violence—United States—Addresses, essays, lectures. 2. Wife abuse—United States—Addresses, essays, lectures. 3. Child abuse—United States—Addresses, essays, lectures. 4. Child molesting—United States—Addresses, essays, lectures. 5. Rape in marriage—United States—Addresses, essays, lectures.
I. Finkelhor, David
HQ809.3.U5F35   1982   306.8'7   82-21496
ISBN 0-8039-1934-4
ISBN 0-8039-1935-2 (pbk.)

FOURTH PRINTING, 1984

40,794

Contents

What Factors Shape Professional and Social Responses?

TO: Murray A. Straus

Dedicating a book to someone whose name appears as a co-editor is an unconventional gesture. We believe there is a sound explanation for this.

The field of family violence research, and three of the co-editors of this volume, owe a particular debt to Murray Straus. Murray was already a leading scholar in the field of family studies when he began his work on family violence. His own research blazed the trail for, and inspired the work of, most of the contributors to this volume. The volume itself grew out of a conference convened to mark the tenth anniversary of the University of New Hampshire Family Violence Research Program, which itself grew out of the work of Murray Straus.

We, the co-editors of this book were all trained by Murray Straus. We each could have chosen one of our own books to dedicate to him. But this book is the proper volume in which to make that dedication. We hope that Murray and the readers of this book will accept and understand this dedication.

David Finkelhor
Richard J. Gelles
Gerald T. Hotaling

Preface

This book has many names on the cover, still more names in the Table of Contents, and there are yet more people who helped make it possible. The book grew out of the National Conference for Family Violence Researchers held in Durham, New Hampshire in the summer of 1981. Nearly 160 researchers participated in that conference, and the quality of the presentations and discussion was high. We wish we could have included more of the papers in the present volume. Many had to be excluded only, because of space limitations and the fact that in some cases they did not fit readily into the ultimate organization of the volume. We want to thank all those who participated in the conference and all those who submitted papers for consideration. The quality of their work was the inspiration behind this book.

Several people played key roles in the preparation of the conference and the manuscript. The enterprise was set in motion by Richard Gelles, who first proposed holding a conference to take stock of where we are in research on family violence, and to mark the tenth anniversary of the Family Violence Research Program at the University of New Hampshire. Conferences, however, take more than ideas. There must also be a dedicated staff to handle an endless amount of paper, starting with 16 copies of a grant application and ending on that happy day when the final manuscript was put together for mailing to the publisher. No one could have done this better than Sieglinde Fizz, Ruth Miller, and Elaine Hashem.

Financial assistance for the conference and book came from two sources. The Elliott Trust Fund Committee of the University of New Hampshire provided the initial grant that allowed us to plan the conference. The Center for Crime and Delinquency at the National Institute for Mental Health provided a major portion of the funds that made the project possible. In particular we would like to thank Saleem Shah and Tom Lalley for enthusiastic support all the way through.

A special word is needed about the important role that was played in the whole project by Gerry Hotaling. Much of the positive reaction to the conference was due in no small part to his effort as conference coordi-

Editors' Note: *The names of editors of this volume are listed alphabetically to reflect their shared work on this project.*

nator. Through careful planning and attention to detail, he anticipated many of the potential problems and solved them before they arose. He put in long hours tracking down and communicating with conference participants. His efforts built a reservoir of good humor and goodwill that infused the proceedings.

Gerry also coordinated the assembly of this volume. His colleagues want to thank him for handling the correspondence, the phone contacts, and much of the dirty work that goes into putting a book like this together. Above all, we are indebted to him for the knowledge and theoretical insight which he brought to the editing of this book.

SECTION I

INTRODUCTION

This volume is a collection of writing by some of the best-known authorities on family violence and abuse. It contains not only some of the newest research and theoretical perspectives on family violence and abuse, but also articles from a wide range of academic disciplines. Contributors include sociologists, psychologists, psychiatrists, physicians, human developmental theorists, social work researchers, social policy researchers, and others. In addition to the diversity of its authors, this is one of the only works on this topic that pays attention to many of the forms family violence and abuse take. The book covers a broad spectrum of issues and controversies in wife abuse, child abuse, the sexual abuse of children, and marital rape. Two of these subjects, sexual abuse and marital rape, have not been widely researched or written about previously.

The selection of articles for this volume was guided by three broad objectives: first, to create a state-of-the-art volume on family violence and abuse; second, to crystallize the key interdisciplinary issues confronting family violence and abuse researchers; and third, to lay out a research agenda for the coming years.

Taken singly, the chapters are quite diverse. But the diversity is misleading. A number of common themes and issues are focused on in this volume. First, many chapters share the perspective that violence and abuse grow out of the nature of social arrangements. Second, even though many different forms of family violence and abuse are written about, several articles explore the commonalities and important etiological differences among these forms (Finkelhor, Chapter 1; Gelles, Chapter 9; Berkowitz, Chapter 10; Sebastian, Chapter 11; and Straus, Chapter 13). Relatedly, several articles examine the common effects of victimization across forms of family violence and abuse (Walker, Chapter 2; Sheilds and Hanneke, Chapter 8; Finkelhor and Yllo, Chapter 7; and Stark and Flitcraft, Chapter 21).

A third theme that runs through this volume is an expansion of research concern to groups other than victims of family violence and abuse. There are chapters that examine the individual and social characteristics of male perpetrators of both wife abuse and child abuse (Walker, Chapter 2; Fagan et al., Chapter 3; and Martin, Chapter 18) and chapters that focus on the attitudes and behaviors of professional groups concerned with the treatment of victims of family violence and abuse (Stark and Flitcraft, Chapter 21; and O'Toole and Turbett, Chapter 22). The motivations of those who conduct family violence research are also the focus of examination (Wardell et al., Chapter 4; and Washburne, Chapter 17).

Perhaps the most important shared aspect of this volume is the greater methodological diversity and attention to theoretical detail evidenced by the chapters. Compared to past research, the chapters included here reveal distinct signs of a more comprehensive social science approach to the study of family violence and abuse.

Past research on family violence has certainly not been atheoretical or devoid of methodological rigor. However, past research was primarily concerned with more pressing problems, such as definitions of terms like "violence" and "abuse" and establishing estimates of the prevalence of forms of family violence.

The state of family violence and abuse research during the 1970s was the focus of two recent review articles by Zigler (1979) and Gelles (1980). These authors concur that theoretical and methodological refinement is critical in the years ahead for progress in this field of study.

The more prominent recommendations made by Zigler (1979) and Gelles (1980) are the following:

(1) linking the study of forms of family violence and abuse to more well-established research literatures;
(2) the use of more nonclinical samples;
(3) increased diversity of measurement instruments, data collection techniques, and research designs; and
(4) systematic theory building and testing.

Based on these criteria, the chapters in this volume represent a step toward greater theoretical and methodological sophistication in research on family violence and abuse.

LINKS TO BETTER-ESTABLISHED RESEARCH LITERATURES

In an article directed to child abuse researchers, Zigler (1979) called for an expansion of theoretical horizons. He urged researchers to move from a view of abuse as an isolated phenomenon to one that orders data from better-developed research traditions. His remarks are just as applicable to research on other forms of family violence and abuse.

It is evident that the articles presented here reflect this advice. Authors have borrowed propositions from a number of theoretical perspectives and applied them to the family violence and abuse literature. For example, Berkowitz (Chapter 10) looks at family violence in light of his vast work in the social psychology of human aggression. Sebastian (Chapter 11) examines violence in families from work in the social psychology of aggression—specifically attraction theory and attribution theory. Herzberger (Chapter 20) takes a social cognitive approach to the issue of the cross-generational transmission of abuse. She pays particular attention to the merits of attribution theory for this issue. In an attempt to tie together findings from several forms of family violence and abuse, Gelles (Chapter 9) uses sociological propositions from exchange theory and social control theory. Burgess and Garbarino (Chapter 5) apply an evolutionary-biological perspective to tie together a number of disparate findings from the literature on child abuse. A model for the study of child sexual abuse is presented by Tierney and Corwin (Chapter 6), who borrow heavily from systems theory. O'Toole and Turbett (Chapter 2) apply propositions from societal reaction or labeling theory in their interpretation of the diagnostic behavior of medical personnel in cases of presumed child abuse.

THE USE OF NONCLINICAL SAMPLES

The use of samples consisting of only publicly identified cases of family violence and abuse can confound the search for causal explanation. As Gelles (1980) stated in his review article on family violence research:

> By using more nonclinical samples, researchers can begin to overcome the confusion that arises out of confounding factors which lead to public identification of family violence with those factors causally related to violent behavior in the home. (p. 883)

The exclusive use of samples of violent family members and victims from clinics, hospitals, and police and other societal agents may produce an incomplete data base on which to build explanations of family violence and abuse. It is interesting to note that articles reporting data from nonclinical samples produce some of the most controversial findings reported in the volume. They present a challenge to some so-called facts that are taken for granted in the violence and abuse literature. For example, Straus (Chapter 13), on the basis of data from over 2100 nationally representative families, presents evidence to suggest common causal factors related to violence against children regardless of the severity of the violence. His data suggest that spanking a child and abusing a child are part of the same continuum of violent actions. Herrenkohl et al. (Chapter 19) conducted a ten-year follow-up study of over 500 families composed of those publicly cited for child abuse and ones in which there was no reason to believe abuse was occurring. They dispute the notion that violence breeds violence. Their data reveal that parental neglect for the growth of self-esteem in children is a more critical factor than severe parental discipline in accounting for the use of violence when these children became adults. Greenblat (Chapter 14), in a number of intensive interviews with men and women about the "meaning" of violence in intimate relationships, presents a real challenge to the idea that norms play a significant role in approving the use of violence between family members.

INCREASED DIVERSITY OF RESEARCH DESIGNS, MEASUREMENT INSTRUMENTS, AND DATA COLLECTION TECHNIQUES

This volume represents a diversity of methodological approaches to the study of family violence and abuse. The "one-shot" survey still predominates, but there are some optimistic trends in the designs used by many of the authors included here.

Herrenkohl et al. (Chapter 19) utilize a longitudinal design analyzing data at two points in time over a ten-year period. Their findings are quite different from previous studies of this issue. Other articles show a broadening of methodological approaches. O'Toole and Turbett use an experimental design to investigate how social factors, especially race and socioeconomic status, affect the "typifications" of child abuse held by medical professionals.

Martin (Chapter 18) utilizes a content analysis of existing child abuse literature to investigate why mothers are so often characterized as the abusing parent in spite of evidence that males constitute a sizable portion—if not a majority—of perpetrators of child maltreatment.

Some of the articles outline a methodological approach for a macrosociological study of forms of family violence. Dobash and Dobash (Chapter 15) propose a context-specific approach to the study of wifebeating, paying attention to both situational factors and broader historical and institutional trends.

Yllo (Chapter 16) uses state-level indicators in her approach to the study of wife-beating. Rates of violence toward women are interpreted as a consequence of the status of women in particular American states. Her independent variable is measured by rates of female participation in various institutional realms. The same state-level approach is employed by Kalmuss and Straus (Chapter 23) in their attempt to account for variations in the provision of wife abuse services in American states.

SYSTEMATIC THEORY BUILDING AND TESTING

There are a number of efforts in this volume toward a program of theory building. Perhaps the best example is the work of Burgess and Garbarino (Chapter 5). These authors seek to explain a number of findings in the child abuse and neglect literature using propositions derived from evolutionary biology. Gelles (Chapter 9) distills a number of propositions from several theoretical traditions and applies them to a number of issues in family violence and abuse research.

These efforts are very important in ordering and understanding the growing number of facts about family violence and abuse. In conjunction with these efforts, several articles report research specifically designed to test competing propositions. By way of skillful statistical analyses, Berk (Chapter 12) tests two competing points of view for explaining the severity of injuries that result from husband-wife violence. Straus (Chapter 13) tests whether minor and severe forms of violence in the family are the result of common etiological factors or should be viewed as governed by unique causal variables. Greenblat (Chapter 14) tests for the existence of norms approving the use of violence between family members. Her article provides data which greatly assist in understanding the complexity of cultural norms in explaining violence in the home.

The theoretical and methodological questions raised about family violence and abuse research in the late 1970s have been asked again about the chapters in this volume. While the field still lacks well-developed theories about family, forms of violence and abuse, and society, there is evidence of a strong interdisciplinary borrowing of propositions and theories from established literatures. Methodologically, greater attention to the value of nonclinical samples and the use of a broader array of research designs that characterize many chapters in this volume bode well for family violence and abuse literature. It can only be hoped that this trend continues through the 1980s.

REFERENCES

Gelles, Richard J. Violence in the famfly: A review of research in the seventies. *Journal of Marriage and the Family,* 1980, *42*(4).

Hotaling, Gerald T., & Straus, Murray A. Culture, social organization, and irony in the study of family violence. Chapter 1 in Murray A. Straus & Gerald T. Hotaling (Eds.), *The social causes of husband-wife violence.* Minneapolis: University of Minnesota Press, 1980.

Zigler, E. Controlling child abuse in America: An effort doomed to failure?" In R. Bourne & E. H. Newberger (Eds.), *Critical perspectives on child abuse.* Lexington, MA: D. C. Heath, 1979.

1

Common Features of Family Abuse

DAVID FINKELHOR

There are actually very few professionals and researchers whose work reflects an interest in family violence and abuse as a whole. For the most part, one finds in this field people who concern themselves with either spouse abuse or child abuse or sexual abuse as individual problems, not all of them together.

If one looks around the country, one can see separate groups of people talking about, writing about, lobbying for, and intervening in each of these separate areas. Each problem has its separate set of agencies, separate set of theories, and separate history of how it was "discovered." Perhaps most seriously, in this day of waning public policy interest and waning public resources for social problems, there are sometimes bitter rivalries and political infighting among the proponents of these separate problems, as each tries to get policymakers to give priority to their particular kind of family abuse.

It may be important, both for the benefit of research and theory, and also to counteract some of the divisive tendencies, for researchers on the disparate forms of family violence to see what they can find in the way of commonalities. That is one of the purposes of this volume of research and theory devoted to the variety of forms of family violence. It is also the purpose of this introductory chapter, which will attempt to point out some of the insights to be found from examining the commonalities and also differences among forms of family violence and abuse.

Author's Note: *I would like to thank Carole Watkins for the idea behind this chapter, Ruth Miller and Lee Fraser for help in preparing the manuscript, and the members of the Family Violence Research Seminar for useful criticisms of a first draft. This work is supported by grants MH30939 and 34109 from NIMH. The Family Violence Research Program has a series of papers on topics related to family violence; a list of these can be obtained by writing to the Program Assistant.*

ABUSE AS ABUSE OF POWER

One commonality among forms of family abuse lies in the power dynamics of these situations. What we call abuse within the family is not simply aggression or injury committed by one family member against another. Family abuse is more precisely the abuse of power.

In part, this is the way abuse is defined. We do not classify as abuse the young child's lashing out at his mother when she deprives him of something he wants. We consider abuse to be a situation where a more powerful person takes advantage of a less powerful one.

Simple abuse of power is not even the full story. Even within the range of behaviors we define as abuse, the most common patterns in family abuse are not merely for the more powerful to abuse the less powerful, but for the most powerful to abuse the least. This is an interesting commonality: Abuse tends to gravitate toward the relationships of *greatest power differential.*

This principle is clearest in sexual abuse of children. The most widespread form of reported sexual abuse consists of abusers who are both male and in authority positions within the family victimizing girls in subordinate positions (Finkelhor, 1979, 1982c). This is a case of abuse across the axis of both unequal sexual power (males victimizing females) and unequal generational power (the older victimizing the younger). Abuse of boys by males appears to be much less common, and abuse of either boys or girls by female family members is extremely rare in comparison.

In physical child abuse a similar principle of the strongest victimizing the weakest operates. First, statistics show that the greatest volume of abuse is directed against the most powerless children, those under the age of six (Gil, 1979; Maden and Wrench, 1977; Straus, Gelles, and Steinmetz, 1980). Moreover, the statistics should also probably be interpreted to show the more common vulnerability to be at the hands of the more powerful parent—the father. Although raw statistics tend to show roughly equivalent numbers of pure incidents of physical child abuse committed by men and women (American Humane Association, 1978; Maden and Wrench, 1977), these figures are deceptive because they do not take into account the fact that women spend a great deal more time with children than do men. If we were to calculate vulnerability to abuse as a function of the amount of time spent in contact with a potential abuser, I think we would see that men and fathers are more likely to abuse.

In the case of spouse abuse, too, again the strongest are shown to victimize the weakest. Research by Straus et al. (1980), for example, shows that in families where a woman has less power by virtue of not being in the labor market, by virtue of being excluded from participation in decision making, and by virtue of having less education than her husband, she is at higher risk of abuse. Once again, abuse gravitates to the greatest power differential.

This suggests the need for more research on the dynamics of power and how it operates in facilitating all forms of family abuse.

ABUSE AS A RESPONSE TO
PERCEIVED POWERLESSNESS

Although family abuse is behavior of the strong against the weak, some people who have clinical experience with abusers sometimes find this an ironic description. Many abusers give a sense of being pathetic and ineffectual, not always people who would be described in objective terms as socially powerful.

This is another commonality among the different kinds of abuse: Although they are acts of the strong against the weak, *they seem to be acts carried out by abusers to compensate for their perceived lack of or loss of power.* In the cases of spouse abuse and the sexual abuse of children, this attempt to compensate is often bound up in a sense of powerlessness, particularly with regard to masculine ideals in our society. Men, it has been noted, often start to beat their wives when their wives try to assert themselves in some way or establish some degree of independence (Gelles, 1974). It has also been noted that men often start to sexually abuse their children when they are unemployed or failing financially or have suffered some other setback (Meiselman, 1978). Reflecting a similar theme, it has been observed that the physical abuse of children tends to start with a feeling of parental impotence (Spinetta and Rigler, 1972). Mothers resort to violence, for example, when they sense that they have lost control of their children and of their own lives.

These are all examples of the uses of abuse to compensate for a perceived lack or loss of power. However, the abuse may not always be instrumental (i.e., intended to restore power): it may also be expressive. Abuse can be a way of venting anger against another family member who is seen in some way as responsible for that loss of power. Or it can be a way of trying to regain control by using coercion or exploitation as the resource for having one's will carried out. In either case, the abuse is a response to perceived power deficit. I suggest that this as another interesting feature of power dynamics in family abuse that should receive greater theoretical attention.

SHARED EFFECTS ON VICTIMS

Another important way in which all family abuse is tied together is in the effect it has on its victims. There are striking similarities in how the victims of family abuse experience their situations. These characteristic responses stem in part from the nature of families and family relationships and do not occur to such an extent in victimization that occurs outside the family.

All forms of family abuse seem to occur in the context of psychological abuse and exploitation, a process victims sometimes describe as "brainwashing." Victims are not merely exploited or physically injured: their abusers use their power and family connection to control and manipulate victims' perceptions of reality as well. Thus abused children are told that they are bad, uncontrollable, and unlovable (Herbruck, 1979). Abused wives are persuaded by their husbands that they are incompetent, hysterical, and frigid (Walker, 1979). Sexually abused children are misled to believe that their father's sexual attentions are normal and testimony of his great and genuine affection (Armstrong, 1978).

This brainwashing that accompanies with family abuse is potent because families are the primary group in which most individuals construct reality. Family members often do not have enough contact with other people who can give them countervailing perceptions about themselves. The distortion of reality and self-image is generally one of the most devastating effects of family abuse.

One result of the psychological manipulation common among all types of family abuse is the tendency among victims to blame themselves. It is difficult for victims to avoid identifying with the rationalizations of the abuser in accounting for what is happening to them. They commonly see themselves as having provoked the abuse or having deserved it, no matter how severe or arbitrary the abuse seems to have been.

Thus it is not uncommon to hear abused women say things like, "I needed it," "I provoked him," "I was being a bad housekeeper and a bad mother" (Gelles, 1974). Among children one often hears, "My dad would lay into me but I needed it to keep me in line." Sexual abuse victims report thinking to themselves, "I must have been leading him on," "It was because my own needs for affection were so strong that I didn't make him stop." Although victims of violence and exploitation in other settings also blame themselves, it is particularly severe for victims in families, where the abuser is an influential person who has had a powerful effect on shaping a victim's perceptions.

One additional result of abuse in the family context is that many of the victims often maintain a rather incredible allegiance to their abusers in spite of all the damage they do. Many battered wives profess that they love their husbands, that they know their spouses really love them and that abuse is evidence of that (Gelles, 1974). Many victims of sexual abuse insist they are more angry at their mother for not protecting them than at their father who had sex with them for years despite their protestations (Herman and Hirschman, 1977). This attachment to the abuser is often combined with a belief that the abuse will stop if only the victim could reform herself. "If I could only be a better housewife," says the abused woman, "he would stop beating me" (Walker, 1979). "If I could only be a good little girl my father would stop punishing me," thinks the child.

Another common pattern among abuse victims is the extreme sense of shame and humiliation they harbor and the belief they have that other people could not possibly understand or identify with them. They often think they are the only ones who have undergone this kind of experience (Butler, 1978). They go to great lengths to keep it secret and often suffer from the sense of stigma and isolation.

In addition, there is a kind of entrapment that stymies the victims of all kinds of family abuse. The abuse often goes on over an extended period of time and the victims have difficulty either stopping it, avoiding it, or leaving entirely. This is one thing that people unfamiliar with family abuse are continually amazed by: victims of spouse abuse, child abuse, and sexual abuse often do not try to escape their abusers. In fact, in many instances, they want to go back and go to great lengths to protect their abusers from outside intervention (Gelles, 1976).

This entrapment is connected to the unequal power balance in most abusive situations, to the lack of social supports that are available to victims of abuse, and also to our potent ideology of family dependency, which makes it difficult for victims to contemplate surviving outside their family, no matter how abusive it is. This entrapment process common to all kinds of family violence has not been adequately researched and articulated in a way that accurately represents how it is experienced by the victims. It clearly deserves more attention.

Of course, as a final area for research on the common experience of victims of family abuse, there is the question of their long-term effects. Victims of the different kinds of family abuse report surprisingly similar long-term patterns: depression, suicidal feelings, self-contempt, and an inability to trust and to develop intimate relationships in later life (Herman and Hirschman, 1977; Walker, 1979). Such effects might well be the common result of the experience of being betrayed, exploited, and misused by someone on whom they were profoundly dependent. More in-depth investigation can be conducted on the common effects of abuse within families.

SHARED CHARACTERISTICS OF ABUSING FAMILIES

Still other things tie various forms of abuse together. Some of the available research, for example, shows that the type of family situation in which one kind of abuse occurs is also the type of family situation in which other abuse occurs. For example, all forms of abuse appear to be higher in the lower socioeconomic strata (Finkelhor, 1980; Pelton, 1981; Straus et al., 1980). All forms of abuse appear to be more common in families where unemployment and economic deprivation are serious problems (Meiselman, 1978; Straus et al., 1980). There is some evidence that all forms of abuse are more common in families that are more patriarchically organized (Finkelhor, 1981; Gelles, 1974; Meiselman, 1978; Star, 1980; Straus et al., 1980). And all forms of abuse have been associated with families that are isolated and that have few community ties, friendships, or organizational affiliations (Finkelhor, 1978, 1981; Garbarino & Gilliam, 1980; Gelles, 1974; Straus et al., 1980).

Not enough research has yet been done to decide to what extent the presence of one form of abuse is a good predictor of the presence of another. But there are suggestions of some high correlations. In particular, the National Survey on Family Violence (Straus et al., 1980) found evidence that men who abuse their wives are much more likely to abuse their children and vice versa. The connection between sexual abuse and physical abuse or spouse abuse, however, is less well established. From case histories we know that sexual abuse victims do report having been beaten and having watched their mothers been beaten by their fathers, but no strong empirical evidence yet exists. So although we can say there are commonalities in the social characteristics of abusing families, we do not know to what extent they actually are the same families.

COMMONALITIES IN SOCIAL RESPONSE

One of the most interesting commonalities shared by the various forms of family abuse is the way in which they emerged as social problems. Even though each emerged separately at a somewhat different moment and in response to somewhat different political pressures, each type of family abuse has gone through a similar evolution as a social problem. For example, all of the abuses emerged as social problems from historical contexts where they had been minimized and where people believed that they did not occur frequently. It is now recognized that all of these forms of abuse occur with great frequency in the general population (Finkelhor, 1979; Straus et al., 1980).

Moreover, when these forms of abuse began first to come to public attention, in all cases they were analyzed as extremely pathological behaviors. Incest offenders were seen as backwoods degenerates and feebleminded freaks (Gebhard, Gagnon, Pomeroy, & Christenson, 1965). Child beaters were seen as depraved (Gelles, 1979). Wife beaters were seen as alcoholic rogues and psychopaths and were considered to come from only extremely lower class and disorganized families (Walker, 1979). Today research sees these offenders as far less deviant that they were once viewed.

Another similarity in the popular mythology around all of these problems was the tendency to implicate the victims of the abuse as well as, or rather than, the offenders. The tendency was perhaps the strongest in the case of spouse abuse. Victims were described clinically as provoking, asking for it, women with masochistic needs for bullying spouses (Gelles, 1976). Early analyses of the problem of sexual abuse had great similarities.

Abused children were seen as seductive and flirtatious to such an extent that they brought the sexual abuse on themselves (Armstrong, 1978).

Perhaps this tendency to blame the victim was weakest in the history of the concern about physical child abuse. It was harder to blame a one-, two-, or three-year-old child than an adolescent or adult woman. But even in this case one can find evidence of a belief that abused children were, in fact, extremely aggressive and provoking and if it had not been for their waywardness, they would not have been abused. In all cases these "blaming the victim" stereotypes took a long time to abate and continue to reappear from time to time in various guises.

In each of the kinds of abuse, a social movement arose which drew attention to the abuse that was occurring (Finkelhor, 1979; Pfohl, 1977). But in each case some ambiguity remained about how to define the normative boundaries of the abuse. In the case of child abuse, there remains much public ambiguity about where to draw the line between what is often referred to as strict discipline and child abuse (Straus et al., 1980). In the case of spouse abuse, there is a belief among large segments of the population and even the professional community that certain forms of violence between couples, such as slapping or pushing, is normative and should not be labeled spouse abuse. In the case of sexual abuse, there are large grey areas. Parents and even professionals are in substantial disagreement about whether bringing children into bed, parading in front of them naked, or exposing them to various kinds of explicit sexual material constitute a form of sexual abuse (Finkelhor, 1982). The ambiguity about normative boundaries is a problem common to all forms of family abuse.

DIFFERENCES AMONG FORMS OF ABUSE

I have discussed these commonalities among the different types of family abuse because I think they suggest some processes common to abuses within the family that should be studied as such. But even though these different types of abuse are similar in some ways, they are quite different in others. Contrasting the differences can also lead to some important insights. Often by contrasting characteristics of one form of abuse with another we note some interesting facts or processes which deserve an explanation.

Although there are many ways in which the different forms of family abuse are different, I want to focus on a few and illustrate how the "compare and contrast" approach can be used to theoretical advantage.

Age and Status of Victims

One important difference among the kinds of abuse concerns the age and social status of its principal victims. The victims of spouse abuse are adults. The victims of physical abuse are children, particularly young children. The victims of sexual abuse are somewhat older than the victims of physical child abuse; on average more of them fall into the preadolescent and adolescent age group (National Center for Child Abuse and Neglect, 1981).

Some important questions about the nature of each kind of abuse are suggested by comparing the ages of the principal victims. For example, should we expect that the effects of abuse occurring at a younger and more impressionable age will be more long-term, profound, and irreversible? This might suggest more serious long-term consequences attendant to physical child abuse.

Is popular mobilization around the problem affected by the relative degree of helplessness suggested by the stereotypical victim? In other words, is public alarm more easily aroused by abuse to a young child than to a mature adult? Is concern about the sexually victimized (stereotypically adolescent) child more problematic because of the ambivalent attitudes people have about children of this age? The age range of typical victims may be useful in understanding some of the differences among types of abuse.

Differences in Support Groups

Another difference that is theoretically interesting in thinking about family abuse concerns the coalitions of groups that have been responsible for the promotion of these problems. Very different groups using very different approaches have mobilized to promote the different kinds of family abuse. For example, the concern about battered women has grown primarily out of the women's movement (Martin, 1976). Workers in this field are volunteers, and funding is shoestring and community-based. Concern about child abuse, by contrast, originated to a much greater extent among professionals, people with paid jobs relating to children, and has relied on state action, welfare bureaucracy, and federal funding to implement its objectives (Pfohl, 1977).

These groups have conducted the politics of their social problems in very different ways. They have also drawn on different theoretical frameworks to analyze these problems; the feminists casting family violence into a feminist theoretical framework, the professionals and child welfare workers casting their analyses of family violence more in terms of family disorganization and dysfunction.

These two approaches provide a fascinating study on contrasting histories of social problem mobilization, but little attention has yet been paid to this matter.

Sexual abuse is interesting from this perspective because it has been mobilized at the intersection of these two movements (Finkelhor, 1979,

1982b). It contains a delegation from both the feminist side and from the child welfare side. The presence of these two elements has provided the wherewithal for a rapid deployment around the problem of sexual abuse, but it has also set the stage for some of the most important tensions within the community of concern about the problem.

Institutional Responses

Perhaps one of the other most important differences among types of abuse is the way in which public institutions, agencies, and professions have responded to them. If there is a somewhat unnatural separation among efforts to deal with each type of family abuse, the divergent institutional responses may be partly to blame. They have made it difficult to develop any concerted approach.

For example, physicians as a group played an instrumental role—in recent years at least—in the mobilization around and intervention into the problem of child abuse (Pfohl, 1977). However, they have been much less prominently involved in the problem of sexual abuse—in part because there is little physical injury attendant to the problem of sexual abuse, and also because of the ambivalence to the problem that is the legacy of the medico-psychiatric ideology (Finkelhor, 1982b). Similarly, in regard to spouse abuse, physicians appear to have shown a low level of consciousness about the problem. In fact, they may contribute significantly to the continuing victimization of some women (Stark et al., 1979). The full reasons for these differential responses on the part of the medical community to different kinds of family violence and abuse have yet to be explored.

Similarly, the role of the police and prosecutors can be examined for the contrasting manner of their relationship to each of these forms of abuse. Police appear to be most heavily involved in the problem of spouse abuse, to a lesser extent in the problem of sexual abuse, and to a very minor extent in the problem of physical child abuse. Although it is in general true that the criminal justice system has been reluctant to get involved in domestic matters of any kind, in some cases of sexual abuse, for example, the response has been swift, massive, and extremely punitive. No one has yet really analyzed the variety of criminal justice responses to different areas of family violence and tried to account for some of these differences.

RESEARCH ON FAMILY ABUSE

In the matter of what research approaches are used to study these issues, the field of family violence and abuse is probably best characterized here by its divergences rather than by its commonalities.

It is true that the research on all kinds of family abuse has been interdisciplinary, and this has been one of its great strengths. But this is not to obscure the fact that there has been a substantial degree of specialization by discipline. For example, medical research has focused almost exclusively on physical child abuse. Sociology, by contrast, has been more heavily represented in spouse abuse than in child abuse research. Psychology, which is well represented in all kinds of family abuse research, probably is more heavily involved in child abuse than in any of the others. These specializations have resulted from such factors as accessibility to research subjects and certain theoretical affinities for certain problems within each discipline. But it is probably a healthy impulse to try to break down these specializations and encourage even more interdisciplinary mixing than currently exists.

There have also been divergences in the methodologies used to conduct research in the areas of family abuse. The patterns are somewhat difficult to gauge accurately, in part because there is a much longer tradition of research in the area of physical child abuse to date than there is in the area of either spouse abuse or sexual abuse. This longer tradition may account for the fact that prospective longitudinal studies and studies based on direct observation of family interaction have been carried out only on the subject of physical child abuse. Child abuse researchers have also been able to do more detailed and quantitative studies of abusers, while sex abuse and spouse abuse researchers have tended to concentrate to a greater extent on detailing the experiences of the victims.

In addition to their longer tradition of research, child abuse researchers have also benefited from a larger network of professionals involved in the identification and treatment of the problem. This has facilitated such things as access to subjects and follow-ups for longitudinal research. Sexual abuse and spouse abuse research, by contrast, have not had such large networks until recently and thus have had more difficulty setting up research designs—like interaction studies and longitudinal research—which require extended contact with and ability to control to some extent the subjects in the research. The fact that the abusers in the case of sexual abuse and spouse abuse are so overwhelmingly male may have something to do with this difficulty, as may the greater involvement of the criminal justice system in these two problems.

CONCLUSION

I have barely scratched the surface in cataloging all of the comparisons that can be made among the different kinds of family violence and abuse. More than any particular idea I have advanced, however, I would like to emphasize the method I am proposing.

I believe there are important theoretical and methodological advances to be made by drawing comparisons and contrasts among the different kinds of family violence and abuse. I hope others carry on this enterprise and emerge with new insights and ideas for all in this field to pursue.

REFERENCES

American Humane Association. *National analysis of official child neglect and abuse reporting.* Denver: AHA, 1978.

Armstrong, L. *Kiss daddy goodnight.* New York: Hawthorn, 1978.

Butler, S. *Conspiracy of silence.* San Francisco: New Glide, 1978.

Finkelhor, D. Psychological, cultural and family factors in incest and sexual abuse. *Journal of Marriage and Family Counseling,* 1978, *4,* 41-49. (Reprinted in Joanne V. Cook & Roy T. Bowles (Eds.), *Child abuse: Commission and omission.* Toronto: Butterworth.)

Finkelhor, D. *Sexually victimized children.* New York: Free Press, 1979.

Finkelhor, D. Risk factors in the sexual victimization of children. *Child Abuse and Neglect,* 1980, *4,* 265-273.

Finkelhor, D. Sexual abuse of boys: The available data. In Nicholas Groth (Eds.), *Sexual victimization of males. Offenses, offenders and victims.* New York: Plenum, 1982. (a)

Finkelhor, D. Sexual abuse: A sociological perspective. *Child Abuse and Neglect,* 1982, *6,* 94-102. (b)

Finkelhor, D. Public definitions of sexual abusiveness toward children. Unpublished paper, University of New Hampshire, 1982. (c)

Garbarino, J., & Gilliam, G. *Understanding abusive families.* Lexington, MA: D. C. Heath, 1980.

Gebhard, P., Gagnon, J., Pomeroy, W., & Christenson, C. *Sex offenders: An analysis of types.* New York: Harper & Row, 1965.

Gelles, R. *The violent home.* Beverly Hills, CA: Sage, 1974.

Gelles, R. Abused wives: Why do they stay? *Journal of Marriage and Family,* 1976, *38,* 659-668.

Gelles, R. *Family violence.* Beverly Hills, CA: Sage, 1979.

Gil, D., *Child abuse and violence.* New York: AMS Press, 1979.

Herbruck, C. *Breaking the cycle of child abuse.* Minneapolis: Winston Press, 1979.

Herman, J., & Hirschman, L. Father-daughter incest. *Signs,* 1977, *2,* 1-22.

Maden, M., & Wrench, D. Significant findings in child abuse research. *Victimology,* 1977, *11,* 196-224.

Martin, D., *Battered wives.* New York: Pocket Books, 1976.

Meiselman, K. *Incest.* San Francisco: Jossey-Bass, 1978.

National Center for Child Abuse and Neglect. *Study findings: National study of the incidence and severity of child abuse and neglect.* Washington, DC: U.S. Department of Health and Human Services, 1981.

Pelton, L. *Social context of child abuse and neglect.* New York: Human Sciences Press, 1981.

Pfohl, S. The discovery of child abuse. *Social Problems,* 1977, *24,* 310-323.

Spinetta, J., & Rigler, D. The child abusing parent: A psychological review. *Psychological Bulletin,* 1972, *77,* 296-304.

Star, B. Patterns of family violence. *Social Casework,* 1980, *61,* 339-346.

Stark, E., Flitcraft, A., & Frazier, W. Medicine and patriarchal violence. *International Journal of Health Sciences,* 1979, *9.*

Straus, M., Gelles, R., & Steinmetz, S. *Behind closed doors: Violence in the American family.* New York: Doubleday, 1980.

Terr, L. C. Family study of child abuse. *American Journal of Psychiatry,* 1970, *127,* 665-671.

Walker, L. *The battered woman.* New York: Harper & Row, 1979.

SECTION II

VIOLENCE AGAINST WIVES

Theories about the causes of wife-beating are legion. The diversity of the approaches is clearly evident in the three chapters in this section. This diversity may be confusing, but it is not necessarily a sign of something amiss. A phenomenon such as wife-beating is likely to have many causes. Consequently, an adequate explanation will have to be based on research which takes a variety of perspectives and which uses a variety of methods. The results will at first seem contradictory, as do the chapters in this section on first reading. More likely, they are complementary. In the long run, they will probably turn out to be interlocking pieces of a larger picture.

It is hard to guess what that picture will look like. But even at this stage, three broad groups of variables have emerged. They can be thought of as "individual" factors, "situational" factors, and "societal" factors. Each is represented by the chapters in this section.

At the individual level are the personal traits or characteristics of the aggressors and victims of marital violence. All three chapters deal with individual-level variables, but the emphasis is different. Fagan, Stewart, and Hansen focus on the characteristics of men who beat their wives. For example, to what extent are they men with a general predisposition to violence? Walker gives attention to this, but even more to the characteristics of beaten women, such as "learned helplessness." Wardell, Gillespie, and Leffler critique the research on such characteristics and are particularly dubious about studies that seek to explain wife-beating by reference to the characteristics of the victims. They point out, for example, that the learned helplessness observed by Walker is more likely a response to their victimization than a cause.

All three of the papers also address situational explanations of violence against wives. Fagan, Stewart, and Hansen, for example, provide evidence on the role of stressful situations when they show a 30% unemployment rate among their sample of battering husbands. Walker provides evidence on the interaction between husband and wife when she shows that it tends to follow a cyclical pattern, alternating between hostility and love. Wardell, Gillespie, and Leffler argue that studies which purport to show that violence is more likely given certain family situations are inherently sexist, despite the good intentions of the researchers. For example, there are studies which show that the rate of wife-beating is greater when the wife has a more prestigious job than her husband. That may be factually correct, but Wardell and her colleagues point out that given the occupational disadvantage of women in American society, such situations are rare.

Finally, we come to societal-level explanations for wife-beating. Wardell, Gillespie, and Leffler explicitly deal with the idea that violence against wives grows out the nature of the society itself. That principle is implicit in the other two chapters as well. There are two main types of societal or social structural variables: social norms and social organization. Wardell, Gillespie, and Leffler's reference to the dual labor market is an example of a social organizational factor. They also call our attention to the existence of implicit social norms which justify male violence against women. One such example is the existence of social categories or stereotypes, such as "the nagging wife," which make women blame worthy victims.

Even if it were true that the discrepencies between the chapters in this section reflect underlying complementarity, there are very real methodological and theoretical weaknesses which will have to be overcome as part of the effort to put the pieces together. Some of the most important of these are brought out in Wardell et al.'s chapter. The authors of the studies they criticize are likely to feel that they have been misrepresented or that the criticisms are incorrect. But to dwell on that would miss the main point and the main contribution of the chapter. Their objective is to reveal the implicit sexism in much of the research on wife-beating, and to force us out of certain established and constricting modes of thinking and research. Since those whose work is criticized are self-consciously and explicitly antisexist, it takes strong medicine to show the implicit sexist assumptions. Wardell, Gillespie, and Leffler administer that needed medicine. It may make some of us squirm, but the end result will be beneficial.

2

The Battered Woman Syndrome Study

LENORE E. WALKER

From July 1978 through June 1981, The Battered Women Research Center at Colorado Women's College undertook a study of battered women in the Rocky Mountain region.[1] The purpose of the study was to learn about domestic violence from the battered woman's perspective. We identified key psychological and sociological factors that composed the battered woman syndrome and tested specific theories by collecting comprehensive data from the women themselves. The two specific theories that were tested were the learned helplessness theory originally proposed by Seligman (1975) and a behavioral cycle theory of violence proposed by Walker (1977-1978). Both of these theories' adaptation to battered women were formulated from previous work of this investigator (Walker, 1979).

The sample for this study consisted of 403 self-identified battered women who lived in the six-state region comprising the federally defined Health and Human Services Region VIII. A woman was considered eligible to participate if she reported that she was battered at least two times by a man with whom she had an intimate or marital relationship. Geographic distribution was constructed to allow for natural selection but with ability to correct for underrepresentation of groups, if it occurred. While the largest number of subjects came from the Metropolitan Denver Area, other areas of Colorado, Montana, South Dakota, North Dakota, Wyoming, and Utah accounted for almost one-third of the final sample. Direct contact was made with minority groups so as to encourage their participation. Women were interviewed on several Indian reservations, in high impact energy areas, in battered women shelters, and in prisons. A special group who had killed their batterers was also obtained.

This sample was generated by a variety of techniques using both referral sources and direct advertising. Most of the staff had contacts within the battered women's movement, as well as human service delivery systems, thus facilitating ongoing advertisement. A carefully detailed intake and scheduling procedure was designed so as to prevent a high no-show and cancellation rate that occurred prior to instituting these procedures. They included establishing one telephone contact staff person, flexibility in rescheduling, accommodating to battered women's unpredictable lifestyle, and confirmation telephone calls the day before the scheduled interview appointment. These procedural details were important in retaining the sample. The quality of the data is considered as reliable as possible for a self-report, retrospective survey.

Special interview techniques were developed to administer the 200-page questionnaire constructed for this purpose, as well as several other standardized psychological scales to measure personality variables. This procedure usually took between six and eight hours to complete in a face-to-face interview. As was predicted, battered women came from all walks of life. They were found in expected proportions for all demographic categories analyzed including race and social class. These data support rejection of the common belief that battered women come from poor, lower-class homes where they learned marginal job skills. Battering behavior was found in several different kinds of relationships, although most victims were married. Over half our sample reported details of a relationship with a nonbatterer, which we used for comparison purposes.

RESULTS AND DISCUSSION

The major purpose of this study has been to learn as much as possible about the nature of domestic violence from the perspective of the battered woman. To this end we have been successful. The 403 subjects shared intimate details of their lives with us. These data indicate that events which occurred in childhood, as well as in the relationship, interact with the violence and affect a woman's current state. After analyzing reported details about the past and present feelings, thoughts and actions of the women, the violent and nonviolent men, our data led us to conclude that there are no specific personality traits which would suggest a victim-prone personality for the women, although there may be an identifiable violence prone personality for the men.

From the women's point of view, the violence pattern which occurred in their relationships was initiated by the batterer because of his inability to control his behavior when angry. Their reports of his previous life experiences indicate that engaging in such violent behavior was learned and rewarded. This view is supported by their reports contrasting the same experiences for nonviolent men. Information, from the woman's perception, about the batterer's childhood and other life experiences follow the psychological principles consistent with his learning to respond to all emotionally distressing cues with angry and violent behavior. The high incidence of other violent behavior, such as child abuse, and correlates, such as a high percentage of arrests and convictions, support this learning theory explanation. These data compel us to conclude that from the woman's point of view, the initiation of the violence pattern in the battering relationships studied comes from the man's learned violent behavior.

SUSCEPTIBILITY FACTORS

Some reported events in the battered women's past occurred with sufficient regularity to warrant further study, as they point to a possible susceptibility factor that interferes with the women's ability to successfully stop the batterers' violence toward them once it is initiated. We originally postulated that such a susceptibility potential could come from rigid sex role socialization patterns, leaving adult women with a sense of learned helplessness so that they do not develop appropriate skills to escape the violence. While our data support this hypothesis, it appears to be more complicated than originally viewed.

For example, we would have expected that women who were so influenced by sex role stereotypes would be traditional in their own attitudes toward the roles of women. Instead, our data indicate that they perceive themselves as more liberal than most in such attitudes. However, they perceive their batterers as very traditional, which probably produces conflict in both the man's and woman's set of expectations for the woman's role in their relationship. They see their batterer's and their father's attitudes toward women as similar, their mother's and nonbatterer's attitudes as more liberal than the others, but less so than their own. The limitation of an attitude measure is that we still do not know how they actually behave despite these attitudes. It is probably safe to assume that the batterer's control forces the battered women to behave in a more traditional role than their reported preference.

Other events reported by the women that suggest a susceptibility factor include early and repeated sexual molestation and assault (48%), a high level of violence by members in the childhood families (67%), perception of critical or uncontrollable events in childhood, and experiencing other conditions which place them at high risk for depression.

The impact of sexual assault is consistent with reports of other studies. Finkelhor's (1979) caution that seriousness of impact on the child cannot be determined by evaluating the actual sex act performed was supported by our data. The trauma seemed to be caused by any act, attempted or completed, and we suspect it negatively influenced the woman's later sexuality and perceptions of her own vulnerability. Incest victims have learned to gain the love and affection they need through sexual activity (Butler, 1978). Perhaps our battered women did too (Thyfault, 1980). At the very least, the fear of losing parental affection and disruption of their home life status quo seen in sexually abused children (MacFarlane, 1978)

TABLE 2.1   Battered Women's Perceptions of the Attitudes Toward Women for Themselves, Their Mothers, Fathers, Batterers and Nonbatterers

Group	N	Mean	S.D.	Normative Sample	Mean	S.D.
Mothers	384	40.26	14.87	Mothers*	41.86	11.62
Fathers	371	27.06	14.59	Fathers*	39.22	10.49
Batterers	391	25.67	14.27	College Males*	44.80	12.07
Nonbatterers	199	42.88	14.57			
Ss Short AWS	383	58.48	11.82	College Females*	50.26	11.68
Ss Full AWS	362	118.24	22.84	College Females**	98.21	23.16

* Norms reported in Spence, Helmreich, & Stapp (1973).
** Norms reported in Spence & Helmreich (1972).

is similar to the battered women's fears of loss of the batterer's affection and disruption of their relationship's status quo.

We also do not fully understand the impact of battering reported in the women's childhood homes. Part of this difficulty is due to definitional problems. We allowed the women to use their own subjective definition of what constituted battering behavior, so we know what is reported to be the impact of their perception of family violence, but not the specific details of the violent acts themselves. This makes it difficult to compare our results with those of researchers such as Straus et al. (1980), who use specific definitions of conflict behavior. In any case, our data indicate the women perceived males as more likely to engage in battering behavior which is directed against women. They perceived the highest level of whatever behavior they defined as battering to have occurred in the batterer's home (81%) and the least amount of it in the nonbatterer's home (24%). The opportunities for modeling effective responses to cope with surviving the violent attacks but not for either terminating or escaping them can be thought to occur in those homes where the women witnessed or experienced such behavior. Certainly, our institutionalized acceptance of violence against women would further reinforce this learned response of acceptance of a certain level of battering provided it was defined as occurring for more socially acceptable reasons, like punishment.

Learned helplessness theory predicts that the perception of helplessness can be learned during childhood from experiences of uncontrollability or noncontingency between response and outcome. Critical events perceived as occurring without much control were reported by the battered women and were found to have an impact on the women's current state. Other factors such as a large family size may also be predictive of less control. It seems reasonable to conclude that the greater strengths the women gained from their childhood experiences, the more resilient they were in reversing the effects of their battering.

In order to determine whether learned helplessness from childhood (Child LH) is a determinant of learned helplessness from the battering relationship (Rel LH), and whether either of these is a determinant of the woman's current state (Current State), a series of path analyses was conducted (Walker, 1981). In the first one, shown in Figure 2.1, the entire sample was included. Results indicate that both Child LH and Rel LH influence current state and that the childhood measure is actually a bit more influential than the relationship measure. (For the final multiple regression analysis on which the path diagram is based, $F(2,400) = 22.56$, $p < .001$.) Contrary to the hypothesis that childhood experiences cause a woman to be more or less vulnerable to helplessness in a battering relationship, there is essentially no relationship between Child LH and Rel LH. Thus, learned helplessness has equal potential to develop at either time in the battered woman's life.

Because the path diagram might differ for women still in an abusive relationship compared with women who have left such a relationship, we recomputed the path analysis for each of these groups separately. The two sets of results are also shown in Figure 2.1. Surprisingly, there is not much difference, despite the fact that the current state of women who are no longer in a battering relationship might be expected to be influenced less by Child LH or, especially, by Rel LH. Even when we look only at women who have been out of the battering relationship for more than a year (an analysis not shown in the figure), the path coefficients remain the same. This suggests either that the influence of Child LH and Rel LH persists, almost regardless of later experiences, or that subjects who selected themselves for our interviews at various distances from battering experiences were still troubled by them.

In order to explore this matter further, we performed an analysis of variance on each of the learned helplessness scores (Child LH, Rel LH, and Current State) with the independent variable being whether the woman was, at the time of the interview, (1) still in the battering relationship, (2) out less than one year, or (3) out more than one year. If large differences were discovered, it might mean that these three groups differ in ways that render the path analyses invalid or misleading. In fact, none of the tested differences was significant. The means, shown in Table 2.2, reveal some interesting trends, however. Women who are still in the relationship report worse (more helpless) childhoods and less current problems with helplessness. If this is true, it might help explain why they are still in a battering relationship. Perhaps they did have somewhat more "training" for helplessness during childhood than women who have left a battering relationship, and either their battering experiences are not as severe or the women do not yet see them as so severe.

Although there seemed to be a potential susceptibility to experiencing the maximum effects from a violent relationship, this did not affect areas

Current State of Woman at Time of Interview
With Childhood and Relationship Variables

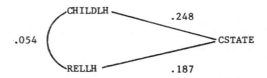

F (2,400) = 22.56, p < .001

Current State of Woman at Time of Interview With
Childhood and Relationship Variables When Woman
was Still "In" the Battering Relationship

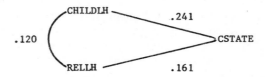

F (2.93) = 4.78, p < .05

Current State of Woman at Time of Interview With
Childhood and Relationship Variables When Woman
was "Out" of the Battering Relationship

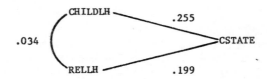

F (2,304) = 18.49, p < .001

Figure 2.1 Learned helplessness predictors of women's current state.

TABLE 2.2   Mean of Learned Helplessness Scores for Battered Women in and out of Relationship

| | *Learned Helplessness Means** | | |
Status of Battering Relationship	*CHILD* Score	*REL* Score	*—CSTATE* Score
In relationship	.2708	−.2904	−.7136
Out less than one year	−.1451	.2087	.3476
Out more than one year	−.0454	.0145	.1922

* A higher score indicates a greater degree of learned helplessness. Scores were normalized z-scores.

of the battered woman's lives other than her family life. Most of the women interviewed were intelligent, well-educated, competent people who held responsible jobs. Approximately one-quarter of them were in professional occupations. In fact, they were quite successful in appearing to be just like other people, provided they were able to contain the batterers' possessiveness and need for control. Once we got to know them, we learned how to recognize the signs that this outward appearance was being maintained at great psychological cost. The women who had terminated the relationship and were not still being hassled by the batterer spoke of the sense of relief and peacefulness of their lives. The others still faced the high-tension situations on a regular basis. For most it seemed that severing the batterer's influence was one of the most difficult tasks to accomplish.

VIOLENCE-PRONE PERSONALITY

Our data confirm that domestic violence does not come from the interaction of the partners in the relationship, or from provocation from irritating personality traits of the battered women, but rather from the batterers' learned behavioral responses. We attempted to find perceived characteristics that would make such violence more predictable than currently has been reported. While we identified a number of such perceived characteristics, the best predictor of future violence was a history of past violent behavior. This included witnessing, receiving, and committing violent acts in the childhood home; violent acts toward pets, inanimate objects, or other people; having a criminal record; being in the military service; and previous violent behavior expressed toward women. Added to that are the following: a history of temper tantrums, insecurity, a need to keep the environment stable and nonthreatening, jealousy, and possessiveness. The man's ability to be charming, manipulative, and seductive to get what he wants and hostile, nasty and mean when he does not succeed,

TABLE 2.3   Violence-Prone Characteristics of Batterers Compared to Nonbatterers as Reported by Battered Women

Variable	Batterers	Nonbatterers
	%	%
Battering in childhood home	81	24
battered by mother	44	13
battered by father	61	23
father battered mother	63	27
battered own children	53	N/A
Was in military	58	46
Drafted	23	32
combat experience?	37	37
number of years	$\overline{X} = 3.2$	$\overline{X} = 1.9$
Was he ever arrested?	71	34
Was he convicted	44	19
Women obtained restraining order	39	1
Frequent alcohol abuse	67	43

makes the risk for battering very high. If alcohol abuse problems are included, the pattern becomes classic.

Perhaps the most telling observation was made by an interviewer: Most of the batterers being described by the women sounded like they all went to the same training school. Perhaps it was in their homes. Many of the men were reported to have experienced similar patterns of discipline in their childhood home. The most commonly reported pattern was a strict father and inconsistent mother. The mother alternated between being lenient, sometimes in a collusive way to avoid upsetting her husband, and being strict in applying her own standards and discipline. Although we did not collect such data, it is reasonable to speculate that if we had, they would have revealed the batterer's mother's pattern of smoothing everything over for the batterer to protect him from his father's potential brutality. Like the battered women, she may have inadvertently conditioned him to expect someone else to make his life less stressful. It is this inability to manage his own world, including his anger, that reinforces his insecurity. Further study into these areas with the batterers themselves is strongly suggested.

RELATIONSHIP ISSUES

There seemed to be certain combinations of factors that would strongly indicate a high risk potential for battering in a relationship. One factor which is often mentioned by other researchers (Berk et al., 1981; Straus et al., 1980) is differences on sociodemographic variables between the batterers and the battered women. Batterers tended to be less educated than their wives, were from a lower socioeconomic class and from a different ethnic, religious, or racial group. There was some indication that the man's earning level was not consistent and below his potential, but since we did not account for the difference in value of dollar income for previous years, we could not statistically evaluate these data. These issues may be measuring fundamental sexist biases in these men that indicates their inability to tolerate a disparity in status between themselves and their wives. Perhaps they used violence as a way to lower the perceived status difference.

Men who are much more traditional than women in their attitudes toward women's roles are also a high risk. With traditionality goes the patriarchal sex role stereotyped patterns that rigidly assign tasks according to gender. Such men seem to evaluate a women's feelings for them by how well she fulfills those expectations. Women who perceive themselves as liberal in their attitudes toward women's roles can be expected to have their values clash with men who do not hold such nontraditional values.

Men who are insecure, need a great amount of nurturance, and are very possessive of women's time can also be at high risk as abusers. Most of the women reported enjoying the extra attention they received initially, only to resent the intrusiveness that it eventually became. Uncontrollable jealousy by the batterer was reported by almost all of the battered women, suggesting this is another critical risk factor. Again, enjoyment of the extra attention and flattery masked these early warning signs for many women. There is a kind of bonding that is reported which has not yet been quantified. The frequency with which the women, men, and professionals report this leads us to speculate that it is a critical factor. Each has an uncanny ability to know how the other would think or feel about many things. Batterers want the women's ability to be sensitive to cues in the environment. At the same time, they view the battered women as highly suggestible and fear outside influences which will support removal of their own influence and control over the women's lives.

Another factor which has a negative impact on relationships and increases the violence risk is sexual intimacy early in the relationship. Batterers are reported to be seductive and charming, when they are not being violent, and the women fall for their short-lived but sincere promises. It seems unusual that one-third of the sample was pregnant at the time of their marriage to the batterer, although we had no comparison data. We did not control for pre- and postliberalization of abortion to determine how battered women felt about the alternatives to marriage, including abortion or giving the child up for adoption.

Finally, the abuse of alcohol and perhaps some drugs is another area that would predict violent behavior. They are similar forms of addiction-type behavior, with the resulting family problems that can arise from them. The clue to note is the increase in alcohol consumption. The more the drinking continues, the more likely it seems violence will escalate. Yet, the pattern is not consistent for about 80% of our group, as only 20% reported abusing alcohol during all four acute battering incidents. It is important to note that the women who reported the heaviest drinking patterns for themselves were in relationships with men who also abused alcohol. Thus, while there is no cause and effect between alcohol abuse and violence, its relationship needs more careful study.

THEORETICAL IMPLICATIONS

Most battered women in our sample perceived three different levels of control over their lives. They scored significantly higher than the norms on the Levinson (1972) IPC Locus of Control Subscales of Internal, Powerful Others, and Chance. These findings suggest that the internal/external locus of control dichotomy does not explain battered women's attributions. Those women still in a violent relationship did not report powerful others as being in control of their lives. Perhaps one reason why a battered woman does not terminate her marriage sooner is this lack of acknowledgement that her batterer really is in control of her everyday activities and of her life.

Seligman's (1978) reformulation of learned helplessness theory would suggest an attributional style of assigning causality for successful experiences to external and specific factors and failures to internal and global ones. Our measurement of attributional style was not designed to test this reformulation, as our study was designed previous to its publication. Therefore, our sample's perception of both internal and external causation may not be unusual in light of this reformulation of learned helplessness theory.

The woman's self-esteem was measured by use of a semantic differential scale. It was predicted that battered women's self-esteem would be quite low; surprisingly, our results show the opposite. They perceived themselves as stronger, more independent, and more sensitive than other women. It is possible that battered women develop a positive sense of self from having survived in a violent relationship which causes them to believe they are equal to or better than others. However, there is incompatibility between these high self-esteem findings and the reports of depression and other learned helplessness measures. From these confusing results, more careful study into the mental health of battered women is recommended.

Depression was measured by the CES-D scale (Radloff, 1977). Our subjects scored higher than the high risk for depression cutoff score. Younger women in the sample were more likely to be depressed than older ones, as were those who were unemployed. An interesting but surprising finding was that women out of the relationship were more likely to be

TABLE 2.4   Battered Women's Attributions of Locus of Control as
Measured by the Levinson IPC Scale

	Battered Women			t Value
	N	Mean	S.D.	
Internal Scale				
Comparison norms	48	35.46	7.41	
Total sample*	386	41.46	6.88	6.12
Total out*	292	41.33	6.79	6.51
Out < 1 year*	112	41.62	6.44	5.26
Out > 1 year*	180	41.14	7.01	4.62
In*	94	41.87	7.13	5.09
Powerful Others Scale				
Comparison norms	48	14.64	6.87	
Total sample*	383	18.01	9.73	9.36
Total out**	291	18.17	9.39	2.76
Out < 1 year**	117	18.43	8.92	2.61
Out > 1 year***	174	17.99	9.72	2.09
In	92	17.52	10.78	1.72
Chance Scale				
Comparison norms	48	13.38	9.05	
Total sample**	383	17.37	9.48	3.14
Total out**	289	17.41	9.32	3.08
Out < 1 year**	113	18.01	8.73	3.03
Out > 1 year***	176	17.03	9.70	2.28
In	94	17.25	9.995	2.30

  * $p < .001$
 ** $p < .01$
*** $p < .05$

more depressed than those still in it. They were also not consistent in demonstrating the negative cognitions and moods we would have expected in other indices within the questionnaire.

Lewinsohn's behavioral reinforcement theory of depression might explain some of our findings on depression (Lewinsohn, 1975; Lewinsohn, Steinmetz, Larson & Franklin, 1981). It postulates that depression occurs when there is a sharp reduction in the amount of positive reinforcement people receive. A lower rate of rewards would result in a lower response rate, or passivity, which then spirals downward into a depressed state. Cognitive or affective disturbances occur simultaneously with the downward spiral or are a consequence of the lowered reinforcement rate. This is similar to the learned helplessness theory, which postulates that the lowered behavioral response rate or passivity is a learned response to uncontrollable trauma. It also postulates that distorted perceptions exist in

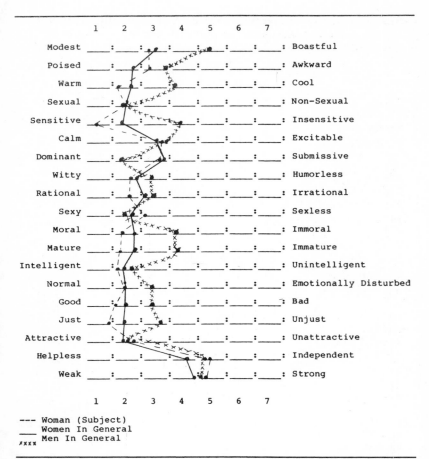

Figure 2.2 Perception of self-esteem for battered women, women in general, and men in general as reported by battered women.

the cognitive and affective domain. While the learned helplessness theory did not specify when these cognitive and affective perceptions occurred, the reformulations suggest an attributional style which serves as a cognitive set for a depressive state to develop.

The findings of a set of factors which could result in childhood learned helplessness and another, responsible for development of learned helplessness in the relationship, supports the application of this theory to battered women. Unfortunately, actual learned helplessness is usually directly measured in a laboratory setting under experimentally controlled conditions. Our research attempted to infer its presence from variables the literature would predict cause it to develop. Although our results are positive, it is strongly recommended that a controlled laboratory setting be constructed

TABLE 2.5 Average Depression Scores (CES—D) for Battered Women by Age, Marital and Employment Status

Variable	N	Mean	S.D.	Comparison Sample Mean
Marital Status				
Married	98	16.86	11.62	
Not married	275	18.67	12.70	
Never married	23	17.13	11.10	12.79[a]
Living together	22	17.05	12.20	
Married	76	16.80	11.53	9.53
Separated/Divorced	243	18.58	12.60	13.71
Widowed	9	18.19	12.44	10.26
Total	373	18.19	12.44	10.10
Employment Status				
Unemployed*	176	21.86	13.14	11.44[b]
Employed*	186	14.78	10.86	9.61
Age				
18-24**	66	21.89	12.48	13.48[b]
25-34	197	18.14	12.55	
35-44**	72	15.65	10.52	
45-49	41	16.95	14.44	
25+				9.62
Total CES—D	376	18.19	12.50	KC 9.62
				WC 9.13

* p < .000
** p < .026

[a] Reported in Radloff (In Press) Table 5.2
[b] Reported in Radloff (In Press) Table 5.3

to test if learned helplessness can be easily induced in a sample of battered women comparable to this one. Such direct measurement is necessary to confirm the theoretical application to battered women.

The Walker Cycle Theory of Violence was also confirmed by our data (Walker, 1979, 1981). There was sufficient evidence to reveal that three phases in battering relationships occur in a cycle. Over time, the first phase of tension building becomes more common and loving contrition, or the third phase, declines. Our results also show that phase three could be characterized by an absence of tension or violence and no observable loving-contrition behavior and still be reinforcing for the woman.

In our interviews with battered women, we asked for detailed descriptions of four battering incidents: the first, the second, one of the worst, and the last (or last prior to the interview). The first two and the last incident, taken together, reflect the temporal course of a stream of acute battering incidents. Each of these is an example of phase two in the cycle theory.

After the description of each incident, basing her judgment on both the open-ended description and a series of closed-ended questions concerning the batterer's behavior before the event ("Would you call it: irritable, provocative, aggressive, hostile, threatening?—each on a 1-5 scale) and after the event ("nice, loving, contrite"), the interviewer recorded whether or not there was "evidence of tension building and/or loving contrition." Comparisons between interviewers' responses indicated a high level of agreement.

In 65% of all cases (including three battering incidents for each woman who reported three) there was evidence for a tension-building phase prior to the battering. In 58% of all cases there was evidence for loving contrition afterward. In general, then, there is support for the cycle theory of violence in a majority of the battering incidents described by our sample.

When the results are broken down chronologically, the pattern in Figure 2.3 emerges. For first incidents, the proportion showing evidence of a tension-building phase is 56%; the proportion showing evidence of loving contrition is 69%. Over time, these proportions change drastically. By the last incident, 71% of battering incidents were preceded by tension building, but only 42% were followed by loving contrition. In other words, over time in a battering relationship, tension building becomes more common (or more evident) and loving contrition declines.

Since our sample included 24% of women who were still in the battering relationship, it is possible that Figure 2.4 marks a difference in pattern between those who were in the relationship and those who had left the relationship by the time of the interview. The former group may not yet have experienced the final battering incident.

Figure 2.4 compares the pattern of these two groups. When we separate them, both show the same decline of loving contrition, but the patterns of tension building are different. Women still in a battering relationship report less evidence of tension building preceding the last incident before our interview. This may be a valid indication of a difference between battering incidents that cause a woman to leave the relationship and battering incidents other than the final one. Or it may indicate a defensive bias on the part of women who choose to remain in the relationship. Our data do not allow us to distinguish between these two possibilities.

It is clear, however, that our data support the existence of the Walker Cycle Theory of Violence. Further, over the course of a battering relationship, tension building before battering becomes more common (or evident) and loving contrition declines.

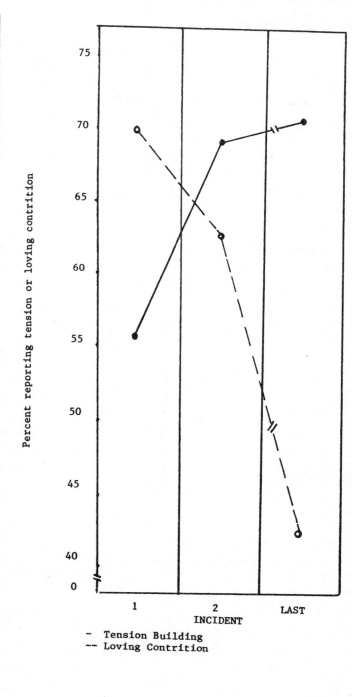

Figure 2.3 Changes over time in tension-building and loving contrition phases of the battering cycle for the total sample (N = 403).

45

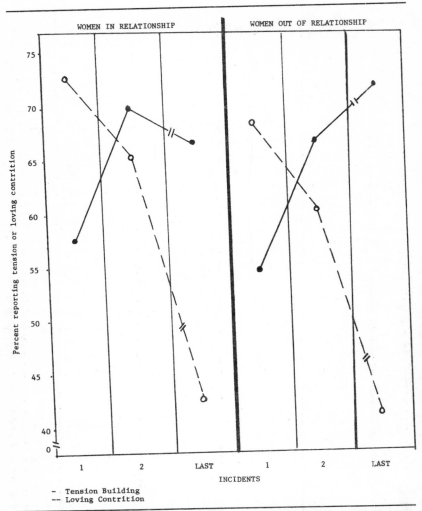

Figure 2.4 **Changes over time in tension-building and loving contrition phases of the battering cycle for women in and out of the battering relationship.**

The analysis of lower reinforcement rates presented with the results of the Walker Cycle Theory of Violence demonstrates that women who were out of the battering relationship left after the ratio between tension-building and loving contrition phases sharply diverged. Women still in the battering relationship reported more positive reinforcement (loving contrition) following the last battering incident they discussed. Thus, these women who were less depressed while still in the relationship may still have been receiving some rewards from it despite the violence. Once the cost-benefit ratio changes, however, and the rate of reinforcement decreases, then the women may be more inclined to leave the relationship but subsequently become depressed as a result of the separation. Further investigation into the psychological costs and benefits of these relationships is still necessary.

CONCLUSIONS

In summary, the results of this study support the hypotheses that battered women develop psychological sequelae that can be considered to constitute a battered woman syndrome. While experiences in childhood and those from living in a violent relationship have an impact on the woman's current state, they appear to interfere with the battered woman's ability to successfully stop the batterer's violence toward them after he initiates it. There are no specific personality traits which would suggest a victim-prone personality for the women, although there may be an identifiable violence-prone personality for the men. When comparing the same woman's reported behavior in both a battering and nonbattering relationship, differences were seen that could not have occurred were there a more stable personality trait pattern for the women. We found sufficient evidence to conclude that the battered woman's terror was appropriate and her fears that separation would make the violence worse were accurate. Our results also support the two main theories tested and suggest further investigation into both the rewards and the destructiveness of battering relationships.

NOTE

1. This report was partially funded by NIMH Grant RO1MH30147, Lenore E. Walker, Principal Investigator.

REFERENCES

Berk, R. A., Berk, S. F., Loseke, D. R., & Rauma, D. *Mutual combat and other family violence myths.* Paper presented at the National Conference for Family Violence Researchers, Durham, New Hampshire, July 1981.

Butler, S. *The conspiracy of silence.* San Francisco: Glide Publications, 1978.

Finkelhor, D. *Sexually victimized children.* New York: Free Press, 1979.

Levenson, H. *Distinctions within the concept of internal-external locus of control: Development of a new scale.* Proceedings from the 80th Annual Convention of the American Psychological Association, 1972, pp. 261-262.

Lewinsohn, P. M. The behavioral study and treatment of depression. In M. Hergen, M. Eider, & P. M. Miller (Eds.), *Progress in behavioral modification.* New York: Academic Press, 1975.

Lewinsohn, P. M., Steinmetz, J. L., Larson, D. W., & Franklin, J. Depression related cognitions: Antecedent or consequence? *Journal of Abnormal Psychology*, 1981, *90*(3), 213-219.

MacFarlane, K. Sexual abuse of children. In J. R. Chapman & M. Gates (Eds.), *The victimization of women.* Beverly Hills, CA: Sage, 1978.

Radloff, L. S. The CES-D scale: A self report depression scale for research in the general population. *Applied Psychological Measurement,* 1977, *1*(3), 385-401.

Seligman, M.E.P. *Helplessness: On depression, development and death.* San Francisco: W. H. Freeman, 1975.

Seligman, M.E.P. Comment and integration. *Journal of Abnormal Psychology,* 1978, *87*(1), 165-179.

Spence, J. T., & Helmreich, R. The Attitudes Towards Women Scale: An objective instrument to measure attitudes towards the rights and roles of women in contemporary society. *JSAS, Catalog of Selected Documents in Psychology,* 1972, *2*(66), 1-51.

Spence, J. T., Helmreich, R., & Stapp, J. A short version of the Attitudes Towards Women Scale (AWS). *Bulletin of the Psychonomic Society,* 1973, *2*(4), 219-220.

Straus, M. A., Gelles, R. J., & Steinmetz, S. K. *Behind closed doors: Violence in the American family.* Garden City, NY: Doubleday, 1980.

Thyfault, R. *Childhood sexual abuse, marital rape, and battered women: Implications for mental health workers.* Paper presented at the annual meeting of the Colorado Mental Health Conference, Keystone, October 1980.

Walker, L. E. Battered women and learned helplessness. *Victimology,* 1977-1978, *2*(3-4), 525-534.

Walker, L. E. *The battered woman.* New York: Harper & Row, 1979.

Walker, L. E. *Final report: The battered woman syndrome.* NIMH Grant #R01 MH30147, 1981.

3

Violent Men or Violent Husbands?

Background Factors and Situational Correlates

JEFFREY A. FAGAN, DOUGLAS K. STEWART, and KAREN V. HANSEN

Despite the numerous theories advanced over the past 30 years to explain violence and, more recently, wife abuse, there is little agreement on the presumed causes and correlates of violent behavior. No single theory or discipline has been able to explain adequately domestic or stranger violence.[1] Many traditions abound, but there is scant evidence to reconcile the apparent differences or to reinforce the preeminence of one school of thought. There is some evidence that actual violence is the strongest predictor of future violence (Wolfgang, Figlio, & Sellin, 1972; Wolfgang, 1977; Monahan, 1977, 1981; Hamparian, Shuster, Dinitz, & Conrad, 1978; Shannon, 1980). Other correlates of domestic violence can be identified, but they are useful only as descriptors of violent behavior or violent individuals and do not significantly contribute to theory construction or modification.

Researchers studying both domestic violence and stranger violence agree that variables representing the characteristics of individuals are insufficient to explain and/or predict violent behavior (Monahan, 1981). Explanations of violence, both inside and outside the home, must incorporate situational or contextual factors as well as an assessment of the relationships of violent individuals to these environments (Dobash &

Authors' Note: *This research was supported by Grants 80-JN-AX-0004 and 78-MU-AX-0049 to the URSA Institute from the National Institute for Juvenile Justice and Delinquency Prevention, Office of Juvenile Justice and Delinquency Prevention, U.S. Department of Justice. The opinions expressed are the authors' and do not represent the views or opinions of OJJDP or the Department of Justice. We wish to thank Sandra Wexler for her meticulous reading of the manuscript and important comments, and Andrew Bundy and Rebecca Cannon, domestic violence workers, who read earlier drafts and made numerous suggestions.*

Dobash, 1979). Finally, a complete analysis and description of violence must incorporate both historical factors (e.g., how often and to what degree violence occurred in the past, who were the victims, in what situations), and an examination of the precipitating events in these previous violent incidents. Such situational factors also include the cognitive and affective processes which usually mediate violent responses to certain individuals or situations.

Until recently, there has been little systematic examination either of violent husbands or the extent to which those engaged in extradomestic violence are also violent at home. The methodological separation of these behaviors may be a misleading artifact of the driving research questions in the prior studies. For example, research on prediction of violence suggests that accurate assessment requires a thorough probing of *all* forms of past violence, with particular attention to the recency, severity, and frequency of violent acts (Fisher, Brodsky, & Corse, 1977). Monahan (1981) argues that at least five indices of violence should be considered:

- arrests and convictions for violent crimes
- juvenile court involvement for violent acts
- mental hospitalizations for "dangerous" behavior
- violence in the home
- other self-reported violent behavior (bar fights, school fights, violence toward animals, property destruction)

The purpose of this chapter is to provide descriptive and analytic information on a sample of men who batter, assessing their backgrounds and behaviors by applying (to the extent possible) the above indices. Such research will be a first step in filling the existing gaps in empirical knowledge on batterers, with potential policy implications for the prevention and control of domestic violence as well as design for models of effective intervention. It will also have broader implications for the study of violence by removing what has previously been a false methodological barrier resulting from the ideological separation of violent crime and spouse abuse. This research focuses on the following questions:

- What are the major actuarial correlates of domestic violence (e.g., background factors, childhood precursors)?
- What are the environmental or situational correlates of domestic violence (e.g., characteristics of the relationship, history of violence in the relationship, reinforcing properties of the environment)?
- Are there "degrees" or indices of violence which are useful in the study of domestic violence? What are the situational and background variables which differentiate those who batter their partners versus those who are "generally" violent?

METHODS

Data Base

The data for this study consist of information obtained from 270 face-to-face interviews with domestic violence victims throughout the country. Respondents were former clients of LEAA-funded family violence programs; the interviews were conducted approximately three months following final contact with one of the projects.

The interview samples were drawn from five projects in four cities offering counseling or shelter services, or both. No direct legal interventions were included, although some of the cases were either prosecuted as a result of shelter support or diverted into therapy. The interviews took place in two waves over a one-year period: March-June 1980 and November 1980-February 1981.[2] Although the data are rich in an area where there is scant knowledge, the following caveats are in order:

- These are *victim* reports concerning batterers.
- Clients of domestic violence projects do not necessarily represent the population of domestic violence victims.[3]
- Those who could be reached and those who consent to an interview do not necessarily represent the population of domestic violence project clients.

Analysis Flow

The data presented make use of regression analysis and "odds ratios."[4] The latter method reflects the odds that a batterer will be abusive under a variety of conditions. This approach is modeled after Goodman's (1972) mode of analysis.

BACKGROUND FACTORS

Background factors or individual characteristics usually are defined to include social structural and demographic factors which are thought by some to be predictive of domestic violence. Although there is considerable disagreement as to the role of such factors in domestic violence, it is generally acknowledged that these factors mediate violent behaviors inside and outside the home, as well as responses to stress or conflict situations. For these analyses, background factors are defined to include the batterer's history of abuse as a child, exposure to spousal violence during childhood, and socioeconomic descriptors.

Demographics

Batterers[5] are typically in their early thirties or younger (67%), male (94%), as likely to be white as nonwhite, and tend not to have attended school beyond the level of high school (74%). Fully 30% of the batterers were unemployed at the time of the interview. They are overwhelmingly spouses or partners of victims (cohabitants).

Batterer's Childhood History

Several researchers have noted the important correlation between growing up in a violent home and violent behavior as an adult (Sorrells, 1977; Alfaro, 1978; Potts, Herzberger, & Holland, 1979). Social learning theories, for example, conceive of violence as learned and reinforced in childhood, as a coping response to stress or a method of conflict resolution, and practiced into adulthood (Bandura, 1973).

The attribution of domestic violence to background factors is termed a "generational" theory. It posits that growing up in a violent home increases the likelihood that an individual will be violent as an adult, both to a spouse and children (violence includes sexual abuse). Thus, an initial series of analyses focuses on the reationship between childhood abuse and several aspects of violence. Overall, 57% were exposed to one form or another of domestic violence as children—either as victims of child abuse or as witnesses to spousal violence. Almost one-third were *both* victims and witnesses to familial violence. Forty-five percent were victims of child abuse, while 43% were witnesses to spousal violence.[6] (Where such violence occurred, more often than not it was in combination.) These data support a generational theory but may also simply indicate the prevalence of violence in the United States.

Of even greater interest and concern is the explanatory power of this legacy in terms of several other attributes of these men, including responsiveness to interventions and both the prevalence (i.e., domestic and extradomestic) and severity of violence. These relationships are explored in later analyses.

SITUATIONAL FACTORS

Dobash and Dobash (1979) have emphasized the importance of analyzing domestic violence in a situational context, where behaviors can best be understood in terms of a range of interacting factors and influences. We investigated several situational factors and describe them below.

Relationship History and Children

The median length of relationship is slightly under five years. However, it is interesting to note that one-fifth of the cases involve relationships of eleven or more years. Separations from the batterers due to domestic violence at some point in time are reported in over 60% of the cases.

Children are present in 80% of the homes. In about one-third of these homes, victims report that the batterers physically punished one or more children "too harshly."

Abuse History and Injuries

The duration of abuse is reported as greater than three years in over half the cases. That is, 56% report three or more years of abuse in the current relationship. Over 40% of the victims report violence occurring weekly or more frequently. Seven percent report daily abuse. In over half the cases, the police were called at least once for a domestic disturbance. Of these cases, 55% report three or more calls for police assistance.

Injury is frequent: One-third report "occasional" injury and over one-fourth report "frequent" injury. Injury is defined here as bruises, lacerations, or more serious harm. Among *all* respondents, 77% report injury (bruises or worse) in the past. Nearly half (43%) report lacerations or worse. Abuse during pregnancy occurred in 44% of the cases. However, the percentage may be underestimated given that we do not know what percent of the total was pregnant during the abusive relationship. Of those who were abused during pregnancy, 18% report miscarriages due to the abuse.

Substance Abuse History

In slightly more than half the cases, the battered women report that drinking is a problem in the relationship, while one-fourth report that drugs are a problem. Drug abuse is reported to be associated with physical abuse (frequently or always) in only one case in six, while alcohol is associated in about half of the cases. This figure is relatively low when compared to other research findings on the association of alcohol and battering behavior (see Walker, 1979).

Extradomestic Violence

Few data exist on the correlation between domestic and extradomestic violence. As mentioned above, evidence suggests that exposure to domestic violence during childhood, as either victim or witness, is the strongest predictor of domestic violence. There is similar evidence to suggest links between childhood violence socialization (witness to or victim of violence) and juvenile delinquency (Alfaro, 1978), juvenile violence (Sorrells, 1980) and rape (Groth, 1979). Thus, an important area of research would explore the extent to which violent partners are also violent against nonfamily members, and the possible overlap of motivations and explanations of violence (such as generational patterns of abuse.) The findings may bear heavily on the development of a theoretical model to enhance our understanding of violence.

In our sample, slightly more than half of the batterers are violent with others as well as with their partners. Using the nomenclature of previous research (Walker, 1979), we will refer to these men as "generally" violent. Victim reports of both incidents and arrests establish the nontrivial nature of the extradomestic violence: Over 80% of those reported to be violent with nonpartners are also said to have been arrested for such behavior. Incidents of extradomestic violence occur at least four times per year (quarterly or more frequently) in nearly half the reported cases.

The Instant Incident

Finally, the instant incident, defined as the incident leading to involvement with the domestic violence intervention project, involved injury (bruises, lacerations, or worse) in two-thirds of the cases. Severity of injury was selected to further describe the violence of the batterer and is not intended to describe the context of the event, nor is it intended to depict any attributes of the relationship or the reactions of the woman involved. In a previous analysis of case data from this evaluation, this variable was found to be a strong predictor both of the type of case (e.g., what interventions were sought) and violence history (e.g., prior help sought, prior injuries; see Fagan, Lewis, Stewart, & Frieze, 1980). Thus, it is included here as a descriptor of the extent of the violence used by the batterer.

UNDERSTANDING VIOLENCE

Stepwise multiple regression analyses are undertaken to determine the situational factors and background characteristics which contribute to the incidence, severity of abuse, and prevalence of "general" violence for this sample of violent men. For each dimension of violence, we first analyze the contributions of background factors, then the role of situational variables, and finally the combined effects of both background and situational factors. These methods of describing individuals and relationships are potentially significant in explaining domestic violence. Ideally, knowledge of the contributions of these two categories of variables, together with environmental variables derived from ecological theory, will greatly enhance predictive accuracy (Monahan, 1981).

Prevalence: Domestic and Extradomestic Violence

One measure of violence is its prevalence—how widespread is an individual's violent behavior. In particular, do men who are violent only with their partners differ from men who are violent with both their partners and others, and in what ways?[7]

Until the 1970s, the study of violence either ignored domestic violence or treated domestic violence and extradomestic violence as separate phenomena. Yet there is evidence here and elsewhere that violence in the family and violence on the street may be part of a more complex continuum of violence (EMERGE, 1981; Ewing, 1982). Certain factors or predisposing characteristics, such as victimization as a child, are shared by batterers and generally violent men. The inhibitors of violence are not well understood. Monahan (1981) suggests that domestic and extradomestic violence must be considered in assessing the potential dangerousness of an individual. Knowledge of the cognitive and affective processes which affect the targeting of violence to specific victims and the severity of such violence could reveal much about these individuals and their location on a violence continuum. Such information would have special policy significance for the future prevention and control of violence.

However, despite the commonalities and shared cultural roots of batterers and generally violent men, it is important to retain the distinction between the groups. Men who batter only their partners may constitute a qualitatively different category of abusers. This large group of men is distinctive precisely because its activity is not perceived as deviant. Battering, if kept private, is in fact sanctioned by societal values of masculinity and sustained through sex role inequalities which subordinate women (see Dworkin, 1974; Straus, Gelles, & Steinmetz, 1980). Thus in struggling to establish an understanding of male violence which is empirically rather than ideologically based, the character of the two types of battering must be acknowledged.

Violence Scale

Such qualitative differences are explored in this analysis, where we examine some of the dispositional and situational characteristics which differentiate violent partners from generally violent men (i.e., those engaging in domestic and extradomestic violence). A simple dichotomous variable is used for this initial inquiry, which we call the "violence scale." This measure describes whether a batterer confines his physically violent behavior to his partner or whether he is also violent with other members of society.[8] The scale utilizes victim reports of extradomestic violence of the assailant.

Regression analyses are used first to determine the background factors which predict the "violence scale." Table 3.1, part A, shows that exposure to violence as a child strongly influences the probability of being generally violent as an adult. The predictive power of these variables is strong ($R^2 = .37$) and significant ($p \leqslant .01$). General violence is positively correlated with both the batterer witnessing spousal abuse as a child and being a victim of child abuse. Involvement in extradomestic violence is greater for men who are young and white. This latter finding is consistent with the

TABLE 3.1   Regression Analysis on Violence Scale as a Function of Background Variables and Situational Variables

A. Background Variables	r*	β
Physical violence between batterers' parents	.51	.60
Batterer's race	.42	.50
Batterer's age	−.27	−.01
Batterer abused as child	.29	.12
Batterer's employment status	−.01	.05
Batterer's education	−.04	−.03
B. Situational Variables	r**	β
Most serious injury − instant incident	.59	.59
Abuse during pregnancy	.36	.61
Most serious past injury	.35	.09
How often abused	.26	.04
Number of prior calls to police	.07	.01

*R^2 = .37, $F_{6,48}$ = 4.73, p ≤ .01 (Panel II only)
**R^2 = .52, $F_{5,49}$ = 10.71, p ≤ .01

sampling biases in the evaluation: Rural and younger men are overrepresented. However, the issue of race remains enigmatic.

The next set of analyses examine situational factors associated with extradomestic violence. Table 3.1, part B, shows that both frequency and severity of domestic violence are predictive of being generally violent. The most serious present injury, the most serious past injury, and abuse during pregnancy are strongly correlated with involvement in extradomestic violence. An extremely strong age-old taboo is being broken by those men who batter pregnant women. A greater incidence of this type of abuse indicates a high likelihood that the batterer will also be violent with others. The frequency of abuse appears to be a suppressor variable, but it is nevertheless also correlated with the batterer being generally violent. Thus, it appears that the batterers who inflict the most injurious and frequent abuse on women are also those who are violent with others.

Having confirmed that childhood experiences contribute to extradomestic violence, we need to examine more closely the relationship between the violence scale and the two indices of exposure to violence as a child. This revealed that 67% of the men who were abused as a child were also violent outside the home, as compared to 46% of the batterers who were not abused as a child (chi-square = 9.6, df = 1, p < .01). A nearly identical relationship was found by cross-tabulating the violence scale by whether the batterer had witnessed spousal violence as a child: Those who had this experience were more likely to be violent outside the home as well as violent toward their wives (61% versus 44%; chi-square = 15.3, df = 1, p < .01).

These data support a social learning theory of violence and corroborate other data showing that such experiences predict adult violence. Violence is learned in the home and reinforced during the child's early socialization experiences. An important research question would examine the reinforcing properties or contingencies of the environment which lead to the learning of violence as a behavior. For example, sex role inequalities may be an important concept that is learned during such episodes. In addition, a contextual study of the uses of violence in and outside the home would yield empirical knowledge on whether these behaviors are "coping responses to stress," "conflict resolution tactics," or the result of other cognitive processes which mediate violence.

The final regression on this scale combines both situational and background factors to predict extradomestic violence (i.e., the violence scale). The results are shown in Table 3.2 and are statistically significant (R^2=.45, df=1, p $\leq$ .05). Again, exposure to violence during the batterer's childhood is a major explanatory variable. As in the previous analyses, both childhood victimization and witnessing parental abuse are correlated. However, one of these variables has a low beta (abuse as a child), indicating that perhaps these variables are explaining the same portion of the variance.

Abuse during pregnancy is again a predictor of extradomestic violence, as is age. Younger men are more often violent against both their spouses and others. Length of abuse in the relationship is another suppressor variable—it "extracts" a portion of the variance from the age variable. Younger men in shorter but violent relationships may be more likely to be involved in extradomestic violence. Again, the more severe the domestic violence, both in type and duration, the more likely the man will also be violent with others.

Severity of Violence: Most Serious Past Injury to Victim

We next seek to represent severity of abuse by examining the most serious injury to the victim. Again, stepwise multiple regression is used to predict severity, with three sets of candidate variables: background factors, situational factors, and a combination of these.

Among the background variables for the batterer, abuse as a child, education, employment (negatively), and age predict most serious past victim injury. Again, violence between the batterer's parents appears to overlap with the abuse of the batterer as a child. Batterers with higher educational attainment appear to inflict more severe injuries, as do unemployed batterers. Age is a suppressor variable, operating on both education and employment. Closer examination of the correlations between age and these two sociodemographic variables shows that age has

TABLE 3.2   Regression Analysis on Violence Scale as a Function of
Background and Situational Variables Combined

Background/Situation	r^*	β
Violence between batterer's parent	.51	.51
Batterer's race	.42	.60
Number of prior calls to police	.07	.18
Abused during pregnancy	.36	.24
Batterer's age	−.27	−.009
Length of abuse in relationship	.03	.16
Length of cohabitation	−.08	−.11
Drinking accompanies abuse	.26	.20
Drug use accompanies abuse	−.10	.15
Number times separated due to violence	.05	−.10
Batterer's education	.04	.05
Batterer's employment status	−.01	.04
How often injured	.22	.04

$^*R^2 = .45$, $F_{13,41} = 2.59$, $p \leqslant .05$ (Panel II only)

a zero-order correlation of r=−.21 with employment and a zero-order correlation of r=.24 with education. We suspect that age is extracting some variance from employment, probably due to younger unemployed batterers, and from education, again due to younger but more highly educated batterers.

The finding on education is not surprising, given prior research (Walker, 1979). Educational attainment and employment are moderately correlated in our sample (r=.27), but they act in opposite directions on the criterion variable. It is possible here that younger but more highly educated men may produce this result. Since youth seems to predict violence, we would otherwise expect a stronger contribution of the age variable. Its low correlation indicates that the variance in age remains. Again, we suspect that younger men with higher educational attainment, as well as younger unemployed men, may inflict more severe injuries. Contextual analyses of these cases may reveal some of the cognitive processes underlying this finding.

Next, we analyze severity of violence as a function of situational variables. Part B of Table 3.3 shows again that the frequency of injury and abuse to the victim, and abuse during pregnancy, are strong predictors of the *severity* of past injury. Prior calls to police is a suppressor variable. The results are again strong and significant ($R^2 = .48$, $p \leqslant .01$).

Prior calls to police and abuse during pregnancy show a zero-order correlation of $r = -.09$, indicating a slight tendency for calls to the police to be associated with a lower incidence of abuse during pregnancy. We

TABLE 3.3 Regression Analysis on Most Serious Past Injury as a Function of Background and Situational Variables

A. Background Variables	r^*	β
Batterer abused as child	.46	.40
Batterer's education	.20	.30
Batterer's employment status	−.12	−.28
Batterer's age	.04	.22
Batterer's race	.16	.16
Violence between batterer's parents	.37	.11

B. Situational Variables	r^{**}	β
How often injured	.60	.43
Abuse during pregnancy	.34	.31
How often abused	.41	.07
Number of prior calls to police	.02	−.08
Length of cohabitation	.13	.12
Drug use accompanies abuse	−.14	−.11
Length of abuse in relationship	.18	−.08
Number of times separated due to violence	.18	−.22
Drinking accompanies abuse	.07	−.03

* $R^2 = .36$, $F_{6,164} = 15.3$, $p - .01$ (Panel II only)
** $R^2 = .48$, $F_{9,145} = 4.63$, $p - .01$ (Panel II only)

suspect that calls to the police occur more often when the victim is not pregnant but are fairly infrequent during pregnancy. Men who abuse women during pregnancy are also generally violent. A simple cross-tabulation between abuse during pregnancy and extradomestic violence shows that men who abuse women during pregnancy are 3.83 times as likely to also be violent outside the home.

Finally, we analyzed both background and situational variables as predictors of most severe past injury to the woman. The results are consistent with other analyses of prior injury and also with previous analyses of extradomestic violence. Table 3.4 shows that the frequency of domestic abuse and prior injury predicts the most serious past injury to the victim. As the frequency of domestic violence increases, so does severity of injury.

Again, socioeconomic variables are also contributors: the batterer's employment status is a negative contributor to severity of injury (i.e., when unemployed, the batterer inflicts a greater severity of injury), while education is positively correlated. Other nontrivial contributors include the batterer's childhood violence experience (i.e., abuse as a child), the batterer's age, the length of the relationship, and abuse during pregnancy.

TABLE 3.4   Regression Analysis on Most Serious Past Injury to Victim as a Function of Situational and Background Variables Combined

Background/Situational	r^*	β
How often injured	.60	.49
Abused as child	.46	.15
Batterer's employment status	−.12	−.28
Batterer's education	.19	.37
How often abused	.41	.20
Length of cohabitation	.13	.13
Number of prior calls to police	.02	−.11
Abuse during pregnancy	.34	.14
Batterer's age	.04	.15
Drinking accompanies abuse	.07	−.10
Violence between batterer's parents	.37	.10
Drug use accompanies abuse	−.14	−.03
Length of abuse in relationship	.18	−.03
Batterer's race	.17	.01
Number of times separated due to violence	.18	−.01

$^* R^2 = .62$, $F_{15,155} = 19.33$, $p \leqslant .01$ (Panel II only)

Younger men in longer relationships appear to be inflicting greater injury on victims.

Comparing the results of this composite analysis with the analysis in Table 3.4 of extradomestic violence, we see some similarities in the role of childhood exposure to violence and abuse during pregnancy. However, factors such as race and drinking are contributors to extradomestic violence but not to severity of injury. Conversely, the batterer's educational status is a strong contributor to severity but not to extradomestic violence.

A richer contextual analysis of the ecological and situational factors in these families or couples is required to understand specifically why higher educational attainment is apparently associated with severity of injury. For example, we suspect that the comparative educational attainment of victim and batterer may be theoretically more important than the educational level of either individual alone. We have observed this in analyses of postproject abuse data (Fagan, Friedman, Stewart, & Lewis, 1982).

Frequency of Involvement in Extradomestic Violence

The third violence dimension analyzed was the frequency of partner involvement in nondomestic violence. As in the previous two dimensions, we analyzed this dependent variable first with respect to batterers' background factors, then situational or relationship factors, and finally both.

TABLE 3.5   Regression Analysis on Frequency Batterer Involved in Nondomestic Violence as a Function of Background and Situational Variables

A. Background Variables	$r*$	β
Batterer's education	.24	.26
Violence between batterer's parents	−.10	−.31
Batterer abused as child	.12	.29
Batterer's age	−.04	−.07
Batterer's employment status	.06	−.04
Batterer's race	−.10	−.03
B. Situational Variables	$r**$	β
How often abuse	−.29	−.06
Number prior calls to police	−.11	−.008
Most serious past injury	−.11	.09
How often injured	−.25	−.13

* $R^2 = .13$, $F_{6,164} = 4.12$, $p \leqslant .01$ (Panel II only)
** $R^2 = .12$, $F_{4,50} = 1.68$, $p =$ n.s. (Panel II only)

TABLE 3.6   Regression Analysis on Frequency Batterer Involved in Nondomestic Violence as a Function of Background and Situational Variables Combined

Background/Situational	$r*$	β
How often abused	−.29	−.07
Batterer abused as child	.12	.26
How often injured	−.25	−.19
Drinking accompanies abuse	−.23	−.18
Batterer's education	.24	.26
Batterer physically punished children too harshly	.08	.23
Violence between batterer's parents	−.10	−.18
Drug use accompanies abuse	−.12	−.12
Batterer's employment status	.06	−.06
Length of cohabitation	.18	.25
Number of prior calls to police	−.11	−.14
Abuse during pregnancy	.00	−.05
Batterer's age	−.04	−.12
Length of abuse in relationship	.13	−.15
Number of prior separations due to violence	−.14	−.07
Batterer's race	−.10	−.07

* $R^2 = .24$, $F_{16,154} = 4.38$, $p \leqslant .01$ (Panel II only)

The results, shown in Tables 3.5 and 3.6, are statistically significant, but only a small percentage of the variance is explained by the regression. Given this caveat, we will discuss the results only in general terms, identifying the commonalities with previous analyses.

Among the background variables, the batterer's education again was a major negative predictor, with both the highest zero-order correlation and a high beta. Also, the variable of batterers' childhood exposure to parental violence was the strongest contributor but was weakly correlated. (It should be noted, however, that the batterer's history of abuse as a child is a negative predictor.) Among situational variables, frequency of injury and abuse had the highest correlations with frequency of extradomestic violence. However, all beta weights are very low. The regression for situational variables is not significant. Combining situational and background variables, the results show that the batterer's childhood abuse history (negatively), his parents violence, and his educational attainment (negatively) are again strong contributors, as is frequency of injury to the spouse. The length of cohabitation is a strong predictor of the dependent variable, as is length of abuse in the relationship (both negative contributors).

Comparing these results to the results of the previous two sets of analyses, we again see some striking similarities among explanatory variables (e.g., the batterer's childhood exposure to violence, frequency of injury and abuse to the victim, batterer's education) and some emerging relationships (e.g., length of abuse in relationship, drinking during domestic abuse). That the duration of domestic abuse is negatively correlated with frequency of stranger violence is consistent with the previous finding on age and extradomestic violence. A likely explanation is that we are observing mostly younger couples with shorter (but violent) relationships, where either domestic violence may be recent or stranger violence only recently known by the victim. Since the findings are only marginally significant, and given sample biases, we again caution readers to regard these as initial inquiries needing further study.

Comparing Three Dimensions of Violence

To this point, we have analyzed three dimensions of domestic and extradomestic violence as a function of batterer background factors and situational variables. Next, we turn to the relationship between these three scales. That is, what is the relationship among severity, prevalence, and frequency of domestic and extradomestic violence? Simple cross-tabulations are compiled for each pair of the scales used to measure violence. For example, the first of these tables revealed that 59.6% of the men who were involved in four or more incidents of nondomestic violence had seriously injured their wives, compared to 39.7% of the men who were violent outside the home three or fewer times (chi-square = 5.0, df=2, $p < .10$).

Overall, the results of the three cross-tabulations are important in two ways. First, severity of injury and the violence scales are all dimensions which appear to distinguish different segments of the sample of violent men. Second, and most important, it establishes a significant association between the two scales. Whereas previous analyses identified commonalities between these scales in terms of explanatory variables, these analyses show a strong association between the two scales.

SUMMARY AND CONCLUSIONS

Based on victim reports of batterer's histories and behaviors, three scales were assessed as indices of the frequency, prevalence, and severity of violence. There appears to be a strong relationship between severity of violence inside the home and involvement in extradomestic violence. Although frequency of extradomestic violence was associated with severity of victim injury, it did not prove to be a useful scale to identify explanatory variables for violent behavior.

Among background variables, exposure to violence during childhood was a strong and consistent predictor of both severity and prevalence. Exposure in this case is defined as witnessing spousal violence as a child or being physically abused as a child. These data support a social learning theory of violence, where early socialization to violence teaches and reinforces violence as a method of conflict resolution or as a coping mechanism.[9] Violence is transmitted through the generations. Of interest for future research are the environmental properties which provide such reinforcement and the cognitive processes associated with violent responses to certain situations. Equally important is an understanding of the factors which enable abused children to avoid violence as adults. The more we know about abused individuals who successfully resist learning or overcome having learned violence, the more effective our future prevention and intervention efforts will be.

Age also is both a strong predictor and a suppressor variable, with younger men at risk for more severe and widespread violence. Education predicts severity of victim injury, particularly for younger batterers, but not involvement in extradomestic violence. There are indications that whites are more often generally violent, but this may result from a sampling artifact. As expected, unemployment, which in this sample is high, is associated with severity of victim injury. The correlation between education and severity of injury suggests that there are factors associated with social mobility or job-related factors which may contribute to severity of injury. A more complete analysis of this variable should examine both the batterer's educational level relative to the victim's and job-satisfaction issues. With respect to race, it is interesting to note that the association reported here (for batterer's) with respect to extradomestic violence involvement is contrary to that reported for the general population: Nonwhites (and blacks in particular) are more violent than whites (see Wolfgang et al., 1972). Despite sampling biases, these findings suggest that among spouse abusers, whites are more violent both in and out of the home. Future research should carefully investigate this question.

Among situational variables, several attributes of violence in the relationship are predictive of severity of violence in the home and prevalence of violence outside the home. Frequency of violence, frequency of injury, and abuse during pregnancy are predictive of both prevalence and severity of abuse. As suggested by Walker (1979), the relationship between frequency and severity is indicative of a possible escalation. However, longitudinal data via a panel study is needed to fully analyze such escalations of violence. The data also suggest that frequency of violence in the home is predictive of the incidence of violence outside the home as well. Abuse during pregnancy also indicates that a batterer is more likely to injure the victim seriously and be violent with others. Moreover, such violence may cause miscarriage of the unborn child.

Actual violence appears to be a strong predictor of subsequent violence. However, these data also suggest a relationship between the frequency and severity of violence and its prevalence. The data suggest that severity of violence in the home is indicative of violence on the street. Future research needs to explore the degree to which the reverse is true. Do men who are incarcerated for crimes against persons, especially career criminals, also perpetrate abuse against women at home? Finally, severity of violence may not only predict future violence; it may also predict an increase in the number of victims.

Policy Implications

The data hold several implications for prevention and control of both domestic and extradomestic violence. First, those wishing to counteract violence in society should look first to violence in the home. As suggested earlier, a thorough assessment of violence potential must take into account not only past extradomestic violence (e.g., in bars, schools, the workplace) but also—and perhaps most important—prior violence in the home. Where there is also evidence of extradomestic violence, the artificial separation of domestic and extradomestic violence in research efforts creates a biased view of violent men, void of a contextual understanding of the relationships among sex roles, violence, and underlying social norms. However, in examining these relationships, we must not lose sight of the fact that in the majority of cases, violence occurs only in the home.

Second, risk factors for violence both inside and outside the home include both age and a history of violence in childhood and adulthood. It also depicts the correlates of domestic violence as consistent with other findings on violent behavior, which have been based primarily on studies of stranger violence. This, of course, requires further study with a wider sample of violent men, including those violent only outside the home.

Third, a study of "spontaneous recovery" will contribute to our knowledge of violent men and should further inform the development of intervention models. Such research has proven extremely valuable in follow-up studies of "treated" and "untreated" heroin addicts (Waldorf & Biernacki, 1980) and alcoholics (Roizen, Cahalan, & Shanks, 1975). Comparable phenomena have been observed among violent delinquents (Wolfgang et al., 1972). Similar research with violent spouses or partners may enhance the development of prevention strategies and intervention programs.

Finally, if in fact violence is learned in childhood and carried forth into adulthood, it suggests an intervention model for violent behavior which "unlearns" such behavior. Moreover, evidence in this research and elsewhere points overwhelmingly to men as the perpetrators of domestic violence (Pagelow, 1978). Thus, both future research efforts as well as intervention models should focus on batterers in conjunction with providing shelter and support for women. Programs for batterers such as EMERGE in Boston and MOVE in San Francisco attempt to implement this unlearning of male violence. Evaluation of these programs and assessment of ensuing behavioral changes can significantly contribute to the practical efficacy of such theory and models.

NOTES

1. Violence is defined for analytic purposes as physical violence. Thus, psychological abuse and verbal threats are not included in our definition of violence. This does not imply that these behaviors are not seriously abusive or injurious—on the contrary. However, given the research objectives, accounts of actual physical violence proved most methodologically sound. In this chapter, domestic violence refers to a man battering his spouse or partner. Extradomestic violence refers to the batterer's involvement in violence outside the home, as reported by the victim of the domestic incident.

2. In the subsequent tables, the first wave will be referred to as Panel I and the second wave as Panel II. Some data were collected for only Panel II due to the addition of questions and modifications to the questionnaire.

3. Battered women's shelters tend to be populated by the victims of more severe battering (Fagan et al., 1982). Also, the demographic distributions are skewed toward the lower end of the economic scale and toward a younger age group.

4. Odds ratios are used in lieu of percentages in the analysis of contingency tables because they more clearly communicate the analytic (causal) asymmetry as well as higher order (interactive) associations.

5. Throughout this chapter the term "batterer" refers to those who perpetrated the violence on the women interviewed. Because the vast majority are male, the term "violent men" is used interchangeably with batterer. This does not discount the importance of the minority of cases where a mother or grandmother is beaten by her daughter/granddaughter or the role of violence in some homosexual couples. However, a majority of cases involve the victimization of a woman by her male partner.

6. An interesting question which these interviews do not ask addresses the issue of witnessing parental abuse against siblings. This form of abuse would accurately fall

under the rubric of domestic violence and constitute another form of a violent childhood environment.

7. A third obvious category suggests itself for this analysis—those men violent outside the home. However, this study did not allow for the inclusion of this group in this sample. Future research should include such a sample to complete this inquiry.

8. The scale classifies cases who had exhibited violent behavior only in the *instant incident* leading to referral to the domestic violence project. Thus batterers who had threatened or psychologically abused their partners were not classified for this analysis, although they may have been physically violent in previous incidents of domestic abuse. The result was a sample of N = 230.

9. Patriarchy is a structural dimension of the social learning environment which perpetuates violence against women. Although it is difficult to operationalize as a set of variables, further research needs to examine the way in which social learning transmits an ideology which results in the systematic physical abuse of women.

REFERENCES

Alfaro, J. *Child abuse and subsequent delinquent behavior.* New York: State Select Committee on Child Abuse, 1978.

Bandura, A. *Aggression: A social learning analysis.* Englewood Cliffs, NJ: Prentice-Hall, 1973.

Boudon, R. A new look at correlational analysis. In H. M. Blalock, Jr. & A. Blalock (Eds.), *Methodology in social research.* New York: McGraw-Hill, 1968.

Dobash, E., & Dobash, R. *Violence against wives: A case against the patriarchy.* New York: Free Press, 1979.

Dworkin, A. *Woman hating.* New York: E. P. Dutton, 1974.

EMERGE. *Organizing and implementing services for men who batter.* Boston: EMERGE, 1981.

Ewing, W. The civic advocacy of violence. *M: Gentle Men for Gender Justice,* Spring 1982.

Fagan, J., Lewis, V., Friedman, E., Mersky, J., & Kaplan, G. *National family violence evaluation: First interim report—History and Development.* San Francisco: URSA Institute, 1979.

Fagan, J., Lewis, V., Stewart, D. K. & Frieze, I. *National family violence evaluation: Second interim report—Process evaluation.* San Francisco: URSA Institute, 1980.

Fagan, J., Friedman, E., Stewart, D., & Lewis, V. *National family violence evaluation—Final report (Volume I: Analytic findings).* San Francisco: URSA Institute, 1982.

Fisher, B., Brodsky, S., & Corse, S. Monitoring and classification guidelines and procedures. Unpublished manuscript, Center for Correctional Psychology, Department of Psychology, University of Alabama, 1977.

Goodman, L. A. A modified multiple regression approach to the analysis of dichotomous variables. *American Sociological Review,* 1972, *37.*

Griffin, S. Rape, the all American crime. *Ramparts,* 1971.

Groth, N. A. with Birnbaum, H. J. *Men who rape: The psychology of the offender.* New York: Plenum, 1979.

Hamparian, D. M., Shuster, R., Dinitz, S., & Conrad, J. *The violent few.* Lexington, MA: D. C. Heath, 1978.

Martin, D. *Battered wives.* San Francisco: Glide, 1976.

Monahan, J. The prediction of violent behavior in juveniles. Paper presented at the National Symposium on the Serious Juvenile Offender, Department of Corrections, State of Minnesota, Minneapolis, 1977.

Monahan, J. *Predicting violent behavior: An assessment of clinical techniques.* Beverly Hills, CA: Sage, 1981.

Morgan, R. *Going too far.* New York: Random House, 1974.

Pagelow, M. D. Social learning and sex roles: Violence begins in the home. Paper presented at the annual meeting of the Society for the Study of Social Problems, San Francisco, 1978.

Potts, D. A., Herzberger, S. D., & Holland, A. E. Child abuse: A cross-generational pattern of child rearing." Paper delivered at the annual meeting of the Midwestern Psychological Association, 1979.

Roizen, R., Cahalan, D., & Shanks, P. "Spontaneous remission" among untreated problem drinkers." Paper presented at Conference on Strategies of Longitudinal Research on Drug Abuse, San Juan, Puerto Rico, April 1976.

Shannon, L. Assessing the relationship of juvenile careers to adult criminal careers." Unpublished draft submitted to OJJDP, 1980.

Sorrells, J. M., Jr. Kids who kill. *Crime and Delinquency,* 1977, *23*(3).

Sorrels, J. M., Jr. What can be done about juvenile homicide? *Crime and Delinquency,* 1980, *26*(2).

Straus, M. Wife beating: Causes, treatment, and research needs. In *Battered women: Issues of public policy.* Washington, DC: U.S. Civil Rights Commission, 1978.

Straus, M. A., Gelles, R., & Steinmetz, S. *Behind closed doors: Violence in the American family.* New York: Doubleday, 1980.

Waldorf, D. & Biernacki, P. Natural recovery from opiate addiction, *Journal of Drug Issues,* Winter 1981, 61-74.

Walker, L. *The battered woman.* New York: Harper & Row, 1979.

Wolfgang, M. From boy to man—From delinquency to crime. Paper presented at the National Symposium on the Serious Juvenile Offender, Department of Corrections, State of Minnesota, Minneapolis, 1977.

Wolfgang, M., Figlio, R., & Sellin, T. *Delinquency in a birth cohort.* Chicago: University of Chicago Press, 1972.

4

Science and Violence Against Wives

LAURIE WARDELL, DAIR L. GILLESPIE, and ANN LEFFLER

INTRODUCTION: THE EMPEROR'S NEW CLOTHES

Before the reemergence of the women's movement in the late 1960s, the social science literature was largely oblivious to the possibility that women were being assaulted in familial relations with men. It was generally assumed that marriage, especially middle-class marriage, was a "companionate," egalitarian, peaceful affair in which violence played no part. O'Brien (1971) reports that the major family journal, *Journal of Marriage and the Family,* included not a single article with "violence" in the title from its founding in 1939 through 1969, and Gelles (1980) adds that violence against *adults* in families was especially invisible in the rarified atmosphere of social science literature.

The growth of the women's movement, current family violence researchers agree, has helped to stimulate major doubts about this tranquil view of American families (Straus, Gelles, & Steinmetz, 1980). Within the last decade, many professionals have acknowledged that power may routinely be distributed unequally inside the family as well as outside it, that the relationship between spouses is affected by the relationship between the genders, that the war between the sexes does not necessarily stop where conjugal relations begin (Gillespie, 1971). Social science has noticed gender stratification. It has noticed wife-beating. It has even acknowledged a connection between these two phenomena.

Authors' Note: *Copyright © 1982 by L. Wardell, D. L. Gillespie, and A. Leffler. Address correspondence to D. L. Gillespie, Department of Sociology, University of Utah, Salt Lake City, UT 84112, or A. Leffler, Department of Sociology, Utah State University, Logan, UT 84322. Leffler's work on this paper was supported in part by a Faculty Research Grant from Utah State University, and in part by a USDA/Agricultural Experiment Station grant.*

The question to be addressed in this chapter is whether these recent literature shifts indeed represent a more feminist analysis of gender relations in marriage. Have the old anti-woman biases of the literature diminished under the impact of feminism, or does the literature mainly retain its misogynist assumptions? The answer suggested will be that basically very little has changed. It is true that the analyses have been altered in what are claimed to be basic ways. It is also true that a dramatic shift has occurred in the sentiments and intentions of the literature. Writings in the area explicitly and continually call for an end to sex roles, an end to the victimization of women, a feminist rather than victim-blaming analysis of wife-beating. But underneath the new analyses and the good intentions flourish the same misogynist assumptions the literature believes it attacks.

Furthermore, it will be argued, there is more to alarm us here than just the fate of the wife-beating issue, urgent though that issue is. The continuation of sexism in the scientific battery literature illustrates the sexist basis of science itself. For with reference to the classic value-neutrality issue, were science in fact value-neutral or objective, an antiseptic tool for the discovery of pure facts, this consistent anti-woman bias could not recur. Moreover, were science simply a craft shaped by the intentions of its practitioners, were the values of science created by its participants rather than vice versa, the plethora of good intentions among the woman-battery researchers would surely produce a pro-woman literature. The anti-woman biases of the scientific literature, then, suggest that science is an institution located in a particular social system at a particular point in time. As such, it patterns the actions of we who are in it much more than vice versa. Since it is currently an institution in a sexist society, its workings reflect and contribute to the maintenance of that sexism.[1] The misogynist tilt of the battery literature, then, affords reasons to despair not only about battery but also about the possibility of moving science beyond its institutional basis in male domination.

The sexist assumptions and victim-blaming focus of the new battery literature can be seen in discussions about the role of the woman involved (for convenience, we will call her the "wife"), in proposals for solving the problem, and in the general context in which wife abuse is studied. In all three areas, battery ends up being treated more as an aberrant deviance on the wife's part than as an illumination of how male dominance works in heterosexual partnerships. What follow are discussions of this interpretative shift in each area.

THE SEARCH FOR DIFFERENCES

With respect to the role of the wife in wife abuse, the literature is preoccupied by the search for ways in which beaten wives differ from unbeaten wives. When differences are found, they are assumed to have caused assault fates. We will have a great deal to say shortly about the questionable status of specific claims that beaten and unbeaten wives differ. But first it must be mentioned that raising this "differences" issue at all exemplifies the tendency in the literature to isolate as deviant not only wife-beating but also beaten wives. The fact is that wife-beating is ordinary, and while it may not be true that every American family encompasses an adult male who is at some point violent to an adult female, still the phenomenon is very common.[2] In this context, what is called for, in Ryan's (1971) terms, is a "universalistic" rather than "exceptionalistic" analysis, a focus on family structure and male/female relationships rather than on ways in which we may speculate beaten wives differ from all other wives. Indeed, the literature generally agrees that what is required is a look at families and social structure rather than a search for some—any—distinguishing pathology on the part of the victimized woman (Straus, 1977). So much for good intentions. But in fact what are compared are not American families to families in other cultures or times, or heterosexual couples to other couples, or the well-being of women alone compared to women with men. Rather, what are compared are women categorized as victims of battering to women who have somehow escaped such categorization. And, of course, in this comparison of official victims to official nonvictims, any differences that can be found are assumed to reveal reasons why abuse starts or continues.

Since the search for differences is so popular, it is worth mentioning that this quest is methodologically indefensible. First, adequate comparison data are often missing. For instance, one version of the "cycle of violence" argument asserts that abused daughters become abused wives. But the fact is that we have no incidence studies on daughter abuse in families of origin; and using other data to proxy these rates, while common, is inappropriate. Doron (personal communication, 1981) points out another way in which comparison data are eschewed: Claims that beaten and unbeaten wives differ often rest on single-case studies of beaten wives alone, with the characteristics of unbeaten wives assumed but not documented to differ. A second problem in the differences search is that since the data are and must be based on self-report, we do not know what populations are being compared when we compare self-reported victims to self-reported nonvictims, and so we do not know whether differences between the two groups reflect the experience of being victimized, the self-perception, the interview comportment, or some other distinction entirely. Third, the data are correlational, which means that any differences between the groups may be results or accompaniments of violence rather than causes of it. Fourth, there is, of course, substantial risk of Type II errors in any wide-scale dredging for differences and throwing away similarities, and we can expect to find some apparent differences between official victims and nonvictims just by looking persistently, even if both groups are actually identical.[3]

In sum, that the question of the wife's role arises so consistently, and that official victims are so frequently compared to official nonvictims, illustrate a priori assumptions that beaten wives are deviant and somehow complicit. Indeed, there is no reliable evidence for any strong distinctions between officially battered and officially unbattered women. Associations which appear in one study disappear in the next, and those which recur tend nonetheless to be very weak (see, for instance, Gelles, 1980; Star, 1978). Given the intrinsically flawed nature of the data and the lack of clean results, if science were in fact an antiseptic search for truth, surely it would have been concluded long since that the wrong question was being asked. But the search for differences between battered and unbattered women continues, and with it the implication that battered women contribute to their own plight.

FOUR DIMENSIONS OF WIFELY COMPLICITY

Four specific analyses of the wife's role are especially popular in the literature. These include the "traditional sex-role socialization" approach (Martin, 1979; Moore, 1979; Pagelow, 1981b; Shainess, 1977; Walker, 1979b), the "provocative wife" argument (Gayford, 1978; Gelles, 1972), the "learned helplessness" analysis (Ball & Wyman, 1977-78; Walker, 1977-78, 1979a), and the "personal resource" theory (Bowker, 1981; Goode, 1974; O'Brien, 1971; Rounsaville, 1978).

In the traditional sex-role socialization approach, wives are complicit because they do not change their situation. They should leave, or let hubby know enough is enough. If they don't do this—and we know they don't because they're still being beaten—it is because they think the situation is inescapable. And if they think that, it is because they believe men have a right to beat women, or it is women's fault if men beat them, or women have no right to protest, or the like. And if they believe this, it is because they mindlessly accept that mythically monolithic "sex-role ideology," which everyone knows is delivered in a pink or blue blanket by the socialization stork. They may be married to men who are sex-role devotees, too. Possibly their traditional views were nurtured by violent families of origin, and they now are resigned to abuse because they consider it commonplace (Roy, 1977). Probably other causes also intervene, but a wife's musty attitudes definitely contribute to her assault.

The socialization line is very popular (see Moore and Pepitone-Rockwell's respondents, 1979). Nonetheless, the literature offers no evidence that battered women are any more consistent traditionalists than those legendary creatures, wives who "don't take shit." Ditto for any evidence of differences in creed between battering husbands and the legendary feminist husbands. Ditto for evidence that husbands' and wives' beliefs covary, or that hers matter at all. And ditto, of course, for evidence that any differences we could find caused rather than resulted from violence, or evidence that how individual members of the genders treat each other mainly reflects variance in sex-role ideology (Gillespie & Leffler, 1981; Kanter, 1977). Indeed, the socialization argument begs the huge questions of social psychology altogether as to whether childhood socialization as opposed to adult socialization affects adult behavior very much (Becker, Geer, Hughes, & Strauss, 1961) and whether ideations— attitudes and beliefs—do in fact cause behavior (Liska, 1975). Given all this, there is no reason to believe traditional sex-role socialization has any bearing on wife abuse. That the literature continually and groundlessly invokes it does not demonstrate that the wife's ideas play any role in her victimization.

In the second specific analysis of the wife's role, the provocative wife argument, she asks for it. Thus, marital violence is sometimes divided into "victim-precipitated violence" and "non-victim-precipitated violence," with victim-precipitated violence construed to occur when victims "contribute" through "actions defined as illegitimate by the offender or through provoking their antagonist" (Gelles, 1972, pp. 85-86). For instance, it has been suggested that researchers rate men on frustration tolerance and women on provocation potential, with the following outcome predicted:

> If men with high frustration tolerance were paired with women of high provocation, violence could not be likely to arise, but women of high provocation with men of low frustration would produce a combination where violence could be predicted. (Gayford, 1978, p. 33)[4]

Included as possibly irksome are her dowdiness, inability to manage the family and home, good home management, intelligence, sullen silence, nagging, depression, frigidity, and incapacity for deep emotional warmth (Gayford, 1978).

Like the socialization analysis, provocation theory also assumes wifely culpability. But the very nature of what is being explained here—*his* violence—means that it is the husband who gets to decide in print what he decides in fact: her guilt. After all, the only way for the provocation theorist to determine a wife's innocence is to see whether her husband is beating her. And so, under the rubric of "provocation," she may be charged in the literature with a wide array of behaviors, some of which are antonyms. Bad home management is sometimes an irritant; so is good home management. Silence can be aggravating; so can nagging. Whenever he swings, a way can be found to claim she drove him to it. Indeed, according to one argument, she may irritate him beyond bearing without doing anything at all (Gayford, 1978). This is called "passive provocation." Thus the operational definition of provocation becomes empirically equivalent to "anything she does or does not do which, after hitting her, he reports disliking." Even overlooking the by now familiar problems of data based on self-reports and of causal arguments about correlational evidence, the provocation argument is unacceptable because, being unfalsifiable, it violates a basic requirement of scientific theorizing. It thus amounts to a priori victim-blaming, not to an empirical demonstration of the wife's complicity.

Martin (1979) points out that provocation theory also constitutes a double standard for evaluating wife and husband:

> Most research into the cause of marital violence concentrates on external influences of the husband's behavior. He was under stress, he lost his job, he drank too much, his mother had an extramarital affair. Whatever the rationalization, it serves to excuse the husband's behavior and remove his responsibility for his own acts. The wife's condition is not seen in its totality, but only in terms of what she may have said or done to provoke her husband's anger. The triggering of violent events is almost always trivial (for example, she wore her hair in a ponytail, she prepared a casserole instead of fresh meat for dinner, she said she did not like the pattern of the wallpaper). In no way do any of these events warrant a violent response. Even if the woman did provoke her husband's anger, there can be no justification for these severe beatings. Furthermore, any approach that attempts to change the wife's behavior, in order to change the husband's behavior, only further victimizes her. (p. 40)

Again, by seeing him whole but her only as a gadfly, provocation theory simply axiomatizes her guilt.

One possible provocation deserves special mention for its popularity in the literature: nagging. Thus arises the argument that there is some truth to the image of the "nagging wife who finally drives her husband to belting her in the mouth" (Gelles, 1972, p. 158). Indeed, the introduction of personal resource or exchange theory (see below) to the area of wife abuse began with the claim that spouses may become verbal vampires, especially the wife, and it is when the husband can no longer tolerate her semantic attacks that he physically retaliates (Goode, 1974, p. 38). This image of the nagging wife may correspond to research stereotypes, but hardly to research findings. In the first place, with respect to verbosity in general, research on nonverbal behavior indicates that males talk more than females, "chatterbox" preconceptions notwithstanding (Henley, 1977). Second, with respect to verbal aggression, Steinmetz reports no significant differences between wives and husbands on "verbal violence" (1977a,

p. 89). Third, with respect specifically to the connection of verbal and physical aggression in the family, correlations between them have been reported (Straus et al., 1980), but these are not broken down by sex or type of verbal aggression; in addition, of course, they leave open the question of causality. In Gayford's (1975) sample, violence was *not* preceded by verbal arguments in 77% of the cases.[5] Fourth, even ignoring all this and focusing only on female nagging, it is not clear what bearing female nagging has on female abuse. Researchers sometimes point to TV situation comedies and other media depictions of nagging wives, and to beaten wives' own testimonies, as evidence that wifely vociferousness provoked husbandly violence. But it does not follow that because some women believe they might have avoided violence by keeping "silent," silence actually would have deterred it. The women who believe this, after all, have seen the same situation comedies the researchers have. And before concluding that it is provocative for women to voice complaints against their spouses, it should be remembered that even if she keeps quiet, he may hit her anyway, this time for "sullen silence" or a lack of "deep emotional warmth." It is also worth asking whether he possibly may deserve "nagging"—also known as a female voicing a grievance. If he does deserve it, then it would seem the original provocation, and the blame, are his. Of course, the usual correlational problem may apply: Even if female nagging is loutish, perhaps battered naggers scold to retaliate for the physical victories their husbands have already won. In any case, what is clear is that the fault is not the wife's, nagger or no.

In sum, the provocative wife analysis amounts to accepting the husband's own self-aggrandizing version that it is all her fault. And when the literature offers examples of her provocation, it is unclear what the "Parfait Wif" can do to avoid provoking her aggrieved husband into beating her and the provocation theory social scientists into claiming she asked for it. By the same token, however, if whatever she does is interpreted to encourage violence, then no particular thing she does can be blamed. As with socialization theory, here again we reach the conclusion that the wife does not play a role in her own abuse.

In the learned helplessness analysis, women remain in battery situations because they have acquired poor self-images and now believe they cannot end or escape the abuse. In the first place, however, wives' feelings of helplessness may be valid, as Campbell (1978) illustrates:

> People take the attitude that anyone who does not walk away from such terrible treatment is too spineless or stupid to be bothered about, that they only have themselves to blame. They have no conception of the soul-destroying, grinding quality of the terror experienced by these women. The battered wives are afraid to stay, and terrified to leave for fear of inescapable reprisals.

> Husbands display diabolical cunning in finding women who have left them. They track them down—sometimes after years—to beat them and terrorise them, sometimes to kill them. They threaten to blow up and burn the women's homes, which frequently house their own children. They kidnap the children and abuse them, threatening worse if the wives do not return. (pp. 150-151)

In such situations, to notice that one lacks alternatives signifies rationality, not a poor self-image. Significantly, battered women neither feel nor appear helpless about other aspects of their lives (Rounsaville, 1978). Indeed, violence may increase rather than diminish their independence (Prescott & Letko, 1977). But regardless of ego robustness, frequently there is nothing wives can do (Waites, 1977-78), and frequently they know that because they have already tried everything but to no avail (Pagelow, 1981a). The first reason wives may feel helpless about battery, then, is that they may be helpless.

In the second place, no doubt some victims overlook some alternatives open to them. But before concluding that such shortsightedness suggests the complicity of a learned failure to cope syndrome, wives' resignation must be compared with that of other groups who make erroneous judgments in ambiguous situations. It is no more valid to assume that characterological dysfunctions cause battered women to remain with their assaulters than to assume that such dysfunctions are the reasons why people retain lemon cars, for instance, or keep their houses although the neighbors have been robbed twice, or get Ph.D.s when universities are not hiring. Once disaster strikes, such decisions may seem irrational and foolish. But in the absence of hindsight or pure objectivity, they may well be reasonable when they are made. And once made, they tend to generate more of the same objectively mistaken decisions. Having paid to reline the brakes, for example, it seems foolish to junk a car which now needs an engine overhaul. Similarly for battered wives—he may in truth stop hitting her after this. Thus, there is no more evidence of a characterological disorder in a wife's mistakenly staying than in the common cross-population phenomenon of erroneous judgments in general. Of course, often she is staying because of a correct evaluation that she lacks alternatives. The theory of learned helplessness merely labels as a peculiarity of the battery victim what is in fact a reasonable response to an unreasonable situation, and thus diverts attention to her from it.

The final common way of attributing a causal role in wife-beating to the wife is the personal resource theory, in which he isn't man enough to rule the roost in the normal way, so she outshines him, so he hits her and becomes boss again. Or, in social science phrasing:

> One should find that violence is most common in those families where the classically dominant member (male-adult-husband) fails to

possess the superior skills, talents or resources on which his preferred superior status is supposed to be legitimately based. Hence it was expected that violent behavior would be disproportionately prevalent in families where the husband-father was deficient relative to his wife-mother in achieved status characteristics. (O'Brien, 1971, p. 68)

The problem with this theory is that, as the copious literature on gender stratification implies, families in which she outscores him in status are very rare (Gillespie, 1971). Women are discriminated against in employment, promotions, job titles, and pay, not to mention the John/ Joan McKay kind of double standard in which women's performance is systematically denigrated compared to men's (Goldberg, 1968; Stromberg & Harkness, 1978). Under these circumstances, it would be astounding were researchers to find many of the purportedly wife-dominant or wife-superior families which supposedly drive husbands berserk. In fact, researchers do not find such families. Nor, of course, do they abandon the personal resource theory. What they do instead is change the operational definition of "wife-dominant/wife-superior" so that it is a contest the husband can lose.[6] Thus, he may be compared to her on a variety of dimensions, and if he loses on one—any one—she wears the pants in the family, even if he wins on the rest. Or he may be compared not to her but to her father. Or he may be compared to her expectations of what an ideal husband should be: If he falls short in her mind, it becomes stressful and he hits her. Or the deficient husband may be compared to his own expectations of what an ideal husband or ideal man should be. (Notice, incidentally, that earlier we learned if she falls short of his expectations concerning perfect wives, that's stressful and he hits her. In other words, if anyone falls short of anyone's expectations, it's all her fault and we can see why he hits her.) Or, finally, if no comparison within the relationship shows him henpecked, the analysis can move outside the relationship and contrast him to other men. If he has less resources than they, or less power over her than they have over their wives, we may conclude that there is a personal resource imbalance in her favor after all, and he is using violence to right the scales. For instance, there is the claim that lower-class husbands "may be impelled to use overt force because they lack other resources that yield power and force to middle or upper class parents and husbands" (Goode, 1974, p. 32). Fittingly, this last version of Nomenclatural Ways to End Male Dominance is most often used to explain why wife-beating occurs mainly in the lower classes, a fact which does not need explaining, since the evidence is contradictory (Martin, 1976; conflicting evidence is found, for instance, in Gelles, 1980, and in Straus et al., 1980).

In sum, the way the literature depicts the battered wife illustrates its sexism. She is considered to differ from officially unbattered women, and her purported differences are assumed to play some role in her own victimization. The particular role it is argued she plays has to do with her supposed traditional sex-role socialization, provocative behavior, learned helplessness, and/or superiority in personal resources. But given the lack of empirical support for these depictions, this persistent emphasis on the wife simply reveals an a priori assumption of victim-blaming. It functions only to divert emphasis from male domination as the cause of wife-beating.

SOLUTIONS: INDIVIDUAL-LEVEL REFORMS

The same things happen with respect to the way the literature handles solutions to wife abuse, and the general context in which it imbeds the problem. With respect to solutions, the literature does call for changes in sex roles, but a closer examination of this proposal reveals that it is mainly the wife's role that is to change. The direction of change is to be that the wife get her head straight and liberate herself from antiquated sex role ideology (the solution implied by socialization theory), that she stop goading her husband into beating her (provocation theory), that she become more assertive and self-accepting (learned helplessness theory), or that she abandon her purported possibility of resource threat within the marriage so that her husband will no longer seize upon violence as a way to right the balance (personal resource theory). What is being called for here is a set of individual-level changes, not changes in the social structure. And as we have already seen, there is no particular reason to believe that any of these solutions can help. Instead, each encourages a continued focus on the wife and a continued view of wife-beating as an aberrant phenomenon which occurs only in deviant families. Thus, with respect to solutions, again the literature blames more than befriends the beaten wife.

We cannot justify this victim-blaming predilection in the scientific choice of solutions by arguing that, after all, we need short-term individual-level reforms while we simultaneously fight for long-term structural changes. This may be true, but one still must choose one's short-term reforms. The particular reforms advocated in the literature rest on analyses that are impediments to long-term structural change rather than harmonious accompaniments to it. It is also true that the literature freely supports other proposals for change as well: shopping lists of them, in fact. But many of the items on these lists appeared in movement documents before social science discovered wife-beating.[7] And if the main contribution of science was to fluff out movement demands with its own wife-focused solutions, again the question is whether science is more a hindrance than a help.

WIFE ABUSE IN SOCIOPOLITICAL CONTEXT

The final issue with respect to which this question arises is the general context in which wife-beating is studied. Here the sexist bias of the literature reveals itself in parallels drawn between wife abuse and other social phenomena. These parallels commonly analogize wife abuse to attitudes about violence in general, or to any other kind of violence at all (including female violence against men), rather than to other forms of male violence against women. The result is that wife abuse is stripped of its behavioral outcome and gender basis.

The most famous example of bowdlerization-by-analogy involves husband-beating, occasionally claimed to be as pervasive and serious as wife abuse (e.g., Steinmetz, 1977-78). This argument has been strongly challenged by a number of critics, who have pointed out that since wife-beating is actually much more pervasive *and* serious, to equate the two is to take wife-beating lightly (Fields & Kirchner, 1978; Pleck, Pleck, Grossman, & Bart, 1977-78). But most other analogies have fared better in the literature. Thus, wife abuse is analogized to public support for the death penalty and other attitudinal measures of support for violence in general (e.g., Gelles, 1975; Steinmetz, 1977a), as if a husband's actually beating his wife is essentially the same phenomenon as a "yes" response to the question, "Do you approve of capital punishment?" Similarly, parallels are drawn between violence against children and violence against wives, without distinguishing the nature of the violence used or the circumstances in which it occurs, and thus with the implication that a mother's spanking her child, or siblings' coming to blows, is equivalent to a husband's breaking his wife's ribs (Gayford, 1975; Gelles, 1972, 1978). What is left out in these inappropriate analogies is the context in which wife abuse occurs: the nature of the abuse, the situation itself, and the supposed role obligations of members within each relationship (Dobash & Dobash, 1979; Klein, 1979; McGrath, 1979; Pagelow, 1979). An adult male's assaulting an adult female is not like answering "yes" on a survey question, mildly disciplining a wayward child whose father assumes few parenting responsibilities, or siblings' tussling. Because of the context in which wife abuse occurs, more appropriate analogies would be between wife-beating and rape, sexual assault, incest, sexual harassment, and possibly the abuse of elderly women.[8] But this latter form of analogy rests on a feminist analysis of wife abuse as occurring in the social context of male domination,[9] and it is this context which the literature does not recognize, despite its calls for changes in sex roles.

THE SCIENTIFIC CONTEXT:
THE ROAD TO MISOGYNY IS PAVED
WITH GOOD INTENTIONS

In sum, despite its genuinely benevolent intentions, the wife-beating literature is riddled with misogyny. Its sexist biases may be seen with respect to its analyses of the causes, solutions, and context of the problem.

Far from representing an alternative to sexist depictions of the family, the literature on wife abuse reiterates them. Under the rubric of concern for victims, it merely continues the tradition of victim-blaming it purports to challenge. In consequence, it offers no thoroughgoing challenge to the myth of domestic tranquility, or an insightful analysis of how male dominance operates in the specific context of heterosexual domiciles. The women's movement may well have helped prod science into addressing the issue of wife-beating, as the literature acknowledges. But scientific gratitude, its own desires notwithstanding, does not extend to eschewing misogyny in its analyses.

In examining the case of wife-beating, we find grounds for concern not only with this specific literature but also with science itself. The wife-beating literature is self-consciously and explicitly anti-sexist; its creators are sincerely and openly committed to advancing the situation of battered wives and of women in general. But what has resulted is sexism as usual. Were science purely objective, this could not have occurred. Were science itself simply a tool that could be put to whatever use its practitioners choose, this could not have occurred. Were science the product of its producers' wills and intentions, this could not have occurred. The only circumstances that can explain the sexism of the wife-beating literature are, first, that science itself is an institution rather than an independent realm of ideas, and second, that as an institution, science itself is shaped by and reinforces the sexism of the society in which it exists. In the process, it molds what we as scientists do much more than our good intentions appear to mold it.

NOTES

1. Some progressives, believing the scientific method superior to all other epistemologies, suggest that we can rescue science from elite control and use it for democratic purposes (e.g., Nelson, 1981; Weisstein, Blaisdell, & Lemisch, 1975). Trained scientists ourselves, we too reject nonscientific epistemologies, but we also are forced by such cases as the battery literature to reject the notion that science currently *or potentially* reflects some abstract "scientific method." Nor do we see any reason to exempt those of us who "mean well" from the effects of institutional science.

2. For a variety of acknowledged methodological problems in the literature, it is not known precisely how common, but it is accepted that violence against women is a common feature of families.

3. A similar set of criticisms has been raised in the sociology of gender literature concerning the search for male/female differences. See, for example, Tresemer (1975).

4. Unfortunately, Gayford does not predict the outcome of matches between high-frustration men and low-provocation women. If the result were violence—and many examples in the literature suggest it may be—then the role of provocation is questionable. See Martin (1976) for illustrative examples.

5. This sample is not representative, but neither are most of the other data bases used in the area.

6. Neatly, this is often justified by means of socialization theory. As tots, husbands were habituated to continuous success. If the researcher can now devise a contest they may lose, so can they. This disgruntles them, and they hit.

Unfortunately, since it is the human lot occasionally to lose, and the human experience mainly to bear it, this theory does not explain why husbands hit wives. Nor does it explain why wives should be called winners on any excuse in order that husbands may be called losers.

Incidentally, even when family power is scored in such a way that he may lose, it is not clear this produces battery: Wives seem to be victimized most often in husband-dominated marriages (Adler, 1981; Straus et al., 1980).

7. See, for instance, the anthologies edited by Babcox and Belkin (1971) and Morgan (1970).

8. The possible parallel between wife and elderly abuse was brought to our attention by B. Pitcher (personal communication, 1981). The parallel seems to extend to the two data bases as well, both literatures exhibiting similar empirical as well as theoretical problems.

9. Similarly, expanding the analysis from sexism to oppression in general, wife abuse can be likened to any routine deployment of violence one group can call up to keep another subordinate. This would include routine violence in the maintenance of white hegemony, upper-class and heterosexual superordinance, and the like.

Using this focus on power imbalances, one could also support the analogy in the literature between wife abuse and violence against children, concluding with a condemnation of both. However, we ourselves consider that the child/parent relation, though in many ways indeed a power imbalance, differs somewhat from such types of imbalance as wife abuse. More important, the literature itself rejects the notion of power imbalances entirely when it analogizes wife-beating with violence against children and, therefore, for the purposes of this chapter, the issue is moot. When the literature likens wives to children, the purported similarities have to do with the victims' irresponsibility, unacceptable comportment, or personal defenselessness, rather than with a common political subordinance. The idea is that wives, like children, may be irksome, but they still deserve protection. It is this context to which we are objecting.

REFERENCES

Abramson, C. *Spouse abuse: An annotated bibliography.* Washington, DC: Center for Women Policy Studies, 1977.

Adler, E. S. The underside of married life: Power, influence, and violence. In L. H. Bowker (Ed.), *Women and crime in America.* New York: Macmillan, 1981.

Allen, C. M. & Straus, M. A. Resources, power, and husband-wife violence. In M. A. Straus & G. T. Hotaling (Eds.), *The social causes of husband-wife violence.* Minneapolis: University of Minnesota Press, 1980.

Anonymous. Working with battered women: An interview with Lisa Leghorn. *Victimology,* 1977-78, *3*(1-2), 91-107.

Babcox, D., & Belkin, M. (Eds.). *Liberation now! Writings from the women's liberation movement.* New York: Dell, 1971.

Baker, J. *Stopping wife abuse.* Garden City, NY: Doubleday, 1979.

Ball, P. G., & Wyman, E. Battered wives and powerlessness: What can counselors do? *Victimology,* 1977-78, *2*(3-4), 545-552.

Bard, M., & Zacker, J. The prevention of family violence: Dilemmas of community intervention. *Journal of Marriage and the Family,* 1971, *33*(4), 677-682.

Becker, H. S., Geer, B., Hughes, E. C., & Strauss, A. L. *Boys in white.* Chicago: University of Chicago Press, 1961.

Bowker, L. H. Wife beating. In L. H. Bowker (Ed.), *Women and Crime in America*. New York: Macmillan, 1981.

Campbell, M. Battered wives. In V. D'Oyley (Ed.), *Domestic violence: Issues and dynamics*. Toronto: Ontario Institute for Studies in Education, 1978.

Carroll, J. C. A cultural-consistency theory of family violence in Mexican-American and Jewish-ethnic groups. In M. A. Straus & G. T. Hotaling (Eds.), *The social causes of husband-wife violence*. Minneapolis: University of Minnesota Press, 1980.

Clarenback, K. F., & Wilson, C. F. *Violence against women: Causes and prevention— A literature search and annotated bibliography* (2nd ed.). Rockville, MD: National Clearinghouse on Domestic Violence, 1980.

Dobash, R. E., & Dobash, R. *Violence against wives*. New York: Free Press, 1979.

Fields, M. J., & Kirchner, R. M. Battered women are still in need: A reply to Steinmetz. *Victimology*, 1978, *3*(1-2), 216-222.

Fleming, J. B. *Stopping wife abuse*. Garden City, NY: Doubleday, 1979.

Gayford, J. J. Wife-battering: A preliminary survey of 100 cases. *British Medical Journal*, 1975, *25*, 194-197.

Gayford, J. J. Battered wives. In J. P. Martin (Ed.), *Violence and the family*. Chichester, England: John Wiley, 1978.

Gelles, R. J. *The violent home: A study of physical aggression between husbands and wives*. Beverly Hills, CA: Sage, 1972.

Gelles, R. J. Family experience and public support of the death penalty. *American Journal of Orthopsychiatry*, 1975, *45*, 496-513.

Gelles, R. J. No place to go: The social dynamics of marital violence. In M. Roy (Ed.), *Battered women: A psychosociological study of domestic violence*. New York: Van Nostrand Reinhold, 1976.

Gelles, R. J. Violence in the American family. In J. P. Martin (Ed.), *Violence and the family*. Chichester, England: John Wiley, 1978.

Gelles, R. J. Violence in the family: A review of research in the seventies. *Journal of Marriage and the Family*, 1980, *42*(4), 873-885.

Gelles, R. J., & Straus, M. A. Violence in the American family. *Journal of Social Issues*, 1979, *35*(2), 15-39.

Gillespie, D. L. Who has the power? The marital struggle. *Journal of Marriage and the Family*, 1971, *33*(3), 445-458.

Gillespie, D. L., & Leffler, A. Idealist explanations of gender stratification. Working paper, 1981.

Goldberg, P. Are women prejudiced against women? *Trans-Action*, 1968, *5*(5), 28-30.

Goode, W. J. Force and violence in the family. In S. K. Steinmetz & M. A. Straus (Eds.), *Violence in the family*. New York: Harper & Row, 1974.

Hake, L. J. *Diary of a battered housewife*. Independence, KY: Feminist Publications, 1977.

Handelman, P. J. Book review of *Battered women*. (M. Roy, Ed.) *Journal of Marriage and the Family*, 1979, *41*(2), 432-433.

Henley, N. *Body politics: Power, sex, and nonverbal communication*. Englewood Cliffs, NJ: Prentice-Hall, 1977.

Hotaling, G. T., & Straus, M. A. Culture, social organization, and irony in the study of family violence. In M. A. Straus & G. T. Hotaling (Eds.), *The social causes of husband-wife violence*. Minneapolis: University of Minnesota Press, 1980.

Kanter, R. M. *Men and women of the corporation*. New York: Basic Books, 1977.

Klein, D. Can this marriage be saved? Battery and sheltering. *Crime and Social Justice*, 1979, *12*, 19-33.

Langley, R., & Levy, R. *Wife-beating: The silent crisis.* New York: E. P. Dutton, 1977.

Marquardt, J. A., & Cox, C. Violence against wives: Expected effects of Utah's Spouse Abuse Act. *Journal of Contemporary Law,* 1979, *5*(2), 277-292.

Martin, D. *Battered wives.* San Francisco: Glide, 1976.

Martin, D. What keeps a woman captive in a violent relationship? The social context of battering. In D. M. Moore (Ed.), *Battered women.* Beverly Hills, CA: Sage, 1979.

McDonald, G. W. Book review of S. K. Steinmetz, *The cycle of violence. Journal of Marriage and the Family,* 1979, *41*(1), 197-199.

McGrath, C. The crisis of the domestic order. *Socialist Review,* 1979, *43,* 11-30.

Menzies, K. S. The road to independence: The role of a refuge. *Victimology,* 1978, *3*(1-2), 141-148.

Moore, D. M. Editor's introduction: An overview of the problem. In D. M. Moore (Ed.), *Battered women.* Beverly Hills, CA: Sage, 1979.

Moore, D. M., & Pepitone-Rockwell, F. Experiences with and views about battering. In D. M. Moore (Ed.), *Battered women.* Beverly Hills, CA: Sage, 1979.

Morgan, R. (Ed.). *Sisterhood is powerful.* New York: Random House, 1970.

Nadeau, O., & Kent, S. *Resource handbook for abused spouses.* Salt Lake City, UT: Department of Social Services, 1978-79.

Nelson, H. A. *Sociology in bondage: An introduction to graduate study.* Saratoga, CA: Century Twenty One, 1981.

O'Brien, J. E. Violence in divorce-prone families. *Journal of Marriage and the Family,* 1971, *33*(4), 692-698.

Pagelow, M. D. Research on woman battering. In J. B. Fleming (Ed.) *Stopping wife abuse.* Garden City, NY: Doubleday, 1979.

Pagelow, M. D. Secondary battering and alternatives of female victims to spouse abuse. In L. H. Bowker (Ed.), *Women and crime in America.* New York: Macmillan, 1981. (a)

Pagelow, M. D. Sex roles, power, and woman battering. In L. H. Bowker (Ed.), *Women and crime in America.* New York: Macmillan, 1981. (b)

Pizzey, E. *Scream quietly or the neighbors will hear.* Baltimore, MD: Penguin, 1974.

Pleck, E., Pleck, J. J., Grossman, M., & Bart, P. B. The battered data syndrome: A comment on Steinmetz article. *Victimology,* 1977-78, *2*(3-4), 680-683.

Prescott, S., & Letko, C. Battered women: A social psychological perspective. In M. Roy (Ed.), *Battered women: A psychosociological study of domestic violence.* New York: Van Nostrand Reinhold, 1977.

Rounsaville, B. J. Theories in marital violence: Evidence from a study of battered women. *Victimology,* 1978, *3*(1-2), 11-31.

Roy, M. A current survey of 150 cases. In M. Roy (Ed.), *Battered women: A psychosociological study of domestic violence.* New York: Van Nostrand Reinhold, 1977.

Russell, D.E.H., & Van deVens, M. (Eds.). *Crimes against women: Proceedings of the international tribunal.* Millbrae, CA: Les Femmes, 1976.

Ryan, W. *Blaming the victim.* New York: Random House, 1971.

Scanzoni, J. H. *Sex roles, life styles, and childrearing.* New York: Free Press, 1975.

Shainess, N. Psychological aspects of wifebattering. In M. Roy (Ed.), *Battered women: A psychosociological study of domestic violence.* New York: Van Nostrand Reinhold, 1977.

Sprey, J. On the management of conflict in families. *Journal of Marriage and the Family,* 1971, *33*(4), 722-731.

Star, B. Comparing battered and non-battered women. *Victimology,* 1978, *3*(1-2), 32-44.

Steinmetz, S. K. *The cycle of violence.* New York: Praeger, 1977. (a)

Steinmetz, S. K. Wife-beating, husbandbeating—A comparison of the use of physical violence between spouses to resolve marital fights. In M. Roy (Ed.) *Battered women: A psychosociological study of domestic violence,* New York: Van Nostrand Reinhold, 1977. (b)

Steinmetz, S. K. The battered husband syndrome. *Victimology,* 1977-78, 2 (3-4), 499-509.

Steinmetz, S. K. Services to battered women: Our greatest need. A reply to Fields and Kirchner. *Victimology,* 1978, *3*(1-2), 222-226.

Steinmetz, S. K., & Straus, M. A. (Eds.). *Violence in the family.* New York: Harper & Row, 1974.

Straus, M. A. A sociological perspective on the prevention and treatment of wifebeating. In M. Roy (Ed.), *Battered women: A psychosociological study of domestic violence.* New York: Van Nostrand Reinhold, 1977.

Straus, M. A. Measuring intrafamily conflict and violence: The conflict tactics (CT) scales. *Journal of Marriage and the Family,* 1979, *41*(1), 75-88.

Straus, M. A. Sexual inequality and wife beating. In M. A. Straus & G. T. Hotaling (Eds.), *The social causes of husband-wife violence.* Minneapolis: University of Minnesota Press, 1980. (a)

Straus, M. A. Wife-beating: How common and why? In M. A. Straus & G. T. Hotaling (Eds.), *The social causes of husband-wife violence.* Minneapolis: University of Minnesota Press, 1980. (b)

Straus, M. A., Gelles, R. J., & Steinmetz, S. K. *Behind closed doors.* Garden City, NY: Doubleday, 1980.

Stromberg, A. H., & Harkness, S. *Women working: Theories and facts in perspective.* Palo Alto, CA: Mayfield, 1978.

Tresemer, D. Assumptions made about gender roles. In M. Millman & R. M. Kanter (Eds.), *Another voice: Feminist perspectives on social life and social science.* Garden City, NY: Doubleday, 1975.

Waites, E. A. Female masochism and the enforced restriction of choice. *Victimology,* 1977-78, *2*(3-4), 535-544.

Walker, L. *The battered woman.* New York: Harper & Row, 1979. (a)

Walker, L. How battering happens and how to stop it. In D. M. Moore (Ed.), *Battered women.* Beverly Hills, CA: Sage, 1979. (b)

Walker, L. E. Battered women and learned helplessness. *Victimology,* 1977-78, *2*(3-4), 525-534.

Weisstein, N., Blaisdell, V., & Lemisch, J. *The godfathers: Freudians, Marxists, and the scientific and political protection societies.* New Haven, CT: Belladonna, 1975.

Whitehurst, R. Violence in husband-wife interaction. In S. K. Steinmetz & M. A. Straus (Eds.), *Violence in the family.* New York: Harper & Row, 1974.

SECTION III

PHYSICAL AND SEXUAL ABUSE OF CHILDREN

Child abuse is the aspect of family violence that has the longest tradition of theory and research. Much of our contemporary research and clinical concern about child abuse date from the early 1960s, the era when Henry Kempe and his colleagues published their first papers on the phenomenon they identified as the "battered child syndrome."

Given this 20-year history, it is not surprising that the status of knowledge about child abuse seems more advanced than other areas of family violence, such as wife abuse. Child abuse research has benefited from such advanced research opportunities as longitudinal prospective studies aimed at identifying both predictors for abuse (Hunter, 1978) and some of the long-term effects of abuse (Elmer, 1977). It has benefited from the passage of laws which instituted the official reporting of child abuse and the collection of nationwide data about its incidence (American Humane Association, 1978). It has also benefited from the existence of a special federal agency, the National Center for Child Abuse and Neglect, which has funded research on the subject.

The tradition of research on child abuse has not been so long, however, that surprising discoveries do not still await researchers of this problem. As recently as the late 1970s, a number of important developments changed researchers' basic perspective about child abuse. One development was a recognition of the extent of abuse committed against adolescents (Garbarino & Gilliam, 1980).

Another development was recognition of the extent of sexual abuse committed against children. Sexual abuse was not frequently noticed by clinicians prior to 1975. Since the first collection of national statistics in 1976, however, sexual abuse has grown faster than any other form of child abuse and neglect (MacFarlane, 1980). Prevalence studies indicate that a substantial number of children are sexually victimized, and, depending on definitions, it can be argued that sexual abuse is even more common than physical abuse (Finkelhor, 1979, 1982a, 1982b; Russell, 1981).

Unfortunately, however, research on sexual abuse is not very advanced, in part because it has only recently been discovered as a social problem. Chapter 6, "Exploring Intrafamilial Child Sexual Abuse: A Systems Approach" by Kathleen Tierney and David Corwin, presents an overview and critique of the current status of this research.

One way in which research on sexual abuse may benefit from the tradition of child abuse research that has preceded it is by avoiding the temptation to apply oversimplified and single-factor explanations to a complex phenomenon. A very important point made by Tierney and Corwin is that a host of factors from a variety of levels need to be taken into consideration in accounting for the occurrence of sexual abuse.

Sexual abuse, like child abuse when it was first discovered, is thought of as such an outrageous and threatening behavior that people easily turn to explanations which ascribe it to offenders who are sick and bizarre. In showing how a variety of sociological, familial, and individual factors can create pressures leading toward sexual abuse, Tierney and Corwin reject a psychopathological model of sexual abuse.

However, they give somewhat insufficient consideration to one important set of variables that need to be incorporated in explaining sexual abuse: sociocultural factors and socialization experiences. We need to understand, for example, how sexual abuse may be promoted by pornography, the sexualization of children in the media, the sexualization of power and dominance in the society as a whole, and the fact that males in our society are given little preparation for nurturant and affectionate interchanges with children which contain no sexual component (Finkelhor, 1982a, 1982b; Herman, 1981; Rush, 1980).

In addition to new insights about its nature and scope, the 1970s have also brought some important new *theoretical* developments to the understanding of child abuse. One was the development of an "ecological" perspective on child abuse—a model that integrated knowledge about child development, familial and community processes in the etiology of child abuse (Garbarino, 1977). Another was the adaptation of sociobiological thinking to the problem of child abuse, the theme of Chapter 5.

Robert Burgess and James Garbarino's "Doing What Comes Naturally? An Evolutionary Perspective on Child Abuse" presents child abuse in the context of the insights of evolutionary biology. In so doing, it advances even further the trend in theorizing about child abuse that moves away from a clinical focus on the individual abuser. Not only may sociocultural factors, such as attitudes approving of violence, play a role in child abuse, but so may even broader cross-species biological factors, such as the desire of organisms to maximize their own genes' chance for reproduction.

Discussions of child abuse from the perspective of evolutionary biology are still rather recent, but Burgess and Garbarino's provocative speculations prompt some important questions. Parents of our species may be impelled, as they argue, to harm their own children, particularly "high cost" or low reproductive potential children, as a way of "conserving parental resources" or minimizing investment in these children. But clearly, then, the best strategy for these parents—according to the theory at least—is to kill the children. By eliminating the children, parents are truly free to concentrate investment on better risks. If, however, they only maim or injure or further disable a child, they have probably increased the amount of child-caring investment they are going to have to make in the child in the future, while at the same time further compromising the likelihood that the abused child will be able to reproduce effectively. In terms of parental investment and the inclusive fitness model, infanticide makes some sense but child abuse does not.

Ironically, in our own society, at least, nonlethal child abuse is much more common than infanticide. Moreover, many of the acts of child abusers cannot really be interpreted as simply half-inhibited attempts to kill the child. Child abuse and infanticide appear to be somewhat distinct phenomena. In what we actually see in most cases of child abuse, parents are doing things that would seem disadvantageous to their opportunities for differential reproduction. Why they should behave this way is a perplexing problem from the point of view of evolutionary biology, but one that grows out of thought-provoking work of Burgess and Garbarino in the next chapter.

REFERENCES

American Humane Association. *National study of child abuse and neglect reporting.* Denver, CO: AHA, 1978.

Elmer, E. A follow-up study of traumatized children. *Pediatrics,* 1977, *59,* 273-279.

Finkelhor, D. *Sexually victimized children.* New York: Free Press, 1979.

Finkelhor, D. *Child sexual abuse in a Boston survey.* Paper presented at the National Conference on Child Sexual Victimization, Washington, D.C., 1982. (a)

Finkelhor, D. Sexual abuse: A sociological perspective. *Child Abuse and Neglect,* 1982. (b)

Gaines, R. et al. Etiological factors in child maltreatment: Multivariate study of abusing, neglecting and normal mothers. *Journal of Abnormal Psychology,* 1978, *87,* 531-540.

Garbarino, J. The human ecology of child maltreatment. *Journal of Marriage and the Family,* 1977, *39,* 721-735.

Garbarino, J., & Gilliam, G. *Understanding abusive families.* Lexington, MA: D. C. Heath, 1980.

Herman, J. *Father-daughter incest.* Cambridge: Harvard University Press, 1981.

Hunter, R. Antecedents of child abuse and neglect in premature infants: A prospective study in a newborn intensive care unit. *Pediatrics,* 1978, *61,* 629-635.

Kempe, C. H. et al. The battered child syndrome. *Journal of the American Medical Association,* 1962, *181,* 17-24.

MacFarlane, K. Remarks to the Advisory Committee to the National Center for the Prevention and Control of Rape, June 1980.

Rush, F. *The best kept secret.* Englewood Cliffs, NJ: Prentice-Hall, 1980.

Russell, D. *Preliminary report on some findings relating to the trauma and long-term effects of intrafamily childhood sexual abuse.* Paper presented at the Conference on Child Prostitution and Pornography, Boston, 1981.

5

Doing What Comes Naturally?

An Evolutionary Perspective on Child Abuse

ROBERT L. BURGESS and JAMES GARBARINO

Child abuse refers to any nonaccidental injury sustained by a child under 18 years of age resulting from acts of commission or omission by a parent, guardian, or other caretakers, although our concern here lies only with abuse perpetrated by adults in the parental role. Such acts range from violent, impulsive, extreme physical assault to nonimpulsive, seemingly deliberate torture of a child to intentional psychological deprivation. The definition of child abuse in the abstract is much easier to accomplish, however, than its documentation in particular instances. One reason for this is that each specific case implies the application of community standards and individual expertise (Garbarino & Gilliam, 1980). Another reason for this difficulty in the determination of child abuse is that the actual events are rarely observed by anyone other than immediate family members in the case of abuse by parents. Child abuse typically occurs behind closed doors. Most often a child's physical injuries are the only indicators of abuse. And since the child is often persuaded that he or she has received just and correct punishment or that drawing attention to the injury would result in further abuse, it is often only in cases of severe or repeated injury that a determination of child abuse can be made. Consequently, it would be especially advantageous to be able to identify situations that are particularly likely to result in abuse. Understandably, many behavioral and social scientists have been motivated by this concern.

Over the past decade especially, we have taken large strides in our effort to discover the causes of child abuse in particular and domestic violence in general. With regard to the area of child abuse, much of the research portrays parents as the source of the problem. Therefore, research has focused on identifying factors that distinguish abusive from non-abusive fathers and mothers. The personal characteristics that were found to place a parent at risk for child maltreatment included emotional disturbances (Elmer, 1967), difficulty in dealing with aggressive impulses (Wasserman, 1967), a tendency to be rigid and domineering (Johnson & Morse, 1968), and low self-esteem (Spinetta & Rigler, 1972). Other factors linked to abusive parental behavior include alcoholism (Blumberg, 1974) and a history of having been abused or neglected as a child (Kempe, Silverman, Steele, Droegemueller, & Silver, 1962; Steele & Pollock, 1974).

Recently, attention has shifted away from such psychiatric profiles of abusive parents to a more social psychological approach. Investigators adopting this perspective seek to determine interpersonal characteristics of parents that are antecedents of child maltreatment. Results of such work suggest that there are styles of parent-child interaction associated with increased likelihood of abuse. These styles include lower than normal frequencies of overall family interaction, especially lower levels of positive behaviors such as praise, words of affection, and otherwise polite modes of address. Moreover, this relative absence of positive affect combines with higher than normal levels of coercive behavior such as verbal threats, complaints, and words of dislike and disapproval (Burgess, Anderson, Schellenbach, & Conger, 1981).

Research also indicates that those patterns of family interaction are themselves correlated with other social events, often resulting from social structural conditions such as a high level of life stress (Conger, Burgess, & Barrett, 1979; Garbarino, 1977), and that these associations may be complicated. For example, life crisis seems to have its most significant impact on those parents who had a history of being mistreated when they were children (Conger et al., 1979). In addition, stress produces abuse more often in a family having only kinship associations than in a family that has outside social associations (Straus, 1980). Life change, physical and emotional health, plus life experiences of a particular type are predisposing events that may turn the similar situations all parents face into an abusive encounter.

Clearly, we have made considerable headway in our attempt to discover the causes of child maltreatment. But the discovery, statement, and test of relationships between events in nature is just one of the tasks facing science. As George Homans (1969) noted:

> Although the statement and test of [relationships] is the condition that must be satisfied if a human activity is to be judged a science, we should be much disappointed if that were all a science did. (p. 2)

The other major task that science addresses is explanation, of course, and Homans goes on to say that we generally are not "satisfied with science unless it explains as well as discovers, unless it tells us not only *that* relationships hold good but *why* they hold good" (p. 2).

The explanation of a phenomenon is essentially the theory of that phenomenon, a goal we achieve when we are able to demonstrate that specific empirically derived relationships (or propositions) about the phenomenon follow logically from, or are deducible from, other more general propositions. In this chapter, we will argue that we already have available a set of general propositions that can aid us in constructing a comprehensive theory of domestic violence and child maltreatment.

EVOLUTIONARY THEORY

When we look beyond the press of public concern, the clamor of the news media, and the incentives of federally financed research grants, it becomes evident that violence, aggression, and the severe mistreatment of children dates from antiquity (Dart, 1948; Bigelow, 1969; Blac, 1962; Radbill, 1980). When we examine the history of humankind, whether from paleontological evidence, documentary accounts such as the Bible, or culture-specific myths and fairytales, we see evidence of children being mistreated, abandoned, sacrificed, or eaten to go along with evidence of their being cuddled, nurtured, and encouraged. Anthropologists have frequently reported harsh treatment of children, including disfigurement and infanticide, in culture after culture (Korbin, 1977), although cultures differ significantly in their treatment of children (Garbarino & Ebata, 1981). Nor is the mistreatment of youngsters limited to humans. The zoological literature contains some rather gruesome accounts of infanticide in such species as lions and langurs (Schaller, 1972; Hrdy, 1974).

Given the long history of child abuse as well as its generality across cultures and species, we clearly need theoretical propositions that derive from a broadly historical perspective, that transcend interspecific differences, that are sufficiently general to permit parsimonious interpretations of the diverse data currently available, and yet that are precise enough to generate specific predictions. It is our view that modern evolutionary theory meets these criteria.

To begin with, evolutionists develop their research around the assumption that all of life from the beginning of time has been subjected to a continual process of natural selection or *differential reproduction.* Thus, within each generation there have been individuals who contributed more offspring to the next generation than others in the same population. It is almost tautological, but nonetheless true, that an individual's evolutionary fitness is measured in part by his or her reproductive success relative to other members of the population. The processes of environmental ("natural") selection determine which individuals have such a reproductive advantage. *On average,* individuals better adapted to their physical and social environment have higher fitness. A crucial component of adaptation is behavior. How an individual behaves evidences and shapes his or her fitness. Behavioral responses to physical, biotic, or social stimuli necessarily affect the likelihood of gene replication. Because behavior results from the interactions among genetic, developmental, and situational factors, child abuse may have a heritable basis and thus a relation to evolutionary processes.

It is clear that individuals continually affect one another's fitness, in that they compete for as well as create resources (Williams, 1966). Occasionally, however, individuals exhibit behavior that appears to contradict this prediction of the theory of natural selection. Individuals sometimes interact with others to what appears to be their own disadvantage.

Alexander (1979), an evolutionary biologist, has discussed the critical role that altruistic or nepotistic behavior toward close relatives has played in the evolution of human social relationships. His argument pivots on the assumption that humans have evolved to be altruistic toward their offspring, their other genetic relatives, and their primary social group. But paradoxically this altruism is fundamentally self-serving. Our altruism is not indiscriminate. Rather, by being directed principally (but not exclusively) toward our children and relatives, such behavior has had the function of increasing the probability that our genes are represented in succeeding generations. Technically, this is the principle of *inclusive fitness.* As outlandish as this notion may appear to persons unfamiliar with evolutionary biology, a growing body of evidence drawn from interspecific comparisons as well as historical analyses shows that the probability of altruistic behavior varies proportionately with the degree of relatedness (Alexander, 1979; Barash, 1977; Wilson, 1975). Thus, there is reason to suspect that much of our behavior today, including the tendency to court potential mates, to establish relatively enduring bonds with each other, to produce and care for offspring, to be jealous, and to mourn the loss of loved ones can ultimately be explained in terms of the contributions those behaviors make to our inclusive fitness—that is, to the transmission of our genes to succeeding generations.

We should emphasize our use of the adverb "ultimately" in the preceding sentence. For while evolutionary biologists emphasize ultimate explanations (that is, the phylogenetic history of behaviors and traits), there are other important levels of explanations. Indeed, Niko Tinbergen, a Nobel laureate, has argued that there are four separate yet complementary levels of causal analysis (Tinbergen, 1951). Three of these levels are developmental, immediate, and adaptive. The developmental, or ontogenetic, history of a phenomenon focuses on, for example, how an individual grows up to behave in a particular manner. This form of causal analysis is of particular importance to developmental psychologists and other students of socialization processes concerned with the acquisition of behavior. A second level of causation deals with the immediate or proximal antecedents of a phenomenon—for instance, the kinds of events that prompt or elicit a behavior at a particular point in time. Examples include the role of goal interference or frustration in eliciting an aggressive response or the way contextual features surrounding violent events contribute to their maintenance (Dobash & Dobash, 1979). The final level of causal analysis, according to Tinbergen (1951), focuses on the adaptive significance of a phenomenon—the functions it performs for the individual actor. The role of behavioral consequences has been most systematically investigated by behaviorists in their analyses of contingencies of reinforcement and punishment (in sociology see Burgess & Bushell, 1969). The point of all this is that a complete understanding of a phenomenon, such as a class of behavior like family violence, requires that we eventually address each of these four levels of causal analysis. It seems apparent that students of domestic conflict have concentrated on developmental, descriptive, and functional levels of analysis (Burgess, 1979). Therefore, in this chapter we focus on features of child abuse that derive from a concern for ultimate causation, specifically for evolutionary significance.

Before doing so, however, we must consider two important concepts in evolutionary theory. The first is the concept of *parental investment* (Trivers, 1972; Williams, 1966). Parental investment refers to behavior displayed by a parent that increases the reproductive potential of the child toward whom the behavior is directed, at the cost of similar investment by the parent toward other or future offspring. Implicit in this definition is the notion that a parent has limited resources and a finite life span to expend those resources in the rearing of children. Knowing this, we can predict that some basis for the preferential distribution of resources and energies will be established simply because random behavior would not be adaptive in an evolutionary sense once any more selective strategy was introduced.

Examples of this adaptive quality of selective parental investment abound in the ethological literature. For example, the bonding of mother to infant has been reported for most species where there is any period of relative dependency of young on parental nurture for survival (Cairns, 1979). Bonding has the effect of making a parent selective with regard to the distribution of limited resources. Moreover, there is evidence that parental nurturance is neither dispensed indiscriminately to all conspecific young (e.g., Hrdy, 1974) nor invariant over a parent's reproductive lifetime (Barash, 1977). Some children receive greater parental investment than others. If this line of reasoning is correct, if an individual parent's investment in his or her offspring varies in a way that has adaptive significance, then we should expect that parental care of young would be limited by circumstances that predict a reduced probability of inclusive fitness payoffs or that involve intolerable costs for the parental effort.

A prime circumstance under which parents might adaptively discontinue or diminish their care involves children of doubtful parenthood. This second important concept of evolutionary theory—*parental certainty*—has been used to explain important differences in male-female gender roles ranging from mate selection to marital interaction (Alexander, 1974; Barash, 1977). In any event, parental care appears to be selective as a function of whether or not circumstances are such that parents are likely to be exposed to unrelated young and thus run the evolutionary risk of investing in offspring who share none of their genes (Alexander, 1974). For example, individual recognition of eggs and chicks is commonly observed in species with dispersed nest sites (Wilson, 1975). Furthermore, such parental discrimination usually develops at precisely that stage of the youngster's developing mobility when the likelihood of confusion becomes a real possibility. For example, female flying squirrels will accept alien pups (an unlikely event in normal circumstances) up to 40 days post-partum—the age at which young squirrels become capable of leaving the nest. From that moment on, strange juveniles approaching a female's nest are attacked (Muul, 1970).

However, even when parents can reliably identify their own offspring, their optimal strategy, in the sense of inclusive fitness, would be to refrain from providing parental care should the prospects of those young surviving and reproducing be poor. Such a circumstance may be brought about by an inadequate resource base or by some deficiency in the offspring (Daly & Wilson, 1980). As Barash (1975) has noted, a parent's decision to cut losses should occur as early in the reproductive process as possible. However, once parents have already invested a sizable amount in offspring, they should be willing to tolerate substantial risks before abandoning their young. And even marginal offspring may receive care from a resource-rich parent. Thus, the concepts of differential parental investment and parental certainty each have potential relevance for specifying conditions that may increase the probability of parents abusing or neglecting their offspring. Specifically, if child abuse is a behavioral response shaped by natural selection, then it is more likely to occur when the situation is one of reduced inclusive fitness payoffs due to uncertain relatedness or low benefit-cost ratios. Let us now turn to the evidence for what turns out to be an illuminating look at the evolutionary parameters of child abuse.

PARENTHOOD

That there should be a positive correlation between the frequency and quality of parental investment and biological parenthood derives from the assumption that there are selection pressures against squandering parental resources on nonkin (Daly & Wilson, 1980). Moreover, we assume that several proximal mechanisms encourage discriminative parental care, such as the attachment bond resulting from early parent-infant contact. It follows that surrogate parents will find it more difficult to develop deep affection for their charges. Consistent with this prediction, Duberman (1975) reports that only 53% of stepfathers and 25% of stepmothers admitted having "parental feelings" toward their stepchildren. Such data suggest that the risk of abuse would be greater for stepchildren than for natural children; they are also consistent with Bronfenbrenner's (1970) observation on the difficulties inherent in professional child care: "You can't pay a person to do what a mother will do for free."

In support of such a prediction, Daly and Wilson (1980) report data from four samples of physical abuse cases drawn from England, New Zealand, and the United States. In each case, only about one-half of the abused children lived in homes with both natural parents present. Although no satisfactory data on the living arrangements of children in the population at large are available, indirect information suggests that considerably more than half of all children live in two natural parent households in the above three countries. According to the U.S. Bureau of the Census (1977), 80% of all children lived with two parents in 1976. Glick (1976) estimated that 10% of those families included stepparents, while Daly and Wilson (1980) estimated that approximately 15% of such families had a stepparent in the home. If we can assume that these figures are correct, then clearly stepchildren are especially at risk for potential abuse.

We find a similar pattern in the series of studies of abusive, neglectful, and normal families reported by Burgess (1978). In over one-half of the abusive families he studied, there were stepchildren in the home. In 11 of those 16 cases (69%), the stepparent was the official perpetrator of the abuse. Significantly, in those families where a stepparent was also a natural parent (9 of the 11 families), the abuse was of a stepchild rather than a natural child in all but one case. Again, we see that there is reason to suspect that stepparent households may be more at risk for potential child abuse than households containing only biologically related family members, at least in cultures like our own that emphasize biological parenthood.

PARENTAL RESOURCES

In addition to biological parenthood influencing the likelihood of an adult investing in young, we suggested earlier that an inadequate resource base may similarly decrease the probability of parental investment and thus increase the risk of child abuse by a parent or other caretaker. We will examine such a possibility by looking at the relationship between child abuse and socioeconomic status, family size, and single parenthood.

There are strong reasons to believe that child abuse, especially physical abuse, is correlated with social class (Garbarino & Gilliam, 1980; Garbarino & Ebata, 1981). Gil's national survey (1970) indicated that child abuse is more likely in lower-class homes. He reported that over 48% of the abusive families had an annual income under $5000, while the percentage of all families at this level was only around 25%. Moreover, less than 1% of the abusive mothers were college graduates and only 17% had graduated from high school. Similarly, Straus, Gelles, and Steinmetz (1980) reported that parents earning less than $6000 annually admitted abusing their children at a rate 62% higher than other parents. Importantly, these latter data relate to abuse admitted to by parents through anonymous questionnaires rather than cases involving the legal system. Garbarino and his colleagues (Garbarino & Crouter, 1978; Garbarino & Sherman, 1980) found the same pattern for rates of child maltreatment across neighborhoods. Similarly, insufficient income was cited as a factor in almost 50% of child abuse and neglect cases in statistics compiled by the American Humane Association (1978). The same document reported that the median family income for child abuse cases was $6886 and for neglect cases $4249 in contrast to the $15,388 median income for all families with children in the population at large (U.S. Bureau of the Census, 1978). The recently completed National Incidence Study (Bergdof, 1981) used a survey methodology to uncover cases of abuse, with the same pattern of socioeconomic results.

A second way to examine parental resources is in terms of family size. Holding resources constant, increasing the membership of a family should result in fewer resources available per family member, thus increasing conflicts of interest over those resources. Gil (1970) and Young (1964) reported data indicating that the proportion of abusing families with four or more children is twice that found in the general population. Light's (1973) data indicate a similar pattern in England and New Zealand.

In his observational study comparing abusive, neglectful, and normal families, Burgess (1978) reported data indicating that the characteristic interaction patterns of abusive and neglectful families increase in intensity with increases in the number of children in the home. For example, Burgess's study found that there was a strong *inverse* correlation between family size and the frequency of verbal and physical contact between a parent and any one child in the home. This was true for all forms of contact combined, and for positive kinds of contacts such as physical affection and verbal praise. On the other hand, he found that the frequency of negative forms of parent-child interaction such as fights and verbal punishment remained stable across families of varying size. Thus, given that the other forms of parent-child contact diminished, the emotional climate in the larger families was clearly of a more negative nature. Such a pattern would probably be especially likely in low-income families where resources are already relatively scarce. In any case, accumulating evidence indicates the coercive styles of family interaction and resultant child abuse and neglect are more likely the larger the family and the greater the concomitant drain on a family's resources.

Our third way of examining parental resources is to compare single-versus two-parent households. Current estimates are that approximately 50% of all first marriages end in divorce. It is also true that divorce hits women hardest, since over 70% of them must work and close to 85% must also care for children (Campbell, 1975). They do so without the psychological investment resources of a partner, but also without the costs that a conflictual marriage entails. The positive outcomes of divorce seem to arise when it results in a net gain in personal resources; the negative, when it results in a net decrease. Given the generally lower income and social isolation of many single mothers, we should not be surprised that single-parent households are significantly implicated in cases of abuse (Friedman, 1976; Gil, 1970; Johnson, 1974) and neglect (Daly & Wilson, 1980). These findings receive support in a report by Kimball, Stewart, Conger, and Burgess (1980), where it was found that mothers in single-parent families displayed rates of negative contacts with their children over twice those found in two-parent families. They also reported that in two-parent abusive, neglectful, and normal families combined there was a 26% higher rate of positive than negative interaction, whereas in single-parent families there was a 45% higher rate of *negative* than positive interaction. These data suggest that those patterns of family interaction found to be typical of two-parent abusive and neglectful families are especially likely given the permanent absence of one parent. Kimball and colleagues (1980) qualify their data by noting that this pattern may be limited to low-SES families, such as those they studied, where resources are strained. But it should also be noted that in 1978 nearly one-half of all poor families were headed by women, and more than two-thirds of poor black families were headed by women (U.S. Bureau of the Census, 1979). In sum, an inadequate parental resource base may substantially decrease the probability of parental investment whether we measure the lack of resources by income, education, the presence of many children in the home, or single parenthood.

CHARACTERISTICS OF THE CHILD

Earlier in this discussion we argued that circumstances associated with a reduced probability of inclusive fitness payoffs for the parent or with exceptionally high costs for parental effort would limit parental solicitude of young children. With regard to the former, we have already seen that abuse is associated with such characteristics of a child as his or her step-relationship to an abusive adult. A number of studies indicate that other child characteristics are implicated in abuse and that these characteristics usually involve either low reproductive potential for those children later in life—for example, retardation and Down's Syndrome (Martin, Beezley, Conway, & Kempe, 1974; Sandgrund, Gaines, & Green, 1974)—or they require care costly in terms of financial and psychological resources. For instance, Johnson and Morse (1968) reported that 70% of their child abuse cases showed some form of developmental problem ranging from poor speech to physical deformities and handicaps. Moreover, even the child welfare workers who dealt with these children found them hard to handle and saw them as being fussy, demanding, stubborn, negativistic, and unsmiling. "The child who represents an unwanted pregnancy, or who resembles a disliked or unfaithful spouse, the chronically sick child, the hyperactive child or the otherwise difficult-to-handle child may incite abusive behavior" (Burgess, 1979, p. 160).

While positive parental feelings toward a child may be inhibited by overt signs of child abnormality, it is important to note that these characteristics of the child may sometimes be the consequence as well as the antecedent of parental responses to the child. In addition, these deficient parental responses may be due to factors that interfered with the mother-infant attachment process, such as perinatal separation of the infant from its mother for medical reasons as occurs with premature infants. Indeed, it is quite possible that the major factor determining whether a parent develops strong parental affection for a handicapped child is the child's early and prolonged separation from the mother at or soon after birth (Daly & Wilson, 1980). Certainly, there is strong evidence that premature children stand at risk for abuse and neglect (Klaus & Kennell, 1976; Martin et al., 1974; Hunter, Klstrom, Kraybill, & Loda, 1978). Moreover, O'Connor and her colleagues (1977) have experimentally demonstrated an ability to reduce substantially the risk of parental mistreatment simply by providing a few extra hours of contact in the first two days after birth. Other studies also show that a more "family-centered" approach to childbirth can do much to permit the "natural" process of early attachment to move forward (Garbarino, 1980a). These results are consistent with an evolutionary interpretation of parent-child relationships.

CONCLUSION

While we have not stated the propositions of evolutionary theory formally or in strict deductive order, we have tried to suggest that some general theoretical principles are currently available. Not unimportantly, attending to the issue of our evolutionary past reminds us that we spent more than 90% of our history as a species in technologically simple, hunting and gathering communities. The driving force behind evolution in these communities was "inclusive fitness"—that is, the differential transmission of one's genes by investing in one's own offspring and those of close relatives. The principle of inclusive fitness allows for the explanation of altruism (sacrificing oneself so that one's relatives may live and subsequently reproduce) and the traditional structure and dynamics of most families (i.e., lactating women protected by male hunters and surrounded by supportive kin). Parental investment shapes family functioning. And because it is biologically greater for females than for males, it suggests a basis for sex differentiation in parental roles. The significant role of the nonparental male adult family member in abuse may be evidence of this.

An evolutionary approach to the family suggests that the modern, Western, isolated nuclear family is "unnatural" in the sense that it is at odds with our evolutionary history (Rossi, 1977). Social isolation of the family (particularly the mother-infant relationship) is perhaps the most significant way in which modern cultural evolution is at odds with our evolutionary past. It is little wonder, then, that Rohner's (1975) cross-cultural study of parental acceptance and rejection found that isolation of the mother-child relationship appears to present a transcultural or universal threat by increasing risk of rejection. Rejection is itself a psychological malignancy that undermines basic features of individual development and social competence (Garbarino, 1980b). This perspective on human development resonates with primate research linking social isolation to abuse and neglect (Nadler, 1979; Rock, 1978). It is the basis for Rossi's (1974) assessment:

> By neglecting the biosocial dimension of human life . . . society may set the stage for unprecedented stress in the lives of young mothers and an impoverishment of their children. (p. 21)

Thus, in this chapter we have taken the biological principle of inclusive fitness and have presented evidence to support the prediction that a parent's investment in young children varies inversely with doubtful or stepparenthood, scarce parental resources, and unusually high costs for parental effort.

If we social and behavioral scientists can overcome our "trained incapacity" to consider the ideas and techniques of other disciplines (Homans, 1969), including our overreaction to the excesses of the Social Darwinists, we can begin the next important step of linking the theoretical propositions of evolutionary theory with sociological, psychological, and social psychological theories of child abuse. What we are as organisms plays a significant role in shaping what we are as people. We should embrace the Aristotelian proposition codified by Spinoza that the human being is indeed "the social animal."

REFERENCES

Alexander, R. D. The evolution of social behavior. *American Review of Ecology,* 1974, *5,* 325-383.

Alexander, R. D. Natural selection and social exchange. In R. L. Burgess & T. L. Huston (Eds.), *Social exchange in developing relationships.* New York: Academic Press, 1979.

American Humane Association. *National analysis of official child neglect and abuse reporting.* Englewood, CA: AHA, 1978.

Barash, D. P. Evolutionary aspects of parental behavior: The distraction behavior of the apline accentor, *Purnella Collaris. Wilson Bulletin,* 1976, *87,* 367-373.

Barash, D. P. *Sociobiology and behavior.* New York: Elsevier, 1977.

Bergdof, K. The National Study of the Incidence and Severity of Child Abuse and Neglect. Washington, DC: National Center for Child Abuse and Neglect, 1981.

Bigelow, R. *The dawn warriors.* Boston: Little, Brown, 1969.

Blanc, A. C. *Some evidence for the ideologies of early man.* London: Methuen, 1962.

Blumberg, M. L. Psychopathology of the abusing parent. *American Journal of Psychotherapy,* 1974, *28,* 21-29.

Bronfenbrenner, U. *Two worlds of childhood: U.S. and U.S.S.R.* New York: Russell Sage Foundation, 1970.

Burgess, J. M., Kimball, W. H., & Burgess, R. L. *Family size and family violence.* Paper presented at the biannual meeting of the Southeastern Conference on Human Development, Atlanta, 1978.

Burgess, R. L. *Project interact: A study of patterns of interaction in abusive, neglectful and control families.* Final report to the National Center on Child Abuse and Neglect, 1978.

Burgess, R. L. Child abuse: A social interactional analysis. In B. B. Lakey & A. E. Kazdin (Eds.), *Advances in clinical child psychology.* New York: Plenum, 1979.

Burgess, R. L., Anderson, E. S., Schellenbach, C. J., & Conger, R. D. A social interactional approach to the study of abusive families. In J. P. Vincent (Ed.), *Advances in family intervention, assessment and theory: An annual compilation of research (Vol. 2).* Greenwich, CT: JAI Press, 1981.

Burgess, R. L., & Bushell, D. *Behavioral sociology.* New York: Columbia University Press, 1969.

Cairns, R. B. *Social development: The origins and plasticity of interchanges.* San Francisco: W. H. Freeman, 1979.

Campbell, A. The American way of mating. *Psychology Today,* May 1975, 37-43.

Conger, R. D., Burgess, R. L., & Barrett, C. Child abuse related to life change and perceptions of illness: Some preliminary findings. *The Family Coordinator,* 1979, 73-79.

Daly, M., & Wilson, M. I. Abuse and neglect of children in evolutionary perspective. In R. D. Alexander & D. W. Tinkle (Eds.), *Natural selection and social behavior.* New York: Chiron Press, 1980.

Dart, R. A. The Makapansgat proto-human *Australopithecus promethus. American Journal of Physical Anthropology,* 1948, *6,* 259-281.

Dobash, R. E., & Dobash, R. *Violence against wives.* New York: Free Press, 1979.

Duberman, L. *The reconstituted family: A study of remarried couples and their children.* Chicago: Nelson-Hall, 1975.

Elmer, E. *Children in jeopardy: A study of abused minors and their families.* Pittsburgh: University of Pittsburgh Press, 1967.

Friedman, R. Child abuse: A review of the psychosocial research. In Hefner & Co. (Eds.), *Four perspectives on the status of child abuse and neglect,* 1976.

Garbarino, J. The human ecology of child maltreatment. *Journal of Marriage and the Family,* 1977, *39,* 721-736.

Garbarino, J. Changing hospital childbirth practices: A developmental perspective on prevention of child maltreatment. *American Journal of Orthopsychiatry,* 1980, *50,* 588-597. (a)

Garbarino, J. Defining emotional maltreatment: The message is the meaning. *Journal of Psychiatric Treatment and Evaluation,* 1980, *2,* 105-110. (b)

Garbarino, J., & Crouter, A. Defining the community context of parent-child relations: The correlates of child maltreatment. *Child Development,* 1978, *49,* 604-616.

Garbarino, J., & Ebata, A. *Ethnic and cultural differences in child maltreatment.* Paper presented at the conference on Research Issues in Prevention sponsored by the National Committee for the Prevention of Child Abuse and the Johnson Foundation, Wingspread, Racine, Wisconsin, June 1981.

Garbarino, J., & Gilliam, G. *Understanding abusive families.* Lexington, MA: D. C. Heath, 1980.

Garbarino, J., & Sherman, D. High-risk families and high-risk neighborhoods. *Child Development,* 1980, *51,* 188-198.

Gladston, R. Observations of children who have been physically abused and their parents. *American Journal of Psychiatry,* 1965, *122,* 440-443.

Gelles, R. J. Child abuse as psychopathology: A sociological critique and reformulation. *American Journal of Orthopsychology,* 1973, *43,* 611-621.

Gil, D. G. *Violence against children: Physical abuse in the United States.* Cambridge: Harvard University Press, 1970.

Glick, P. C. Living arrangements of children and young adults. *Journal of Comparative Family Studies,* 1976, *7,* 321-331.

Homans, G. D. Prologue. In R. L. Burgess & D. Bushell, Jr. (Eds.), *Behavioral sociology: The experimental analysis of social process.* New York: Columbia University Press, 1969.

Hrdy, S. B. Male-male competition and infanticide among the langurs (*Presbytis entellus*) of Abu Rajasthan. *Rolia Primatologica,* 1974, *22,* 19-58.

Hunter, R. S., Klstrom, N., Kraybill, E. N., & Loda, F. Antecedents of child abuse and neglect in premature infants: A prospective study in a newborn intensive care unit. *Pediatrics,* 1978, *61,* 629-635.

Johnson, C. F. *Child abuse in the Southeast: Analysis of 1172 reported cases.* Athens, GA: Regional Institute of Social Welfare Research, 1974.

Johnson, B., & Morse, H. A. Injured children and their parents. *Children,* 1968, *15,* 147-152.

Kempe, C. H., & Helfer, R. E. *Helping the battered child and his family.* Philadelphia: J. B. Lippincott, 1972.

Kempe, C. H., Silverman, F. N., Steele, B. B., Droegemueller, N., & Silver, H. K. The battered-child syndrome. *Journal of the American Medical Association,* 1962, *181,* 17-24.

Kimball, W. H., Stewart, R. B., Conger, R. D., & Burgess, R. L. A comparison of family interaction in single versus two parent abusive, neglectful and normal families. In T. Field, S. Goldberg, D. Stern, & A. Sostek (Eds.), *Interactions of high risk infants and children.* New York: Academic Press, 1980.

Klaus, M. H., & Kennell, J. H. *Maternal-infant bonding.* St. Louis: C. V. Mosby, 1976.

Korbin, J. Anthropological contributions to the study of child abuse. *Child Abuse and Neglect: The International Journal,* 1977, *1,* 7-24.

Light, R. J. Abused and neglected children in America: A study of alternative policies. *Harvard Educational Review,* 1973, *43,* 556-598.

Martin, H. P., Beezley, P., Conway, E. F., & Kempe, C. H. The development of abused children. Part I. A review of the literature. Part II. Physical, neurologic, and intellectual outcome. *Advanced Pediatrics,* 1974, *21,* 25-73.

Muul, I. Intra- and inter-familial behavior of *Glaucomys volans* (Rodentia) following paturition. *Animal Behavior,* 1970, *18,* 20-25.

Nadler, R. Child abuse in gorilla mothers. *Caring,* 1979, *5*(3), 1-3.

O'Connor, S. M., Vietze, P. M., Hopkins, J. B., & Altemeir, W. A. Post-partum extended maternal-infant contact: Subsequent mothering and child health. *Pediatric Research,* 1977, *11,* 380.

Radbill, S. A history of child abuse and infanticide. In R. Helfer & C. H. Kempe (Eds.), *The battered child* (3rd ed.). Chicago: University of Chicago Press, 1980.

Rock, M. Gorilla mothers need some help from their friends. *Smithsonian,* 1978, *9*(4), 58-63.

Rohner, R. *They love me, they love me not.* New Haven, CT : HRAF Press, 1975.

Rossi, A. A biosocial perspective on parenting. *Daedelus,* 1977, *106,* 1-31.

Sandgrund, A. R., Gaines, R., & Green, A. Child abuse and mental retardation: A problem of cause and effect. *American Journal of Mental Deficiency,* 1974, *79,* 327-330.

Schaller, G. B. *The Serengeti lion: A study of predator-prey relations.* Chicago: University of Chicago Press, 1972.

Spinetta, J. J., & Rigler, D. The child-abusing parent: A psychological review. *Psychological Bulletin,* 1972, *77,* 296-304.

Steele, B. B., & Pollock, C. B. A psychiatric study of parents who abuse infants and small children. In R. E. Helfer & C. H. Kembe (Eds.), *The battered child.* Chicago: University of Chicago Press, 1974.

Straus, M. A. Stress and physical child abuse. *Child Abuse and Neglect,* 1980, *4,* 75-88.

Straus, M. A., Gelles, R. J., & Steinmetz, S. K. *Behind closed doors: Violence in the American family.* Garden City, NY: Doubleday, 1980.

Tinbergen, N. *The study of instinct.* London: Oxford University Press, 1951.

Trivers, R. L. Parental investment and sexual selection. In B. Campbell (Ed.), *Sexual selection and the descent of man 1871-1971.* Chicago: Aldine, 1972.

U.S. Bureau of the Census. *Marital status and living arrangements: March 1976.* Current Population Reports P-20, No. 306. Washington, DC: Government Printing Office, 1977.

U.S. Bureau of the Census. *Money income in 1976 of families and persons in the United States.* Current Population Reports P-60, No. 114. Washington, DC: Government Printing Office, 1978.

U.S. Bureau of the Census. *Twenty facts on women workers.* Washington, DC: Government Printing Office, August 1979.

Wasserman, S. The abused parent of the abused child. *Children,* 1967, *14,* 175-179.

Williams, G. C. *Adaptation and natural selection.* Princeton: Princeton University Press, 1966.

Wilson, E. O. *Sociobiology: The new synthesis.* Cambridge: Harvard University Press, 1975.

Young, L. *Wednesday's children: A study of child neglect and abuse.* New York: McGraw-Hill, 1964.

6

Exploring Intrafamilial Child Sexual Abuse

A Systems Approach

KATHLEEN J. TIERNEY and DAVID L. CORWIN

This chapter presents a model for explaining intrafamilial child sexual abuse, using concepts at the socioecological, structural, interpersonal, and intrapersonal levels. The discussion of factors contributing to sexual abuse of children in the family is based on a review of the literature and on data and clinical impressions obtained by the staff of the Family Support Program (FSP) at the University of California, Los Angeles. The FSP has been involved in the treatment of intrafamilial abuse cases for the last three years.

In this discussion, we define intrafamilial child sexual abuse as *contact between a child and an adult member of the same household, where sexual stimulation of the adult initiator or another person is the objective.* This definition is similar to the one advanced by the National Center on Child Abuse and Neglect (1978), except that the focus is on perpetrators who share a home with the child, rather than on adults in general. While we occasionally use the term "incest" as a synonym for intrafamilial child molestation, our definition differs from the strict legal conception of incest, in that it covers incidents of molestation by stepparents and other parent figures (e.g., common law spouses, live-in companions) as well as blood relatives. In our discussion, it is the relationship of authority and trust between adult and child, and not primarily the biological tie, that distinguishes this form of sexual abuse from others. We expand our focus beyond cases of "true" incest and exclude sex play involving siblings who are close in age, because we believe sexual abuse of a child initiated by an adult authority figure in the family is distinct in its etiology, dynamics, and effects from molestation by strangers and from sexual contact

Authors' Note: *We wish to thank Gloria Powell, Roland Summit, Virginia Kiehlbauch, David Finkelhor, and Jill Korbin for their comments and suggestions.*

between children. Because it uses the term "contact," but leaves the nature of the contact unspecified, the definition is broad enough to include a range of illicit sexual behavior, including seductive speech and conduct, exhibitionism, fondling, oral-genital contact, the exploitation associated with child pornography, and prostitution and sexual intercourse.

METHODOLOGICAL PROBLEMS

Explaining child sexual abuse initiated by adult family members has proved extremely problematic for researchers, for several reasons. First, there is a lack of knowledge of the true prevalence of the phenomenon and the characteristics of the persons involved. To an even greater extent than child abuse and wife abuse, sexual molestation of children in the family does not readily lend itself to study by standard survey techniques (see Gelles, 1979, for a cogent discussion of the problems inherent in doing traditional kinds of research on families). To date, the topic has been grossly underresearched. Estimates of the incidence of this type of victimization in our society vary, depending on the data used and the type of sample from which estimates are derived. An early study (Weinberg, 1955) estimated the incidence of incest at 1.9 per million people in the population per year. Research by the American Humane Association (DeFrancis, 1969) makes a higher projection—40 cases per million. Finkelhor (1979) reports that nearly one-fifth of college women he surveyed reported sexual victimization during childhood; of these, one-half indicated family members were the perpetrators. The estimate of the National Center on Child Abuse and Neglect (1978) for all cases of child sexual abuse is between 60,000 and 10,000 cases per year. In Gagnon's reanalysis of retrospective Kinsey Institute interviews with adult women, nearly one-quarter recalled involvement in sexual activity prior to puberty, and relatives were involved in a significant proportion of nonaccidental contacts. Sarafino (1979), extrapolating from reported incidents of sexual offenses against children in four U.S. locales, estimates the national rate of reported and unreported offenses to be just over 336,000 per year.

Despite these differences in the estimated incidence of sexual abuse of children in American society, the literature seems to suggest strongly that (1) the rate of child sexual victimization is much higher than it was once believed to be; (2) females are victimized more than males during childhood[1]; and (3) a significant proportion of child sexual abuse occurs within the family, with fathers, stepfathers, and mothers' male companions comprising the largest category of perpetrators. Beyond this, there is considerable lack of consensus with regard to the influence of such factors as social class, psychological traits, and situational factors on the behavior (Henderson, 1972; National Center on Child Abuse and Neglect, 1978; Groth, 1978).

Second, serious methodological problems plague the area. As is the case with much research on sexual behavior and deviance, those interested in child sexual abuse have had to resort to obtaining data on small samples, usually made up of prescreened populations such as prisoners and persons in psychotherapy. This type of data is subject to bias from several sources. Detected cases and reported offenses are likely to be unrepresentative of the range of child sexual abuse, and conclusions based on such samples are likely to be distorted. Discovery and conviction are likely to be associated with a host of confounding factors, including social class, race, extreme and overt psychopathology or violence, and the severity of the offense.

Approaches used to examine the problem of intrafamilial child sexual abuse also render the generality and precision of the findings questionable. The use of case studies and small samples is quite understandable, given the low rate of discovery of this form of abuse and the meager resources of those interested in the issue, but this approach rules out the use of data-analytic techniques that would control for the effects of particular variables. The tendency for researchers not to use control groups raises further questions about their conclusions.[2] While we can be somewhat more confident regarding findings based on data from larger, more representative, "normal" groups, such as those used in the Gagnon (1965) and Finkelhor (1979) surveys, such data are still subject to a degree of bias. Because these surveys are retrospective, there is a strong possibility that respondents' recollections of events are selective or distorted. The fact that data come from only one source—the victim—limits the extent to which investigators can probe such important issues as the tone of family relationships and the motives of the perpetrator.

Third, those wishing to explore intrafamilial child sexual abuse have been handicapped by the extreme difficulty of separating out the antecedent conditions, correlates, and effects of molestation. This problem, present to some degree in all nonexperimental research, is particularly acute in the study of incest because of the secret, shameful nature of the act, the fact that it can go undisclosed for long periods, and the strength and complexity of the emotions that accompany it. Is sex play between a parent and a child traumatic in and of itself, or is it exposure and the subsequent response by parents and significant others that are more damaging? Did the parents of sexually abused children experience unsatisfactory sexual relations before the abuse occurred, or are claims of dissatisfaction with the partner merely post hoc rationalizations? What influence does molestation have on psychosexual development and later adjustment of victims? What is the role of alcohol use in intrafamilial molestation? Use of alcohol by the parent-molester is frequently cited as a contributing factor in incest (Browning & Boatman, 1974; Virkunnen,

1974), but drinking may be a precipating factor, an activity used by perpetrators to justify their loss of control, or a behavior that is only accidentally or indirectly associated with abuse. Because most incest research has been conducted at a single point in time, often a long time after the fact, answers to questions like these are virtually impossible to obtain.

Further, even when detected early, intrafamilial child sexual abuse presents special challenges to the researcher. It is an area in which the weaknesses of cross-sectional and survey analysis are emphasized. Survey respondents are known to bias their responses in the direction of social desirability, particularly when discussing sensitive topics such as marital and sexual adjustment (Laws, 1971), and incest is probably the prototypical "sensitive topic" (Gelles, 1979). This fact, together with the fact that families involved in incest situations often manifest high levels of repression and dissociation, may lead to serious measurement errors if parent or victim attitudes are measured at only one point in time by means of standard survey instruments. For example, preliminary analysis of data obtained on patients in UCLA Family Support Program, with which the authors are associated, indicates that couples involved in incest report good marital adjustment and that partners score high on measured self-esteem *at the time of intake*; however, their defensiveness is also high, and later work with these couples indicates they frequently display substantial conflict and poor sexual and marital adjustment. Measures taken later in the course of treatment, when couples are not so defensive, are quite different from those obtained earlier. While it is impossible to say how much of this difference is due to treatment itself, such results do suggest that a great deal can be learned if families are studied in depth and on a long-term basis, rather than superficially and at a single point in time.

Finally, our knowledge of intrafamilial child sexual abuse is fragmented because of the varied backgrounds and different objectives of the scholars who work in the area. Studies tend to be confined to selected aspects of the problem or to specific populations. Varying theoretical perspectives and approaches to research have been taken by persons from anthropology, psychiatry, clinical psychology, sociology, social work, medicine, and criminology (see literature reviews by Henderson, 1972, and Meiselman, 1978, as well as the bibliography by Schultz, 1979, for an idea of the research tradition in different fields).[3] In part because of the use of so many different frames of reference, an almost bewildering array of possible causes, associated factors, and outcomes has been advanced. Persons attempting to review and assess the literature confront large amounts of descriptive, qualitative data and discussions of possible explanatory variables, with no clear basis for judging which explanations have merit.

At present, some of the most solid contributions to the literature are those which attempt to make some order out of this variegated set of findings. Research and treatment can benefit from work by writers who caution against oversimplification and mythologizing where incest is concerned (see Meiselman, 1978), present well-grounded discussions of clinical aspects of the problem (see Cormier, Kennedy, & Sangowicz, 1962; Herman & Hirschman, 1977), and develop typologies which suggest the range of behaviors and motives involved (Weinberg, 1955; Groth, 1978; Summit & Kryso, 1978).

A SYSTEMS MODEL

The research plan we outline here goes well beyond descriptive and taxonomic approaches. It is designed to overcome the problems that handicapped earlier work on child molestation. Our recommended approach assesses the effects of a small number of selected variables by gathering data on families in which sexual abuse of the child has occurred and on two matched control groups—a set of nonincestuous families in the community and a group of families with children in treatment for reasons other than sexual molestation.

Rather than viewing intrafamilial child sexual abuse as originating solely from adjustment problems of the perpetrator or family disorganization or victim characteristics, we approach incest as behavior influenced by factors at several different levels. According to our perspective, a particular outcome (in this case, incest) is the product not of single preconditions acting independently, but rather of the combined or cumulative influence of a set of factors. This "system" approach has been used in the explanation of family violence (Straus, 1973), but to our knowledge no one has explicitly advanced it as a framework for studying child sexual molestation in the home.

Rather than attempting to generalize about a large number of possible etiological factors, we limit our focus to a few key variables. The variables were selected according to several criteria. First, we included variables for which there seemed to be significant support in the literature. Second, we considered variables which seemed to clinicians working in the area to have the greatest heuristic or explanatory value. Third, other things being equal, we chose variables which suggest potentially efficacious prevention, treatment, and policy-making strategies.

The variables in our explanatory model fall into several broad conceptual categories: socioecological or family climate factors; aspects of family structure; predisposing factors in the perpetrator, victim, and spouse; and precipitating or situational factors. The variables are discussed individually below. They are presented with full awareness that their apparent association with incest may, in fact, be spurious. The only way to determine whether such factors do help explain the phenomenon is to test hypotheses based on the model.

Socioecological Factors

It seems justified on both theoretical and empirical grounds to argue that features of the family environment or living situation are related to the occurrence of intrafamilial child molestation, because they either reduce normative constraints or increase the opportunities for illicit sexual contact. Renshaw and Renshaw (1977) and Lukianowicz (1972) cite household crowding as a possible factor in incest, although the latter also points out that research findings are not in agreement on this point. Booth (1976) found household congestion to be slightly related to both the frequency of sibling quarrels and the incidence of physical child abuse, and it seems reasonable to assume *household density* and practices such as bedroom-sharing may be background conditions for sexual molestation as well.

Geographic isolation is another frequently mentioned correlate of intrafamilial sexual deviance. Henderson (1972) reviews a fairly sizable set of studies suggesting that isolation and rural lifestyles promote the seeking of social and sexual satisfaction within the family.

In addition to geographic isolation, family members can also experience *social isolation.* Many researchers stress the importance of a lack of individual social connectedness in the etiology of intrafamilial molestation. Finkelhor (1979), for example, notes that having few friends during childhood is associated with a higher risk of sexual abuse. We believe that an entire family can also be characterized as socially isolated when, for example, the family group does not participate in friendship networks or community activities or when there is a family history of high geographic mobility.

Social isolation may provide a context for illicit sexual contact with children in the family for three reasons. First, since social support appears to be an important factor reducing the negative physiological and psychological impact of stress (Cobb, 1976; Liem & Liem, 1978), an absence of support may leave affected family members more vulnerable to stressful situations. Second, regular contact with friends, relatives, and neighbors can both validate parental role performance and exert a measure of social control. Where such ties are absent, there may be no one to whom the adult perpetrator feels accountable in the role of parent/protector. Third, as is also the case with geographic isolation, social isolation may weaken inhibitions against molestation because it renders discovery by outside parties less likely.

Family Structure

Like the aspects of family environment mentioned above, various features of family organization may serve to loosen the constraints against illicit sexual contact in the home. *Family composition* is one such variable.

In particular, reconstituted or stepparent families appear to be more prone to episodes of child sexual exploitation than intact families (Poznanski & Blos, 1975; Finkelhor, 1979). This may be a result of the comparative weakness of the taboo against incestuous contact for nonblood relatives.[4]

Writings on families in which illicit child molestation occurs point to other structural features that are believed to be atypical. One is *role disturbance,* particularly mother-child role reversal (see Lustig, Dresser, Spellman, & Murray, 1966; Herman & Hirschman, 1977; Browning & Boatman, 1974; Summit & Kryso, 1978). According to observations by researchers and clinicians, illicit contact with a daughter is facilitated by the mother's abdication of, or inability to perform, many of the tasks associated with the female role and the daughter's assumption of those tasks. Another possibly atypical feature of incest families is the *absence of an affectionate mother-child relationship* within the family unit, that would otherwise be a source of support and protection for the child. Herman and Hirschman (1977) state that many of the female incest victims they studied recalled being estranged from their mothers throughout childhood, and clinicians in the UCLA Family Support Program have also received reports from mothers whose daughters became victims of molestation, indicating the mothers felt "cool" toward these particular daughters for some time prior to the incident. This lack of perceived closeness is also reported by adult women, currently in treatment at the Family Support Program, who were victimized as children.

The distribution of *power* in the marital dyad is another area that merits exploration. The literature offers few clear statements on the nature of the power relationship between the male and female partners in homes characterized by child victimization, but it does provide some clues. Cormier et al. (1962), for example, claim the father-perpetrator in incest cases feels a need to live up to the authoritarian role, despite his inadequacy and immaturity. Summit and Kryso (1978) note the existence of a type of incest they label "imperious," which is based on the male's need to elicit obedience within the family unit. Such observations, together with findings that suggest intrafamilial child victimization is associated with patriarchal-authoritarian subcultures or modes of family organization (Lukianowicz, 1972; Maisch, 1973; Finkelhor, 1979), leads us to hypothesize that some problem families are strongly male-dominated, with most household decisions and family resources controlled by the male household head. In other cases, however, the opposite pattern may occur. There may be a subgroup of families in which the male spouse shows his hostility for a "domineering" wife who controls family decision-making by exploiting one of the children. The fact that such cases have been reported by clinicians in the FSP suggests that marked *power imbalances* may be characteristic of families in which child sexual abuse occurs.

Individual Predispositions

While some discussions of incest tend to highlight both family and individual pathology as causal factors, there is no indication that persons involved in intrafamilial child sexual abuse suffer from psychoses or any other easily diagnosed psychological disorders. However, there is evidence that certain maladaptive personality characteristics may be present. Depending on the clinical experience and interests of the writer, various personality traits are used to characterize initiators, spouses, and victims. For example, male molesters are described as coming from socially deprived backgrounds (Kaufman, Peck, & Taguiri, 1954; Henderson, 1972); as emotionally dependent, isolated, and sexually hyperactive (Groth, 1978; Gebhard, Gagnon, Pomeroy, & Christenson, 1965; Ferracuti, 1972); and as prone to alcohol abuse. Female spouses are frequently characterized as emotionally dependent and as lacking influence within the family (Henderson, 1972)—that is, as incapable of protecting the child. Marital dissatisfaction and sexual estrangement of the adult partners is also a frequently mentioned correlate of abuse (Weinberg, 1955; Lustig et al., 1966; Molnar & Cameron, 1975). Child victims are described as isolated (Finkelhor, 1979) and emotionally neglected (Burgess & Holmstrom, 1978; Rosenfeld, 1979). As mentioned earlier, clinicians in the FSP have noted a high frequency of subtle characterological problems that are often overlooked in cross-sectional evaluations but which become more and more apparent in the course of long-term contact with the parties involved in intrafamilial child sexual abuse. These problems include a range of symptoms, such as splitting, denial, projection, "clinging," and the projective identification often reportedly associated with so-called borderline syndromes.

Our explanatory model attempts to synthesize such findings into a brief list. The qualities we hypothesize should characterize individuals involved in illicit intrafamilial sex are as follows:[5]

> Male parent or parent figure: psychosexual immaturity, low impulse control, few social ties (contacts with friends, ties to the workplace), childhood experience of deviant sex contact within the family, and low marital and sexual satisfaction.

> Female spouse: poor self-concept, low marital and sexual satisfaction, emotional distance from victim, and history of abuse.

> Victim: Few social ties with high need for affection and attention.

Precipitating Factors

The sets of factors discussed above may be present in families and yet may not lead to child molestation, except in the presence of changes that place even more strain on family members. One such situational factor may be *life stress.*[6] A series of major life changes within the family could, in the absence of positive coping actions, lead to an increase in aggressive or otherwise inappropriate acting-out behaviors, including sexual abuse, by predisposed persons.

Unlike life stress, which is a more general precipitating condition, *parental absence* may channel acting-out behavior in a more overtly sexual direction. Some writers emphasize the importance of the father's absence and subsequent return to a changed home situation as a triggering factor in incest (Kaufman et al., 1954; Cormier et al., 1962). Others argue that departure or incapacitation of the mother—for example, through desertion, travel, hospitalization, or prolonged illness—is a critical variable (Herman & Hirschman, 1977). Parental absence prior to or at the time of molestation may be an important contributing factor because it could relax normative constraints on the participants, make detection of the activity less likely, provide justification for impulsive behavior, exacerbate the perpetrator's feeling of sexual deprivation, or increase the loneliness and isolation of the victim.

The variables discussed above should be seen as affecting behavior in combination rather than singly. Molestation cannot be explained or predicted on the basis of the personality traits of those involved, or through the identification of pathological family patterns. Rather, it should be seen as occurring in a context consisting of family living patterns that offer an opportunity for such behavior, a family history which does not rule out the sexual objectification of children, and an absence of outside contacts which encourage role-appropriate behavior. Where contextual factors are present, specific events or changes that place further strains on the family may increase the probability of overt sexual behavior toward children on the part of persons who are predisposed to find such contact gratifying.

SUGGESTIONS FOR FUTURE RESEARCH

At present, there is considerable justified concern that, like other social problems, sexual abuse in the family is about to enter a period of "benign neglect" as far as research funding and the provision of services are concerned. This would be unfortunate, because very little is known about the frequency, causes, and effects of the problem and about how to treat and prevent it. We know that the kind of comprehensive research effort we outline below is probably too "ambitious" to be carried out in toto at this time, given the prevailing political attitudes about social scientific research funding. Nevertheless, we hope it provides an overall sense of direction for future research and suggests a way for integrating or coordinating small-scale, partial investigations of the problem.

The ideal research strategy in this area is one that is rigorous enough to lead to solid conclusions and flexible enough to alert investigators to unexpected patterns in the data. Further, there is a practical need for research focusing on aspects of behavior that are amenable to change through intervention. The research strategy we outline here has a qualitative, exploratory dimension, but it still focuses on systematic measurement and intergroup comparisons on key variables. We give the most emphasis to factors that have implications for prevention and treatment, such as social support.

The strategy we recommend uses multiple data-gathering methods, including interviews, questionnaires and psychometric instruments, and systematic observation. Ideally, work on intrafamilial child sexual abuse should be carried out by a multidisciplinary team composed of clinicians and social scientists who are trained in therapy and research methods.

One way to make a comprehensive study manageable is to compare a relatively large group of families in treatment for child sexual molestation with similar families receiving counseling for other problems, as well as with a comparable group of nontreatment families recruited from the community. The "in treatment-nonmolestation" comparison group is used to determine the extent to which the variables in the model can distinguish families in which child sexual molestation has occurred from "problem families" in general. The three sets of families should be matched as closely as possible on characteristics such as family size, socioeconomic status, age and sex of children, and family structure (intact versus stepparent families). Families containing obviously psychotic members and manifesting gross disorganization would not be included in the study.

Ideally, research on the factors contributing to incest would be conducted with undetected cases of intrafamilial molestation rather than with families in treatment. However, we believe there are several advantages to conducting research with acknowledged incest cases: (1) it affords an opportunity to follow families for a period of time, making for a fuller understanding of relationships in the family; (2) a therapeutic setting offers subjects a measure of confidentiality and the possibility of trust relationships with researchers, which should increase the level of candor; (3) families admitting that molestation has occurred will almost certainly be more willing to participate in the research and less likely to resist taking part; and (4) perhaps most important, working with families in treatment gives researchers the opportunity to gather data from all family members, including perpetrators.

Figure 6.1 lists variables at different levels of analysis that may contribute to illicit sexual conduct with children in the family. It also indicates sources from which data may be obtained (family records, individual members) and suggests methods for gathering data. In some cases, specific research instruments are listed as good candidates for inclusion in a comprehensive study. These instruments have the advantage of known reliability and could give badly needed uniformity to studies on intrafamilial child molestation.

Level of Analysis	Variable	Suggested Measure/Data Source
SOCIOECOLOGICAL	Geographic location	Family place of residence
	Household density	Family interview: family life space
	Geographic mobility	Times moved, last five years
Family		
A. Support Networks	Social support	Friendship networks measure: perpetrator/spouse/victim
	Social participation	Index of family social participation
	Decision-making power	Decision Power Index (Blood and Wolfe, 1960)
B. Structure	Role/task performance	Family Interaction Schedule (Straus, 1965)
	Mother-child bonds	Perceived quality of mother-victim relationship
	Structure, quality of communication	Coding of videotaped interviews
C. Interaction	Patterns of dominance, latent hostility, etc.	
INDIVIDUAL		
A. Quality of Marriage	Partner marital satisfaction	Marital Satisfaction Scale* (Locke and Wallace, 1959)
	Partner sexual satisfaction	Sexual Satisfaction Questionnaire*
	Perpetrator impulse control	Clinical interview
	Perpetrator overcontrol of hostility	Minnesota Multiphasic Personality Inventory
B. Personality Factors	Perpetrator socio-pathy	Minnesota Multiphasic Personality Inventory
	Parent self-concept	Tennessee Self Concept Test: Perpetrator/Spouse
	Victim-perceived need for affection	Clinical interview
C. Sexual Attitudes/ Knowledge	Parent sexual attitudes	Sexual Attitude Questionnaire Perpetrator/Spouse
	Victim experience with sex education	Clinical Interview

Figure 6.1: Factors affecting severity and duration of abuse.

D. Experience of Abuse	Parent history of sexual abuse in childhood	Interview: Perpetrator/ Spouse
PRECIPITATING FACTORS	Parent separation	Parent absence, reported in interview, questionnaire
	Life stress	Social Readjustment Rating Scale (Holmes and Rahe, 1967)

Figure 6.1 Continued

* As noted earlier, parent marital satisfaction measures should be obtained more than once.

CONCLUSION

Research on the problem of intrafamilial child sexual abuse indicates it is a complex phenomenon that arises from a variety of sources. Although it is possible that such activity stems in part from psychological traits or conflicts in the perpetrator, clinical investigations have failed to uncover particular personality characteristics associated with abuse. Instead, the evidence favors an interpretation based on multiple conditions at the level of the individual, the family unit, and the family environment. Our review of the literature has identified a number of factors that appear to be related to intrafamilial child molestation. Future research in the area should strive for comprehensiveness and should test specific hypotheses on comparison groups of incest, "normal," and nonincest "problem" families, with the goal of determining which factors or sets of factors (if any) are characteristic of families in which incestuous activities occur.

NOTES

1. This pattern may be more common in cases of intrafamilial abuse than child sexual abuse in general. There is some evidence indicating that boys are less willing to disclose sexual abuse and that they are victimized more by strangers and acquaintances than by family members. Groth (personal communication), for example, reports that in one of his projects, boys initially reported lower sexual victimization; however, after participating in a brief program designed to facilitate reporting of abuse, boys reported being sexually molested at about the same rate as girls. Several factors might explain the combination of high victimization and low reporting for boys: the tendency for habitual pedophiles to seek out boys; the fact that in our society, boys are allowed more independence and given less supervision than girls; and the reluctance of boys to see themselves as victims and to report having been exploited.

2. For example, Meiselman (1978), in her review of the literature, lists 46 studies on overt incest. In 24 of these studies, the number of persons involved is less than 10; 8 studies involve single cases only. Meiselman notes that because such small samples

are frequently used, writers tend to be guided more by theory and intuition than actual data.

3. Additionally, there is a growing "applied" literature in psychiatry, psychology, social work, and law that focuses on methods of recognizing cases of child sexual molestation (Kempe, 1978; Rosenfeld, 1979; Summit, n.d.), strategies for treating victims and perpetrators (Pittman, 1976; Giaretto, Giaretto, & Srogi, 1978; Weitzel, Powell, & Penick, 1978; Paulson, 1978), and related topics.

4. It is difficult to determine whether this pattern mirrors the true prevalence of intrafamilial child sexual abuse or whether it is an artifact produced by other factors. It could be that incest is equally common in intact families but that the pressure against disclosing it are stronger than in reconstituted families. On the other hand, the atmosphere in stepparent families may be more conducive to greater rates of abuse. Since blood ties between the parent and child are not present, the incest prohibition could be weaker; role confusion may be more common in such families; or the lifestyles associated with seeking a new spouse (and later remarriage) could put the child at greater risk due to increased contact with adults or decreased supervision.

5. We have attempted to offer a short, manageable list of individual factors. The literature contains numerous references to the mental status, needs, and motives of different family members—so many that assessing each individual in a sample would probably be impossible from a practical standpoint. Rather than trying to obtain in-depth knowledge of the psychological profile of each party in the molestation, our perspective emphasizes focusing on a few potentially strong explanatory variables.

6. Incest families appear to experience a great deal of stress before and during the *disclosure* of the sexual abuse; there may be an arrest, family members may move, and so on. However, to be considered a precipitating factor, stressful life events must be shown to have come before the illicit sexual contact was *initiated*.

REFERENCES

Blood, R. O., Jr., & Wolf, D. M. *Husbands and wives.* New York: Free Press, 1960.

Booth, A. Crowding and family relations. *American Sociological Review,* 1976, *41,* 308-321.

Browning, D., & Boatman, B. Incest: Children at risk. *American Journal of Psychiatry,* 1974, *134,* 69-72.

Burgess, A., & Holmstrom, L. Accessory-to-sex: Pressure, sex, and secrecy. In A. Burgess, A. Groth, L. Holmstrom, & S. Sgroi (Eds.), *Sexual assault of children and adolescents.* Lexington, MA: D. C. Heath, 1978.

Cobb, S. Social support as a moderator of life stress. *Psychosomatic Medicine,* 1976, *38,* 300-314.

Cormier, B., Kennedy, M., & Sangowicz, J. Psychodynamics of father-daughter incest. *Canadian Psychiatric Association Journal,* 1962, *7,* 203-217.

DeFrancis, F. *Protecting the child victim of sex crimes committed by adults.* Denver: American Humane Association, 1969.

Ferracuti, F. Incest between father and daughter. In H. Resnik and M. Wolfgang (Eds.), *Sexual behaviors: Social, clinical, and legal aspects.* Boston: Little, Brown, 1972.

Finkelhor, D. *Sexually victimized children.* New York: Free Press, 1979.

Gagnon, J. Female child victims of sex offenses. *Social Problems,* 1965, *13,* 176-192.

Gebhard, P., Gagnon, J., Pomeroy, W., & Christenson, C. *Sex offenders.* New York: Harper & Row, 1965.

Gelles, R. Methods for studying sensitive family topics. In R. Gelles (Ed.), *Family violence.* Beverly Hills, CA: Sage 1979.

Giaretto, H., Giaretto, A., & Sgroi, S. Co-ordinated community treatment of incest. In A. Burgess, A. Groth, L. Holmstrom, & S. Sgroi (Eds.), *Sexual assault of children and adolescents.* Lexington, MA: D. C. Heath, 1978.

Groth, A. Patterns of sexual assault against children and adolescents. In A. Burgess, A. Groth, L. Holmstrom, & A. Sgroi (Eds.), *Sexual assault of children and adolescents.* Lexington, MA: D.C. Heath, 1978.

Henderson, D. Incest: A synthesis of data. *Canadian Psychiatric Association Journal,* 1972, *17,* 299-313.

Herman, J., & Hirschman, L. Father-daughter incest. *Signs: Journal of Women in Culture and Society,* 1977, *2,* 735-756.

Holmes, T. H., & Rahe, R. H. The social readjustment rating scale. *Journal of Psychosomatic Research,* 1967, *11,* 213-218.

Kaufman, K., Peck, A., & Taguiri, C. The family constellation and overt incest relations between father and daughter. *American Journal of Orthopsychiatry,* 1954, *24,* 266-277.

Kempe, C. Sexual abuse, another hidden pediatric problem: The 1977 Anderson-Aldrich lecture. *Pediatrics,* 1978, *62,* 382-389.

Laws, J. L. A feminist review of the marital adjustment literature: The rape of the Locke. *Journal of Marriage and the Family,* 1971, *33,* 483-516.

Liem, R., & Liem, J. Social class and mental illness reconsidered: The role of economic stress and social support. *Journal of Health and Social Behavior,* 1978, *19,* 136-156.

Locke, H. J., & Wallace, K. M. Short marital adjustment and prediction tests: Their reliability and validity. *Marriage and Family Living,* 1959, *21,* 251-255.

Lukianowicz, N. Incest. *British Journal of Psychiatry,* 1972, *120,* 301-313.

Lustig, M., Dresser, J., Spellman, S., & Murray, T. Incest: A family group survival pattern. *Archives of General Psychiatry,* 1966, *14,* 31-40.

Maisch, H. *Incest.* London: Andre Deutsch, 1973.

Meiselman, K. C. *Incest.* San Francisco: Jossey-Bass, 1978.

Molnar, G., & Cameron, P. Incest syndromes: Observations in a general hospital psychiatric unit. *Canadian Psychiatric Association Journal,* 1975, *20,* 373-377.

National Center on Child Abuse and Neglect. *Child sexual abuse: Incest, assault, and sexual exploitation.* Pub. No. (OHDS) 79-30166. Washington, DC: U.S. Department of Health, Education and Welfare, 1978.

Paulson, M. Incest and sexual molestation: clinical and legal issues. *Journal of Clinical Child Psychology,* 1978, *7,* 177-180.

Pittman, F. Counseling incestuous families. *Medical Aspects of Human Sexuality,* 1976, *10,* 57-58.

Poznanski, E., & Blos, P. Incest. *Medical Aspects of Human Sexuality,* 1975, *9,* 46-76.

Renshaw, D., & Renshaw, R. Incest. *Journal of Sex Education and Therapy,* 1977, *3,* 3-7.

Rosenfeld, A. Endogamic incest and the victim-perpetrator model. *American Journal of Diseases of Children,* 1979, *40,* 159-164.

Sarafino, E. An estimate of the nationwide incidence of sexual offences against children. *Child Welfare,* 1979, *58,* 127-134.

Schultz, L. The sexual abuse of children and minors: A bibliography. *Child Welfare,* 1979, *58,* 147-163.

Straus, M. A. *The family interaction schedule test and manual.* Minneapolis, MN: Family Study Center, 1965.

Straus, M. A general systems theory approach to a theory of violence between spouses. *Social Science Information,* 1973, *12,* 105-125.

Summit, R. Typical characteristics of father-daughter incest: A guide for investigation. Torrance, CA: Community Consultation Service, Harbor-U.C.L.A. Medical Center, n.d.

Summit, R., & Kryso, J. Sexual abuse of children: A clinical spectrum. *American Journal of Orthopsychiatry,* 1978, *48,* 237-250.

Virkunnen, M. Incest offenses and alcoholism. *Medicine, Science, and the Law,* 1974, *14,* 124-128.

Weinberg, S. *Incest·behavior.* New York: Citadel Press, 1955.

Weitzel, W., Powell, B., & Penick, E. The clinical management of father-daughter incest: A critical examination. *American Journal of Diseases of Children,* 1978, *132,* 127-130.

SECTION IV

MARITAL RAPE

Marital rape is the newest form of family violence to emerge as a social problem. As a research issue, marital rape is so new that virtually all the citations to research on it mentioned in this section were still (at the time of writing, May, 1982) unpublished papers.

The research yet to be done on the topic of marital rape promises to have a dramatic impact on thinking about both rape and marriage. For example, public opinion and scientific research about rape have for a long time assumed that stranger rape was the paradigm of rape. Now prevalence studies are suggesting that rape by intimates is far more common than rape by strangers and that sexual assaults in marriage may be the most common kind. This conclusion is not so surprising for family violence researchers, who have long recognized the greater vulnerability of individuals to assaults by intimates than assaults by strangers. But conceptual frameworks about rape are sure to change under pressure from these new empirical findings.

Research on marital rape should also put pressure for change on accepted notions of marriage and marital sexuality. Sex therapists, for example, have generally considered the major sexual dysfunctions of marriage to be problems of passivity—impotence, inability to be aroused, lack of desire for sex, lack of orgasm. Research on marital rape suggests that a widespread, largely unrecognized, and perhaps more important sexual issue in marriage is aggressivity—the desire to hurt, humiliate, and dominate through sex. Treatment and research on sexual dysfunction needs to incorporate this new insight into its framework.

The two chapters presented in this section give a sampling of some of the empirical and theoretical issues posed by the subject of marital rape. One of the strengths of David Finkelhor and Kersti Yllo's "Marital Rape: A Sociological Perspective" is its attempt to delineate a typology among kinds of marital rape. Nancy Shields and Christine Hanneke, in "Battered Wives' Reactions to Marital Rape," show some of the complex methodological and conceptual issues that need to be addressed in understanding the effects of marital rape as a separate form of violence and injury.

A latent issue below the surface of both chapters is the question of what conceptual framework to use in thinking about marital rape. Some have argued that the problem is best framed in terms of wife-battering; others, that it is best framed in terms of rape. For example, some of the effects of marital rape are perhaps best understood through the wife-beating literature. Marital rape victims, like battery victims, are trapped with their abusers, subject to repeated assaults, victimized by the psychological abuse that goes along with the physical abuse, and more likely to require the services of a battered women's shelter than a rape crisis hotline.

On the other hand, some people have pointed out the danger of assuming too close an affinity between marital rape and battering. A great deal—perhaps too much—of what we know about marital rape comes from studies of battered women. This may lead to a misestimation of the importance of what Finkelhor and Yllo called the "nonbattering marital rapes." It may be through study of such rapes that we will discover the most about the roles of dominance and violence in the typical marriage in our society. Certainly, unless we think about the specifically sexual insult and violation that goes along with marital rape, researchers may miss the kind of special trauma that it causes, a trauma that Shields and Hanneke try to isolate. Obviously, researchers and theorists need to borrow from both the wife abuse and rape literature in order to develop their ideas about this most recently revealed form of family violence.

7

Rape in Marriage
A Sociological View

DAVID FINKELHOR and KERSTI YLLO

The subject of marital rape is cropping up with increasing frequency in the media in recent years. Yet, attention has focused almost entirely on court cases—such as those of John Rideout in Oregon and James Chretien in Massachusetts—and on state legislatures, where efforts have been made to criminalize this form of sexual assault (Celarier, 1979; Croft, 1979; Laura X, 1980).

While lawyers and legislators debate the issue, those in positions best suited to understanding this form of abuse and to offering help to victims have generally remained silent. Surprisingly little attention has been paid to the problem of marital rape by researchers, counselors, therapists, and doctors. Even feminist recognition of marital rape is coming well after other types of violence against women became national concerns.

Nonetheless, public and professional awareness that marital rape exists is growing. The slowly accumulating evidence suggests that rape in marriage is not a rare crime that may blossom into a headline-grabbing trial, but that it is a persistent problem in a large number of marriages.

PREVALENCE OF MARITAL RAPE

Evidence about violence against wives in general leads to a suspicion that forced sex in marriage is fairly commonplace. For a long time, wife abuse also was considered a rather unusual crime, but results of recent large-scale surveys have reversed this notion. Straus, Gelles, and Steinmetz (1980) found that 16% of all American couples admitted to a violent episode in the course of the previous year, and for 4% the violence was severe enough to qualify as wife-battering.

Authors' Note: *Funds from NIMH grants MH15161, MH30930, and MH34109, as well as from the research office of the University of New Hampshire, helped make this research possible. Ruth Miller assisted in the preparation of this manuscript. Portions of this chapter were presented to the Society for the Scientific Study of Sex in Dallas, November 1980, and to the American Orthopsychiatric Association in New York, April 1981.*

Testimony from battered women confirms their high vulnerability to marital rape. Spektor (1980) surveyed 304 battered women in 10 shelters in the state of Minnesota and found that 36% said they had been raped by their husband or cohabitating partner. Giles-Sims (1979) found a similar proportion of women in shelters reporting a forced sex experience, and Pagelow (1980) reported a figure of 37% based on a sample of 119 women in California. Forced sex is clearly a common element in the battering situation.

Diana Russell (1980) has gathered some of the first direct evidence about the prevalence of marital rape experiences in the population at large. Russell surveyed a random sample of 930 women residents of San Francisco, 18 years and older, about any incident of sexual assault they had had at any time throughout their lives. Fourteen percent of the 644 married women in the sample reported a sexual assault by a husband. Twelve percent had been forced to have intercourse, and two percent experienced other types of forced sex. *Sexual assaults by husbands were the most common kinds of sexual assault reported, occurring over twice as often as sexual assault by a stranger.*

It is important in evaluating Russell's finding to realize that she did not ask any of her respondents whether they had been "raped," a stigmatizing term that many women are reluctant to use to describe sexual assault experiences. Instead, she asked women to describe any kind of unwanted sexual experience with a husband or ex-husband, and then only included in her tally those women who described encounters that met the legal definition of rape: "forced intercourse, or intercourse obtained by physical threat(s) or intercourse completed when the woman was drugged, unconscious, asleep, or otherwise totally helpless and hence unable to consent."

Russell's finding that marital rape is the most common kind of rape cannot thus be ascribed to semantics. She used the same definition of sexual assault in tabulating the experiences with husbands as she did with strangers.

The findings from Russell's study are bolstered by results from a survey we recently completed in Boston. In a study on the related subject of childhood sexual abuse, we also asked a representative sample of 326 women whether a spouse or person they were living with as a couple had ever used physical force or threat to try to have sex with them. *Ten percent* of the women who had been married (or coupled) answered "yes." These women, too, reported more sexual assaults by husbands than assaults by strangers (10% versus 3%). Forced sex in marriage is a frequent—perhaps the most frequent—type of sexual assault.

WIVES AVOID RAPE LABEL

Few women whose husbands have forced them to have sex define themselves as having been raped (Gelles, 1979). Most women see rape as something that primarily happens between strangers. They too share the cultural and legal assumption that there is no such thing as rape between husband and wife. Violent and unpleasant as a husband's assault might have been, most wives would resist calling it rape. No doubt raped wives, like battered wives, use many self-deceptions to avoid facing the realities of an intolerable marriage because the alternatives—loneliness, loss of financial security, admission of failure—are so frightening (Gelles, 1979).

For these reasons, asking women whether they have been raped by their husbands is an unpromising course. To use a term that more victims could identify with, we used the term "forced sex" rather than "marital rape" throughout our research.

VARIETIES OF COERCION

Another definitional problem concerns the question of when sex is forced. It has been argued that given the power inequality in the institution of marriage, *all* marital sex is coerced (Brogger, 1976). It may be that when sex is not explicitly desired it should be considered forced. Obviously, many different sanctions and pressures are brought to bear by husbands to gain sexual access. Although all these sanctions have elements of coercion, some important distinctions can be made among them.

Four basic types of coercion can be identified. Some women submit to sex in the absence of desire because of social pressure—because they believe it is their wifely duty. This can be considered *social coercion.* Other wives comply because they fear their husbands will leave them if they do not, or because their husbands have threatened to cut off their source of money or humiliate them in some way. In these cases husbands use their resource and power advantage to force their wives. This second type of coercion, *interpersonal coercion,* refers to threats by husbands that are not violent in nature. The third type involves the *threat of physical force.* Threatened force can range from an implied threat that a woman could get hurt if she doesn't give in to an explicit threat she will be killed if she doesn't comply. For many women, the memory of previous beatings is enough to ensure cooperation.

The fourth kind of coercion, *physical coercion,* requires little explanation. Instances of physical coercion range from physically holding a woman down to striking her, choking her, tying her up, or knocking her out to force sex on her.

FOCUS ON PHYSICAL FORCE

The varieties of sexual coercion in marriage would be the subject of an intriguing study; however, it is beyond the scope of this research. We have limited our study to physical force for two main reasons. First, such force is most life- and health-threatening and in that sense most extreme. Second, the presence or absence of physical threats and actual violent coercion is somewhat easier to determine empirically than is the presence or absence of other, more subtle forms of coercion. This is not meant to imply that other forms of coercion cannot be brutal or that "marital rape" can occur only when physical force is involved.

IN-DEPTH INTERVIEWS

The following sections represent an overview of our exploratory study of marital rape from the victim's perspective. Our findings are based on 50 in-depth interviews with women whose husband or partner had used force or threat of force to try to have sex with them. Our interviewees were recruited from a number of sources. The majority (56%) were clients of Family Planning agencies in northern New England. These clinics routinely take a limited sexual history from each client. For the purposes of this study an additional question was added to the form: "Has your current partner (or a previous partner) ever used force or threat of force to try to have sex with you?" If the answer indicated that the client had had such an experience with a spouse or cohabitant, she was asked to participate in an additional interview for research purposes, for which she would be paid $10.

Other interviewees (16%) were recruited through area battered wives shelters. When it was determined that a woman's violent experiences included forced sex, she was asked to participate in the research, if shelter staff felt that she was up to an interview. Additional interviewees (28%) were self-referrals. These women heard of our research in the media or through our public speaking and contacted us, offering to discuss their experiences. Finally, a few interviews (10%) were arranged as a result of an ad placed in *Ms.* magazine requesting interviews.

Although the sample is not a representative one, we do not regard this as a serious drawback because of the nature of this research. Our goal in this exploratory study was not to determine incidence rates or demographic data (our Boston survey provides such information). Rather, our purpose was to talk at length with women who were willing to discuss their forced sex experiences so that we could gain a qualitative understanding of marital rape and begin to outline issues for further research. The clinics and shelters were sites where these intimate subjects could be raised fairly easily and where intervention services could be made available to women needing them.

THREE TYPES UNCOVERED

The forced sex experiences of the women we interviewed can be divided roughly into three types. One group can be described as typically "battered women." These women were subject to extensive physical and verbal abuse, much of which was unrelated to sex. Their husbands were frequently angry and belligerant to them and often had alcohol and drug problems. The sexual violence in these relationships appeared to be just another aspect of the general abuse. Along with the other kinds of anger and physical pain which these men heaped on their wives, they also used violent sex.

Let us quote briefly from a case study of one of these "*battering rapes*":

The interviewee was a 24-year-old woman from an affluent background. Her husband was a big man, over six feet tall, compared to her 5'2". He drank heavily and often attacked her physically. The most frequent beatings occurred at night after they had had a fight and she had gone to bed. She would awaken to find him physically abusing her. Such attacks, at their worst, occurred every couple of weeks. After one incident her face was so bruised that she could not attend class for a full week.

Their sexual activities had violent aspects, too. Although they shared the initiative for sex and had no disagreements about its timing or frequency, she often felt that he was brutal in his love-making. She said, "I would often end up crying during intercourse, but it never seemed to bother him. He probably enjoyed my pain in some way."

The most violent sexual episode occurred at the very end of their relationship. Things had been getting worse between them for some time. They hadn't talked to each other in two weeks. One afternoon she came home from school, changed into a housecoat and started toward the bathroom. He got up from the couch where he had been lying, grabbed her, and pushed her down on the floor. With her face pressed into a pillow and his hand clamped over her mouth, he proceeded to have anal intercourse with her. She screamed and struggled to no avail. Afterward she was hateful and furious. "It was very violent . . .", she said, ". . . if I had had a gun there, I would have killed him."

Her injuries were painful and extensive. She had a torn muscle in her rectum so that for three months she had to go to the bathroom standing up. The assault left her with hemorrhoids and a susceptibility to aneurisms that took five years to heal.

The second group of women have somewhat different relationships. These relationships are by no means conflict-free, but on the whole, there is little physical violence. In this group, the forced sex grew out of more specifically sexual conflicts. There were long-standing disagreements over some sexual issue, such as how often to have sex or what were appropriate sexual activities. The following is an exerpt from a case study of a "*nonbattering rape*":

> The interviewee was a 33-year-old woman with a young son. Both she and her husband of ten years are college graduates and professionals. She is a teacher and he is a guidance counselor. Their marriage, from her report, seems to be of a modern sort in most respects. There have been one or two violent episodes in their relationship, but in those instances, the violence appears to have been mutual.
>
> There is a long-standing tension in the relationship about sex. She prefers sex about three times a week, but feels under considerable pressure to have more. She says that she is afraid that if she refuses him that he will leave her or that he will force her.
>
> He did force her about two years ago. Their love-making on this occasion started out pleasantly enough, but he tried to get her to have anal intercourse with him. She refused. He persisted. She kicked and pushed him away. Still, he persisted. They ended up having vaginal intercourse. The force he used was mostly that of his weight on top of her. At 220 pounds, he weighs twice as much as she.
>
> "It was horrible," she said. She was sick to her stomach afterward. She cried and felt angry and disgusted. He showed little guilt. "He felt like he'd won something."

In addition to the sexual assaults we classified as battering and nonbattering, there were a handful that defied such categorization. These rapes were sometimes connected to battering and sometimes not. All, however, involved bizarre sexual obsessions in the husbands that were not evident in the other cases. Husbands who made up this group were heavily involved in pornography. They tried to get their wives to participate in making or imitating it. They sometimes had a history of sexual problems, such as difficulty in getting aroused, or guilt about earlier homosexual experiences. Sometimes these men needed force or highly structured rituals of sexual behavior in order to become aroused. A case study of one of these *obsessive rapes* is illustrative:

> The interviewee was a thirty-one-year-old marketing analyst for a large corporation. She met her husband in high school and was attracted to his intelligence. They were married right after graduation because she was pregnant.
>
> After the baby was born, he grew more and more demanding sexually. "I was really just his masturbating machine," she recalls.

He was very rough sexually and would hold a pillow over her face to stifle her screams. He would also tie her up and insert objects into her vagina and take pictures which he shared with his friends.

There were also brutal "blitz" attacks. One night, for example, they were in bed having sex when they heard a commotion outside. They went out in their bathrobes to investigate to discover it was just a cat fight. She began to head back to the house when her husband stopped her and told her to wait. She was standing in the darkness wondering what he was up to when, suddenly, he attacked her from behind. "He grabbed my arms behind me and tied them together. He pushed me over the log pile and raped me," she said. As in similar previous assaults, he penetrated her anally.

The interviewee later discovered a file card in her husband's desk which sickened her. On the card, he had written a list of dates, dates that corresponded to the forces sex episodes of the past months. Next to each date was a complicated coding system which seemed to indicate the type of sex act and a ranking of how much he enjoyed it.

FORCE AND RESISTANCE

The incidents uncovered in our study so far varied both in the amount of force used by the men and the amount of resistance offered by the women. In some cases the man applied massive force, dragging the woman somewhere, tearing off her clothes, and physically beating her. In other situations, particularly where the couple was already in bed, the force was more moderate. In several cases the women mentioned the men's weight and their persistent attempts to penetrate them as the main elements of force.

Many women said they did not put up much of a fight, however. They felt that it was no use or wasn't worth it. This is an important point to understand better, because so many victims of sexual force have been ridiculed for not meeting the masculine stereotype of how vigorously a threatened person should resist. Lack of violent resistance is often interpreted as a sign that the victims really "wanted" sex on some level or that it wasn't so traumatic.

There appear to be three main factors that inhibited the women's attempts to ward off sexual aggression from their partners. First, many of the women felt they could not ward off their partners' aggression no matter how hard they tried. They perceived their partners to be very strong. Indeed, we were struck by the large size disparity between our subjects and their partners. Women who are much smaller than their husbands may be a particularly vulnerable group, not only because they *are* weak in comparison but because they *feel* weak as well.

Second, many of the women feared that if they resisted they would be hurt even worse, especially the women who had been beaten before. They expected that if they resisted they would be punched, bruised, and manhandled and that the sexual act itself would be more painful and damaging.

Third, many of the women believed that they themselves were in the wrong. In several cases, their husbands had convinced them that they were frigid. They believed that they were at fault for whatever marital dispute was in process, and felt responsible for their husband's mood or frustration. Although they did not want the sexual act, they were not armed with the conviction that they were *justified* in not wanting it. This made it difficult for them to put up a fight.

In general, it seemed that certain kinds of ultimate resistance tactics seemed out of the question for these women. Most did not run out of the house or physically resist by gouging at the partner's eyes or kicking him in the groin. No doubt they were hampered by their socialization not even to consider such actions. Moreover, unless they were prepared to leave, they knew that they would have to face this man later on, in the morning or the next day. Since most were not prepared to make it on their own, a central goal was "keeping the peace." They were not willing to bring out the ultimate weapons, because they had to continue living with this person. And they wanted to make things more tolerable for themselves. So appeasement rather than massive resistance appeared to be the preferable approach from their immediate point of view.

TRAUMA OF MARITAL RAPE

Many people fail to get alarmed about the problem of marital rape because they think it is a rather less traumatic form of rape. Being jumped by a stranger in the street, they imagine, must be so much more damaging than having sex with someone you have had sex with several times before.

This misconception is based on a failure to understand the real violation involved in rape. Those who see rape primarily in sexual terms think the degradation comes from the woman having been robbed of her reputation. Although this element can be present, what is most salient for rape victims is most often the violence, the loss of control, and the betrayal of trust.

Women raped by strangers often go through a long period of being afraid, especially about their physical safety. They become very cautious about being alone, where they go, and who they go with (Burgess & Holmstrom, 1974). Women raped by husbands, however, are often traumatized at an even more basic level: in their ability to trust. The kind of violation they have experienced is much harder to guard against, short of a refusal to trust any man. It touches a woman's basic confidence in forming relationships and trusting intimates. It can leave a woman feeling much more powerless and isolated than if she were raped by a stranger.

Moreover, a woman raped by her husband has to live with her rapist, not just a frightening memory of a stranger's attack. Being trapped in an abusive marriage leaves many women vulnerable to repeated sexual assaults by their husbands. Most of the women we interviewed were raped on multiple occasions. These women do not have the option of obtaining police protection (as do other rape victims) because these rapes are legal in most states.

The research bears out the traumatic impact of marital rape. Russell found that the marital rape victims in her study rated their experiences as having a more serious impact on their lives than did the victims of stranger rape (Russell, 1980). Other studies, too, have shown that rape by intimates in general is more, not less, traumatic than rape by strangers (Bart, 1975).

FORCED MARITAL SEX AND THE LAW

While research cited earlier has highlighted the high prevalence of forced marital sex, and this research has documented some of its human cost, the criminal justice system is locked in anachronistic view of the subject. As of January 1982, approximately 36 of the 50 states and the District of Columbia exempt a husband from prosecution for the rape of a wife with whom he is currently living. (An excellent review of the laws on a state-by-state basis is available from the National Center on Women and Family Law; see Schulman, 1980.) Most states have a so-called spousal exemption in their rape laws, and 13 states extend this exemption not just to husbands but also to cohabiting lovers (Schulman, 1980). Such laws effectively deny the possibility of charging a husband with rape, no matter how brutal or violent he may have been in the pursuit of sex. They also contain the implicit assumption that upon marrying a woman gives permanent and irrevocable (short of divorce) consent to any and all sexual approaches a husband wishes to make.

Changing such laws has been vehemently opposed in some quarters on the grounds that it will result in a rash of fabricated complaints or that such behavior is already adequately prohibited under existing assault laws. However, evidence from countries and states where marital rape is a crime shows that few frivolous complaints are brought (Geis, 1978). Moreover, as this and other research on rape shows, sexual assault is a crime different from other assaults, with particular motives and particularly humiliating effects on its victims. Marital rape, just like other rape, deserves special classification within the legal system (New York University Law Review, 1977).

PUBLIC ATTITUDES ABOUT MARITAL RAPE

However, it would be naive to think that the simple removal of the spousal exemption will dramatically reduce the occurrence of marital rape. Evidence suggests that even where such laws exist, they are infrequently used (Geis, 1978). Even the minority of women who may recognize that their husbands have committed a crime against them, for various reasons—loyalty, fear, unwillingness to go through a grueling public exposure—are still extremely reluctant to press charges. The lesson of spouse abuse is that laws alone have relatively little effect (Field & Field, 1973). Physical spouse abuse is a crime and has been for many years; yet in spite of such laws, all evidence suggests that such abuse is epidemic.

The spousal exemption is merely one manifestation of a complex of social attitudes surrounding the physical and sexual abuse of wives. Until these attitudes also change, the problem will remain critical with or without a law. These social attitudes portray marital rape as acceptable behavior, at least under some circumstances, and even if sometimes objectionable, at least not very seriously so.

For insight on these attitudes, we asked groups of undergraduate students for their opinions about marital rape, and some of their replies are revealing.

Some denied entirely that the phenomenon could occur: "No. When you get married, you are supposedly in love and you shouldn't even think of love making as rape under any circumstances."

Others expressed the view that implicit in the marriage contract is an acceptance of the use of force. "Sexual relations are a part of marriage and both members realize this before they make a commitment," said one in explaining why there was no such thing as marital rape.

A number of students believed that forced sex was a reasonable solution to marital conflict. "If the wife did not want to have sex . . . after many months the husband may go crazy. [Rape] would be an alternative to seeking sexual pleasure with someone else."

"If she doesn't want sex for a long amount of time, and has no reason for it—Let the old man go for it!"

Besides expressing the opinion that force is an acceptable way of trying to salvage a marriage, such statements reveal other attitudes which work to justify marital rape: for example, the belief in a man's overpowering need for sex and the belief that women withhold sex from their husbands for no good reason. Note also the myth, discussed earlier, that forced sex is primarily a response to a woman who is denying satisfaction to her husband.

The refusal on the part of politicians and the public to see marital rape as a crime is also based on the belief that it is not a very serious offense. Peter Rossi presented a random sample of people living in Baltimore with descriptions of 140 offenses ranging from the planned killing of a policeman to being drunk in a public place. While the respondents ranked "forcible rape after breaking into a home" as the fourth most serious of all 140 offenses, just *above* the "impulsive killing of a policeman," they ranked "forcible rape of a former spouse" sixty-second, just above "driving while drunk" (Rossi, Waite, Bose, & Berk, 1974).

So while people consider some rape a serious offense, rape of a former spouse is not seen as very serious. Imagine how low the ranking would have been had Rossi asked about rape of a "current" rather than a "former" spouse. This corresponds with what we know about attitudes toward violence: The more intimate the victim, the less serious the assault is considered to be.

This can be read as rather sobering evidence that the "marriage license is a raping license." Not only is it true that by marrying, a man gains immunity (a form of license) to the charge of rape, but it also appears true that people are much less likely to disapprove of sexually violent behavior, if he directs it against a woman to whom he is married rather than some other woman.

If people do not think that spousal rape is a serious offense, it certainly contributes to a climate where husbands feel they can do it with impunity. The climate also affects the victims who conclude from such social attitudes that they are wrong to be so upset and that few people will sympathize with them, so why bring it up.

Although changing the spousal exemption law is unlikely to bring many offenders to court for their offenses, it may have some effect on the general climate of acceptance of marital rape. For one thing, the political debate should alert the community, the criminal justice system, and mental health professionals about the existence of this problem. The change in the law may also put on notice some potential husband rapists that their behavior is not generally acceptable and in fact is a crime. Finally, the change may give vulnerable women a potential tool in protecting themselves.

The deterrent effect of changing the law was illustrated in the case of one woman we interviewed. Her recently separated husband kept returning and trying to have sex with her, and he was becoming more and more aggressive in his attempts. When she told some friends about the problem, they counseled her to tell him that if he tried it again she would have him prosecuted for marital rape. Apparently the husband was familiar with the recent publicity around the marital rape trials, because after she made her threat he relented and did not molest her again. This is an encouraging incident and shows that legal changes and the public discussions they stir need not be measured merely by the number of new arrests and convictions they produce.

CONCLUSION

This review of current information about marital rape and our findings regarding wives' forced sex experiences are a first step toward a full understanding of this social problem. Our research shows that "marital rape" is not a contradiction in terms, but rather a form of violence against wives which is not rare, just rarely discussed.

The case studies and typologies developed here are intended to encourage the generation of hypotheses and further analysis of forced sex in marriage, its antecedents, consequences, and implications. As a whole, our research is intended to add to the groundswell of concern about violence against women and to signal that the time has arrived for concerted investigation and discussion of the problem of rape in marriage and for action in political, legal, academic, and clinical arenas.

REFERENCES

Bart, P. Rape doesn't end with a kiss. *Viva,* 1975, 40-42, 101-107.

Brogger, S. *Deliver us from love.* New York: Delacorte, 1976.

Burgess, A., & Holmstrom, L. *Rape: Victims of crisis.* Bowie, MD: Brady, 1974.

Celarier, M. I kept thinking maybe I could help him. *In These Times,* January 1979, 10-16.

Croft, G. Three years in rape of wife. *Boston Globe,* September 15, 1979.

Doron, J. *Conflict and violence in intimate relationships: Focus on marital rape.* Paper presented at the annual meetings of the American Sociological Association, New York.

Field, M., & Field, H. Marital violence and the criminal process: Neither justice nor peace. *Social Service Review,* 1973, *47*(2), 221-240.

Geis, G. Rape-in-marriage: Law and law reform in England, the U.S. and Sweden. *Adelaide Law Review,* 1978, *6,* 284-302.

Gelles, R. *Family violence.* Beverly Hills, CA: Sage, 1979.

Giles-Sims, J. *Stability and change in patterns of wife-beating: A systems theory approach.* Unpublished Ph.D. dissertation, University of New Hampshire, 1979.

Hunt, M. *Sexual behavior in the 1970's.* Chicago: Playboy Press, 1974.

New York University Law Review. Marital rape exemption. 1977, *52,* 306-323.

Pagelow, M. D. *Does the law help battered wives? Some research notes.* Madison, WI: Law and Society Association, 1980.

Rossi, P., Waite, E., Bose, C., & Berk, R. The seriousness of crimes: Normative structures and individual differences. *American Sociological Review,* 1974, *39,* 224-237.

Russell, D. *The prevalence and impact of marital rape in San Francisco.* Paper presented at the annual meetings of the American Sociological Association, New York, 1980.

Schulman, J. The marital rape exemption. *National Center on Women and Family Law Newsletter,* 1980, *1*(1), 6-8. (a)

Schulman, J. Expansion of the marital rape exemption. *National Center on Women and Family Law Newsletter,* 1980, *1*(2), 3-4. (b)

Spektor, P. Testimony delivered to the Law Enforcement Subcommittee of the Minnesota House of Representatives, February 29, 1980.

Straus, M., Gelles, R., & Steinmetz, S. *Behind closed doors: Violence in the American family.* Garden City, NY: Doubleday, 1980.

Wolfe, L. The sexual profile of the Cosmopolitan girl. *Cosmopolitan,* 1980, *189*(3), 254-257, 263-265.

X, Laura. *The Rideout trial.* Women's History Research Center, mimeo.

8

Battered Wives' Reactions to Marital Rape

NANCY M. SHIELDS and CHRISTINE R. HANNEKE

A major focus of both the literature on wife-battering and the literature on nonmarital rape of women (i.e., rape by friends, acquaintances, strangers, etc.) has been the question of the impact of the violence on the victim. Of the two literatures, possible reactions of battered wives have probably been studied more fully. Some behaviors that have been thought to be reactions to battering have included (1) seeking help from others to end or avoid the violence (Hirsch, 1981; Martin, 1976; Gelles, 1976; Straus, 1976; Frazier, 1977); (2) retaliatory violence against the husband (Hirsch, 1981; Gelles, 1974; Truninger, 1971) as well as physical abuse of their own children (Gelles, 1974; Martin, 1978); (3) separating from or divorcing their husbands (Truninger, 1971; O'Brien, 1971; Gelles, 1976); (4) increasing "social isolation" in terms of seeing others socially less often and not discussing their victimization with others (Gelles, 1974; Straus, 1977; Martin, 1978); (5) depression (Hirsch, 1981; Gelles, 1974; Truninger, 1971) and the use of alcohol for depression (Martin, 1978); (6) attempted suicide (Hirsch, 1981; Martin, 1978; Gelles, 1974); (7) an increase in physical illnesses, some psychosomatic in nature (Frazier, 1977; Hilberman & Munson, 1977); (8) increasingly negative attitudes toward their husbands, marriage in general, and men in general (Prescott & Letko, 1977; Martin, 1978; Gelles, 1974; Truninger, 1971) and changes in attitudes toward their sexual relationships with their husbands, including withholding sex (Gayford, 1975); (9) increasingly negative self-esteem (Truninger, 1971; Straus, 1976); (10) legal action against the husband, such as filing for a restraining order or having him arrested (Shields & Fox, 1978); (11) self-blame for victimization (Davidson, 1978; Martin, 1976); and (12) involvement in lesbian relationships (Hirsch, 1981). Many of these reac-

Authors' Note: *This research was funded by a grant from the National Institute of Mental Health, Center for Studies in Crime and Delinquency (Grant # 5R01-MH33297-02).*

tions are thought to be related to the stress produced by victimization. In a recent case study of a severely battered woman, nearly all of the reactions cited were experienced by the woman (McNulty, 1980).

Research on reactions of female rape victims has dealt primarily with victims of rape other than marital rape. Sutherland and Scherl (1970) identified a three-stage process of response to rape. In the acute phase (occurring a few hours to one to two weeks after the rape), victims experience feelings of shock, disbelief, and dismay and are fearful that their own "poor judgment precipitated the crisis." They are also fearful of telling others, especially family members, about the incident. In the second stage, "pseudoadjustment," the victim tries to deny that the event occurred and/or rationalizes why it happened to her. In the third stage, integration, the victim is depressed and must resolve her feelings of anger at the assailant and her own self-blame.

Burgess and Holmstrom (1974) have also developed a model of reaction to rape called the "rape trauma syndrome." This two-state process involves an acute phase in which the victim experiences fear, shock, and disbelief at what has occurred as well as feeling humiliation, embarrassment, and self-blame. The woman may also experience somatic reactions from physical trauma of general soreness and bruising to skeletal muscle tension—for example, headaches, fatigue, sleep problems; gastrointestinal irritability—such as lack of appetite, feeling nauseated; or genitourinary disturbances of vaginal discharge, itching, or burning sensation at urination. The second stage in the process is one of reorganization which occurs two to three weeks after the rape. In this stage, the woman takes such actions as changing residence or her phone number, getting support from family and friends, as well as experiencing nightmares and developing phobias related to the rape experience, such as fear of being indoors, being outdoors, being alone, being in crowds, or sexual fears.

In order to test the models and stages suggested by Burgess and Holmstrom and Sutherland and Scherl, more recent studies on reactions of rape victims have utilized standardized measures of relevant variables in order to determine any changes in victims' anxiety levels and mood states (Kilpatrick, Veronen, & Resick, 1979a, 1979b), depression (Atkeson, Calhoun, Resick, & Ellis, 1982), and sexual functioning (Feldman-Summers, Gordon, & Meagher, 1979) over time. In comparison with control groups of women, the victims' scores on the measures of mood states and sexual functioning approximated the scores of the control groups for the first several months after being attacked. However, the fear and anxiety scores of the women remained at high levels through one-year postrape, with most fears being related to the initial rape experience and fear of subsequent attack (Kilpatrick, Resick, & Veronen, 1981). Atkenson et al. (1982) found that victims were significantly more depressed than control group women and found less enjoyment and satisfaction in life for the first several months after being attacked. Feldman-Summers et al. (1979) found similar effects in the area of sexual functioning. The victims in their study reported less satisfaction with sex than did control group women from two months to seven years after their rape experience. Ellis et al. (1981) report that some victims experience "sexually-induced" flashbacks of the rape situation when engaging in postrape sex and that these flashbacks produce intense anxiety attacks in the women.

Since marital rape has only recently been identified as an area of study, research on reactions of marital rape victims is much more limited than the general battering research or nonmarital rape research. What data are available suggest that reactions to marital rape are similar to reactions to both nonmarital rape and nonsexual battering. Finkelhor and Yllo (1980) found reactions to marital rape of humiliation, anger, depression, and self-blame, as well as physical symptoms of illness. Others have also found a lack of interest in sex and/or problems in maintaining an enjoyable sexual relationship with the perpetrator (Russell, 1980; Finkelhor & Yllo, 1980; Doron, 1980; Frieze, 1980; Gelles, 1977). Russell (1980) found a strong association between frequency of marital rape and negative long-term effects on the lives of the women—for example, some become paranoid of men and of starting new relationships with men, as well as develop negative attitudes toward sex. Doron (1980) found that although women who had been raped and battered by their husbands were more likely to discuss the violence with others than women who had been battered but not raped, she, as well as others (Finkelhor & Yllo, 1980), found that the rape victims were reluctant to discuss the rape incident with family or friends. These results are consistent with Frieze's (1980) findings that victims of marital rape were more likely to seek help from relatives and social service agencies for marital problems than were women who were battered but not raped. Frieze (1980) also found that marital rape victims were more likely than battering victims to call the police for protection and more likely to file charges against their husbands for violence. These women were also more physically violent with their children than were women who had been battered but not raped. Finally, Russell's (1980), Finkelhor and Yllo's (1980), and Frieze's (1980) findings suggest that leaving and subsequent divorce might also be a common reaction of marital rape victims.

Researchers examining marital rape have also suggested that being raped and battered by one's husband may be an even more traumatic and disallusioning experience than being "battered" but not raped, and that marital rape may produce more negative long-term effects than rape by a stranger (Russell, 1975, 1980; Frieze, 1980; Doron, 1980). Weis and Borges (1973) hypothesized that when a woman is raped by a nonstranger whom she trusted, she must reinterpret and redefine not only the situation in which the rape occurred but also her relationship with this individual.

Women experience shock and betrayal at what has occurred and in many cases experience self-accusatory guilt for having placed themselves in the situation to begin with (Weis & Borges, 1973). Furthermore, self-blame may be a greater problem among marital rape victims than nonmarital rape victims, because these women may not want to disrupt their relationships with their husbands and therefore may submit to his sexual advances to avoid an argument or other violence. Marital rape may also be more stressful than nonsexual battering, in the sense that the wife may feel she has the right to refuse sex yet also believes that her husband has the right to request sex from her at any time, a cognitive ambiguity that may contribute to stress (Weis & Borges, 1973). Ambiguity about the definition of the situation may increase the resultant trauma of the event and could lead to more traumatic responses of victims of nonstranger (especially marital) rapes (Weis & Borges, 1973). This trauma is increased if the woman must continue to interact with the individual (Weis and Borges, 1973); and if the assailant is her husband, one might hypothesize that the daily interaction with the husband produces strain and stress in the form of a constant reminder of the incident as well as possible fear of another attack.

STATEMENT OF PURPOSE

The apparent similarity of reactions of victims of nonsexual battering, marital rape, and nonmarital rape raises the question of the extent to which these three phenomena produce different or more or less severe reactions on the part of victims. In particular, given that some victims of battering are also victims of marital rape (Frieze, 1980; Doron, 1980; Elbow, 1977; Gelles, 1977; Ball, 1977; Hilberman & Munson, 1977; Finkelhor & Yllo, 1980), we were interested in the extent to which the phenomenon of marital rape has an impact on the victim separate from the impact of nonsexual battering. That is, we were interested in the question of whether or not marital rape is a distinct phenomenon or one form of the general phenomenon of battering.

Different or more severe reactions on the part of women who have been raped and battered versus women who have been battered but not raped appear to be dependent on the women perceiving the act of marital rape in a different way from nonsexual acts of violence. As was suggested earlier, there are reasons to expect that being a victim of battering and rape might be perceived differently and be more stressful than being a victim of battering but not rape. The act of marital rape may be perceived by the victim as the ultimate attack on the woman's ideal of the romantic marital/sexual relationship, even more severe than the attack the other physical violence represents. It may also be perceived as the ultimate violation of her body or sexual self.

On the other hand, some researchers (Russell, 1975; Finkelhor & Yllo, 1980; Gelles, 1977) have suggested that many women are dependent both financially and emotionally on their husbands and to define them as rapists and continue to live with them would be too painful. Therefore, a woman may redefine the event as not involving forced sex at all, or as one involving battering but not rape, which may be less humiliating for her (Groth, 1979). In this sense, the act of rape might be perceived in the same way as the other violence she has experienced and therefore not produce more severe "reactions."

Accordingly, the major purpose of this chapter is to assess the extent to which marital rape (in the presence of nonsexual battering) produces different or more or less severe reactions on the part of the victim compared with victims of nonsexual battering.

METHODS

Preliminary data on marital rape are available to us from our previous research ("Violent Husbands and Their Wives' Reactions"). The general purpose of this project was to identify correlates of three violence patterns of husbands (violent only with family members, violent only with non-family members, and violent with both family and nonfamily members), and differential reactions among their wives or female cohabitants. Women who participated in the study had been married to or lived with a man (for at least 6 months) who had been violent with an adult during the time they were living together.

As part of this project, standardized, in-depth interviews were conducted with 92 wives of violent men. Women were referred to the study for participation by several public and private social service agencies and self-help groups. The number of women referred by different sources is as follows: self-help groups for alcoholics and families of alcoholics (12), a local police department (4), a halfway house for women on probation or parole (14), a private therapist (7), two shelters for abused women (30), an occupational redevelopment program for abused women (7), a local university (1), and an attorney (2). Fifteen women were obtained through "snowballing." Although not a representative sample of wives of violent husbands, the variety of referral sources produced a sample of wives of varying ages, marital status, and socioeconomic status.

One section of the interview schedule was devoted to sexual aspects of the respondent's relationship with her husband/partner. Respondents were asked if (1) there was ever a prolonged period of time during the relationship when they didn't want to have sex with their partners; (2) if they had ever withheld sex from their partners for a prolonged period of time; (3) if their partners had ever physically forced them to have sex; and (4) if they had ever had sexual relations with another man while living with their partners. Data on other specific acts of violence against the woman (besides forced sex) were obtained in a different section of the interview dealing with the man's violent behavior against others. A description of the measurement of the women's reactions that were studied and the nonsexual violence can be found in Appendix A.

A preliminary analysis of the data revealed a substantial number of women reporting that their partners had physically forced them to have sex with them at some time during their relationships. Of all the women participating in the study, 11% (married to "nonfamily only" husbands) reported no violence (rape or nonsexual violence) directed toward them, 41% reported rape and other forms of violence, and 48% reported only nonsexual violence. None of the women reported being raped with no other forms of violence. Excluding the "nonfamily only" group, *46% of the women had experienced marital rape.* However, it should be noted that the interview schedule did not differentiate among violent *episodes*—that is, if any other form of violence accompanied the rape (such as shoving or pushing), the woman was classified as a victim of rape *and* nonsexual violence. Therefore, it is possible that for a particular person, all the violent episodes involved rape, and in that sense the victim could be considered a victim only of rape.

Accordingly, our data provide three comparison groups—a group of women who have been raped and experienced other forms of violence, a group of women who have experienced only nonsexual forms of violence, and a small nonvictimized comparison group. Due to the small number of nonvictimized women ($N = 11$), the bulk of the analysis to be presented will focus on a comparison between the raped and battered and battered only groups. Given these two groups, we were able to determine whether or not marital rape (in the presence of other violence) has an impact on the victim that is different or more severe than the impact of nonsexual violence alone. *Because we do not have the third logical comparison group—women who have been raped but not experienced other violence—we are unable to determine whether or not marital rape produces a truly separate impact, or if any impact is due to the interaction of rape and other forms of nonsexual violence.*

FINDINGS

In order to investigate the question of the impact of marital rape in comparison with the impact of nonsexual violence, it was necessary to examine the zero-order relationships between whether or not the woman had been raped and the various measured reactions. Preliminary analysis of the data did suggest that a number of the variables were related to marital rape. However, another measured variable—the severity of the nonsexual violence—was also found to be related to whether or not the woman had been raped ($r = .37$; $p < .01$); that is, *those women who had been raped had experienced both more severe forms of nonsexual violence and more*

TABLE 8.1 Zero-Order Correlations Between Severity of Violence and Reactions, and Partial Correlations Controlling for Rape

Variables	Severity of Violence	Severity, Controlling for Rape
Self-Esteem	−.29*	−.08
See others socially	−.04	−.11
Discuss nonsexual violence	.31*	.27**
Attitudes toward own marriage	.20***	.07
Attitudes toward marriage in general	.05	.02
Attitudes toward men in general	−.05	.06
Number of psychosomatic illnesses	.28*	.25**
Felt depressed	.20**	.11
Attempted suicide	−.02	−.06
Filed for legal separation	.02	.03
Filed for divorce	.22***	.09
Used alcohol for depression	.18***	.01
Used drugs for depression	.03	−.10
Mad at children	.07	−.03
Sought help for violence	.20***	.17
Sought help for marital problems	.08	−.01
Sought help for drug/ alcohol problem	−.05	−.11
Sought help for personal problem	.05	−.09
Filed for restraining order	.03	.01
Had husband arrested	.23**	.09
Retaliatory violence	.29*	.02
Didn't want sex with husband	.37*	.18
Had extramarital sex	.30*	.23**
Withheld sex form husband	.05	−.07

*p less than or equal to .01
**p less than or equal to .05
***p less than or equal to .10

reactions. Using Pearson's correlation coefficient, severity of violence was related to a number of reactions at the .10 level or beyond, even though most of the coefficients were only moderate to weak (see Table 8.1). Variables that were related to severity of violence at the .10 level of significance or beyond were as follows. The more severe the violence: (1) the lower the woman's self-esteem; (2) the more likely she was to discuss the nonsexual violence with others; (3) the more negative her attitudes toward her own marriage had become; (4) the more psychosomatic reactions she had; (5) the more likely she was to be depressed; (6) the more likely she was to have used alcohol for depression; (7) the more likely she was to have sought help for the nonsexual violence; (8) the more likely she was to have had her partner arrested; (9) the more likely she was to have been violent with her husband; (10) the more likely she was to have not wanted sex with her partner for a prolonged period of time; and (11) the more likely she was to have engaged in extramarital sexual relations. These findings introduced a "rival hypothesis," in that it seemed possible that more severe reactions on the part of marital rape victims could be due to the fact that they had experienced more severe forms of nonsexual violence, rather than to the rape itself. To test the possibility that the ractions were due to severity of nonsexual violence rather than marital rape, it was necessary to examine the relationships between marital rape and the reactions, controlling for severity of nonsexual violence.

Because the control variable (severity of violence) and some of the dependent variables are technically measured at the ordinal rather than the interval level, it may seem more appropriate statistically to use an ordinal measure of partial association to investigate the question of interest. However, Blalock (1972) warns that in the present of ties, ordinal measures of association such as Kendall's tau, gamma, and so on can be misleading, and that the theoretical underpinnings of such procedures are not strong. He recommends that such procedures be accompanied by the use of Pearson's partial correlation. Given the problems associated with ordinal partialing procedures, and the robustness of Pearson's correlation coefficient, the following results were computed using Pearson's partial correlation coefficient.

As was stated, at the zero-order level, a number of reactions were significantly (at the .10 level or beyond), although not strongly, related to whether or not the woman had been raped as well as experienced nonsexual violence (see Table 8.2). Compared with nonraped victims, victims of marital rape were more likely to (1) have lower self-esteem; (2) have discussed the nonsexual violence with others; (3) have more negative attitudes toward men; (4) have filed for a divorce; (5) have used alcohol for depression; (6) not wanted sexual relations with their partners for a prolonged period of time; (7) have had their partners arrested; (8) have engaged in extramartital sexual relations; (9) have experienced depression; and (10) have withheld sex from their husbands. However, when the severity of the nonsexual violence was controlled (by partial correlation), only the relationships between marital rape and self-esteem, negative attitudes toward men, using alcohol for depression, having the husband

TABLE 8.2 Zero-Order Correlations Between Rape and Reactions, and Partial Correlations Controlling for Severity of Violence

Variables	Rape	Rape, Controlling for Severity
Self-Esteem	−.32*	−.28*
See others socially	.06	.09
Discuss nonsexual violence	.20***	.09
Attitudes toward own marriage	.05	.01
Attitudes toward marriage in general	.09	.08
Attitudes toward men in general	.22**	.19***
Number of psychosomatic illnesses	.17	.07
Felt depressed	.20***	.15
Attempted suicide	.13	.09
Filed for legal separation	−.07	−.06
Filed for divorce	.22***	.18
Used alcohol for depression	.19***	.18
Used drugs for depression	.05	.09
Mad at children	.17	.17
Sought help for violence	.11	.04
Sought help for marital problems	.06	.06
Sought help for drug/ alcohol problem	.04	.07
Sought help for personal problem	.07	.10
Filed for restraining order	.07	.06
Had husband arrested	.26**	.21***
Retaliatory violence	.02	.02
Didn't want sex with husband	.21***	.23**
Had extramarital sex	.26**	.17
Withheld sex from husband	.21***	.22**

*p less than or equal to .01
**p less than or equal to .05
***p less than or equal to .10

arrested, withholding sex, and not wanting sexual relations remained statistically significant at approximately the same level. This seems to indicate that in some cases, the reaction appears to be due to more extreme forms of violence rather than marital rape.

If this interpretation were correct, when the relationships between severity of nonsexual violence and the reactions (controlling for whether or not the woman had been raped) are examined, the relationship between severity and the reaction should hold. Otherwise, it would be an indication that marital rape is an intervening variable, in the sense that more severe violence might lead to marital rape, which tends to result in more severe reactions. When these partial associations are examined, the latter interpretation tends to be supported by the data. With the exception of the number of psychosomatic reactions, help-seeking for nonsexual violence (marginally significant), discussing nonsexual violence, and involvement in extramarital sex, the zero-order relationships between severity and the reactions disappear.

In combination, the data seem to suggest that *marital rape has a* separate direct impact on self-esteem, developing negative attitudes toward men, not wanting sexual relations with their partners, using alcohol for depression, withholding sex, and having their partners arrested, while severity of nonsexual violence has a separate direct impact on producing psychosomatic reactions, discussion of nonsexual violence, seeking help for violence, and involvement in extramarital sex. For the other variables— depression and filing for divorce—rape and severity of nonsexual violence seem to have a joint impact. Although the relationships between retaliatory violence and severity of nonsexual violence, and negative attitudes toward own marriage and severity of nonsexual violence also tend to disappear when marital rape is controlled, the interpretations of these findings are not as straightforward because marital rape is not strongly related to either of these reactions. Variables which were not affected by rape or severity of nonsexual violence were attitudes toward marriage in general, filing for a restraining order, seeing others socially, attempting suicide, filing for a legal separation, seeking help for marital problems, seeking help for a drug or alcohol problem, and seeking help for a personal or psychological problem.

In addition to asking respondents about whether or not they had been victims of marital rape, we also asked for a subjective estimate of how often they had experienced marital rape (once or twice, a few times, many times, or all the time). (We had found during pretesting that women were generally unable to provide absolute numbers, especially in cases where the violence might have occurred weekly or biweekly over a period of many years). Of the 38 women who were victims of marital rape, 13.2% had been raped once or twice, 50%, a few times; 34.2%, many times; and 2.6%, all the time. Given these estimates of the frequency of marital rape, we were able to do some separate analysis with the subgroup of women who had been victims of marital rape (see Table 8.3). Frequency of rape was correlated with many of the reactions. Again, the zero-order results indicated that the more often the woman had been raped, the lower was her

TABLE 8.3 Zero-Order Correlations Between Frequency of Rape and Reactions, and Partial Correlations Controlling for Severity of Violence

Variables	Frequency of Rape	Frequency, Controlling for Severity of Violence
Self-Esteem	−.36**	−.36**
See others socially	−.19	−.19
Discuss nonsexual violence	.18	.17
Attitudes toward own marriage	.40*	.41*
Attitudes toward marriage in general	.03	.03
Attitudes toward men in general	.21	.21
Number of psychosomatic illnesses	.29***	.29***
Felt depressed	−.07	−.08
Attempted suicide	.30***	.32***
Filed for legal separation	−.08	−.12
Filed for divorce	.20	.19
Used alcohol for depression	.09	.09
Used drugs for depression	.04	.04
Mad at children	.12	.12
Sought help for violence	.21	.21
Sought help for marital problems	.17	.16
Sought help for drug/ alcohol problem	−.01	.01
Sought help for personal problem	.22	.23
Filed for restraining order	.14	.14
Had husband arrested	.09	.09
Retaliatory violence	.19	.11
Didn't want sex with husband	.25	.27***
Had extramarital sex	.09	.09
Withheld sex from husband	.22	.24

*p less than or equal to .01
**p less than or equal to .05
***p less than or equal to .10

self-esteem, the more negative were her attitudes toward her own marriage, the more psychosomatic reactions she experienced, and the more likely she was to have attempted suicide. All these relationships were moderately strong at the .10 level or beyond. When severity of nonsexual violence was controlled, these relationships remained essentially unchanged and the significance level for the positive relationship between not wanting sex and frequency of rape increased to a significant level.

Finally, in order to compare reactions of the two victimized groups with a somewhat comparable nonvictimized group (women from the same referral sources who were married to nonfamily violent men), 24 one-way analyses of variance were performed with group membership as the independent variable and the reactions as the dependent variables (see Table 8.4). However, it should be noted that these nonvictimized women were included in the sample because of their husband's involvement in nonfamily violence. Duncan's multiple range test was used to suggest significant differences between the three groups. This analysis is considered tentative due to the small number of cases in the comparison group, which is likely to produce unreliable results.

Variables for which the one-way ANOVA showed significant differences (at the .10 level or beyond) between the three groups were (1) self-esteem, (2) attitudes toward men, (3) depression, (4) use of alcohol for depression, (5) retaliatory violence, (6) divorce, (7) having the husband arrested, (8) not wanting sex, and (9) extramarital sex. (The variables of discussion of nonsexual violence, help-seeking for violence, and filing for a restraining order were not included because they were not applicable to the comparison group.) Duncan's multiple-range tests showed the following. (1) For self-esteem, having the husband arrested, not wanting sex, and extramarital sex, the comparison group was significantly different from the "raped and battered," but not the "battered only" group. (2) For attitudes toward men, depression, and divorce, the comparison group did not differ significantly from either victimized group. (3) For use of alcohol for depression and retaliatory violence (violence against husband), the comparison group differed significantly from both victimized groups. However, in all cases, except attitudes toward men, the comparison group had the least severe reactions of the three groups and in general the raped and battered group showed the most severe reactions, with the battered only group between the other two groups. In the case of negative attitudes toward men, the comparison group actually had the most negative attitudes. Further analysis is needed to explain this anomaly, but it could be related to the husbands' violence outside the home. This analysis is highly tentative, but it does suggest likely differences between victimized groups (especially victims of marital rape) and a somewhat comparable nonvictimized group.

LIMITATIONS OF THE DATA

The design of this study allows only limited analysis, since the original purpose was not to study marital rape in relation to battering. The effects

TABLE 8.4   One-Way Analyses of Variance with Group Membership as the Independent Variable and Reactions as Dependent Variables

| | Group Means | | | |
	Raped & Battered	*Battered Only*	*Non-victimized*	*Probability of F−Ratio*
Self-Esteem	3.00	3.55	3.96	*
See others socially	−11.26	−25.04	−22.7	
Attitudes toward own marriage	4.16	4.05	3.3	
Attitudes toward marriage in general	3.82	3.6	3.6	
Attitudes toward men in general	3.84	3.41	4.1	**
Number of psychosomatic illnesses	4.76	3.95	3.2	
Felt depressed	.87	.70	.60	***
Attempted suicide	.55	.42	.66	
Filed for legal separation	.03	.06	.00	
Filed for divorce	.55	.33	.16	***
Used alcohol for depression	.58	.39	.20	***
Used drugs for depression	.55	.50	.50	
Mad at children	2.65	2.41	2.16	
Sought help for marital problems	.47	.41	.3	
Sought help for drug/ alcohol problem	.21	.18	.2	
Sought help for personal problem	.5	.4	.3	
Had husband arrested	.47	.23	.10	**
Retaliatory violence	.76	.75	.2	*
Didn't want sex with Husband	.87	.59	.30	*
Had extramarital sex	.47	.23	.10	**
Withheld sex from husband	.5	.3	.3	

*p less than or equal to .01
**p less than or equal to .05
***p less than or equal to .10

of marital rape which appear to be independent of battering may be due to an interaction between rape and battering, since we had no rape only victims for comparison, at least to our knowledge.

Regarding the time sequence of victimization and reactions, we, like other researchers, can only assume temporal order. However, we do have some indication (Shields & Hanneke, 1982) that although some reactions of some women occurred prior to victimization, the incidence of reactions tends to increase significantly during victimization and continues to increase even after the relationship has ended. Information about when events occurred is essential for developing a causal model of victimization and reactions.

The measurement of the presence of marital rape in this study was crude. We did not specify to respondents what behaviors were to be included under "forced sex," and it is possible that many included only forced intercourse. We did not include psychological coercion—for example, the woman knew she would be severely beaten if she resisted.

Finally, we were studying reactions to battering, not marital rape per se. Our preliminary findings suggest the usefulness of exploring more reactions regarding sexual attitudes and variables related to self-esteem and social competence.

DISCUSSION

Given these limitations, the data suggest that a significant number of battering victims are also victims of marital rape and that marital rape and nonsexual violence seem to be perceived differently by victims, in that both produce some apparently separate and direct reactions on the part of victims. The data also seem to suggest that when sexual violence occurs in a relationship, it is not an isolated incident—that is, most of the marital rape victims in our sample were raped more than once or twice. The unique reactions to marital rape seem to have to do primarily with negative attitudes toward self and men and with reducing the victim's desire to engage in sex with her partner. These findings are consistent with existing research on marital rape (Russell, 1980; Finkelhor & Yllo, 1980; Doron, 1980; Gelles, 1977; Frieze, 1980). Furthermore, it appears that the more often the victim experiences marital rape, the more serious are the reactions (e.g., greater number of psychosomatic reactions and attempted suicide). The apparent separate impact of severe nonsexual violence on discussing nonsexual violence, psychosomatic reactions, help-seeking for violence, and extramarital sex is also consistent with existing wife-battering research (Gelles, 1979; Gayford, 1975; Frazier, 1977; Hilberman & Munson, 1977). However, the results also seem to suggest the possibility that marital rape researchers will mistake effects of severe nonsexual violence for effects of marital rape (e.g., Doron's finding that raped and battered women were more likely to discuss nonsexual violence and Frieze's finding of more extramarital sex among raped women). Finally, the comparison of the two victimized groups with the nonvictimized group also suggests that victimized women show more reactions than do nonvictimized women, but it also suggests that at least some battering researchers have drawn conclusions regarding reactions in the absence of a comparison group.

An important finding of this research is that marital rape seems to co-occur with more severe forms of nonsexual violence. The findings point to a need to clarify the interrelations between rape, nonsexual violence, and reactions of victims. Collectively, our findings seem to suggest that when sexual violence occurs, nonsexual violence escalates to encompass sexual violence as well as nonsexual violence, but both sexual and nonsexual violence seem to produce some independent effects. In general, it appears that as the severity or frequency of violence increases, so does the severity of the reaction. For example, although severe nonsexual violence produced more psychosomatic reactions, so did increased frequency of marital rape. Marital rape seems to have the greatest impact on victims' feelings and emotions (especially self-esteem and *feelings* about sex), while severe battering seems more likely to produce an *action* response—for example, extramarital sex. It seems plausible that the clear effect marital rape has on lowering self-esteem might produce some of the very serious psychological reactions related to more frequent marital rape victimization—psychosomatic illnesses and suicide attempts. That marital rape and nonsexual violence appear to be so interrelated also points to the need to study both phenomena concurrently.

APPENDIX A:
VARIABLES AND BRIEF DESCRIPTION OF MEASUREMENT

Victim/Nonvictim of Rape

Marital Rape—Yes/no question about whether respondent was ever physically forced to have sex with her husband/partner against her will. 1 = yes; 0 = no.

Reactions to Battering and/or Marital Rape

Self-Esteem—The mean of 5 items measured on 6-point agree/disagree scales. Items revised from Coopersmith's (1967) self-esteem inventory. Higher scores indicate higher self-esteem. Scale reliability Alpha = .52.

Attitudes Toward Own Marriage/Relationship—One item measured on a 5-point scale (much more positive to much more negative) measuring the change, if any, in respondent's attitudes toward her own marriage/relationship during the time she was experiencing physical violence. Higher scores indicate more negative attitudes.

General Attitudes Toward Marriage—One item measured on a 5-point scale (much more positive to much more negative) measuring the change, if any, in respondent's attitude toward marriage in general during the time she was experiencing physical violence. Higher scores indicate more negative attitudes.

General Attitudes Toward Men—One item measured on a 5-point scale (much more positive to much more negative) measuring the change, if any, in respondent's attitude toward men in general during the time she was experiencing physical violence. Higher scores indicate more negative attitudes.

Psychosomatic Reactions—Ten yes/no questions about if respondent had ever had any unusual trouble with headaches, not being able to sleep, having a poor appetite, gaining a significant amount of weight within a few months, losing a significant amount of weight within a few months, intestinal problems, high blood pressure, problems with menstrual periods, skin disorders, or allergies. The number of items the respondent had problems with is the measure of psychosomatic reactions. The higher the score, the more problems she experienced.

History of Depression and Suicide Attempts—Yes/no questions about if respondent ever felt so depressed that she did not want to go on living, and if so, if she ever tried to take her own life. 1 = yes; 0 = no.

Use of Drugs/Alcohol for Depression—Yes/no questions about if respondent ever used drugs or alcohol because of depression or a bad mood. 1 = yes; 0 = no.

Social Isolation—Difference between the frequency with which respondent saw friends or relatives socially without her husband/partner at the beginning of their relationship, and the frequency with which she saw them during the battering. Higher scores indicate greater social isolation.

Discussion of Nonsexual Violence—The mean of seven items measured on 4-point scales ranging from never discussed to discussed many times. Items included discussion of nonsexual violence with her family members, his family members, their children, a friend, a co-worker, co-members of clubs or organizations, and with husband/partner. Higher scores indicate more discussion.

Upset with Children—One item measuring the frequency with which respondent became angry with her children because she was depressed or in a bad mood. Higher score indicates higher frequency of occurrence (never to all the time). This variable was intended to tap the possibility of violence against children. We were not able to question the respondent about her violence against children due to a conflict in confidentiality of response and the Child Abuse Reporting Law in the area in which the research was conducted.

Retaliatory Violence—Yes/no question about whether respondent was ever violent with her husband/partner. 1 = yes; 0 = no.

Loss of Interest in Sex—Yes/no question about if, for a prolonged period of time (subjectively defined), the respondent did not feel like having sex with her husband/partner. 1 = yes; 0 = no.

Withheld Sex—Yes/no question about whether the respondent ever withheld sex from her husband/partner for a prolonged period of time. 1 = yes, 0 = no.

Extramarital Sex—Yes/no question about if respondent ever had sex with a man other than her husband/partner while living with her husband/partner. 1 = yes; 0 = no.

Separation/Divorce—If married, yes/no questions about if respondent ever filed for a legal separation or for a divorce from her husband. 1 = yes; 0 = no.

Legal Action Against Husband/Partner—Yes/no questions about if respondent ever filed for a restraining order against her husband/partner or if she ever had him arrested. 1 = yes; 0 = no.

Help-Seeking—Yes/no questions about help-seeking from family, friends, or professionals for violence or marital problems, or help-seeking from professionals for drug/alcohol or personal/psychological problems. 1 = yes; 0 = no.

Nature of Violent Behavior

Violent Behaviors—Yes/no questions about if respondent's husband/partner had ever (1) shoved, pushed or grabbed, (2) slapped, (3) scratched, (4) kicked, (5) hit with fist, (6) hit with object, (7) (tried to) choke/strangle, (8) bit, (9) burned, (10) threatened with weapon, (11) stabbed/cut, (12) shot/shot at, (13) threw an object at, (14) (tried to) smother, (15) (tried to) drown, (16) forced sexually, or (17) used any other types of violent behaviors against her.

Severity of Violence—Violent behaviors were divided into three categories based on combined rankings of six expert judges: (1) minor—shove/push/grab, slap, scratch, kick, bite; (2) moderate—hit with fist, hit with object, burn, threaten with weapon, throw object at; and (3) severe—choke/strangle, stab/cut, shot/shot at, tried to smother, tried to drown. Judges were asked to rank behaviors according to their life-threatening potential. Severity of the husband's/partner's violence was determined by which of the three categories his most severe violent behavior against the woman fell into. Higher scores indicate more severe violent behavior.

REFERENCES

Atkeson, B. M., Calhoun, K. S., Resick, P. A., & Ellis, E. M. Victims of rape: Repeated assessment of depressive symptoms. *Journal of Consulting and Clinical Psychology*, 1982, *50*, 96-102.

Ball, M. Issues of violence in family casework. *Social Casework*, 1977, *58*, 3-12.

Blalock, H. M. *Social statistics*. New York: McGraw-Hill, 1972.

Burgess, A., & Holmstrom, L. Rape trauma syndrome. *American Journal of Psychiatry*, 1974, *131*, 981-986.

Coopersmith, S. *The antecedents of self-esteem*. San Francisco: W. H. Freeman, 1967.

Davidson, T. *Conjugal crime: Understanding and changing the wife-beating pattern*. New York: Hawthorn Books, 1978.

Doron, J. B. *Conflict and violence in intimate relationships: Focus on marital rape*. Paper presented at the annual meetings of the 1980 American Sociological Association, New York, August 1980.

Elbow, M. Theoretical considerations of violent marriages. *Social Casework*, 1977, *58*, 515-526.

Ellis, E. M., Atkeson, B. M., & Calhoun, K. S. An assessment of long-term reactions to rape. *Journal of Abnormal Psychology*, 1981, *90*, 263-266.

Feldman-Summers, S., Gordon, P., & Meagher, J. The impact of rape on sexual satisfaction. *Journal of Abnormal Psychology*, 1979, *88*, 101-105.

Finkelhor, D., & Yllo, K. *Forced sex in marriage: A preliminary research report*. Paper presented at the annual meetings of the American Sociological Association, New York, August 1980.

Frazier, W. H. *Medical contexts and sequelae of domestic violence*. NIMH grant application, November 1977.

Frieze, I. H. *Causes and consequences of marital rape*. Paper presented at the annual meetings of the American Psychological Association, Montreal, September 1980.

Gayford, J. J. Wife battering: A preliminary survey of 100 cases. *British Medical Journal*, 1975, *25*, 194-197.

Gelles, R. *The violent home*. Beverly Hills, CA: Sage, 1974.

Gelles, R. Abused wives: Why do they stay? *Journal of Marriage and the Family*, 1976, *38*, 659-668.

Gelles, R. Power, sex and violence: The case of marital rape. *Family Coordinator*, 1977, *26*, 339-347.

Gelles, R. *Family violence*. Beverly Hills, CA: Sage, 1979.

Groth, A. N. *Men who rape: The psychology of the offender*. New York: Plenum, 1979.

Hilberman, E., & Munson, K. Sixty battered women. *Victimology: An International Journal,* 1977, *2,* 460-470.

Hirsch, M. *Women and violence.* New York: Van Nostrand Reinhold, 1981.

Kilpatrick, D. G., Resick, P., & Veronen, L. Effects of a rape experience: A longitudinal study. *Journal of Social Issues,* 1981, *37*(4), 105-122.

Kilpatrick, D. G., Veronen, L. J., & Resick, P. A. The aftermath of rape: Recent empirical findings. *American Journal of Orthopsychiatry,* 1979, *49,* 658-669. (a)

Kilpatrick, D. G., Veronen, L. J., & Resick, P. A. Assessment of the aftermath of rape: Changing patterns of fear. *Journal of Behavioral Assessment,* 1979, *1,* 133-148. (b)

McNulty, F. *The burning bed.* New York: Harcourt Brace Jovanovich, 1980.

Martin, D. *Battered wives.* San Francisco: Glide, 1976.

Martin, J. P. (Ed.). *Violence and the family.* Chicester, England: John Wiley, 1978.

O'Brien, J. E. Violence in divorce-prone families. *Journal of Marriage and the Family,* 1971, *33,* 692-698.

Prescott, S., & Letko, C. Battered women: A social psychological perspective. In M. Roy (Ed.), *Battered women.* New York: Van Nostrand Reinhold, 1977.

Russell, D.E.H. *The politics of rape: The victim's perspective.* New York: Stein & Day, 1975.

Russell, D.E.H. *The prevalence and impact of marital rape in San Francisco.* Paper presented at the annual meetings of the American Sociological Association, New York, August 1980.

Shields, N. M., & Fox, S. *Violent husbands and their wives' reactions.* NIMH grant application, October 1978.

Shields, N. M., & Hanneke, C. R. Violent husbands and their wives' reactions. Final report, NIMH Grant No. 5R01 MH33297-02, 1982.

Straus, M. A. Sexual inequality, cultural norms, and wife-beating. *Victimology: An International Journal,* 1976, *1,* 54-70.

Straus, M. A. Societal morphogenesis and intrafamily violence in cross-cultural perspective. In L. L. Adler (Ed.), *Issues in cross-cultural research.* Annals of the New York Academy of Sciences, 1977, *285,* 717-730.

Sutherland, S., & Scherl, D. Patterns of response among victims of rape. *American Journal of Orthopsychiatry,* 1970, *40,* 503-511.

Truninger, E. Marital violence: The legal solutions. *Hastings Law Journal,* 1971, *23,* 259-271.

Weis, K., & Borges, S. Victimology and rape: The case of the legitimate victim. *Issues in Criminology,* 1973, *8,* 71-115.

SECTION V

TOWARD A THEORY OF INTRAFAMILY VIOLENCE

There has been no shortage of attempts to explain and understand the tragic problems of child abuse, wife abuse, and family violence. The emotions that are stirred by descriptions and photographs of victims of family violence cry out for answers to the question "why?" or "who could do such a thing?" And while many have tried to answer the questions, there has been precious little in the way of theory and theory building in the study of family violence.

The first chapter in this section, "An Exchange/Social Control Theory" by Richard J. Gelles, begins with a brief review of the theoretical notions about intrafamily violence. Gelles traces the development of theoretical positions on family violence, from the earliest postulations which linked child and wife abuse to psychopathology, to fully developed causal models. In an earlier work with Murray Straus, Gelles inventoried 15 theories that appeared to have relevance for understanding violence between family members. Reflecting on that process, Gelles notes in Chapter 9 that the final integrated theory was so complex that it ultimately was more useful as an inventory of factors associated with family violence than as a full-fledged, testable theory. Now Gelles borrows theoretical propositions from family studies and work on juvenile delinquency to develop his exchange/social control theory of intrafamily violence. The propositions from exchange (or choice) theory come from a tradition of family research developed by John Scanzoni and F. Ivan Nye. Travis Hirschi's work on control theory and juvenile delinquency form the second body of work used for Gelles's theoretical presentation. Gelles's theory has a pragmatic side, as he proposes direct implications of the theory for both clinical work and policy formulation.

A review of much of the theoretical work on family violence reveals that many researchers tend to work in a kind of theoretical vacuum. There is a tendency to see family violence as "special" and thus in need of its own unique theory. The long tradition of experimental social psychological research on aggression and violence may be alluded to or referenced, but a great number of researchers who study family violence fail to see the relevance of experimental social psychological research to the study of the social problem of family violence. Leonard Berkowitz has had a long and important career as an experimental psychologist concerned with aggression and violence. His chapter "The Goals of Aggression," makes a significant contribution to family violence theory building (and our understanding of violence in general). Berkowitz bridges the tradition of laboratory research on aggression with social research on family violence by first considering the aims of aggressive behavior, in general and in the family. Berkowitz finds that a first commonality is that aggression (in and outside the home) is carried out to achieve a particular end—to hurt another person. From here Berkowitz goes on to demonstrate the applicability of findings from experimental research on aggression to the subject of family violence.

Finally, in "Social Psychological Determinants," Richard Sebastian continues Berkowitz's attempt to apply the findings of laboratory research on aggression to family violence. Sebastian rounds out the link between the two traditions of research by considering two important aspects of aggression—inhibitory factors and instigation—and discusses how these factors come into play in the unique setting of the family. Sebastian suggests that inhibitions against aggression are especially weak in the family. Moreover, the special nature of family relations means that instigations can be extremely potent.

Together, the three selections in this section provide a brief glimpse at the nature of theoretical development in the field of family violence research; but more important, they point the way for more refined theoretical development in future research. Instead of assuming that because the family is special and unique, one needs a special theory to explain violence in the home, these authors imply that the task of theory building can be enhanced by drawing on research and theory developed by those studying aggression and violence outside the home. The findings and principles from these studies can be applied to the family by noting how the special nature of the family influences, impinges on, or enhances the factors that are related to acts intended to cause pain and hurt other people.

9

An Exchange/Social Control Theory

RICHARD J. GELLES

The study of child abuse, wife abuse, and other forms of domestic violence emerged as a publicly recognized problem and a scientific issue during the late 1960s and early '70s. Erin Pizzey, author of the first book-length treatment of battered wives, *Scream Quietly or the Neighbors Will Hear,* wrote in 1976 that those concerned with any form of social caring should empty their shelves and make space for a massive onslaught of literature on the subject of domestic violence. She was correct. In the next three years there was an exponential increase in the number of books and articles published on the various aspects of domestic violence.

A review of popular and professional literature reveals that social scientists and the public alike have asked questions and pursued knowledge along parallel lines. The first major question asked about domestic violence is, "How common is it?" A great deal of attention has been directed toward estimating incidence of child abuse, wife abuse, husband abuse, and even parent abuse—almost as if domestic violence could not be considered a legitimate social problem unless it had an incidence in the millions. The second major question asked was, "What causes people to be violent and abusive toward family members?" Answers from both the public and the research community tended toward myths, conventional wisdom, and simplistic theoretical models. With few exceptions (noted later), the answer to this question, as presented by social scientists, has tended to be a summary of factors found to be related to family violence. These associations and correlations, while illuminating, do not yet provide a corpus of knowledge that could be considered theoretical insight into the causes of domestic violence.

Author's Note: *This chapter is part of a program of research on family violence conducted at the University of Rhode Island. Funding for this research has been provided by NIMH Grant MH 227557 and OCD/NCCAN grants 90-C-425 and 90-C-1792. A revised version was presented at the annual meetings of the American Society of Criminology, Philadelphia, 1979.*

This chapter briefly reviews and summarizes the popular theoretical notions about domestic violence. The methodological dilemmas that have inhibited the development of a knowledge base which could be used to test theoretical propositions about the causes of family violence are then reviewed. The existing theories of violence and aggression that can be brought to bear in explaining family violence are briefly reviewed. Finally, I advance the outline of an exchange/social control theory of intrafamily violence.

THEORETICAL NOTIONS ABOUT INTRAFAMILY VIOLENCE

Psychopathology: The Intraindividual Level of Analysis

Public presentations on domestic violence frequently begin with graphic black and white or even color slides of battered and abused women and children. These slides produce, nearly without fail, gasps, groans, and exclamations of disbelief on the part of the audience (irrespective of its sophistication and experience). On a cognitive level, the reaction is also similar—that is, members of the audience tend to view the slides in disbelief and assume that people who inflict such injuries are psychologically deranged. The reaction of audiences is much the same as the response of clinicians who encounter cases of child and wife abuse—the offender must be psychologically ill. The early writing on both child abuse (e.g., Kempe et al., 1962; Steele & Pollock, 1974; Galdston, 1965) and wife abuse (e.g., Snell, Rosenwald, & Robey, 1964) portrayed the causes of domestic violence as arising from offenders' psychological problems. After ten years of continued research and administration of countless psychological tests, the summary evaluation of the psychopathological approach to domestic violence is that the proportion of individuals who batter their family members and suffer from psychological disorders is no greater than the proportion of the population in general with psychological disorders (Straus, 1980; Steele, 1978).

A unique aspect of the theoretical approach to wife-battering is the popular view (and a view alluded to in some of the professional literature—see Snell et al., 1964) that violence arises out of psychological problems of the victims. "Women like to be beaten," we are told. Or "battered women are crazy." There are, however, no scientific data to support either of these points of view, and if, indeed, battered women do behave strangely, it is probably as a consequence (not a cause) of being battered (Walker, 1979).

The Determining Effects of Learning and Stress

The earliest research on child abuse found that abusive adults were likely to have been raised in abusive homes (Steele & Pollock, 1974; Bennie & Sclare, 1969). The explanation for this finding was that being abused as a child produces a personality disorder which predisposes the individual to a life pattern of violence and aggression. The more contemporary interpretation of the relationship is that experience with, and exposure to, violence serves as a learning experience which teaches that violence can and should be used toward family members. Indeed, the research results have been so consistent that an aura of family determinism has begun to surround the data, such that many people expect that *all* victims of childhood violence will grow up to be violent adults. And it is expected that individuals who are not exposed to violence as children will grow up to be nonviolent. Such is not the case. Indeed, if it were, we would have one of the truly rare social scientific findings—a unicausal phenomenon.

While the relationship between exposure to and experience with violence as a child and violent behavior as an adult is consistent, and the time order clear, the relationship is not as strong as some reviews of the literature would argue (Potts & Herzberger, 1979). The relationship between experience with abuse as a child and later abusive behavior as an adult can be considered deterministic only under certain conditions (e.g., environmental stress) that would have to be specified by a larger theory.

The same can be said of the relationship between stress and family violence. Skolnick and Skolnick (1977) have stated that "family violence seems to be a product of psychological tensions and external stresses affecting all families at all social levels." While investigators find a consistent relationship between stress and violence, again there is the danger of accepting the relationship in its simplistic deterministic form.

Thus, while social learning and social psychological stress are found to be related to family violence, and probably are part of the causal flow of events which explains family violence, they have only been demonstrated as associations. Neither relationship is satisfactorily explained or empirically examined so as to constitute a theoretical explanation of family violence. While they may be necessary factors, they are not sufficient.

Ideology: Sexism and Racism

A number of theoretical themes have emerged at the sociocultural level of analysis. Official statistics on child abuse and wife abuse indicate that women, blacks, minorities, and the poor are overrepresented victims of domestic violence. Research that is not limited to studying only officially labeled cases of domestic violence also finds relationships between income and family violence (an inverse relationship), race and violence, and minority status and violence (Straus, Gelles, & Steinmetz, 1980).

Some have argued that these data support the notion that the real cause of family violence is not psychological disorders or social learning; rather, it is oppressive sexism, racism, and a patriarchal social organization of capitalistic societies (see U.S. Commission on Civil Rights, 1978).

While it is easy for liberal-minded social scientists to sympathize with these conceptualizations, the jump from the relationship between income and violence to a theory of racism or sexism is large and not yet fully supported by the available empirical evidence.

The use of ideology in place of scientifically informed theory has become increasingly common in the emotion-charged field of domestic violence and has partially inhibited a serious scientific program of theory construction in this area.

Fully Developed Causal Models

Despite the fact that one of the earliest and most widely read studies of child abuse concluded that violence toward children was the product of a complex multidimensional process (Gil, 1970), the current state of the art in theory construction consists of profiles of abusers and abused (see for example Steinmetz, 1978) and simplistic, unicausal models. Fully developed causal models are rare. One exception is Garbarino's ecological model (1977); another is Justice and Justice's symbiosis model (1976). Interestingly, both of these theories have been applied only to child abuse. Straus's general system model of family violence (1973) is perhaps the only comprehensive theoretical model which attempts to explain all forms of family violence.

The next section reviews some of the methodological problems that have retarded the development of adequate multidimensional causal models of family violence.

METHODOLOGICAL DILEMMAS AND
THEORY CONSTRUCTION

There are numerous reasons for the lack of sophisticated theoretical models in the study of domestic violence. First, most investigations concentrate on one aspect of family violence—either child abuse, wife abuse, or even husband or parent abuse. Only a minority of investigations conceptualize the problem of violence between family members at the family level of analysis. Thus, while theoretical models are applied to child abuse or wife abuse, few efforts attempt a general model of family violence.

Defining Violence and Abuse

One important difficulty is the problem of nominally defining violence and abuse. Both terms are perhaps more suited as political concepts than scientific ones—that is, they are pejorative, emotion-charged terms used to draw attention to behavior considered deviant. The terms "abuse" and "violence" have been applied to the narrow issue of physically striking a family member and causing injury (Kempe et al., 1962, Gil, 1970), to the act of striking a person with the intent of causing harm or injury—but not actually causing it (Gelles & Straus, 1979), to acts of violence where there is the high potential of causing injury (Straus et al., 1980), and to acts where there is no actual hitting at all—such as verbal abuse or psychological and emotional violence.

Because of the wide variation in nominal definitions of violence, there is a resulting lack of comparability among various investigations of types of domestic violence. A study that examines hitting children cannot be directly compared with another study of child abuse that defines abuse as sexual, psychological, emotional, and physical exploitation of children.

The lack of comparability means that a large base of knowledge of one uniform type of behavior has not been, and is not being, developed.

Operationalization of Abuse and Violence

Perhaps the most difficult methodological problem facing those studying child abuse, wife abuse, and family violence has been to select an adequate sample of abusive and violent families to study. Social service providers and researchers tend to agree that it is extremely difficult for a family to admit to an interviewer that they are violent or abusive. Thus, nearly all investigations of child abuse and wife abuse operationalize "abuse" as those individuals or families who come to public attention and are publicly labeled as abusers. Child abuse cases are located in hospital and protective service agency records, while samples of abused women are drawn from residents of shelters for abused women.

Exceptions to this pattern are the studies of family violence conducted by Straus and Steinmetz (Steinmetz, 1974; Straus, 1974a, 1974b). They sampled college students and asked them to report on the level of violence in the students' homes during the last year they lived at home. Steinmetz (1977) conducted one of the earliest studies based on a representative sample of families, but the sample was small (57 families) and the families were drawn from only one county in Delaware. More recently, a study of family violence using a nationally representative sample of 2143 families has been completed (Straus et al., 1980).

It is crucial to consider the problems of theory development in an area where the primary mode of operationalizing the dependent variable (abuse or violence) is to choose individuals and families who have been publicly labeled as abusers or violent. Simply stated, this method of operationalizing the dependent variable does not allow investigators to partial out the variables that make an individual or family vulnerable to being labeled "abusive" from the variables that led the individual or family to be abusive (Gelles, 1975).

The criticism that the family violence knowledge base suffers from the inadequate operationalization of the dependent variable and nonrepresentative sampling of subjects is similar to Polsky's critique of the knowledge base in the area of crime and delinquency. Polsky (1969) states that knowledge in this area is limited by the tendency of investigators to study only adjudicated or incarcerated criminals. Just as Polsky argues that criminologists know a great deal about people who are failures as criminals and delinquents (by virtue of getting caught), it appears that there is considerable information on which families are vulnerable to being labeled "abusers" and very little knowledge about which factors actually cause abuse.

AVAILABLE THEORETICAL MODELS

The methodological problems impinging on the study of intrafamily violence and the fact that the detailed scientific study of family violence really began at the beginning of this decade have combined to limit the amount of theory construction on the issue of family violence.

Even though there has been little in the way of theoretical work on the specific issue of family violence, theoretical frameworks and propositions have been developed from the study of violence and aggression that are applicable to the issue of family violence. Gelles and Straus (1979) inventoried 15 theories which seemed to have relevance for understanding violence between family members.

The theories considered ranged from intrapsychic theories to macrosociological. The paper also attempted to develop an integrated theory of violence between family members. Unfortunately, simplicity was not possible, and a model which articulated the key elements of each theory of violence resulted in an integrated model long on heuristic value and equally long and complex to examine.

As a consequence of the large effort that was devoted to developing the integrated model, we learned that it would be wiser and more useful to work with a more "middle-range" theory and set of theoretical propositions. Exchange theory appeared to be the approach which best integrated the key elements of the diverse theories used to explain human violence. Moreover, exchange theory also has the virtue of providing a suitable perspective to explain and answer a variety of questions and issues in the study of family violence, such as "Why do women who are battered remain in violent marriages?" (Gelles, 1976).

AN EXCHANGE/SOCIAL CONTROL MODEL
OF FAMILY VIOLENCE

An assumption of exchange theory which is relevant in explaining family violence is that human interaction is guided by the pursuit of rewards and the avoidance of punishment and costs (Gelles & Straus, 1979). In addition, an individual who supplies reward services to another obliges him to fulfill an obligation, and thus the second individual must furnish benefits to the first (Blau, 1964). If reciprocal exchange of rewards occurs, the interaction will continue. But if reciprocity is not received, the interaction will be broken off. However, intrafamilial relations are more complex than those studied by traditional exchange theorists. In some instances, it is not feasible or possible to break off interaction, even if there is no reciprocity. When the "principle of distributive justice" is violated, there can be increased anger, resentment, conflict, and violence.

Many students of family violence tend to view violence as the last resort to solving problems in the family (Goode, 1971). Nye (1979), however, notes that this need not be the case. Spanking, for instance, is frequently the first choice of action by many parents.

A central (and perhaps greatly oversimplified) proposition of an exchange/social control theory of family violence is that *people hit and abuse other family members because they can.* In applying the principles of general exchange theory we expect that people will use violence in the family if the costs of being violent do not outweigh the rewards. From social control theory we derive the proposition that family violence occurs in the absence of social controls which would bond people to the social order and negatively sanction family members for acts of violence.

The most difficult aspect of applying the propositions from the form of social control theory that has been used to explain juvenile delinquency (see Conger, 1980; Hirschi, 1969; Kornhauser, 1978) is that there are conflicting norms concerning the use of violence in families—and thus some confusion as to whether the normative social order in families is one of harmony and peace or conflict and violence. Publicly, at least, we think of the family as a loving, tranquil, peaceful social institution to which one flees *from* stress and danger. Privately, the family is perhaps society's most violent social institution (Straus et al., 1980). There exist mores and folkways which accept and even mandate the use of violence in families (such as the phrase "spare the rod and spoil the child" or the English law "rule of thumb" which gave husbands the right to strike their wives with sticks no larger than their thumbs). Thus, there is the dilemma as to whether social control is exerted to maintain a certain level of violence in families, or whether social control is designed to keep violence from occurring.

For purposes of the exchange/social control theory presented in this chapter, social control is assumed to be efforts to *prevent* intrafamilial violence. This assumption follows from exchange principles which we use to propose that while violence in families can be normative under some circumstances, there are *costs* for being violent. First, there could be the potential of the victim hitting back. Second, a violent assault could lead to an arrest and/or imprisonment. Finally, using violence could lead to a loss of status. Thus, there are significant costs involved in being violent (Goode, 1971).

Inequality, Privacy, Social Control, and Violence

The first, overly simple proposition that people hit and abuse family members because they can may be expanded to the following:

(1) Family members are more likely to use violence in the home when they expect that the costs of being violent are less than the rewards.
(2) The absence of effective social controls over family relations decreases the costs of one family member being violent toward another.
(3) Certain social and family structures serve to reduce social control in family relations, and therefore reduce the costs and/or increase the rewards of being violent.

The private nature of the modern family serves to reduce the degree of social control exercised over family relations (Laslett, 1973, 1978). Inequality in the home can reduce both social control and the costs of being violent. Finally, the image of the "real" man in society also reduces social control in the home and increases the rewards of being violent.

Inequality

The normative power structure in society and the family and the resulting sexual and generational inequality in the family serves to reduce the chances that victims of family violence can threaten or inflict harm on offenders.[1] Husbands are typically bigger than wives, have higher status positions, and earn more money. Because of this, they can use violence without fear of being struck back hard enough to be injured. Moreover, they do not risk having their wives take economic or social sanctions against them. Parents can use violence toward their children without fear that their children can strike back and injure them. The fact that the use of violence toward children by mothers decreases with the child's age

(Gelles & Hargreaves, 1981) can be interpreted as a consequence of the greater risk of being hit back as the child grows older and larger.

Women and children may be the most frequent victims of family violence because they have no place to run and are not strong enough or do not possess sufficient resources to inflict costs on their attackers.

Privacy

Victims of family violence could turn to outside agencies to redress their grievances, but the private nature of the family reduces the accessibility of outside agencies of social control. Neighbors who report that they overhear incidents of family violence also say that they fear intervening in another person's home. Police, prosecutors, and courts are reluctant to pursue cases involving domestic violence. When these cases are followed up, the courts are faced with the no-win position of either doing nothing or separating the combatants. Thus, to protect a child, judges may view as their only alternative to remove the child from the home. To protect the woman, the solution may be a separation or divorce. Either situation puts the legal system in the position of breaking up a family to protect the individual members. Because courts typically view this as a drastic step, such court-ordered separations or removals are comparatively rare, unless there is stark evidence of repeated grievous injury.

Violence and the "Real Man"

One last cost of being violent is the loss of social status that goes along with being labeled a "child beater" or a "wife beater." However, there are subcultures where aggressive sexual and violent behavior is considered proof that someone is a "real man" (Toby, 1966). Thus, rather than risk status loss, the violent family members may actually realize a status gain. Moreover, that notion that "a man's home is his castle" reduces external social control over family life.

In situations where status can be lost by being violent, individuals employ accepted vocabularies of motive (Mills, 1940) or "accounts" (Lyman & Scott, 1970) to explain their untoward behavior. Thus, violent fathers or mothers might explain their actions by saying they were drunk or lost control. Parents who shared the same desire to batter their children might nod in agreement without realizing that a real loss of control would have produced a much more grievous injury or even death.

Applying Exchange/Social Control Theory

An exchange/social control theory approach to family violence can be extremely helpful in explaining some of the patterns of family violence which have been uncovered in recent empirical investigations.

The child abuse literature notes that certain types of children are at greater risk for abuse. Ill, handicapped, premature, ugly, and demanding children are at greater risk of being abused by their parents (Friedrich & Boriskin, 1976). These children either make great demands on their parents (economically, socially, or psychologically), or, as in the case of deformed children or children seen as ugly by their parents, may be perceived as not providing sufficient gratification in return for the parents' investment of time and energy. In any case, when the parent perceives the costs of parenting to outweigh the rewards, the alternatives are limited. The relationship between parent and child is difficult to break—with the exception of giving the child up for adoption or foster care, or the death of the child or parent. Thus, with few alternatives and high dissatisfaction, the parent may resort to abusive violence.

A similar combination of lack of alternatives and violation of the principle of distributive justice is helpful in understanding conjugal violence. It should be noted that it is easier to explain why a spouse would remain with a violent partner (lack of alternatives) than it is to explain why the one partner adopted violence (see Gelles, 1976, for a discussion of why wives stay with battering husbands). Another facet of conjugal violence that can be seen through the exchange perspective is the use of violence to inflict "costs" on one's partner. Exchange theorists (for example, Homans, 1967) note that to inflict costs on someone who has injured you is rewarding. The idea of revenge being "sweet" can be used to examine why wives resort to extreme forms of violence in response to being punched or hit by their husbands and why husbands resort to violence to silence a wife.

Nye has applied exchange (what he calls choice) theory to family violence and developed a number of theoretical propositions. At the macrosocial level of analysis he states:

> Violence in the family is more frequent in societies that have no legal or other normative structure proscribing it. In societies that proscribe violence against some members (wives) but permit it against others (children), violence will be less frequent towards those members against whom it is proscribed than towards those against whom it is allowed. (Nye, 1979)

Nye goes on to propose that wife-beating and child-beating are less common in families that have relatives and/or friends nearby, while child-beating is more common in single-parent than in two-parent families. I would recast his propositions to read:

> Family violence is more common when nonnuclear family members (e.g., friends, relatives, bystanders) are unavailable, unable, or unwilling to be part of the daily system of family interaction, and thus unable to serve as agents of formal and informal social control.

In terms of the general pattern of relationships among family members, the greater the disparity between perceived investment in a family relationship such as parenting and the perceived returns on the investment, the greater the likelihood that there will be violence. The fact that children three to five years of age and children aged fifteen to seventeen were found to be the most likely victims of child abuse (Straus et al., 1980) could be the result of parents of younger children perceiving a rather large investment in their children while getting little in the way of actual return. Parents who abuse teenage children (and risk being hit back) may do so because they have evidence showing that their investment in rearing the children has yielded disappointing results.

These propositions, again, tend to view violence as a last resort or final alternative to a lack of reciprocity in the family. It is important to note that violence can be the first resort. Spanking children may be common because it is culturally approved and because it is immediately gratifying. Many parents justify the use of violence as a child training technique because it tends to bring with it the immediate emotional reward for the parent and the immediate cessation of the behavior of the child that led to the violence.

Exchange theory is also useful for explaining other findings in the study of family violence. The fact that pregnant women are at risk of physical abuse by their husbands may be due in part to the helplessness of these women and their inability to hit back. Parents who overestimate their children's ability and capabilities may abuse them because these parents expect more out of their relationship with their children than they receive (Nye, 1979).

IMPLICATIONS FOR TREATMENT

It is often difficult for social scientists who seek nomothetic explanations for human social behavior to apply their theories to the idiographic work of clinicians and practitioners who must deal with case-by-case problems of family violence. An exchange/social control theoretical orientation to family violence, however, is a perspective that is directly applicable to both treatment issues and social policy.

Treatment

Applying exchange/social control theory to clinical issues in the treatment of family violence results in the conclusion that if people abuse family members because they can, then a central goal of treatment is to make it so they *can't*. To do this, a clinician needs to increase the degree of social control exerted over family relations and to raise the costs of intrafamilial violence.

Increasing social control and raising the costs is not as easy as it would seem. A consistent finding in child abuse and family violence research is that perpetrators of domestic abuse typically have poor self-concepts. Thus, if we were to raise the costs of family violence by directing the offender to accept the pejorative label "abuser," one of the unanticipated consequences of this approach would be to further undermine the patient's self-concept and further exacerbate the factors causing the abuse.

Nevertheless, it is important to "cancel the hitting license" and move the patient to accept the responsibility for his or her violent and abusive behavior. This means that the clinician cannot accept accounts or rationalizations which attribute the violent behavior to drugs, alcohol, or an inability to control oneself. An example of how a counselor can "cancel the hitting license" by rejecting such accounts is the case of a husband who hit his wife on several occasions:

> Each time he felt he was wrong. He apologized—very genuinely. But still, he did it again. The husband explained that he and his wife got so worked up in their arguments that he "lost control." In his mind, it was almost involuntary, and certainly not something he did according to a rule or norm which gives one the right to hit his wife. But the marriage counselor in the case brought out the rules which permitted him to hit his wife. He asked the husband why, if he had "lost control," he didn't stab his wife! (Straus et al., 1980)

The norms that accept certain levels of permissible family violence are so pervasive that a counselor must be aware not to accept them in the course of therapy.

A variety of innovative treatment approaches to family violence, including EMERGE, the first men's counseling source for domestic violence, now advocate the "canceling of the hitting license" and the acceptance of responsibility for violence as a necessary part of treatment.

A second treatment approach implied by an exchange/social control theory is to reduce the social isolation experienced by violent families. Research finds that child abusers, wife abusers, and their families are more socially isolated than nonviolent families (Straus et al., 1980). Not only does isolation deprive families of social, psychological, and economic resources in times of stress, but it greatly reduces the possibility of external social control over family relations. Families with considerable stress and conflict could be well served by having community linkages on which they could draw for help or assistance in meeting stress and reducing conflict.

Third, research also finds that violence is more likely to occur in homes where the husband (and in some instances the wife) has *all* the power and makes *all* the decisions. Democratically run households with sharing of decision making are the least violent (Straus et al., 1980). This finding implies that if families were helped to change the power structure of their relations and reduce the inequity in decision making, this would reduce the risk of conflict and confrontation escalating into violence and abuse.

Policy

Exchange/social control theory also speaks to necessary policy to reduce and prevent family violence. The following policy recommendations serve to raise the costs of being violent and establish firm, but not unnecessarily intrusive, social control in family relations:

(1) *Elimination of the norms which legitimize and glorify violence in society and in the family.* A reduction of television and other media violence, and passing laws such as implemented by the Swedish Parliament which prohibit hitting children by teachers *and parents* are needed if violent behavior is truly to be considered inappropriate.

(2) *Reducing economic and gender inequity.*

(3) *Increasing the response capacity of the criminal justice system and child welfare system in cases of domestic abuse.* Police frequently are wary of getting involved in family disputes and courts often treat cases of wife abuse less seriously than other forms of assault. Child welfare systems do not have the resources to respond rapidly and effectively to all reports of child abuse. For the costs of family violence to be raised and for the social control to be effective, there must be a certainty of response by agents of social control.

NOTE

1. Earlier I dismissed the notion that sexism caused family violence as being not supported by the data. In this section, I draw on the same theory (sexual inequality causes violence) as that earlier dismissed. My concern in the earlier section was that the proposition about sexism and family violence was being advanced as a *single-factor explanation* of family violence (see for example Dobash & Dobash, 1979). What I reject is the ideological fervor used to advance the argument that sexism causes abuse, rather than the claim that gender inequality is part of a causal model.

REFERENCES

Bennie, E., & Sclare, A. The battered child syndrome. *American Journal of Psychiatry,* 1969, *125*(7), 975-979.

Blau, P. M. *Exchange and power in social life.* New York: John Wiley, 1964.

Conger, R. D. Juvenile delinquency: Behavior restraint or behavior facilitation? In T. Hirschi & M. Gottfredson (Eds.), *Theory and fact in contemporary criminology.* Beverly Hills, CA: Sage, 1980.

Dobash, R. E., & Dobash, R. *Violence against wives.* New York: Free Press, 1979.

Friedrich, W. N., & Boriskin, J. A. The role of the child in abuse: A review of literature. *American Journal of Orthopsychiatry,* 1976, *46*(4), 580-590.

Galdston, R. Observations of children who have been physically abused by their parents. *American Journal of Psychiatry,* 1965, *122*(4), 440-443.

Garbarino, J. The human ecology of child maltreatment: A conceptual model for research. *Journal of Marriage and the Family,* 1977, *39*(4), 721-735.

Gelles, R. J. The social construction of child abuse. *American Journal of Orthopsychiatry,* 1975, *45*(3), 363-371.

Gelles, R. J. Abused wives: Why do they stay? *Journal of Marriage and the Family,* 1976, *38,* 659-668.

Gelles, R. J., & Hargreaves, E. F. Maternal employment and violence toward children. *Journal of Family Issues,* 1981, *2*(4), 509-530.

Gelles, R. J., & Straus, M. A. Determinants of violence in the family: Toward a theoretical integration. In W. Burr et al. (Eds.), *Contemporary theories about the family.* New York: Free Press, 1979.

Gil, D. *Violence against children: Physical child abuse in the United States.* Cambridge: Harvard University Press, 1970.

Goode, W. J. Force and violence in the family. *Journal of Marriage and the Family,* 1971, *33,* 624-636.

Hirschi, T. *Causes of delinquency.* Berkeley: University of California Press, 1969.

Homans, G. C. Fundamental social processes. In N. Smelser (Ed.), *Sociology.* New York: John Wiley, 1967.

Justice, B., & Justice, R. *The abusing family.* New York: Human Sciences Press, 1976.

Kempe, C. et al. The battered child syndrome. *Journal of the American Medical Association,* July 7, 1962, *181,* 17-24.

Kornhauser, R. R. *Social sources of delinquency: An appraisal of analytic models.* Cambridge, England: Cambridge University Press, 1978.

Lang, A. R. et al. Effects of alcohol on aggression in male social drinkers. *Journal of Abnormal Psychology,* 1975, *84,* 508-518.

Laslett, B. The family as a public and private institution: A historical perspective. *Journal of Marriage and the Family,* 1973, *35*(3), 480-492.

Laslett, B. Family membership, past and present. *Social Problems,* 1978, *25*(5), 476-490.

Lyman, S. M., & Scott, M. B. *A sociology of the absurd.* New York: Appleton-Century-Crofts, 1970.

Mills, C. W. Situated actions and vocabularies of motive. *American Sociological Review,* 1940, *5,* 904-913.

Nye, F. I. Choice, exchange, and the family. In W. R. Burr et al. (Eds.), *Contemporary theories about the family* (Vol. 2). New York: Free Press, 1979.

Owens, D., & Straus, M. A. Childhood violence and adult approval of violence. *Aggressive Behavior,* 1975, *1*(2), 193-211.

Pizzey, E. Review of *The violent home* by Richard J. Gelles. *Nursing Mirror,* 1976, January 29.

Polsky, N. *Hustlers, beats, and others.* Garden City, NY: Doubleday, 1969.

Potts, D., & Herzberger, S. *Child abuse: a cross generational pattern of child rearing?* Paper presented at the annual meetings of the Midwestern Psychological Association, Chicago, April 1979.

Schachter, S., & Singer, J. E. Cognitive, social, and physiological determinants of emotional states. *Psychological Review,* 1962, *69*(5), 379-399.

Scheff, T. J. The role of the mentally ill and the dynamics of mental disorder: A research framework. *Sociometry,* 1963, *26,* 436-453.

Skolnick, A., & Skolnick, J. H. (Eds.). *The family in transition* (2nd ed.). Boston: Little, Brown, 1977.

Snell, J. E., Rosenwald, R. J., & Robey, A. The wifebeater's wife: A study of family interaction. *Archives of General Psychiatry,* 1964, *11,* 107-113.

Steele, B. F. The child abuser. In I. Kutash, S. Kutash, & L. Schlesinger (Eds.), *Violence: Perspectives on murder and aggression.* San Francisco: Jossey-Bass, 1978.

Steele, B. F., & Pollock, C. A psychiatric study of parents who abuse infants and small children. In R. Helfer & C. Kempe (Eds.), *The battered child* (2nd ed.). Chicago: University of Chicago Press, 1974.

Steinmetz, S. K. Occupational environment in relation to physical punishment and dogmatism. In S. Steinmetz & M. Straus (Eds.), *Violence in the family.* New York: Harper & Row, 1974.

Steinmetz, S. K. *The cycle of violence: Assertive, aggressive, and abusive family interaction.* New York: Praeger, 1977.

Steinmetz, S. K. Violence between family members. *Marriage and Family Review,* 1978, *1*(3), 1-16.

Straus, M. A. A general systems theory approach to a theory of violence between family members. *Social Science Information,* 1973, *12,* 105-125.

Straus, M. A. Cultural and social organization influences on violence between family members. In R. Prince & D. Barrier (Eds.), *Configurations: Biological and cultural factors in sexuality and family life.* Lexington, MA: D. C. Heath, 1974. (a)

Straus, M. A. Leveling, civility, and violence in the family. *Journal of Marriage and the Family,* 1974, *36,* 13-30. (b)

Straus, M. A. A sociological perspective on the causes of family violence. In M. Green (Ed.), *Violence and the family.* Boulder, CO: Westview Press, 1980.

Straus, M. A., Gelles, R. J., & Steinmetz, S. K. *Behind closed doors: Violence in the American family.* Garden City, NY: Doubleday, 1980.

Toby, J. Violence and the masculine ideal: Some qualitative data. In M. Wolfgang (Ed.), *Patterns of violence. Annals of the American Academy of Political and Social Science,* 1966, *364.*

U.S. Commission on Civil Rights. *Battered women: Issues of public policy.* Washington, DC: Government Printing Office, 1978.

Walker, L. E. *The battered woman.* New York: Harper & Row, 1979.

Washburn, C. *Primitive drinking: A study of the uses and functions of alcohol in preliterate societies.* New Haven, CT: College and University Press, 1961.

10

The Goals of Aggression

LEONARD BERKOWITZ

All those with a serious interest in the study of human behavior obviously must have some understanding of human aggression. Whether their primary focus is on mental health, political institutions, crime and deviant behavior, everyday encounters in ordinary social settings, socialization into one's society, or the impact of family life, behavioral scientists should know why people fight and why they strive to injure others. What prompts the violence, and what are the aggressors trying to accomplish? But although the various human sciences all seek to answer these questions, their disciplinary cultures lead them along different methodological paths and even to different kinds of answers. There is relatively little similarity between investigators trained in experimental social psychology and researchers concerned with social problems in naturalistic settings in the way they conduct their inquiries or even in the nature of the questions they ask. Indeed, to a considerable degree they also make somewhat different assumptions regarding what factors control human behavior generally and violent actions in particular.

In this chapter I will attempt a brief survey of how behavioral scientists have looked at the aims of aggressive behavior. My own approach has, of course, been shaped by long years of experience in the experimental laboratory, but I will not insist on the methodological superiority of laboratory research. As the reader will see, I believe all of the behavioral disciplines can further our understanding of human aggression; moreover, I believe there is no one correct answer to the question, "What is the goal of human aggression?"

IS IT NECESSARY TO CONSIDER
THE AIMS OF AGGRESSION?

To begin, it is important to recognize that all of us do not define aggression in exactly the same way. Furthermore, we also frequently disagree on the major goals of this behavior, or even whether it is necessary to refer to any goals at all. A small minority of psychologists do not want to make any assumptions about the aggressor's objectives. For example, in his book, the first modern survey of psychological research on aggression, Buss (1961) sought to avoid all reference to supposedly mentalistic concepts, choosing to regard aggression only as "the delivery of noxious stimuli to another." This type of formulation runs into an obvious problem: An accidental injury is surely not the same as deliberately inflicted harm, and Buss's definition does not adequately recognize this difference. Bandura's (1973) solution was to say social labeling defines an act as aggressive or not. For him "a full explanation of aggression must consider both injurious behavior and social judgments that determine which injurious acts are labeled as aggressive" (p. 5). Harmful behavior is most likely to be viewed as aggression, he believed, when the response is relatively intense, the recipient expresses pain, and injurious intentions are attributed to the actor. All in all, Bandura seemed to think it is less important to ascertain the aggressor's purpose than to determine why onlookers believe the attack was meant to inflict harm.

A few other psychologists who have adopted what they term "a symbolic interactionist perspective" share Bandura's emphasis on social labeling and his avoidance of motivational notions (Tedeschi, Smith, & Brown, 1974; Kane, Joseph, & Tedeschi, 1976). These writers contend that "no action can be identified as aggressive or violent without taking into account the value system of the perceiver" (Tedeschi et al., 1974, p. 557). Going somewhat further than Bandura, they maintain that observers will not classify an action as "aggressive" *unless* they regard the behavior as deviating from social norms.

This position, adopted by only a few experimental social psychologists, is fairly clear: Aggression is counternormative behavior, and the investigator's task is to determine why this action occurs in spite of social rules or, somewhat differently, why the behavior is seen as deviating from shared norms.

I am troubled by this perspective for a number of reasons. First, it seems that Tedeschi et al.'s position could seriously impede the development of behavioral science if it were taken at face value. We essentially are told that behavioral scientists should not develop their own technical concepts but must always be guided by common parlance. Never mind trying to formulate terms that have a clear and precise meaning for the community of scientists; we have to adopt the meanings involved in everyday language. We as scientists can label an action as "aggression" only if the majority of ordinary people in our society would also apply the term to this behavior—and they presumably believe that aggression is only "bad" behavior.

Moreover, if we were to follow this reasoning seriously, we would have to cut down on our discussion of family violence or at least greatly lessen the number of cases that could be regarded as violent acts. Several authorities have noted that "most Americans see a moral obligation for parents to use physical punishment as a means of controlling children if other means fail" (Steinmetz & Straus, 1975, p. 3). Whether they feel morally obligated to punish their offspring or not, many parents start the abusive incident by trying to impose what is for them fully justified discipline. According to Bell, "abuse is most frequently . . . a consequence of disciplinary action taken by parents or caretakers in response to a specific act of the child" (1975, p. 417). Adding corroboration, Kadushin and Martin (1981) found that almost all of the people in a sample of 66 parents who were reported for child abuse viewed their behavior as "disciplinary procedures required in response" to the child's conduct (p. 190). A good proportion of the American public undoubtedly would agree with them. Similarly, Murray Straus has often referred to the marriage license as a "hitting license" which supposedly gives husbands the right to strike their wives. None of these cases could be classified as aggression in the Tedeschi scheme of things.

This is not to say that morally proper attacks are identical in every respect to illegitimate acts of aggression. We might want to differentiate between these two types of behavior and study them separately. But any comprehensive account of aggression surely must deal with both.

THE GOALS OF AGGRESSION

In contrast to those who would avoid references to the goals of aggression, most behavioral scientists (including virtually all sociologists) agree that aggression is carried out to achieve a particular end. They differ, however, as to what constitutes the main objective of this behavior. The great majority of all these writers generally define aggression, as I do, as a deliberate attempt to harm another. Nevertheless, for many—especially, but not entirely, those with sociological training—the attack is more of an effort to achieve some other, noninjurious outcome than to do harm. In other words, they interpret aggression as primarily instrumental behavior.

Violence as Rule-Following Behavior and the Desire for Social Approval

Normative conceptions think of aggression as instrumental behavior. When someone attacks his victim, according to this popular notion, he is basically acting in conformity to group norms in order to promote or gain acceptance. Such a norm or rule does more than give permission or provide a "license to hit." Theoretically it exerts a positive call for aggression under particular circumstances.

Wolfgang (1959) referred to this type of influence in his discussion of the subculture of violence. "Quick resort to physical combat as a measure of daring, courage or defense of status appears to be a cultural expectation, especially for lower socioeconomic class males of both races" (p. 189). For him, the men living in this subculture of violence presumably attack others mainly because they believe they are expected to do so. If they have been provoked, the only way they can receive the respect and approval they desire from bystanders is to lash out at the offending party. Failure to strike could bring negative consequences. "The juvenile who fails to live up to the conflict gang's requirements is pushed outside the group. . . . The 'coward' is forced to move out of the territory, to find new friends and make new alliances" (Wolfgang & Ferracuti, 1982, p. 160). In much the same way, some parents might hit their children when the youngsters disobey them because the norms in their social circles prescribe physical punishment under these circumstances. They believe any onlookers would think less well of them if they failed to adhere to these rules.

This approach to aggression has been adopted by a number of criminologists (e.g., Clinard, 1974; Gibbons, 1973) and especially by those who believe that almost every socially significant action is rule-governed. From my perspective, however, normative theories exaggerate the extent to which aggression conforms to social rules. As I will suggest later, these notions fail to recognize the impulsivity in many acts of criminal violence (see Berkowitz, 1978). Horowitz and Schwartz (1974) have also criticized normative conceptions, at least indirectly, by arguing that gang violence often arises under conditions of "normative ambiguity" when the teenagers are not sure what rules apply to a given situation. I suspect that the same kind of statement can be made about many cases of family violence. Here, too, one family member may strike a spouse or a child when he or she does not know what to do or what is right.

Self-Oriented Conceptions of Aggression

Where relatively few psychologists have emphasized the importance of normative influences, many more of them agree with their sociological counterparts that self-conceptions play a significant role in aggressive behavior. But whether they come from psychology, sociology, or any of the other behavioral sciences, those stressing the role of the self-concept do not necessarily give the same attention to externally versus internally oriented self-concerns. Some writers have basically assumed the individual attempts to enhance his image in other people's eyes, whereas other discussions place greater emphasis on the person's desire to be true to himself.

Normative analyses of aggression, of course, are especially likely to be in the former camp and often suggest that we adhere to social rules in order to look good to others. A husband may hit his wife in a public argument with her because he thinks he has to live up to his group's idea of how men ought to act toward women. If he didn't "put his wife in her place," the others around him might sneer at him. Claude Brown, author of *Manchild in the Promised Land,* has described how his own violent behavior as a youngster in the Harlem of the late 1940s was affected by social expectations and his desire to adhere to them:

> I knew that they admired me for [being aggressive], and I knew I had to keep on doing it. This was the reputation I was making, and I had to keep living up to it every day that I came out of the house. (excerpted in Steinmetz & Straus, 1975, p. 267)

"Impression management" notions offer just this interpretation of aggressive behavior, of course. In one of the latest statements of impression management theorizing, Felson assumed that "much of human behavior is designed to obtain favorable reactions from an audience" (1978, p. 205). He then maintained that most aggressive actions are an attempt to restore a "favorable situational identity" after this identity has been devalued by a perceived humiliation. Someone who has just been insulted is more likely to retaliate, he insisted, if a third party can observe this attack than if the aggressor is truly anonymous (p. 209).

In my view this conception also exaggerates the extent to which angry violence is governed by the hope of approval from others. Some years ago I conducted an investigation of English violent criminals (Berkowitz, 1978), asking them detailed questions about the violent incident that had led to their arrest. Many of these cases grew out of arguments, most of the time with a stranger and often in or near a tavern. What is most important for us now, none of the 65 men said he had sought approval or tried to preserve his reputation when he hit his antagonist. The Kadushin and Martin (1981) interviews with 66 abusive parents also failed to find any indications that these people had struck their child in the hope of gaining the approval of others. In addition to this absence of supporting evidence, other observations are clearly inconsistent with Felson's expectations. Zimbardo's (1969) examination of the social psychological concept of deindividuation showed that university students attacked an obnoxious person much more severely when they believed they were anonymous than when they thought they could be identified. All in all, the impression management conception of aggression unduly generalized interpretations of youthful violence in conflict gangs to aggression in other settings. Teenagers and young adults in inner-city ghettoes may fight, at least partly, in anticipation of approval or social status, but this does not mean that most aggressors or even most angry aggressors are motivated by the same desires.

(I must be clear about the functioning of social approval in aggressive behavior. Even though angry aggressors might not hit their victim primarily because they are looking for approbation, praising them for such behavior might serve to reinforce this action so that it is more likely to occur again. The approval operates as a reinforcement because most people have learned the general value of being favorably regarded, and not because the aggression was an attempt to gain this regard.)

Even though most aggressive actions may not be motivated primarily by hope of external approval, both sociologists and psychologists believe that this behavior is at least sometimes an effort to regain self-esteem. In this regard, Horowitz and Schwartz (1974) have differentiated between impression management and the desire to preserve one's "honor" very much as I have just done. The former is much more of a "cool" attempt to create a particular outward appearance, whereas the latter is more self-involving. It is this second concern that is more likely to lead to an emotional outburst of violence. Horowitz and Schwartz held that Chicano conflict gangs often fight to protect or restore their honor which has been impugned by a perceived humiliation. The youths' honor is especially at stake, we are told, when they think they are not treated with sufficient respect. The same perception undoubtedly contributes to family violence. According to Martin's analysis of some 800 child abuse cases in Wisconsin (cited in Kadushin & Martin, 1981), the parents were particularly likely to punish their offspring severely when the youngsters were defiant. These extremely abusive adults might have believed that their children had not shown them the proper respect. Feeling humiliated, they became furious and then lashed out at the offender.

As I will discuss later, I do not think that the humiliation-engendered violence is only an attempt to regain one's honor or status. Nevertheless, some persons suffering from an ego-deflating insult may hit their victim in an effort to command respect from him; they may want to show that they are not to be taken lightly but are people worthy of deference. An experiment by Worchel, Arnold, and Harrison (1978) also points to aggression evidently performed to demonstrate self-worth. In this study, male undergraduates who had just been insulted by a fellow student were much more punitive to that person when their victim would know who had punished them than if the victim supposedly would believe someone else was the disciplinarian. (In both conditions the watching audience—but not the victim—supposedly would know who actually administered the punishment.) The angry students evidently regarded the punishment they delivered as an opportunity to show their insulter that they were to be treated with respect, and this could be demonstrated most effectively if the insulter would know that they were doing the punishing.

Most sociologically based self-concept analyses of youthful violence have emphasized how aggression can be used to regain honor or enhance self-esteem. But this is not the only way in which the self-concept can affect aggression. People also try to live up to the ideals they hold for themselves, the way they want to think of themselves. It is important to realize here that the self-image is ever constant and never operative but has to be made highly salient if it is to have an influence. An intriguing series of experiments by Duval, Wicklund, and others (see Wicklund, 1975) has demonstrated that we are especially inclined to adhere to the ideals we have for ourselves when some situational influence causes us to be highly aware of ourselves. In this research the subjects are led to focus their attention on themselves. They then typically become highly motivated to act in keeping with their personal values. As an example, Carver's (1975) men were more likely to live up to their previously expressed attitudes regarding the administration of physical punishment when they were made to be highly self-conscious than when their attention was not focused on themselves. If we transfer all this to a family setting, we would expect men to try harder to be the tough, dominant head of the family if (a) they wanted to picture themselves as this type of male *and* (b) they were highly aware of themselves at the time for some reason. Any aggression they displayed on this occasion is likely to be an attempt to live up to this self-image.

Coercion and Control

Yet another approach contends that aggression is basically an attempt to coerce the victim. Whatever the aggressors do–hurt their opponent physically, criticize him, or threaten some dire outcome in the future– they are supposedly trying mostly to control that individual's behavior. Along with other writers (e.g., Goode, 1971), Ball-Rokeach (1980) adopted this view when she argued that virtually all social violence grows out of the conflict over scarce resources arising from "asymmetric social relations" and is essentially an effort to influence the distribution of these "scarce resources by the threat or exertion of physical force" (p. 46). Aggressors really are not trying to inflict harm for its own sake; they are only seeking to get more of something they want. In applying her analysis to family violence, Ball-Rokeach hypothesized that the decreased asymmetry of the husband-wife relationship as wives increase their own earnings (thus increasing the "power resources of the subordinate wife vis-a-vis her husband") would reduce the likelihood of wife/mother violence against children but would raise the probability that the husband/father would be violent toward the offspring (p. 57).

Space limitations prevent me from mentioning all of the criticisms I could level against Ball-Rokeach's analysis. I will note only that her formulation appears to slight the important role of situational stresses in family violence generally and child abuse in particular (Gelles, 1973; Steinmetz & Straus, 1975). Thus, men who are greatly dissatisfied with their jobs are especially likely to punish their children severely, regardless of their social class level (and perhaps somewhat independently of the asymmetry of their relations with their wives; see Steinmetz & Straus, 1975, p. 9). Nor does the Ball-Rokeach conception adequately account for the relatively great proportion of child abuse incidents in which parents overreact to a child's crying or whining (Kadushin & Martin, 1981).

Patterson (1976; Patterson & Cobb, 1973), on the other hand, paid considerable attention to the effect of stressful conditions but still emphasized what he regarded as the coercive nature of the aggressor's behavior. Patterson based his formulation chiefly on field observations of aggressive youngsters. On recording the actions of these children in their homes, he and his associates found that the youngsters exhibited a wide spectrum of unpleasant behaviors—including hitting, teasing, negativism and refusal to comply with requests, and even open defiance—apparently in order to control the conduct of others in their family. In other words, for Patterson the children's hitting is part of a general coercive pattern. His observations also suggested that these "coercive" behaviors are frequently reactions to aversive conditions, unpleasant events initiated by some other member of the family, and that these reactions are often reinforced when the victim submits to the aggressor.

There can be little doubt that much of the violence occurring in families is at least partly an attempt to control the victim's actions. If we take what parents say at face value, we can see this in the Kadushin and Martin (1981) study of the 66 men and women who had been reported for mistreating their children. Forty-four percent of the sample said they had initiated the abusive incident either in order to teach the youngster a lesson and thereby control his or her behavior or in order to reassert their control over the child, a control that had been threatened or eroded.

But what we must always keep in mind is that a good part of this behavior arises when the youngster's action is decidedly aversive for the parent. Fully one-third of the Kadushin and Martin sample indicated they had lashed out in an effort to reduce or eliminate their offspring's unpleasant conduct (p. 189). I use the phrase "lashed out" advisedly because, as I will discuss more fully later, the reaction to the initial aversive stimulus is often highly emotional and impulsive. The perpetrators are often enraged and strike out in fury; while they may have a general idea of what they want to accomplish, they usually are not as rational and calculating as Ball-Rokeach and others assume.

Aversively Stimulated Aggression and the Desire to Inflict Pain

People do at times hit others in an attempt to coerce their victims, and their aggression may also be spurred by a desire to enhance their self-esteem. The violence can be instrumental to the attainment of a number of different goals. We should also recognize, however, that aggression often is also directed chiefly toward the inflicting of injury rather than being carried out in pursuit of nonharmful objectives.

Just what goal is paramount depends largely on the nature of the condition that produced the aggressor's attack. It is easy to suggest that aggressors are particularly intent on hurting their victim if this person had previously insulted them. Thus, we may be quite reluctant to punish someone who had not provoked us earlier but are much more inclined to harm this individual if he or she had been insulting to us (Rule & Nesdale, 1974).

If we stop and think about it, it is only a matter of common sense that angry people want to hurt those who had provoked them. But a number of studies also attest to this desire. Over 40 percent of the violent criminals I interviewed in my previously mentioned British study (Berkowitz, 1978) said they had wanted to hurt their antagonist when they struck at him (while most of the others indicated they attacked chiefly in search of safety). Even some of the parents in the Kadushin-Martin study admitted they had hit their child because they had wanted to hurt the youngster.

Other evidence that angry aggressors seek to inflict pain comes from laboratory research. Most notably, several experiments have demonstrated that strongly angered people are frequently more punitive than they otherwise would have been on finding that their tormentor is in some pain (Baron, 1977). The information indicative of the victim's suffering (i.e., the pain cues) evidently showed the angry persons they were approaching their goal, the appropriate injury of the one who had provoked them, and thus stimulated them to even stronger aggressive reactions. Further, since the suitable injury of the tormentor is the provoked person's goal, previously neutral stimuli associated with that individual's suffering can acquire the capacity to evoke impulsive aggressive reactions (Berkowitz, 1974). In an experiment by Swart and Berkowitz (1976), for example, angered subjects exhibited the strongest impulsive aggression when they encountered previously neutral stimuli that had been paired with the offender's injury. These stimuli acquired the capacity to evoke aggression-facilitating reactions as a result of their connection with the angry subjects' aggressive goal.

We can think of several reasons why provocations might arouse such a goal. In addition to the more obvious possibilities, in recent years I have noted that provocations are only one kind of aversive event, and have argued that humans are inclined to hurt someone when they are experiencing unpleasant feelings.

This is a broad-ranging principle. In essential agreement with Moyer (1976) and others, I contend that all aversive events, whether frustrations, deprivations, noxious stimuli, or environmental stresses, produce an instigation to aggression as well as a desire to escape or avoid the unpleasant situation (Berkowitz, 1978, 1980; Berkowitz, Cochran, & Embree, 1981). The aggressive tendencies may be oriented partly toward the termination or reduction of the aversive stimulus, but at the human level, they are also directed toward doing injury. That is, those who are in physical or mental pain are inclined to hurt someone even though their aggression cannot lessen their own suffering. As one bit of evidence, Berkowitz et al. (1981) demonstrated that people exposed to an extremely aversive treatment were much harsher to an available target if they believed their punishment would hurt rather than help this individual. They apparently wanted to inflict harm, and the possibility of doing so stimulated heightened aggression, just as the possibility of obtaining food can stimulate a hungry person to increased food-getting behavior.

This notion of aversively stimulated aggression is easily applied to family violence. Investigators have reported repeatedly that a variety of environmental stresses can heighten the level of aggression within the family (Gelles, 1973; Steinmetz & Straus, 1975). We know, for example, that the likelihood of child abuse is increased when the father is unemployed or is extremely unhappy in his job. I suggest that these stressful conditions—whether they are poverty, job dissatisfactions, an unhappy marriage, or anything else—tend to produce an instigation to aggression to the extent that they create feelings of displeasure. This instigation is not always revealed in overt behavior. But if the situation is right, if inhibitions against aggression are weak and there is a suitable target, the aversively instigated aggression can be translated into open violence. What we then see is emotional aggression. All aggression is not carried out in the heat of intense feelings. A good deal, especially instrumental aggression, can be coolly calculating. But just as it is a mistake to deny this instrumental behavior, so is it also wrong to neglect the emotional, aversively stimulated aggression, as some analyses have done.

Furthermore, as I have also suggested, humans who are stimulated to aggression by decidedly unpleasant occurrences are inclined to hurt someone, especially *but not only* the perceived source of their suffering. The aggression they display is goal-directed. This may not be apparent to those who are thinking only of instrumental aggression carried out in pursuit of noninjurious ends, such as social status, approval, or ego-enhancement. Some writers (e.g., Steinmetz & Straus, 1975) have termed all noninstrumental aggression "expressive" aggression, as if the behavior had no goal at all. However, this is not the case; aversively stimulated aggression often pursues a particular objective, the inflicting of injury.

INVOLUNTARY ASPECTS OF AGGRESSION

This matter of expressive aggression brings up what I regard as the major difference between sociologists and "neobehavioristically" oriented psychologists of my ilk. When behavioral scientists talk of expressive reactions, we usually are thinking of involuntary responses, of behavior that does not seem to be guided by any definite aims. I think it is fair to say that sociologists as a group are more likely than psychologists such as myself to assume that almost every action is intended. All behavior is motivated, said Freud, and most sociologists accept this statement as a truism. Expressive behavior is therefore supposedly relatively uncommon. So, in the case of aggression, the father who bruises his child badly when spanking him and the husband who hurts his wife seriously when he hits her in the heat of an argument probably meant to produce this outcome. Expressive aggression probably occurs every once in a while, but not too often. Ball-Rokeach (1980) adopted an extreme, but not an entirely unusual, version of this position when she held that violence was better regarded as "primarily goal-oriented and therefore rational" than as expressive behavior; the former, goal-oriented violence was "social" in nature, she maintained, whereas expressive reactions were "asocial" and supposedly were produced only by "abnormal or deficit" conditions unlike the more rationally governed, goal-oriented violence (p. 47).

There are several problems with this type of conception. For one, at least some of those who believe all behavior is "motivated" are actually equating the notion of "motivation" with "determination"—systematic and predictable influences on action. This is an unnecessary confusion. Behavior can be "determined" even though the actor is not consciously or unconsciously in pursuit of a particular outcome. A person may guess that he will fail on a certain task, not because he wants to do poorly but because he is extrapolating from a past record of inadequate performance.

The view that aggression is usually carried out in pursuit of some rationalistic motive also fails to recognize how much of our everyday behavior is affected by external stimuli. As one illustration, Ball-Rokeach's analysis of hostility displacement is seriously obsolete. Where she thought of displaced aggression as arising from "ego defensive needs" supposedly to "release hostility or frustration," empirical evidence indicates this phenomenon is better understood as an involuntary response to the stimulus characteristics of the people in the surrounding environment (Miller, 1948). If the angry person is afraid to punish the one who had provoked him, he will tend to displace his hostility onto others whose stimulus qualities associate them with the provocateur (Moore, 1964; Fitz, 1976), not because of an ego defensive need but because these targets evoke the aggressive reactions the angry individual is disposed to perform. Moreover, we cannot really say that the aggressor had fully intended to harm the innocent bystanders; he might have wanted to hurt someone, but he had not necessarily intended to harm the bystanders as much as he actually did.

I have taken this approach for almost a generation now (Berkowitz, 1962). While it is not fashionable with the current crop of cognitively oriented social psychologists, it has received a great deal of empirical support from a truly impressive range of studies. Some of the best examples can be found in research on the effects of violent movies

(Berkowitz, 1973; Parke, Berkowitz, Leyens, West, & Sebastian, 1977). The evidence here is fairly clear: The presentation of aggressive scenes heightens the chance that people in the audience will behave aggressively themselves. Several different processes contribute to this effect, but one of them is the type of stimulation I have been discussing. The aggressive stimuli on the screen tend to elicit reactions within the viewers that are semantically associated with aggression—ideas, feelings, and even motor reactions, all of which increase the likelihood that the observers will display aggression themselves (Berkowitz, 1973). Weapons are still another example of aggressive stimuli. Because of the meaning they have for many persons—weapons are objects that can be used to hurt others—the mere sight of a gun can stimulate some people to be more aggressive than they otherwise would have been (Berkowitz & LePage, 1967; Turner, Simons, Berkowitz, & Frodi, 1977).

So far I have been talking about two kinds of situational influences: (1) aversive events that create an instigation to aggression and even a desire to inflict injury, and (2) situational stimuli that have an aggressive meaning. Both of these classes of stimuli, operating together or alone, can contribute to impulsive outbursts of violence. Basically, the unpleasant occurrence causes the individual to want to attack someone, particularly the perceived source of the displeasure, whereas the aggression-associated stimuli can elicit aggression facilitating reactions so that the attack may be stronger than the aggressor intended.

Impulsive Violence

Consider the rapid escalation of violence that sometimes occurs when an angry person starts hitting. Not infrequently, the enraged aggressor seems to get carried away as he or she strikes at the victim so that the attacks quickly mount in fury. Kadushin and Martin (1981) have a quotation that is illustrative. A mother described what happened when she started beating her daughter:

> And I grabbed her and I looked at her. . . . She looked at me like I was poison. And I whupped Julia and I whupped her and I whupped her and it looked like the more I whupped her, the more I wanted to whup her. I couldn't whup her enough. (p. 196)

This type of phenomenon probably occurs more often than one may think. On examining descriptions of the conflicts in 385 married couples, Straus (1974) found that high levels of verbal aggression between husbands and wives were typically accompanied by great amounts of physical aggression; the harsh words the men and women exchanged evidently did not serve to "release" their hostile feelings but instead may have stirred things up even further so they came to blows. We can readily imagine how the fights escalated in these cases: there were increasingly severe insults culminating in an explosion of physical violence. Patterson's (1981) observations of the fighting in families having extremely aggressive children also point to an escalation of aggression. In many of these families the most aggressive youngster first does something unpleasant. Where normal families would either ignore this action or punish it very effectively so that it is quickly stopped, in the distressed families many of the members quickly react with their own aggression. "One, maybe two or three, persons leap into the fray and produce an instant explosion."

Here, too, several different processes undoubtedly contribute to this rapid buildup of violence. First, the initial acts probably lower the aggressors' restraints so that they feel freer to attack their victim even more strongly. Second, the aggressors may even be stimulated to heightened aggression by the sight of their own and others' actions. Just as the sight of people fighting on a movie or TV screen can stimulate aggressive tendencies in the viewers, persons embroiled in violent conflict can be stimulated to attack their opponents ever more strongly by the sight of their own and their antagonists' aggressive actions. This aggression could become even more violent if the antagonists see a weapon. The gun stimulates them even further. And so the fighting escalates in intensity— until someone is hurt so badly that inhibitions finally come into play or one of the opponents capitulates.

Target Selectivity

Still another example of aggression influenced by external stimulation is especially important to those who seek to understand family violence and especially child abuse. While many abusive parents generalize their hostility fairly indiscriminately to almost every member of the family, every now and then one particular youngster tends to become the favorite target for the parents' attacks (Kadushin & Martin, 1981). This child can be picked out for a number of reasons. Sometimes he or she acts especially obnoxiously and quickly provokes the aggressively disposed parent. In other instances, however, the youngster's only "sin" is that he or she is somehow associated with pain and suffering. Recall that an aversive stimulus can evoke aggressive inclinations. By the same token, previously neutral stimuli that just happen to be connected with a decidedly unpleasant event can also acquire the capacity to elicit these aggressive tendencies. We can see evidence of this phenomenon in the nature of the children who seem to bear more than their share of parental violence. Quite often, they have been connected with something unpleasant: a premature birth, an unwanted pregnancy, an unattractive appearance, or even poor health (Parke & Collmer, 1975). What happens in these cases, I suggest, is that the children have become aversive stimuli for the parents because of these unpleasant associations, and as a consequence, they tend to evoke relatively strong aggressive reactions from their mothers and/or fathers when these adults are not feeling well and are thus disposed to violence. In a sense, these youngsters draw out the aggression the unhappy parents are inclined to exhibit.

This possibility has been supported by the findings in two experiments conducted by myself and Frodi (1979). In the second of these studies, university women given the task of supervising a 10-year-old boy were most punitive to him when he was both "funny looking" and had a speech handicap than when he had only one or none of these unpleasant qualities. The doubly stigmatized youngster evidently elicited the strongest aggressive reactions from these people.

CONCLUSION

In this chapter I have tried to present a picture of the multifaceted nature of human aggression. People can be very complex. At one time they might act in rational pursuit of a carefully considered objective. On another occasion they might turn their attention to a very different goal but still pursue this aim thoughtfully. At yet another moment they might react impulsively and with relatively little thought to the situation confronting them. The same thing can be said about aggression. The behavior can be carried out for any number of aims, although, whatever else he or she might be striving to accomplish, one of the aggressor's objectives is the injury of the target. Furthermore, this action is often at least partly an involuntary response to the stimuli in the situation. The different behavioral sciences do not agree as to how much of human aggression is affected by these impulsive reactions. Nevertheless, it is a mistake to neglect the impulsivity of an attack made in intense anger. Sociologists, especially, sometimes forget that a good deal (but not all) of aggression is performed in the heat of strong emotions. Angry persons frequently strike out in rage without much thought (beyond some vague idea that they want to hurt). Theories that pay little attention to the role of emotions, particularly in aggression, rob humans of their full complexity.

REFERENCES

Ball-Rokeach, S. J. Normative and deviant violence from a conflict perspective. *Social Problems,* 1980, *28,* 45-62.

Bandura, A. *Aggression: A social learning analysis.* Englewood Cliffs, NJ: Prentice-Hall, 1973.

Baron, R. A. *Human aggression.* New York: Plenum, 1977.

Bell, R. Q. Reduction of stress in child rearing. In L. Levi (Ed.), *Society, stress and disease, Vol. 2: Childhood and adolescence.* New York: Oxford University Press, 1975.

Berkowitz, L. *Aggression: A social-psychological analysis.* New York: McGraw-Hill, 1962.

Berkowitz, L. Words and symbols as stimuli to aggressive responses. In J. F. Knutson (Ed.), *Control of aggression: Implications from basic research.* Chicago: Aldine, 1973.

Berkowitz, L. Some determinants of impulsive aggression: Role of mediated associations with reinforcements for aggression. *Psychological Review,* 1974, *81,* 165-176.

Berkowitz, L. Is criminal violence normative behavior? *Journal of Research in Crime and Delinquency,* 1978, *15*(2), 148-161.

Berkowitz, L., Cochran, S., & Embree, M. Physical pain and the goal of aversively stimulated aggression. *Journal of Personality and Social Psychology,* 1981, *40,* 687-700.

Berkowitz, L., & Frodi, A. Reactions to a child's mistakes as affected by her/his looks and speech. *Social Psychology Quarterly,* 1979, *42,* 420-425.

Berkowitz, L., & LePage, A. Weapons as aggression-eliciting stimuli. *Journal of Personality and Social Psychology,* 1967, *7,* 202-207.

Buss, A. H. *The psychology of aggression.* New York: John Wiley, 1961.

Carver, C. S. The facilitation of aggression as a function of objective self-awareness and attitudes toward punishment. *Journal of Experimental Social Psychology,* 1975, *11,* 510-519.

Clinard, M. B. *Sociology of deviant behavior* (4th ed.). New York: Holt, Rinehart & Winston, 1974.

Felson, R. B. Aggression as impression management. *Social Psychology,* 1978, *41,* 205-213.

Fitz, D. A renewed look at Miller's conflict theory of aggression displacement. *Journal of Personality and Social Psychology,* 1976, *33,* 725-732.

Gelles, R. J. Child abuse as psychopathology: A sociological critique and reformulation. *American Journal of Orthopsychiatry,* 1973, *43,* 611-621.

Gibbons, D. C. *Society, crime and criminal careers.* Englewood Cliffs, NJ: Prentice-Hall, 1973.

Goode, W. J. Force and violence in the family. *Journal of Marriage and the Family,* 1971, *33* 624-636.

Horowitz, R., & Schwartz, G. Honor, normative ambiguity and gang violence. *American Sociological Review,* 1974, *39,* 238-251.

Kadushin, A., & Martin, J. *Child abuse: An interactional event.* New York: Columbia University Press, 1981.

Kane, T. R., Joseph, J. M., & Tedeschi, J. T. Person perception and the Berkowitz paradigm for the study of aggression. *Journal of Personality and Social Psychology,* 1976, *33,* 663-673.

Miller, N. E. Theory and experiment relating psychoanalytic displacement to stimulus-response generalization. *Journal of Abnormal and Social Psychology,* 1948, *43,* 155-178.

Moore, S. G. Displaced aggression in young children. *Journal of Abnormal and Social Psychology,* 1964, *68,* 200-204.

Moyer, K. E. *The psychobiology of aggression.* New York: Harper & Row, 1976.

Parke, R. D., Berkowitz, L., Leyens, J. P., West, S. G., & Sebastian, R. J. Some effects of violent and nonviolent movies on the behavior of juvenile delinquents. In L. Berkowitz (Ed.), *Advances in experimental social psychology,* (Vol. 10). New York: Academic Press, 1977.

Parke, R. D., & Collmer, C. W. Child abuse: An interdisciplinary review. In E. M. Hetherington (Ed.), *Review of child development research* (Vol. 5). Chicago: University of Chicago Press, 1975.

Patterson, G. R. The aggressive child: Victim and architect of a coercive system. In L. A. Hamerlynch, L. C. Handy, & E. J. Mash (Eds.), *Behavior modification and families. I. Theory and research.* New York: Brunner/Mazel, 1976.

Patterson, G. R., & Cobb, J. A. Stimulus control for classes of noxious behaviors. In J. F. Knutson (Ed.), *The control of aggression: Implications from basic research.* Chicago: Aldine, 1973.

Rule, B. G., & Nesdale, A. Differing functions of aggression. *Journal of Personality,* 1974, *42,* 467-481.

Steinmetz, S. K., & Straus, M. A. *Violence in the family.* New York: Dodd, Mead, 1975.

Straus, M. A. Leveling, civility and violence in the family. *Journal of Marriage and the Family,* 1974, *36,* 13-29.

Swart, C., & Berkowitz, L. The effect of a stimulus associated with a victim's pain on later aggression. *Journal of Personality and Social Psychology,* 1976, *33,* 623-631.

Tedeschi, J. T., Smith, R. B. III, & Brown, R. C., Jr. A reinterpretation of research on aggression. *Psychological Bulletin,* 1974, *81,* 540-562.

Turner, C. W., Simons, L. S., Berkowitz, L., & Frodi, A. The stimulating and inhibiting effects of weapons on aggressive behavior. *Aggressive Behavior,* 1977, *3,* 355-378.

Wicklund, R. A. Objective self-awareness. In L. Berkowitz (Ed.), *Advances in experimental social psychology* (Vol. 8). New York: Academic Press, 1975.

Wolfgang, M. E. *Patterns in criminal homicide.* Philadelphia: University of Pennsylvania Press, 1959.

Wolfgang, M. E., & Ferracuti, F. *The subculture of violence: Towards an integrated theory of criminology* (American ed.) London: Social Science Paperbacks, Beverly Hills, CA: Sage, 1982.

Worchel, S., Arnold, S. E., & Harrison, W. Aggression and power restoration: The effects of identifiability and timing on aggressive behavior. *Journal of Experimental Social Psychology,* 1978, *14,* 43-52.

Zimbardo, P. G. The human choice: Individuation, reason, and order versus deindividuation, impulse and chaos. In W. J. Arnold & D. Levine (Eds.), *Nebraska Symposium on Motivation, 1969.* Lincoln: University of Nebraska Press, 1969.

11

Social Psychological Determinants

RICHARD J. SEBASTIAN

In the main report of their study of a nationally representative sample of American couples, Straus, Gelles, and Steinmetz (1980) wrote: "The American family and the American home are perhaps as or more violent than any other American institution or setting (with the exception of the military, and only then in time of war)" (p. 4). Whether or not this specific position is accurate, the important point it makes is that physical aggression among family members, or to use the more popular terminology, family violence, is very common and frequently quite severe (e.g., Gelles, 1974; Gil, 1971; Parke & Collmer, 1975; Straus et al., 1980; Walker, 1979). The major aims of this chapter are to present some social psychological suggestions for why physical aggression among family members is especially common and to offer some ideas about the interpersonal as well as intrapersonal processes involved in these injurious family interactions. This analysis will also explicitly point out some common features among several forms of family violence.

In this review the physical attacks which family members direct toward one another are viewed as specific examples of physical aggression, not as a special class of physically aggressive behaviors. A special theory of these physically aggressive acts involving family members or a special theory of family violence is therefore unnecessary.[1] Rather, it seems that family violence can be readily and profitably analyzed in terms of extant theory and research in areas of social psychology which have special relevance to physical aggression involving intimates, such as aggression, interpersonal attraction, and person perception and attribution. The application of theory and research from social psychology to the problem of family violence should not only increase understanding of these behaviors but also promote the development of social psychological theory and the production of new knowledge. These latter outcomes will surely follow from the inevitable failures of extant theory to account satisfactorily for all observations of aggressive behavior in the family.

The focus here will be what social psychologists have called hostile or angry aggression (e.g., Berkowitz, 1974; Buss, 1971). For this class of aggressive behaviors, the attacker's *primary* intent is injury of the victim, whereas in instrumental aggression it is the attainment of personally satisfying or societally valued noninjurious ends. This necessarily implies that some forms of family violence are conceptualized in this chapter as hostile aggression. In fact, many instances of wife-beating, child abuse, and attacks against the elderly seem more readily amenable to theoretical analysis when viewed as instances of hostile rather than instrumental aggression,[2] and it is these three forms of family violence which will be emphasized. The focus on hostile aggression toward wives, children, and the elderly does not, however, mean that the ideas presented apply exclusively to hostile aggression. It also does not mean that other expressions of physical aggression carried out for instrumental reasons or performed by or directed at other family members are unimportant. Finally, this emphasis does not mean that a single aggressive behavior cannot be carried out to achieve multiple goals, hostile as well as instrumental.

INSTIGATION AND INHIBITION OF AGGRESSION IN THE FAMILY

At a very general level, a social psychological analysis of aggressive behavior examines the influence of two sets of opposing forces, instigational and inhibitory (e.g., Berkowitz, 1962; Goldstein, 1975; Megargee & Hokanson, 1970). That is, consideration is given to forces which motivate or impel the individual to perform aggressive behavior and to antagonistic forces which restrain or block the person from behaving in an overtly aggressive manner. The strength of an aggressive response, and even the very occurrence of one, depends on the relative strengths of these two sets of forces. Thus, if the strength of the instigation outweighs the strength of the inhibitory forces, then aggressive behavior will occur. If, on the other hand, inhibitions are stronger than the instigational forces, overt aggression will not occur. The major thesis regarding the operation of these forces in the family is that *family violence is more common than other forms because family members have especially great instigational potential for one another and because restraints against aggression are weaker in the family than they are in other social settings.*

Inhibitory Factors

Generaly speaking, many behaviors are less restrained in the family setting than they are in other contexts. In the privacy of their own residence and in the company of those who know them well and accept them basically as they are, people are freer to say and do what they want. The more specific and more pertinent proposition advanced here is that aggressive behavior, especially when directed at some targets, is also weakly inhibited in the home. Before this thesis is developed further, it is worth noting that inhibitions against aggression outside the home seem quite strong. Physical aggression involving adults is infrequent in most settings despite the presence of powerful provocations in some of these settings, such as work. In general, restraints against aggression fortunately are very effective for most individuals most of the time.

This is not, however, true in the family, for a number of reasons. First, despite the fact that most states now have some kind of legislation regarding assaults in families, the legal consequences of assault in this context are minimal in comparison to what would follow a similar attack against a nonfamily member (*Response,* 1980). Assaults in the family, first, doubtlessly are not reported to the police as often as other assaults. Moreover, when they are, the police are frequently reluctant to make an arrest in a domestic assault because, among other reasons, the victim often refuses to press charges or eventually drops them (Lerman, 1981).

As just mentioned, assaults in the home are probably not reported to the police as often as similar attacks outside the home. One reason for this is that they simply are not observed. The absence of observation, evaluation, and control of behavior in the home by nonfamily members is offered as a second determinant of the weak inhibitions against aggression in this setting. The approval, acceptance, and esteem of others, especially others whose evaluations are important, influence our behavior powerfully (Berscheid & Walster, 1978). In particular, that the known or assumed values of those who observe aggressive displays strongly influence these behaviors is now well-established (Baron, 1971; Borden, 1975; Richardson, Bernstein, & Taylor, 1979). Furthermore, although some kinds of physical aggression in the family may be tolerated (e.g., slapping one's wife) and even approved (e.g., spanking one's child), there is little reason to believe that physical attacks which cause or have the potential to cause serious injury to family members are tolerated or approved by the majority of individuals in our society when the attacks are unambiguously perceived and defined by the observers. Instead, attacks which are serious enough to be called abuse are clearly strongly disapproved, as their name attests. The main point here is that the absence of such disapproval from others in the home minimizes or eliminates altogether any influence they might have and makes physical aggression in the family (or any other private setting, for that matter) more probable.[3]

To begin the exposition of the third reason for the weakness of inhibitions against aggression in the home, it should be noted that family members have intimate knowledge of one another. The significance of this obvious assertion for present purposes is that family members will therefore have a rough idea of how much inappropriate aggressive behavior or even abuse their victims will tolerate. They know what they can "get away with." Generally, for reasons to be described momentarily, family members will in fact "put up with" more inappropriate behavior from another family member than others would. Thus, as long as these limits are recognized and as long as the aggressor stays within them, or exceeds them only minimally, it is proposed that some level of aggression will be more probable under these conditions than others where little or no tolerance for aggressive behavior can be expected.

Family members are also interdependent; they rely on one another, to a greater or lesser degree, for the satisfaction of social, psychological, and physical needs. It is the *greater* dependency of some members on others which "forces" them to put up with even serious attacks from others (Gelles, 1976; Kalmuss & Straus, in press). In child, wife, and elderly abuse the victims are frequently highly dependent on the aggressor in one or more ways, an important commonality among these phenomena. Moreover, in some instances of abuse, especially those involving infants, young children, and some elderly, the victims depend on their attackers for their very existence and really have no choice in the matter. In these instances termination of the relationship or its threat is impossible and consequently has no deterrent value whatsoever for the abuser. In other cases, where the dependency is "simply" psychological, not physical or even economic, the victim may still fail to terminate the relationship for any number of reasons. In general, an individual who satisfies needs in a relationship or who, in other words, benefits from it will accept more costs from it than one who does not benefit from the relationship, especially if no good alternatives are known to be available (Thibaut & Kelley, 1959). The critical point here is that this psychological dependency will also weaken the attacker's restraints against hurting.

The final factor which affects inhibitions governing aggression and which may be especially influential in several forms of family violence is the simple ability of the victim to retaliate or defend himself or herself successfully. This capacity is notably absent in the three focal forms of family violence for this chapter: wife, child, and elderly abuse. In all three cases the victims are, on the average, less able to defend themselves or successfully retaliate because of differences in size, strength, or both. For example, men on the average are about 5.2 inches taller and 27 pounds heavier than women (*World Almanac,* 1981). Uncorrected for weight, women possess about 35% of the upper body and trunk strength of men. When corrected for weight, it is still only 80% (Willerman, 1979). Some additional evidence for the importance of size and strength as determinants of victimization can be gleaned from the findings of the National Study of the Incidence and Severity of Child Abuse and Neglect (1981). In this research the incidence of physical abuse of boys was highest for 3-5-year-olds and declined from that age range with especially sharp drops at 12-14 and 15-17 age categories. For girls, on the other hand, the highest levels of physical abuse occurred for those in the 12-14 and 15-17 age categories. As boys mature physically, they can protect themselves more capably, but girls apparently do not gain in this capacity to the same degree. As obvious as this general point is, it is an important common feature of these three focal forms of family violence, and one that has not been given the attention it deserves in discussions of the problem.

In summary, inhibitions against physical aggression in the family are hypothesized to be much weaker than they are in other settings because (1) adverse legal consequences are much less probable; (2) social disapproval from nonfamily members is less likely; (3) aggressors have a fairly accurate sense of how much inappropriate behavior family members will tolerate; (4) victims of physical aggression are often highly and even involuntarily dependent on their assailants; and (5) some of the most commonly victimized family members are weaker and smaller than their attackers. All other things being equal, the weaker an individual's inhibitions, the more probable and the more intense the person's aggressive behavior will be.

Instigational Factors

Not only can inhibitions against aggression be especially weak in the family, but instigation to it can also be potent. To argue that family members have especially great instigational potential for one another does *not* mean that the victims of violence are seen as exclusively or even mainly responsible for many of the attacks they experience. In many instances the victim may have done absolutely nothing objectively (i.e., in the eyes of detached observers) to justify the attacker's anger, let alone the expression of it in serious physical aggression. The "provocation" required for such attacks may be obvious *only to the attacker*. In these assaults the aggressor's anger probably stems from intrapersonal, environmental, and social structural sources for which the victim has no responsibility. For example, unemployment is strongly associated with child and wife abuse (Gil, 1971; Straus et al., 1980). Neither the child nor the woman is responsible for the aggressor's anger and pain, but they are the targets of its aggressive expression. It is also important to remember, as stated earlier, that physically aggressive behaviors in the family are performed for instrumental reasons, many of which the victim has little or no control over (such as "keeping her in her place," "getting respect," etc.). Nonetheless, despite these important qualifications, this analysis of family violence does not remove all responsibility for all attacks from the victims. Social behavior is interactive, and victims can knowingly contribute to their attacks. Finally, responsibility issues aside, the victim's behavior and/or characteristics are sometimes determinants of the attacker's aggression.

Why do family members have this capacity to provoke high levels of anger and aggression? In the first place, most individuals have highly generalized and strongly held expectations for positive treatment from family members and, more generally, intimates. That is, people strongly expect more affectionate, more encouraging, more helpful, and more comforting behavior from their spouses, children, and parents (maybe even siblings) than they do from most other individuals. Disconfirmation of these strong expectations will consequently be very frustrating, thereby creating strong instigation to aggressive behavior (Berkowitz, 1960a; Dollard, Doob, Miller, Mowrer, & Sears, 1939). According to this reasoning, hostility, insults, or physical attacks from an intimate should arouse stronger anger than the same treatment from a stranger or an enemy (Berkowitz, 1960b; Holmes & Berkowitz, 1961). Even neutrality from an intimate can be very provocative because of the expectations held for this person. Friends and intimates may indeed lose their potential to reward one another but not to punish (Aronson & Linder, 1965).

Other strong, albeit often unrealistic or inappropriate, expectations are also dashed by an individual's loved ones, once again arousing high levels of anger. Parents occasionally expect their children to develop too quickly in one or more ways and are badly thwarted by their almost inevitable failure to do so (Parke & Collmer, 1975). Low birth weight infants and those who cry excessively are especially likely to be abused, as are developmentally disabled, retarded, and physically unattractive children (Berkowitz & Frodi, 1979; Parke & Collmer, 1975). One commonality shared by these children is that they frustrate their parents in one way or another. Simply behaving in an appropriate way for their age, which is to say behaving as children, sometimes frustrates parents who want their children to behave like adults. The strongly held expectations for the kind of treatment received from loved ones and for their "performance" in other domains are potential sources of intense instigation to aggression.

The wide range and sheer number of activities shared by family members also contributes to their instigational potential (Gelles & Straus, 1979). Each shared activity carries with it an opportunity for the interactants to frustrate one another. As a result, the number of frustration opportunities available to each family member is high, and the variety of thwartings which the same or a different family member can cause another is great. If a number of frustrations occur in fairly rapid succession, the anger aroused by these individual frustrations can build (Berkowitz, 1962). Whereas the anger aroused by the separate blockings may not have been sufficient to result in open aggression, the combined anger which results from several recent frustrations may well be intense enough to give rise to overt aggressive behavior. Closely related to these circumstances, but even more likely to result in open aggression, given the same time limits (i.e., a fairly restricted time period), are those situations where a purposive response meets with frustration, as do all other nonaggressive responses which are substituted for it. The probability of overt aggression in these circumstances is heightened not only by summated anger but also by the proven inability of nonaggressive responses to remove the obstacle and achieve goal attainment (Berkowitz, 1962; Miller, 1941). One family member's repeated frustration of another's responses has a very good likelihood of stimulating open attacks, especially if the frustrations are viewed as unjust or arbitrary (Baron, 1977).

The instigational potential family members have for one another is also influenced by their special knowledge. Simply stated, intimates possess the information which enables them to hurt one another seriously, and if they exploit this resource to "get" their partner, their chances of success are high. They know their partner's (or sibling's, etc.) sensitivities, shortcomings, and vulnerabilities (Gelles, 1974). Focusing on these features knowingly causes pain and therefore unequivocally establishes one's aggressive intent. Revealing the same confidential information in public should be even more provocative because it also violates the partner's trust (Hotaling, 1980). The knowledge of what hurts and the willingness to use it, especially in the presence of others, gives an intimate great provocative capacity.

To recapitulate, family members have the capacity to block strongly held expectations, to interfere with a wide range of behaviors, and to do so repeatedly. They additionally know what is especially painful to other members. They can be very frustrating and can cause intense pain—they can arouse intense instigation to aggressive behavior.[4]

VICTIM'S PAIN CUES AND
THE ATTACKER'S BEHAVIOR

Aggressive behavior is determined not only by instigational and inhibitory forces but also by its consequences. For present purposes, the victim's signs of suffering, expressions of injury, or pain cues are the consequences of aggressive responses which are especially important. The significance of these particular response outcomes stems, first, from the seemingly plausible assumption that in many instances of child, wife, and elderly abuse the pain, suffering, and injury experienced by the victim are plainly visible. As argued earlier, in all of these forms of family violence, the victim is often incapable of successfully retaliating or defending himself or herself due to size and/or strength differences. Thus, attacks directed against these targets should frequently result in clearly evident injurious consequences. Somewhat surprisingly for many people, casual observation and more systematic evidence suggest that these consequences sometimes fail to inhibit the attacker's ongoing aggressive behavior and to reduce the likelihood of future similar behaviors (Sebastian, 1979). The other main reason for isolating these specific consequences is a theoretical one which finds the failure of the victim's pain cues to stop an attack anything but surprising. This position essentially asserts that an angry aggressor's attacks are actually stimulated and reinforced *because of,* not in spite of, the victim's pain and suffering (Berkowitz, 1974; Sebastian, 1979). As should be even more evident momentarily, these consequences are indeed theoretically the most appropriate ones on which to focus in view of my concern with hostile aggression.

The basic elements of this theorizing follow. Aversive events, such as frustrations, physical attacks, and verbal insults, consistently arouse anger (Rule & Nesdale, 1976). Once an individual is angered, it is assumed that he or she is primarily and specifically motivated to inflict injury on the person perceived as the source of the anger or other suitable targets (e.g., individuals in some way associated with the original provocateur [Berkowitz, 1970]). The individual is, in other words, motivated to perform hostile aggression. Under such circumstances, signs and/or knowledge of the victim's suffering and pain should indicate some degree of goal attainment. That is, appropriate levels of pain cues from the victim should act as reinforcers for the angry aggressor. As reinforcing stimuli, such cues may therefore stimulate more intense, ongoing aggressive behavior, increase the likelihood that the attacker will perform similar responses in the future, and produce positive affective consequences.

The evidence for these views is mixed, and some reviewers conclude that expressions of injury are not reinforcers for aggression and do not stimulate ongoing aggressive behavior (e.g., Bandura, 1973; Zillman, 1979). Nonetheless, the results from a number of laboratory studies are consistent with the basic ideas presented (Baron, 1979; Feshbach, Stiles, & Bitter, 1967; Hartmann, 1969; Perry & Perry, 1974; Sebastian, 1978; Sebastian, Buttino, Burzynski, & Moore, 1981; Swart & Berkowitz, 1976) and lead me to conclude that pain cues' effects are real, albeit subtle and complex.

For some time these ideas and results have struck me as especially relevant to situations in which there is a marked difference in the aggressive capabilities of the attacker and the victim, such as those forms of family violence chosen for emphasis throughout this chapter. Because injury is especially likely in these attacks and because the noninjurious, instrumental value of such attacks is frequently considerably less than obvious, one is left with the theoretically sensible, yet morally unsettling, inference that the attacks are maintained and perhaps intensified by appropriate levels of pain feedback from the victim. The impact of victim reactions on the attacker's aggression is an important theoretical and practical problem.

SUMMARY AND CONCLUSIONS

Physical aggression is commonplace in the family. My central thesis is that physical aggression among family members is relatively more frequent than other forms of aggression because inhibitions against aggression are weak in the family and because intimates can arouse high levels of instigation to aggression. It was also argued that attacks directed against children, women, and the elderly may be maintained and even intensified by the injury and pain these behaviors cause.

Because in many instances of family violence the victim cannot sensibly be viewed as responsible for the aggressor's anger or attack, the weakness of inhibitions in the home have been emphasized over the instigational potential of intimates. This does not deny that the perpetrators of serious physical aggression against loved ones are not highly angry about something. It is only to assert that often their victims have had little, if anything, to do with its arousal. The weakness, vulnerability, and dependency of the common victims of family violence is one central unifying feature of this analysis. A second is the absence of untoward legal and social consequences for family aggressors who cannot be counted on to regulate their own behavior. The benefits of aggression, including injury of the victim, seem clearly to outweigh its costs. Thus, increasing its costs— legal, social, and psychological—will not eliminate family violence, but such steps should reduce its frequency.

NOTES

1. This position in no way diminishes the importance of studying directly, or even exclusively, physical aggression among family members. The importance of the social unit called the family for societal functioning, as well as the potentially detrimental effects of the physical aggression which occurs in this group, forcefully point to the need for such research. Regardless of the value attached to the family, direct investigations of physical aggression between family members are important because of the frequency with which this kind of aggression occurs.

2. In an unpublished study by the author, college students were asked to report on the physically aggressive conflicts they had with their mothers, fathers, and siblings. In 95 cases the students were asked to report how angry the attacker was in the conflict on a 7-point scale, with 1 representing "not at all," 4 "moderately," and 7 "extremely." In every one of these cases the attacker was said to be angry, and the overall mean for these 95 cases was 5.76. These data strongly suggest that angry or hostile aggression is common in the family.

3. This reasoning implies that family members relative to outsiders may have lost their ability to control other family members' inappropriate behavior. This can result for at least two reasons: (1) the approval, acceptance, and esteem of family members are completely taken for granted or simply don't matter any longer; and (2) the attacker (accurately) assumes that the disapproval of a family member will not result in a call to the police, an assumption not as casually made for outsiders. Such questions as which family members have control over others and why are in turn raised by these notions.

4. The instigational notions that have been presented may be especially relevant for "normal" aggression—noncyclical attacks which do not invariably result in serious injury and for which the intensity of the attack is roughly proportional to the intensity of the provocation from the victim. The instigational notions probably have little to do with highly abusive attacks, such as those that occur during phase 2 in Walker's (1979) cycle of violence theory. In these instances there is often no provocation from the victim, and any provocation there might be in no way should instigate an attack of the intensity of the one that occurs. The instigation comes predominantly from intrapersonal sources and other sources external to the familial relationship.

REFERENCES

Aronson, E., & Linder, D. Gain and loss of esteem as determinants of interpersonal attractiveness. *Journal of Experimental Social Psychology*, 1965, *1*, 156-171.

Bandura, A. *Aggression: A social learning analysis.* Englewood Cliffs, NJ: Prentice-Hall, 1973.

Baron, R. A. Aggression as a function of audience presence and prior anger arousal. *Journal of Experimental Social Psychology*, 1971, *7*, 515-523.

Baron, R. A. *Human aggression.* New York: Plenum, 1977.

Baron, R. A. Effects of victim's pain cues, victim's race, and level of prior instigation upon physical aggression. *Journal of Applied Social Psychology*, 1979, *9*, 103-114.

Berkowitz, L. Repeated frustrations and expectations in hostility arousal. *Journal of Abnormal and Social Psychology*, 1960, *60*, 422-429. (a)

Berkowitz, L. The judgmental process in personality functioning. *Psychological Review*, 1960, *67*, 130-142. (b)

Berkowitz, L. *Aggression: A social psychological analysis.* New York: McGraw-Hill, 1962.

Berkowitz, L. The contagion of violence: An S-R mediational analysis of some effects of observed aggression. In W. J. Arnold & M. M. Page (Eds.), *Nebraska Symposium on Motivation* (Vol. 18). Lincoln: University of Nebraska Press, 1970.

Berkowitz, L. Some determinants of impulsive aggression: Role of mediated associations with reinforcements for aggression. *Psychological Review*, 1974, *81*, 165-176.

Berkowitz, L., & Frodi, A. Reactions to a child's mistakes as affected by his/her looks and speech. *Social Psychology Quarterly*, 1979, *42*, 420-425.

Berscheid, E., & Walster, E. H. *Interpersonal attraction* (2nd ed.). Reading, MA: Addison-Wesley, 1978.

Borden, R. J. Witnessed aggression: Influence of an observer's sex and values on aggressive responding. *Journal of Personality and Social Psychology*, 1975, *31*, 567-573.

Buss, A. H. Aggression pays. In J. L. Singer (Ed.), *The control of aggression and violence.* New York: Academic Press, 1971.

Dollard, J., Doob, L. W., Miller, N. E., Mowrer, O. H., & Sears, R. R. *Frustration and aggression.* New Haven, CT: Yale University Press, 1939.

Feshbach, S., Stiles, W. B., & Bitter, E. The reinforcing effect of witnessing aggression. *Journal of Experimental Research in Personality*, 1967, *2*, 281-292.

Gelles, R. J. *The violent home.* Beverly Hills, CA: Sage, 1974.

Gelles, R. J. Abused wives: Why do they stay? *Journal of Marriage and the Family*, 1976, *38*, 659-668.

Gelles, R. J., & Straus, M. A. Determinants of violence in the family: Toward a theoretical integration. In W. R. Burr, R. Hill, F. I. Nye, & I. L. Reiss (Eds.),

Contemporary theories about the family. New York: Free Press, 1979.

Gil, D. G. *Violence against children.* Cambridge, MA: Harvard University Press, 1971.

Goldstein, J. H. *Aggression and crimes of violence.* New York: Oxford University Press, 1975.

Hartmann, D. P. Influence of symbolically modeled instrumental aggression and pain cues on aggressive behavior. *Journal of Personality and Social Psychology,* 1969, *11,* 280-288.

Holmes, D. S., & Berkowitz, L. Some contrast effects in social perception. *Journal of Abnormal and Social Psychology,* 1961, *62,* 150-152.

Hotaling, G. T. Attribution processes in husband-wife violence. In M. A. Straus & G. T. Hotaling (Eds.), *The social causes of husband-wife violence.* Minneapolis: University of Minnesota Press, 1980.

Kalmuss, D. S., & Straus, M. A. Wives' marital dependency and wife abuse. *Journal of Marriage and the Family,* in press.

Lerman, L. G. Criminal prosecution of wife beaters. *Response,* 1981, *4*(3), 1-4.

Megargee, E. I., & Hokanson, J. E. (Eds.). *The dynamics of aggression.* New York: Harper & Row, 1970.

Miller, N. E. The frustration-aggression hypothesis. *Psychological Review,* 1941, *48,* 337-342.

National Study of the Incidence and Severity of Child Abuse and Neglect. Washington, DC: U.S. Department of Health & Human Services, 1981.

Parke, R. D., & Collmer, C. W. Child abuse: An interdisciplinary analysis. In E. M. Hetherington (Ed.), *Review of child development research* (Vol. 5). Chicago: University of Chicago Press, 1975.

Perry, D. G., & Perry, L. C. Denial of suffering in the victim as a stimulus to violence in aggressive boys. *Child Development,* 1974, *45,* 55-62.

Response, 1980, *3*(12), 1-16.

Richardson, D. C., Bernstein, S., & Taylor, S. P. The effect of situational contingencies on female retaliative behavior. *Journal of Personality and Social Psychology,* 1979, *37,* 2044-2048.

Rule, B. G., & Nesdale, A. R. Emotional arousal and aggressive behavior. *Psychological Bulletin,* 1976, *83,* 851-863.

Sebastian, R. J. Immediate and delayed effects of victim suffering on the attacker's aggression. *Journal of Research in Personality,* 1978, *12,* 312-328.

Sebastian, R. J. The influence of a victim's suffering on an attacker's aggression. *USA Today,* 1979, *108,* 49-52.

Sebastian, R. J., Buttino, A. J., Burzynski, M. H., & Moore, S. Dynamics of hostile aggression: Influence of anger, hurt instructions, and victim pain feedback. *Journal of Research in Personality,* 1981, *15,* 343-358.

Straus, M. A., Gelles, R. J., & Steinmetz, S. K. *Behind closed doors.* Garden City, NY: Doubleday, 1980.

Swart, C., & Berkowitz, L. Effects of a stimulus associated with a victim's pain on later aggression. *Journal of Personality and Social Psychology,* 1976, *33,* 623-631.

Thibaut, J. W., & Kelley, H. H. *The social psychology of groups.* New York: John Wiley, 1959.

Walker, L. E. *The battered woman.* New York: Harper & Row, 1979.

Willerman, L. *The psychology of individual and group differences.* San Francisco: W. H. Freeman, 1979.

World almanac. New York: Newspaper Enterprise Association, 1981.

Zillman, D. *Hostility and aggression.* Hillsdale, NJ: Lawrence Erlbaum, 1979.

SECTION VI

AN APPRAISAL OF CURRENT ISSUES

Many of the chapters in this section are concerned with controversies surrounding the "meaning" of violence and abuse. Researchers made much progress during the 1970s developing nominal definitions of these two terms (Goode, 1971; Gelles & Straus, 1979; Giovannoni & Beccara, 1979), but trying to arrive at a consensus about definitions is only part of the problem. Controversy still exists concerning conceptual distinctions between aspects of both violence and abuse. For example, what are the commonalities and important differences between socially approved and illegitimate violence, between instrumental and expressive violence, or between minor and severe violence?

The first group of studies explores the question, Is it best to assume there are several types of violence, or is violence violence regardless of its perceived legitimacy, severity, or the motives for its use? The answer, in part, depends on whether violence is examined in terms of etiological factors, consequences, or how beliefs about violence affect subsequent behavior.

In "Mutual Combat and Other Family Violence Myths," Berk et al. argue that when physical injuries are one's chief concern in the study of spouse abuse, it is very important to make distinctions among types of violence. Their data show that the violence of men against women is more severe and results in greater physical injury than the violence of women toward men. In terms of physical consequences, violence means something very different for men than women.

Recognizing that there are important differences among forms of violence, Straus, in "Ordinary Violence, Child Abuse, and Wife-Beating: What Do They Have in Common?" argues that in terms of etiological factors, violence is violence. He presents data on 2100 nationally representative families showing that the same factors that explain child abuse and wife-beating also explain ordinary violence and minor violence between spouses. His chapter suggests several theoretical and practical implications of this finding. In "A Hit Is a Hit Is a Hit . . . Or Is It? Approval and Tolerance of the Use of Physical Force by Spouses," Greenblat casts doubt on whether it is necessary to make a conceptual distinction between legitimate and illegitimate forms of spouse abuse. Data from intensive interviews with men and women find *no support* for the existence of a norm approving the use of violence between spouses. This chapter contains an important discussion of norms in terms of approval, toleration, and understanding of violent behavior.

The methodological approach of Greenblat, which attempts to understand the many subtle meanings and interpretations people make of violent behavior, is similar to "The Context-Specific Approach" used by Dobash and Dobash. These authors, through intensively interviewing battered women, try to understand violent behavior in the context of relationships. They focus on the history and backgrounds of men and women in violent relationships, as well as the day-to-day activities that mark their lives. This attention to interactional processes is supplemented by a sensitivity to broader historical processes and institutional practices in the explanation of violence against women. Often these macrosociological processes are difficult to gauge empirically. This is precisely what Yllo tries to do in her chapter, "Using a Feminist Approach in Quantitative Research: A Case Study." She outlines a strategy for operationalizing the term "patriarchy" by using American states as her units of analysis. Her strategy shows that patriarchy can be measured and its variable effect on rates of violence against women can be gauged.

The third group of chapters in this section examines the issue of women and child abuse in different but related ways. Washburne, in "A Feminist Analysis of Child Abuse and Neglect," argues that feminist theory has paid little or no attention to problems in child abuse and neglect, especially findings showing that women are more likely than men to be perpetrators of abuse. She argues for the feasibility and necessity of a feminist analysis of child abuse for the advancement of knowledge about violence toward children. Martin, in "Maternal and Paternal Abuse of Children: Theoretical and Research Perspectives," takes a somewhat different position. The gap she sees in the literature on child abuse is the omission of research on the role of male perpetrators. The almost exclusive research concern with women as abusers is inconsistent with Martin's reading of the evidence that men, not women, are more often the perpetrators of child abuse. Martin would agree with Washburne that a feminist analysis of child abuse is necessary, but she would add that such an analysis should begin by asking why men have been relatively ignored in past analyses.

In the same manner that Martin reexamines the taken-for-granted findings relating to gender and the abuse of children, two authors in this section, writing about the intergenerational transmission of abuse, take a fresh look at what gets transmitted from parent to child. Herzberger, in "A Social Cognitive Approach," contends that the evidence supporting a "violence begets violence" argument is not as strong as past research has led us to believe. She suggests the need for greater attention to the meanings and interpretations people attach to violence in order to understand its long-term effects on personality and behavior. The interpretation children make of parental behavior in general may be an important research focus to account for the intergenerational transmission of violence and abuse. Herronkohl et al., in "Perspectives on the Intergenerational Transmission of Abuse," report the results of a ten-year study of 500 families. Their longitudinal data indicate that severe parental discipline is not as important a factor as parental neglect for the growth of self-esteem in children to account for the use of violence by these children when they reach adulthood.

The last group of chapters deals with social responses to forms of family violence and abuse. They investigate aspects of the interpretations professional and policy groups make of family violence and how such interpretations affect their behavior. Stark and Flitcraft, in "Social Knowledge, Social Therapy, and the Abuse of Women: The Case Against Patriarchal Benevolence," argue that the response of medical personnel to battered women is to "reconstitute" the problem of battering into a set of problems consistent with medical and psychiatric ideology. According to Stark and Flitcraft, medical attention focuses on problems that are the result of abuse and selectively ignore the real problem: the violence of men toward women.

O'Toole and Turbett, in "Theories, Professional Knowledge, and Diagnosis of Child Abuse," use an experimental design to investigate the process through which child abuse is labeled by medical professionals. A key issue in Chapter 22 is how knowledgeable medical personnel are about family violence and the extent to which it affects their diagnostic behavior.

Existing services and professional groups may not be as responsive to victims of wife abuse as are services and groups specific to child abuse. The current political and economic climate makes it increasingly difficult for such services to come into being. Kalmuss and Straus, in the final chapter in this section, "Feminist, Political, and Economic Determinants of Wife Abuse Services," use state-level data to investigate what factors account for the greater success in some American states in providing services to one group of victims of family violence: abused women.

REFERENCES

Gelles, R. J., & Straus, M. A. Determinants of violence in the family: Toward a theoretical integration." In W. R. Burr, R. Hill, F. I. Nye, & I. Reiss (Eds.), *Contemporary theories about the family* (Vol. 1). New York: Free Press, 1979.

Giovannoni, J. M., & Beccara, R. M. *Defining child abuse.* New York: Free Press, 1979.

Goode, W. J. Force and violence in the family. *Journal of Marriage and the Family,* 1971, *33,* 624-636.

12

Mutual Combat and Other
Family Violence Myths

RICHARD A. BERK, SARAH FENSTERMAKER BERK,
DONILEEN R. LOSEKE, and DAVID RAUMA

While it is widely acknowledged that spouse abuse is a problem of significant proportion (e.g., U.S. Department of Justice, Bureau of Justice Statistics, 1980), there is lively debate over the appropriate conceptual framework. Some observers place spousal violence within the broader context of male domination (e.g., Hamilton, 1977; Walker, 1979; Martin, 1979); the violence is fundamentally "about" the systematic subjugation of women. Patriarchal ideology and institutions allow men to use force as an instrument of control with but occasional reprimands for particular individuals who show excessive zeal. From this "wife battery" perspective, it is not surprising that attention centers heavily on the consequences of the violent acts and especially the injuries women receive. Others emphasize that husbands, too, are commonly assaulted (Steinmetz, 1977-78) and inquire "how and why women participate in their own victimization" (Straus, 1980, p. 691). Under a rubric of family violence, "mutual combat" becomes a unifying theme. The problem, then, is not violent men, but violent people.

Authors' Note: *Support for this research was provided by the Center for the Study of Crime and Delinquency of the National Institute of Mental Health (Grant No. 34616-010). Thanks go to Nancy Blum and Christopher Sproul for their assistance and to Trina Marks Miller for clerical help. Ann Witte provided a number of helpful suggestions on an earlier draft. The authors are listed in alphabetical order to denote equal contributions.*

Just as in most academic disputes, part of the disagreement reflects differences in emphasis. All reasonable parties would agree, for example, that women sometimes *do* contribute in a nontrivial fashion to confrontations from which they ultimately suffer. However, it does not necessarily follow that the distinction between offender and victim is meaningless, or that there are not important gender differences in motives, tactics, and consequences. Likewise, few would claim that in the usual head-to-head household brawl, the two combatants are equally matched. Yet, compassion for the victim should not preclude the study of potential provocation.

More generally, there is considerable ambiguity in the spouse abuse literature about what kinds of behavior should be the subject of inquiry. For example, there is no inevitable correspondence between "conflict tactics" (e.g., Straus, 1980) and the consequences of the "conflict," and likewise no inevitable correspondence between them and the processes by which a violent episode unfolds. The relations between these and other dimensions of spouse abuse are empirical questions, leaving open the possibility that several different kinds of spousal violence may well exist.

In this spirit, we focus here on the injuries that can result from spouse abuse and, in particular, explore the relative merits of the "wife battery" and "mutual combat" perspectives. Using data from 262 incidents of "domestic disturbance" in Santa Barbara County, California, we build and estimate a two-equation, nonrecursive model of mutual combat with injuries as the outcome of interest. One equation represents the causes of injuries to the woman, and the second equation represents the causes of injuries to the man. Within this causal structure, the injuries to either party are reciprocally related. The strength of these reciprocal effects provide one assessment of the two conceptual approaches.

DATA, MODEL SPECIFICATION, AND STATISTICAL ISSUES

Data

Our data derive from 262 "domestic disturbance" incidents in which police were called and which involved an adult man and an adult woman linked in an ongoing "romantic" relationship.[1] The primary source material included reports filed by the investigating police officers, coupled with supplemental documentation gathered by the district attorney's office. Virtually all information of possible relevance was coded: who called the police, the ages of the participants, prior criminal records, and the like. While there are no doubt important factors for which no information was available, a rich array of potential variables was nevertheless obtained.

For males, there were very few instances in which the police recorded any injuries, and descriptions were typically brief. Therefore, for the male's injuries we will consider only whether or not an injury occurred (i.e., as a dummy variable). For females, there was a far larger number of instances in which injuries were recorded and greater detail about their nature. Consequently, it was possible to evaluate the "severity" of injuries on an 8-point scale, as follows:

0 = no injuries
1 = bruises or cuts or abrasions of a superficial nature (only one type of injury)
2 = some combination of the injuries in 1
3 = 1 or 2 but *not* superficial
4 = broken bones, broken teeth, and/or injury to sense organs (e.g., eyes)
5 = internal injuries and/or concussion
6 = some combination of 3, 4, and 5
7 = high anchor point

The severity scale ranges from no injuries to rather severe injuries for which medical attention would normally be required, but necessarily neglects injuries *not* noted by either police officers or staff from the prosecutor's office. Thus, bruises hidden by clothing, for example, might well be overlooked; we are no doubt underestimating the incidence of at least less serious injuries.

Three of the authors independently scored the documentation on injuries. Intercoder correlations on the severity scale were all well above .90, indicating that the reliability of the coding process was quite high. On the other hand, the precise relationship between the scale and "real" severity, while almost surely substantial and positive, is unknown.

Table 12.1 shows the substantive variables to be used in the analyses and some selected descriptive statistics. At this point, the major question is whether any troubling anomalies have surfaced. Comparing the proportions of injured women and men, Table 12.1 indicates that our data reproduce the common finding that women suffer far more than men from the physical consequences of spousal violence. In particular, while 43% of the women in our sample are reported to have been injured, only 7% of the men are reported to have been injured.[2] When our data on injuries are rearranged to focus solely on *incidents in which injuries are reported,* women are victims 94% of the time compared to 14% of the time for men (allowing for incidents in which both are injured). Moreover, data from the National Crime Survey, collected from a nationally representative sample of households, indicate that for incidents defined much like ours (i.e., between "spouses and ex-spouses"), *when a victimization occurs,* 95% of the time it is the woman who suffers. In only 5% of the incidents is the man victimized (U.S. Department of Justice, Bureau of Justice Statistics, 1980, p. 44). Clearly, the "victimization" rates derived from our data

TABLE 12.1   Selected Descriptive Statistics

(N = 262)

Variable	Mean	Standard Deviation	Minimum	Maximum
Severity of female's injuries	0.97	1.25	0	5
Whether female alone is injured (binary)	0.39	0.49	0	1
Whether male alone is injured (binary)	0.03	0.16	0	1
Whether both female and male are injured (binary)	0.04	0.19	0	1
Whether male drinking (binary)	0.18	0.39	0	1
Whether female drinking (binary)	0.05	0.21	0	1
Male's # alcohol priors	0.27	0.97	0	8
Male's # person crime priors	0.09	0.63	0	8
Male's # spouse/child abuse priors	0.07	0.37	0	3
Share same household (binary)	0.59	0.49	0	1
Divorced or separated (binary)	0.22	0.42	0	1
Property damage (binary)	0.14	0.36	0	1
Male under restraining order (binary)	0.03	0.17	0	1
Male abusive to police (four levels)	0.06	0.38	0	3
Female's age (years)	31.18	11.78	17	82
Male's age (years)	33.33	10.44	18	85
Ratio of male's age to female's age	1.07	0.15	0.75	1.50
White male (binary)	0.45	0.50	0	1
White male – Hispanic female (binary)	0.01	0.11	0	1
More than two people involved (binary)	0.18	0.38	0	1

compare quite favorably to the victimization rates drawn from the National Crime Survey, despite some disparities in the relevant definitions. And it cannot be overemphasized that the national data are not subject to the reporting biases inherent in incidents coming to the attention of the criminal justice system.[3]

Model Specification

We began with a two-equation, nonrecursive model in which the severity of the female's injuries and the presence or absence of the male's injuries were the two endogenous variables. If particular incidents can be properly characterized as mutual combat, these two outcomes should be positively related, other things being equal. Note, however, that we are using the term "mutual combat" to refer to a given incident and not a temporal series of incidents in which first one party and then the other is injured (see Straus, 1980). With this in mind, should there prove to be no relationship between the two injury variables, one formulation of the mutual combat model (i.e., for a given incident) becomes implausible and either a "Battered Wife Syndrome" *or* a "Battered Husband Syndrome" may surface.

Exogenous variables are of six broad kinds. First, two variables are meant to capture a male's tendency to dominate the relationship; we included the ratio of the male's age to the female's age and a dummy variable for households in which the male was white and the female was of Hispanic descent. (There were virtually no blacks in the sample.) For both, we anticipated that males would, on social status grounds alone, be more likely to dominate in such relationships. That is, disparities in age or ethnic status that favored the male would tend to make him more dominant. Unfortunately, it was unclear a priori whether households with more dominant males would experience more or less violence. On one hand, higher-status males might already be fully in control and have no need to employ violence. On the other hand, inequities in status might be an irritant and lead to more violent disputes. Regardless, the use of a dummy variable for households with a white male and a Hispanic female required that we control for the main effect of race. Thus, we also included a dummy variable for whether the man was white. Because of collinearity, we could not include a dummy variable for whether the woman was Hispanic. Similarly, the ages of the participants were introduced to control for any effects beyond those of the age ratio.

Second, we included two dummy variables to capture something of the relationship between the man and the woman. One dummy variable indicated whether the two parties were divorced *or* separated, while a second dummy variable indicated whether they were living under the same roof. Since some have claimed that a "marriage license is a hitting license" (Straus, Gelles, & Steinmetz, 1980), we expected that injuries to both participants would be more likely and more serious when the couple was not divorced or separated. We also anticipated more serious injuries and a greater likelihood of injuries when the couple was sharing the same residence, if for no other reason than "time at risk" is greater.

Third, we introduced a number of variables representing the environment in which the domestic disturbance occurred. We have two dummy variables for whether the male and/or the female had been drinking when the police arrived, anticipating that perhaps through reduced inhibitions there would be a greater likelihood of injuries. In addition, we included a dummy variable for whether the police recorded any property damage associated with the disturbance. Property damage was to be an indicator of a particularly active incident and of an enhanced probability of injuries (and serious injuries). We also employed a variable for the male's behavior toward the police, capturing four levels of hostility: no abuse, verbal abuse, physical abuse, and both physical and verbal abuse (there was no instance of a woman abusing the police). In essence, we were allowing for some of the injuries to males to be a result of confrontations with police officers; such injuries were not explicitly designated in the primary source documents. Finally, we included a dummy variable for the presence of other people at the scene. We believed that additional people would inhibit potential violence, perhaps through their role as potential witnesses, or perhaps as reminders of social convention.

Fourth, we considered several variables capturing important biographical characteristics of the participants. Perhaps most important, for the males we included from police records the number of prior charges for alcohol abuse, the number of prior charges for wife and/or child abuse (these were not distinguished in the primary source documents), and the number of prior charges for other "person" crimes. The latter two were thought to tap a proclivity to violence and therefore to be predictors of the seriousness of the female's injuries. The role of the number of alcohol priors was less clear. However, from impressionistic accounts (e.g., McNulty, 1980), we anticipated a positive relationship between problem drinking and the seriousness of the woman's injuries. In any case, we would have included similar measures on the females, but virtually none was reported to have a prior record (primarily because record checks were not done on victims).

Fifth, many have argued that family violence can be reduced by placing prospective offenders under court order prohibiting any contact with potential victims (e.g., Paterson, 1979; Walker, 1979). While only a few of our males (and none of our females) were under restraining orders, we included the appropriate dummy variable to determine if the female's injuries were reduced.[4]

Finally, the data were organized with the incident as the unit of analysis. Nine couples had more than one police contact, and we included a dummy variable for each of these nine couples. We expected to find a greater likelihood of injuries and more serious injuries among these couples on probabilistic grounds alone; with a greater number of disturbances, there is a greater opportunity for injury. We also suspected that such couples might more readily resort to serious violence to resolve disputes.

It should be readily apparent that a number of other variables of potential importance were not available: factors which contribute to a couple's financial stress (e.g., unemployment), drug abuse, views on the nature of marriage, and the like. Clearly, the analyses to follow are subject to specification errors. At this point, our major rejoinder is that no one has yet directly and systematically tried to explain injuries that result from spousal violence, and even data of modest quality are better than no data at all. We are just beginning to collect new data sets that will in the future allow us to specify more compelling models.[5]

Some Statistical Complications

There are two major econometric problems with the model proposed. First, the severity measure is truncated at zero. Truncated variables are known to yield biased and inconsistent estimates when the usual least squares procedures are applied (e.g., Stromsdorfer & Farkus, 1980, pp. 32-41). Second, because the equation for males rests on a dummy endogenous variable, the usual least squares procedures are vulnerable to a number of difficulties, including inefficiency and biased (and inconsistent) estimates of the standard errors (see, for example, Hanushek & Jackson, 1977, pp. 180-187).

Since both problems exist within our simultaneous equation system, there is no straightforward way in which to proceed. On theoretical grounds at least, we could not effectively use Heckman-like approaches (Heckman, 1979; Olsen, 1980; Ray, Berk, & Bielby, 1981) for the truncation problem because the truncation resulted from "explicit selection" (Goldberger, 1981, pp. 361-363). That is, the severity of injuries must exceed some threshold before the police record that any injuries resulted, and it is also the police who document the severity of the injuries. Heckman-like approaches rest on "incidental selection" (Goldberger, 1981, pp. 363-365) which implies a very different substantive process. Therefore, we employed three alternative strategies. First, we used the square root of the severity index, which at the very least allowed us to fit a functional form that seemed more consistent with the truncated scatter plot (compared to the linear plot). Second, we redefined the severity index as a dummy variable: injured or not. This eliminated the truncation problem at the price of nonnormal and heteroskedastic residuals. Finally, with considerable empirical justification, we focused solely on the equation for the severity of the female's injuries and applied a convenient approximation of MLE Tobit estimation procedures (Greene, 1981a, 1981b). By and large, the story was unchanged under these different formulations.

For the male equation, we supplemented the least squares procedures with logit techniques (solely for that equation). Again, the story did not change significantly. Thus, the least squares procedures do not seem to be leading us astray. In summary, while there are no doubt statistical problems with the least squares procedures whose results we will report, these problems do not seem to have important substantive implications.

One might also be a bit uneasy with the fact that nine couples appear twice in the sample and that correlated residuals can result. However, since only nine observations are affected, the impact of the correlated residuals (even if they existed) is likely to be very small. Indeed, we deleted the redundant cases from the sample and reestimated the two-equation model; very little changed. Once again, statistical problems in principle did not appear to create substantive problems in fact.

Finally, we are proceeding as if our injuries scale has equal interval properties. Technically, of course, the scale is only ordinal, but its departures from a true equal interval scale are probably not serious. Moreover, as noted above, various transformations of the scale lead to very similar results.

FINDINGS

Before turning to the simultaneous equation results, there are several important findings that can be gleaned from Table 12.1. Note that in only 4% of the incidents are both parties injured. Thus, if there is any validity to the mutual combat perspective (for given incidents), it is relevant to a tiny fraction of the cases; there is no evidence that spouses "exchange" injuries in any but a small proportion of the disturbances.

If spouses do not exchange injuries, who is likely to be the victim? From Table 12.1 it is apparent that the woman is far more likely to be injured than the man. In 39% of the cases, the woman alone is injured, while in only 3% of the cases is the man alone injured. This implies that if there is anything to the battered husband syndrome, it either has nothing to do with injuries or is relevant to very few couples.

Table 12.2 shows the simultaneous equation results for the three-stage least squares estimates. (The story is almost the same for two-stage least squares results, and we saw no reason not to capitalize on the greater efficiency of three-stage least squares).[6] Focusing first on the equation for whether the male was injured, the results are disappointing. Only one variable is statistically significant (at the .05 level); males who are abusive to the police face as much as a .33 greater probability of injuries. While this is consistent with our expectations, caution is required. To begin, given the large number of variables in the equation, chances are excellent that the significant t-value reflects nothing more than Type I error. In addition, very few males were at all abusive to police, so it is difficult to argue that we are capturing a widespread phenomenon. Finally, the least squares equation is no doubt seriously undermined by an endogenous variable that is almost a constant: There is virtually no variance to explain.

TABLE 12.2   Three-Stage Least Squares Estimates for the Two-Equation Model of Injuries

Variable	Male's Injuries Metric Coefficient	Male's Injuries t-value	Female's Injuries Metric Coefficient	Female's Injuries t-value
Intercept	0.28	1.55	0.97	1.34
Male drinking (binary)	−0.02	−0.49	0.09	0.46
Female drinking (binary)	−0.09	−1.21	0.19	0.53
Male's # alcohol priors	b	b	0.13	1.47 (1.91**)[a]
Male's # person crime priors	b	b	0.13	1.01
Male's # spouse/child abuse priors	b	b	0.27	1.19
Share household (binary)	0.05	1.15	0.14	0.69
Divorced or separated (binary)	−0.05	−0.79	−0.45	−1.98**
Property damage (binary)	0.02	0.05	−0.11	−0.48
Restraining order (binary)	−0.03	−0.26	0.33	0.67
Male abuse of police (four levels)	0.11	2.28*	b	b
Female's age (years)	−0.00+	−1.15	b	b
Male's age (years)	b	b	−0.00+	−0.92
Male's age/female's age	−0.11	−0.95	−0.07	−0.13
White male (binary)	−0.02	−0.55	0.34	2.08**
White male − Hispanic female (binary)	0.05	0.20	2.13	3.59**
More than two people involved (binary)	−0.00+	−0.16	−0.28	−1.46 (−1.64*)[a]
Repeater Couple 1 (binary)	−0.10	−0.37	−0.64	−0.55
Repeater Couple 2 (binary)	0.03	0.12	2.13	2.50**
Repeater Couple 3 (binary)	−0.11	−0.53	−0.74	−0.87
Repeater Couple 4 (binary)	−0.09	−0.45	0.55	0.63
Repeater Couple 5 (binary)	−0.05	−0.17	1.15	0.98
Repeater Couple 6 (binary)	0.23	1.34	−1.25	−1.48
Repeater Couple 7 (binary)	−0.00+	−0.04	0.83	1.20
Repeater Couple 8 (binary)	−0.00+	−0.04	−0.12	−0.12
Repeater Couple 9 (binary)	0.03	0.15	0.68	0.81
Instrument for severity of females injuries	−0.04	−0.56	b	b
Instrument for severity of male's injuries	b	b	1.62	0.85

$$r_{u_1 u_2} = .12$$

a. t-value for square root of severity index.
b. Coefficient constrained to zero.
 * t-value < .05 for a one-tailed test.
** t-value < .05 for a two-tailed test.

Table 12.2 indicates that we are far more successful explaining the severity of the female's injuries. First, there is some evidence that the man's number of prior charges for alcohol abuse affects how seriously the woman is injured. While the t-value for the linear form of the severity index is only 1.47, the t-value for the square root form is 1.91. Thus, we are inclined to interpret the regression coefficient of .13. This means that for the full range of the number of alcohol priors (0-8), an overall impact of one unit results on the severity index. Since there are meaningful differences in each level of the index, the impact of the number of alcohol priors is nontrivial.

Unfortunately, whether a number of alcohol priors appears on the primary source documents may significantly depend on whether criminal justice personnel bothered to check the offender's record. Perhaps they undertake a search only when the victim is seriously injured. However, the t-values for the number of person crime priors and the number of spouse/child abuse priors[7] hover around 1.0 (in both the linear and square root forms of the severity index). If the alcohol effect were solely a function of the decision to undertake a record search, one should find statistically significant effects here as well. Therefore, there may well be something to the role of problem drinking.

While a history of problems with alcohol seems to affect the severity of the female's injuries, whether (according to the police) either party had been drinking at the time of the disturbance has no impact. Both t-values are well under 1.0; even under the most generous definitions of statistical significance, both effects cannot be distinguished from chance. (There is no evidence that the null findings result from multicollinearity.) While a *history* of problems with alcohol affects the severity of the female's injuries, *drinking associated with the incident proves unimportant.* Whatever the disinhibiting impact of alcohol, it does not seem to trigger more serious incidents. More generally, one might argue that "unhappy" men can become problem drinkers and "unhappy" men may inflict more serious injuries in incidents of spousal violence, but drinking is not an immediate and direct cause of those injuries. This serves to underscore Gelles's observation (1979, p. 173): "thus, the commonly assumed association between alcohol and violence tends to be spurious."[8]

Our efforts to explore the role of dominance in the male-female relationship brings mixed results. The ratio of the male's age to the female's age has virtually no impact, and the male's age by itself does no better.[9] In contrast, we find a very large impact for Hispanic women linked to white men; women in these kinds of relationships experience far more serious injuries. The t-value is 3.59 and the regression coefficient is 2.13. In other words, such women have injuries that are over two units more serious. Moreover, white males are likely to inflict more serious injuries regardless of the ethnic background of the females with whom they have a relationship. The t-value is 2.08, and the regression coefficient is .34. These two effects are not a collinearity artifact, since each remains statistically significant when the other variable is dropped from the equation (Belsley, Kuh, & Welsch, 1980). White men appear to be more brutal, especially if they have the opportunity to victimize a Hispanic woman.[10] This implies that male dominance *increases* violence.

We also find some support for the notion that a marriage license is a hitting license. Holding constant whether the two parties share the same residence (which has no effect itself), couples who are divorced or separated are less likely to be violent; the woman's injuries are less serious (by .45 units). When injuries are used as the outcome of interest, a marriage license is a hitting license *but for men only*. Unfortunately, even if one accepts this finding, the underlying mechanisms are unclear. First, the dummy variable captures the effect of marriages that have either been ended or are in substantial jeopardy. Second, separated couples are still legally married and therefore more than the legal status of marriage is implicated. Future research will have to look closely at the role of marital status, with careful attention to the distinction between legal and behavioral definitions of marriage.

There is also a hint in Table 12.2 that the female's injuries are less serious when others are involved in the domestic disturbance. Using the linear form of the severity index, the t-value is only 1.46, but in the square root form, the t-value increases to 1.64 (statistically significant at the .05 level for a one-tail test). While the regression coefficient is rather small, the negative sign is consistent with our expectations. Perhaps the presence of "observers" does serve as a deterrent.

The rest of the story from Table 12.2 derives primarily from null findings. To begin, while the female in "repeater" couple 2 is more seriously injured, there is certainly no overall tendency for men in repeater couples to inflict more severe injuries. Yet, it is probably unwise to make too much of this finding, since countervailing forces may be at work. In particular, while repeater couples may have greater proclivities to violence, they may also have had greater contact with the criminal justice system; their behavior may be shaped partly by the deterrent potential of arrest, prosecution, and incarceration.

We also find no effect for temporary restraining orders—if anything, the impact is positive. Yet, before one dismisses the deterrent potential of judicial intervention, it is important to note that our statistical controls for the violent potential of men under restraining orders are at best imperfect. Presumably, restraining orders are applied to men with violent histories and to men with a greater likelihood of inflicting serious injuries. To the degree that we have failed to control for such tendencies (primarily through prior police record), we may be substantially underestimating the value of restraining orders. Moreover, orders of protection are effective only if potential offenders have reason to believe that the orders will be enforced. And here there are ample grounds for skepticism. Criminal justice officials may, for a variety of reasons, rarely apply appropriate sanctions, and potential victims may be reluctant to report violations until it is too late.

Finally, we find no evidence that when a man is injured, a woman's injuries are more serious. While the regression coefficient is large and in the predicted direction (i.e., 1.62), the t-value is less than 1.0. On the other hand, the descriptive statistics reported in Table 12.1 indicate that the deck is stacked against finding such effects; the variance in whether the man is injured is very small. Moreover, the reduced form equation for the male dummy variable produced an extremely weak instrument. Consequently, the "purged" regressor used in the female's equation has still less variance. With a reduced form R^2 of .08, only 8% of the variable's original variance was effectively transmitted.[11]

Given the overall null findings for the male equation, we were able to explore the impact of a rather different specification. In particular, we dropped the equation for males, and thus reduced the simultaneous equation system to a single equation. This eliminated the need to construct an instrument for the male injury dummy variable, and it also allowed us to apply a close approximation to MLE Tobit procedures designed to address the truncation problem (Greene, 1981a, 1981b). Table 12.3 shows the OLS and corrected results (Tobit approximation), and it is apparent from the corrected equation that while the size of all the regression coefficients approximately doubles, the story does not change dramatically.

First, since there is a certain arbitrariness in our severity index, doubling of the regression coefficients is not nearly as important as doubling in circumstances where the outcome variable has some well-established, conventional meaning. Second, the additional significant t-values for the repeater couples must be treated with caution. The truncation adjustments applied assume that the regressors are drawn from a multivariate normal density, and dummy variables as skewed as these are a very long way from the normal. Note that for our other dummy variables, which are not as skewed, the adjusted t-values are not especially different. Equally important, there are about as many positive as negative t-values of substantial magnitude; there is still no clear pattern for repeater couples. Third, the impact of the male's number of prior convictions for spouse/child abuse is now statistically significant for a one-tailed test, which makes wife abuse appear more like a "normal" crime. Past criminal records predict future criminal activity. Finally, we now find (in both the corrected and uncorrected equations) a large and statistically significant effect for the male's injuries. When the man is injured, the woman's injuries are nearly three units more severe.

TABLE 12.3   Corrected OLS Results for Female Injuries

Variable	OLS Metric Coefficient	t-value	Corrected OLS Metric Coefficient	t-value
Male drinking (binary)	0.09	0.45	0.21	0.44
Female drinking (binary)	0.18	0.52	0.41	0.52
Male's # alcohol priors	0.13	1.45	0.30	1.92*
Male's # person crime priors	0.11	0.94	0.26	0.97
Male's # spouse/child abuse priors	0.27	1.18	0.62	1.70*
Share household (binary)	0.16	0.88	0.38	0.91
Divorced or separated (binary)	−0.46	−2.07**	−1.07	−2.53**
Property damage (binary)	−0.10	−0.44	−0.23	−0.51
Restraining order (binary)	0.32	0.66	0.73	0.79
Male's age (years)	−0.01	−1.12	−0.02	−1.04
Male's age/Female's age	−0.09	−0.18	−0.21	−0.18
White male (binary)	0.33	2.15**	0.77	2.17**
White male − Hispanic female (binary)	2.47	3.64**	5.74	4.49**
More than two people involved (binary)	−0.28	−1.45	−0.64	−1.52
Repeater Couple 1 (binary)	−0.66	−0.57	−1.79	−3.60**
Repeater Couple 2 (binary)	2.11	2.51**	4.91	15.33**
Repeater Couple 3 (binary)	−0.77	−0.93	−1.80	−3.60**
Repeater Couple 4 (binary)	0.52	0.61	1.20	0.59
Repeater Couple 5 (binary)	1.12	0.96	2.60	5.28**
Repeater Couple 6 (binary)	−1.19	−1.73	−2.77	−6.36**
Repeater Couple 7 (binary)	0.81	1.20	1.89	1.35
Repeater Couple 8 (binary)	−0.12	−0.13	−0.28	−0.20
Repeater Couple 9 (binary)	0.67	0.80	1.55	0.86
Male injured (binary)	1.36	4.60**	3.16	6.15**

* t-value < .05 for a one-tailed test.
** t-value < .05 for a two-tailed test.

Still, the causal meaning of the male's injuries is unclear. Perhaps most important, by giving up the simultaneous equation model, we have no information on what causes the male's injuries. On one hand, the woman may first injure the man, who in turn retaliates with a severe beating. And once the beating begins the woman is unable to defend herself effectively. Such a sequence of events would be consistent with our simultaneous equation results *if* we had found a statistically significant effect for the male's injuries in the equation predicting the severity of the female's injuries. On the other hand, a male assailant who has already injured the female may also be more likely to direct hostility toward the police. And then the police may be inclined to use force. That is, the male's injuries come from actions of the police officers. This would be broadly consistent with our simultaneous equation results, but it implies that one should not use the presence or absence of the male's injuries as a cause of the severity of the female's injuries. In any case, given the few instances in which both parties are injured, the potential role of mutual combat in our data is probably moot.[12]

SUMMARY AND CONCLUSIONS

Several findings stand out from the simultaneous equations. First, while men who have a history of problem drinking are more likely to inflict serious injuries, alcohol does not seem to play a direct role in particular battery incidents. In other words, the causal role sometimes attributed to drinking is probably spurious. Second, we find that marriage may well be a hitting license *for men.* Women do not respond to the marriage bond in this fashion. Third, there is some evidence that in households where the man is more dominant, the woman is more likely to face the prospect of serious battery. It seems that white males are more likely to inflict serious injuries, especially if they are married to Hispanic females. Finally, we find no evidence in our data that restraining orders prevent battery. The null finding, however, may have more to do with the reasons why restraining orders are implemented and the ways in which they are enforced than with restraining orders themselves.

Perhaps more important, from our simple descriptive statistics alone it is apparent that when injuries are one's primary concern, the mutual combat characterization of spousal violence is terribly misleading. "Mutual combat" calls up the image of Rocky Balboa and Apollo Creed going 15 rounds to a split decision. Nothing could be further from the truth. It is equally clear that if by the term "battery" one means assault with physical consequences, we can find no substantial evidence for the battered husband syndrome; our data show that it is *women* who are battered. In this context, therefore, terms like "mutual combat" are at best imprecise, and while there are certainly occasional instances of husbands being battered, it is downright pernicious to equate their experiences with those of the enormous number of women who are routinely and severely victimized. In short, our analysis indicates that, at least when injuries are one's primary concern, spousal violence is about the harm that men inflict on women.[13]

NOTES

1. We are referring to ongoing relationships of the "romantic" variety, but also include couples who are divorced or separated.

2. To arrive at these figures, the "both injured" outcome was added to the "female alone" and "male alone" outcomes.

3. It is interesting to note in passing that according to the National Crime Survey, 43% of the time spousal victimizations are not reported to the police, and that the reason cited most often by respondents for failing to report the incident is that family violence is a "private matter" (U.S. Department of Justice, Bureau of Justice Statistics, 1980, p. 38).

4. Of course, the deterrent value of temporary restraining orders depends on whether or not they are enforced. We have no documentation for whether or not they tend to be enforced in Santa Barbara County.

5. One study, funded by NIMH (Grant No. MH34616-01), involves the collection of data on households that have experienced spousal violence, in part to follow how various public agencies, like the criminal justice system, respond. A second study, funded by the National Institute of Justice through the Police Foundation (Grant No. 80-IJ-CX-0042), involves a randomized experiment undertaken in Minneapolis to determine the effectiveness of various police intervention strategies in incidents of spousal violence.

6. On the other hand, given the correlation of .12 between the residuals in the two equations, the gain in efficiency is no doubt quite small. Note also that both equations are overidentified.

7. The number of priors for person crimes and the number of priors for spouse/child abuse are mutually exclusive.

8. Actually, we are taking even a stronger position than does Gelles. Our analysis suggests that drinking is not associated with injuries, even as a self-serving justification.

9. Due to collinearity, we could not include the male's age and female's age in the same equation.

10. Alternative specifications do *not* suggest that Hispanic women are more likely to be seriously injured regardless of the characteristics of males to whom they are attached.

11. Nothing of substantive interest was apparent in the reduced form equations; therefore we have not bothered to report them.

12. In case the reader is curious about the stability of our overall findings under alternative models, the story remains the same under a number of different specifications. In particular, efforts to reduce the collinearity between the two instruments and the other regressors by dropping subsets of exogenous variables did not affect the significant findings in any meaningful way.

13. It is interesting to speculate why Steinmetz and others have arrived at quite different conclusions. First, by ignoring outcomes, Straus's "Conflict Tactics Scales" neglect the injuries that may result. This is fully acknowledged by Straus and his colleagues. Second, what is not considered is that reports of such actions may be subject to systematic biases. *Regardless of whether the husband or wife is reporting,* "violent" actions by wives may be more likely to be remembered (and reported), while the "violent" actions by husbands may be more likely to be forgotten. Aggressive, physical behavior from the wife may be so out of character and so at variance with prevailing gender stereotypes that even mild outbursts are defined as

violence and hence recalled. In contrast, aggressive, physical behavior from a husband may have a far lower probability of being defined as violence and may also be ignored as nothing beyond "ordinary" behavior (see Straus, 1980). In other words, the reporting bias involves two related processes: a gender-related bias in what actions are defined as violent, and a gender-related selective recall of those acts once they are defined as violent. *Both* husbands and wives are subject to these biases.

REFERENCES

Belsley, D. A., Kuh, E., & Welsch, R. E. *Regression diagnostics.* New York: John Wiley, 1980.

Gelles, R. J. *Family violence.* Beverly Hills, CA: Sage, 1979.

Goldberger, A. S. Linear regression after selection. *Journal of Econometrics,* 1981, *15*(2), 357-366.

Greene, W. H. On the asymptotic bias of the ordinary least squares estimator of the Tobit model. *Econometrica,* 1981, *49*(2), 505-514. (a)

Greene, W. H. Computing an asymptotic covariance matrix for a moment estimator of the Tobit model. Working Paper # 242. Ithaca, NY: Department of Economics, Cornell University, 1981. (b)

Hamilton, R. *The liberation of women.* Boston: George Allen & Urwin, 1977.

Hanushek, E. A., & Jackson, J. E. *Statistical methods for social scientists.* New York: Academic Press, 1977.

Heckman, J. J. Sample bias as a specification error. *Econometrica,* 1979, *47*(1), 153-162.

Martin, D. What keeps a woman captive in a violent relationship? The social context of battering." In D. M. Moore (Ed.), *Battered women.* Beverly Hills, CA: Sage, 1979.

McNulty, F. *The burning bed.* New York: Harcourt Brace Jovanovich, 1980.

Olsen, R. J. A least squares correction for selectivity bias. *Econometrica,* 1980, *48*(7), 1815-1820.

Paterson, E. J. How the legal system responds to battered women. In D. M. Moore (Ed.), *Battered women.* Beverly Hills, CA: Sage, 1979.

Ray, S. C., Berk, R. A., & Bielby, W. T. Correcting sample selection bias for a bivariate logistic distribution. Paper presented at the annual meetings of the American Statistical Association, 1980.

Steinmetz, S. K. The battered husband syndrome. *Victimology,* 1977-78, *2*(3-4), 499-509.

Straus, M. A. Victims and aggressors in marital violence. *American Behavioral Scientist,* 1979, *23*(5), 681-704.

Straus, M. A. Measuring intrafamily conflict and violence: The conflict tactics (C.T.) scales. *Journal of Marriage and the Family,* 1980, *41*(1), 75-88.

Straus, M. A., Gelles, R. J., & Steinmetz, S. *Behind closed doors: Violence in the American home.* Garden City, NY: Doubleday, 1980.

Stromsdorfer, E. W., & Farkus, G. (Eds.). *Evaluation studies review annual,* (Vol. 5). Beverly Hills, CA: Sage, 1980.

U.S. Department of Justice, Bureau of Justice Statistics. *Intimate victims: A study of violence among friends and relatives.* Washington, DC: Government Printing Office, 1980.

Walker, L. E. *The battered woman.* New York: Harper & Row, 1979.

13

Ordinary Violence, Child Abuse, and Wife-Beating
What Do They Have in Common?

MURRAY A. STRAUS

From its beginning, the Family Violence Research Program at the University of New Hampshire has operated on the assumption that there are common elements underlying the occurrence of all types of physical violence. This does not deny the importance of the difference between, for example, physical punishment and child abuse, or between throwing something at a husband or wife versus the brutal and often life-threatening assaults that go under the name "wife-beating." Indeed, a major part of an earlier theoretical work on family violence (Gelles & Straus, 1978) is devoted to specifying a number of dimensions on which violence must be classified to avoid confusion and make family violence research cumulative.

There is no contradiction between the idea that all violence has something in common and the idea that there are important differences between various types of violence. Both approaches are necessary to understand this complex phenomenon fully. Whether one focuses on the common elements in all violence or on the unique aspects of a certain type of violence depends on the purpose. For purposes of emergency intervention services, it makes sense to have a special category of "battered women" or "abused children" so that such cases can be given immediate assistance. Or, to take another example, Kalmuss and Straus (1982) found that the more a wife subjectively perceived herself as dependent on her

Author's Note: *I am indebted to Susan Frankel for the computer analysis, and to the members of the Family Violence Research Program 1981 Seminar for comments and suggestions on an earlier draft. The Family Violence Research Program is supported by the University of New Hampshire and by NIMH grants MH27557 and T32 MH15161. A program bibliography and list of available publications are available on request. The codebook and data tape for this study (Straus & Gelles, 1980) may be obtained from the Interuniversity Consortium For Polical and Social Research, University of Michigan.*

husband, the greater the rate of *minor* violence. However, mere subjective dependency apparently is not enough in respect to *severe* violence. Economic dependency much more than psychological dependency keeps a woman in a severely abusive marriage.

On the other hand, as I will try to show in this chapter, there are common elements underlying physical punishment, child abuse, throwing things at a spouse, and wife-beating. This information throws light on the causes of family violence and is information which may also be extremely important for primary prevention.

THEORETICAL AND PRACTICAL IMPORTANCE OF THE ISSUE

The theoretical issue of this chapter is whether child abuse and wife-beating are unique types of violence that require a separate explanatory theory. Or are they simply more extreme aspects of the everyday violence that goes almost unnoticed in American families? More specifically, I have argued that physical punishment trains children in the use of violence— that is, that this most ordinary of ordinary types of family violence is one of the root causes of child abuse and wife-beating (Straus, 1979a, 1979b; Straus, Gelles, & Steinmetz, 1980, chap. 5). This idea is supported by Frude and Goss (1979), who showed that the more the parents in their sample used ordinary physical punishment, the greater the percentage who were worried that they might get carried away to the point of child abuse. The analyses to be reported are intended to determine if there is more direct empirical support for this theory.

Issues of considerable practical importance are at stake. If ordinary physical punishment is, in fact, related to child abuse and wife-beating, it means that to break the cycle of violence from generation to generation, more attention must be paid to helping parents find alternatives to the use of physical punishment.

Of course, many other factors seem to be part the etiology of child abuse and wife-beating, including, for example, a male-dominant balance of power in the family, the level of stress experienced by the family, and the larger pattern of intrafamily violence, such as violence between siblings and violence by women toward their children and their husbands. These are pervasive types of violence. In fact, children are the most violent members of American families. In early childhood, practically all children hit their brothers or sisters. Even among the 15- to 17-year-olds in this study, two-thirds had hit a sibling during a one-year period, and in about a third of the cases, this was a severe assault. In the case of women, well over 90% of mothers use physical punishment; child abuse rates are at least as high as those for men; and assaults on husbands are almost as high as assaults by husbands on wives (Straus, 1980). It seems reasonable to assume that these are also factors which must be included in any consideration of what is necessary to reduce the level of wife-beating.

But what do they have to do with the question of whether ordinary violence has anything in common with child abuse and wife-beating? The link is indirect but important: If the variables listed above are part of an interrelated system of social relationships that includes ordinary physical punishment, violence between siblings, and ordinary marital violence as key elements, then primary prevention efforts aimed at child abuse and wife-beating will probably be ineffective unless all the component elements are addressed.

SAMPLE AND METHOD

Research Design

The strategy used to investigate whether ordinary physical punishment and child abuse share the same etiology, and whether the ordinary pushes, slaps, and shoves which occur between spouses has the same origins as wife-beating, is to compare the correlates of "abusive" violence with the correlates of ordinary violence. If the same set of variables that statistically explain child abuse and wife-beating also explain ordinary physical punishment and minor acts of violence between spouses (such as pushing, shoving, slapping, or throwing things), this will be taken as support for the idea that ordinary violence has much in common with child abuse and wife-beating.

Sample

The data to be reported are from a nationally representative sample of 2143 American families interviewed in 1976. The sample was restricted to husband-wife and heterosexual cohabiting couples. The characteristics of this sample correspond closely to those of American husband-wife households as reported by the Bureau of the Census. Approximately half of these couples had a child aged 3 through 17 living at home. The data on child abuse and violence by children was obtained by a random selection of one child in each family as the "referent child." Additional information on the sampling design and sample characteristics is given in Straus et al. (1980).

Violence Measures

The Conflict Tactics Scale (CTS)

The instrument used to measure intrafamily violence is the Conflict Tactics Scale (Straus, 1979). Previous publications on the CTS distinguished between the "Overall Violence" rate and the "Severe Violence" rate. The Overall Violence rate is the annual incidence rate obtained by counting a person as violent if he or she engaged in *any* of the acts of violence listed in the CTS during the year covered by the survey. The Severe Violence rate, on the other hand, is the measure used to identify cases of child abuse and spouse abuse. It is restricted to assaults which go beyond pushing, slapping, shoving, and throwing things. Using these two measures, support was claimed for the idea that the same set of etiological variables that were found to statistically explain child abuse and wife-beating also account for family-to-family differences in ordinary violence (Straus et al., 1980, p. 208). Due to a methodological error (described below), that claim was unwarranted.

A New Measure: The "Ordinary Violence" Rate

The error just mentioned occurred because we overlooked the fact that the Overall Violence rate is just that—it includes *all* the violent acts in the CTS, whereas for the purposes of comparing ordinary violence and severe violence a different measure is needed. What is needed is a measure that is restricted to the minor acts of violence so common in American families. Consequently, an "Ordinary Violence" index was computed for this study. It identifies respondents who engaged in pushing, slapping, shoving, and throwing things (items k, 1, and m of the CTS) and did *not* engage in any of the more serious acts of violence listed in the CTS. In addition, when parent-to-child violence is being measured, respondents were classified as having used ordinary violence if they reported using physical punishment during the year.[2]

Frequency of Assault

In addition to distinguishing between ordinary violence and severe violence, another refinement is necessary. Most abused children and most of the women who seek assistance at shelters have been *repeatedly* beaten. It is possible that what distinguishes child abuse and wife-beating from ordinary violence is not just the severity of the assault, but the fact that it is a continuing pattern. Consequently, in relation to husband-to-wife violence, I will distinguish between four groups of husbands: (1) those who seriously assaulted their wife three or more times during the year of the survey, (2) those who engaged in such attacks once or twice that year, (3) those who used only ordinary violence as defined above, and (4) the nonviolent. In the case of parent-to-child violence, the same procedure was followed except that for group 3 the classification is based on both the Ordinary Violence index of the CTS described above and on questions which asked how often the respondent and his or her spouse had used physical punishment during the year covered by this survey. Parents who indicated either some act of minor violence in response to the CTS questions or who reported using physical punishment were classified in group 3, provided they did not report any instance of severe violence.

THE "VIOLENCE BEGETS VIOLENCE" THEORY

The idea that child-abusing parents were themselves victims of abuse, and that wife-beating husbands come from violent families, is now widely accepted. Consequently, that is not the main purpose of this section. Rather, the objective is to determine if the links are confined to violence at an equivalent level: Is it only victims or observers of *severe* violence who have elevated rates of child abuse and wife-beating? Or is merely being subjected to ordinary physical punishment or ordinary minor violence between spouses also associated with a greater probability of being a child abuser or wife beater?

Physical Punishment and Violence by Children

The point plotted in the lower left of Figure 13.1 shows that "only" 15% of children whose parents used no physical punishment or other violence during the year covered by this survey repeatedly and severely assaulted a sibling. By contrast, the point plotted at the upper right corner shows that 76% of the children who were repeatedly abused by their parents repeatedly and severely assaulted a sibling.[3] In general, the more violence experienced by the child, the higher the rate at which such children are violent toward a sibling. It does not take being a victim of child abuse to produce an elevated rate of being violent to others. Ordinary physical punishment also "works." In fact, children who experienced only culturally permissible physical punishment frequently and severely assaulted a sibling at almost three times the rate of children who were not physically punished during the year (42 versus 15).

There are, of course, many problems with these data. By itself, Figure 13.1 cannot be taken as strong evidence. For example, the causal direction may be the reverse of that implied above. That is, children who engage in repeated serious assaults on a sibling may evoke repeated extreme measures on the part of parents who have tried everything else to no avail. Whether this is the case or not is best established by detailed case studies.

Another problem is that the association between the self-reported parental violence and the violence reported for their child may reflect a common tendency to view the world in violent terms, rather than a real causal linkage. Detailed case studies, and especially observational studies, could help settle this issue. More can also be done using the data for this sample. For example, an analysis that uses independent variables which do not involve the possibility of reciprocal violence provide a better test of the common etiology theory. Such analyses will be reported later.

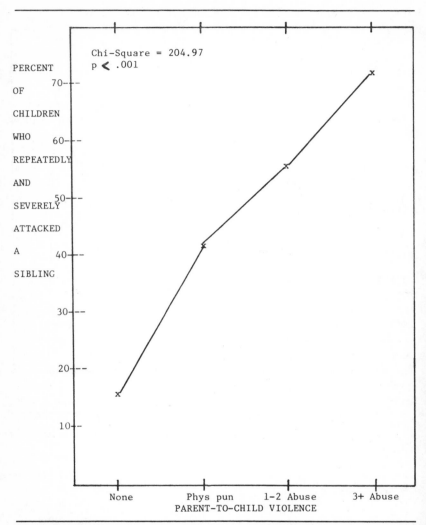

Figure 13.1   Child-to-child violence by parent-to-child violence.

WIFE-BEATING AND CHILD ABUSE

Readers who are not familiar with the base rates for child abuse in previous reports on this research may be startled at the rates in the lower left of Figure 13.2. These show that 7% to 10% of parents who reported *no* instances of marital violence frequently abused their children. However, the issue that Figure 13.2 is designed to investigate is whether the rate of child abuse is even higher in families with ordinary marital violence as well as in families where there was wife-beating.

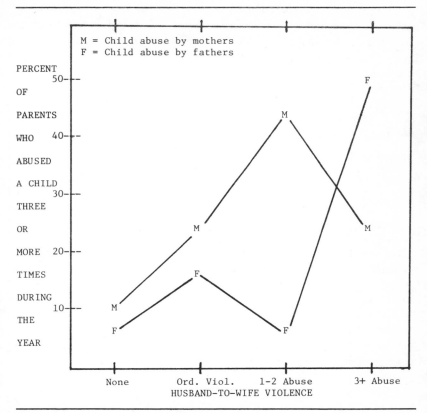

Figure 13.2 Frequent child abuse by husband-to-wife violence.

The answer is "no" for fathers and "yes" for mothers. The data for abuse by fathers (the line of Fs) is contrary to the idea that ordinary violence has the same effect (even though less strongly) as severe violence. Only fathers who frequently abused their wives have elevated rates of frequently abusing their children. For mothers, however, Figure 13.2 shows that the rate of child abuse by those who have been beaten is at least double that of mothers whose husbands did not assault them. Moreover, this is true irrespective of whether the wives were the victims of many severe assaults or only one or two such assaults, or had only been pushed, slapped, or shoved by their husbands.

ANTECEDENTS OF PHYSICAL PUNISHMENT AND CHILD ABUSE

The findings to this point are consistent with the theory that violence in one role is associated with violence in other roles. Furthermore, and most important for the issue of this study, this is true irrespective of whether the violence is within the normal range typical of American society or is more severe. In this section the focus shifts to a more detailed analysis of the etiology of child abuse. Two overlapping analyses will be presented. The first is concerned with whether parents who themselves experienced ordinary nonabusive physical punishment when they were children are more likely to *abuse* a child than others. The second issue is whether the other factors that previous studies have found to be related to child abuse are also related to the use of ordinary physical punishment.

Experience With Physical Punishment and Child Abuse

It is often asserted that abusing parents tend to be people who were themselves abused as children. For the most part, quantitative data demonstrating such an association are lacking. This study also lacks data on whether the parents we interviewed were abused as children. However, we do have data on the extent to which they experienced ordinary physical punishment.[4] Fortunately, this is the critical variable as far as the issue of this chapter is concerned.

The top line of Figure 13.3 shows little or no relationship between the amount of physical punishment experienced by the parents in this sample and using physical punishment on their own children. However, the line labeled A shows that the more parents in this sample were physically punished, the greater the rate of frequently abusing their own child.

These findings seem somewhat odd. Why should experiencing ordinary physical punishment be related to child abuse but not to using ordinary physical punishment? One possibility has to do with the age at which the punishment occurred. Recall data over such a long period are hazardous at best. To minimize this hazard, the physical punishment questions asked how often this happened when the respondent was about 13. However, experiencing physical punishment at age 13 and later might also be an atypical experience, if that is after most parents cease to use this form of discipline. To check on this (at least indirectly), Figure 13.4 indicates the extent to which physical punishment was used by these parents on their own children. It shows that 13 happens to be the age at which a majority (though only a bare majority) stop using physical punishment.

On the other hand, very close to half (49.4%) of children *are* physically punished at age 13. Moreover, a generation or more ago, when these parents were children, physical punishment was probably more widely used than it is today (Bronfenbrenner, 1958; Miller & Swanson, 1958). So they might actually have been part of the majority at that time. Given these pros and cons, it is obvious that additional research will be needed to determine whether experiencing physical punishment does increase the

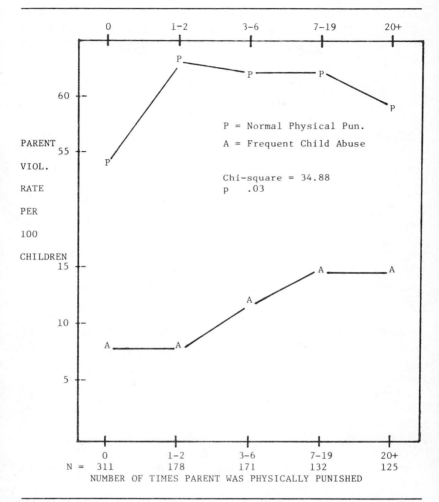

Figure 13.3 Parental violence by amount of physical punishment experienced at about age 13.

probability of abusing one's own children, and if so, what the thresholds are in respect to the amount of physical punishment and whether this applies to children of all ages. Unfortunately, that research will be a long time in coming because a longitudinal study is needed to even approach a reasonably firm answer to these important questions.

Other Factors Associated With Child Abuse

Previous analyses of these data identified a large number of individual and family characteristics that are associated with child abuse. Physical

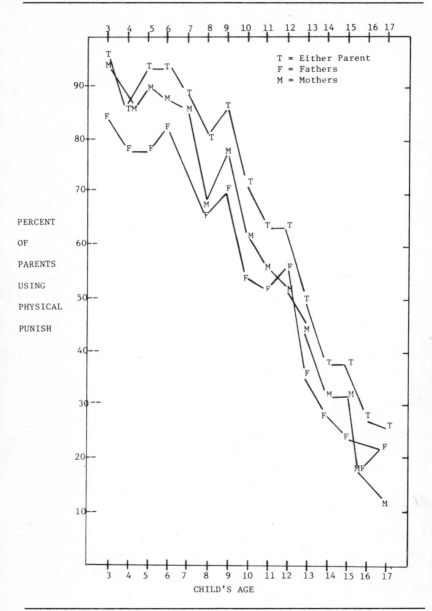

Figure 13.4 Percentage of children physically punished, by age of child and sex of parent.

punishment as a child was one of these. The data on that variable were described in detail in the previous section. Within the limited space of this chapter it is not practical to do this for each of the other variables separately. Instead, a "Child Abuse Checklist" was used to summarize the combined effect of these variables. It consists of 16 variables found to have a statistically significant and nonoverlapping relationship to child abuse.[5] Since these variables were selected long before this study was written, and solely using the criterion of their association with child abuse, they can be considered a reasonable sample of factors associated with child abuse. The question is, do these same factors also account for a significant part of the variance in ordinary physical punishment?

For purposes of this index, the variables were first dichotomized. Families were given one point for each variable that applied. A family with none of these characteristics was scored zero, a family with 6 of them received a score of 6, and so on.

Figure 13.5 shows the relationship of the checklist score to three measures of violence by the parents in this study. The line labeled with A's gives the rate of child abuse. There were no instances of child abuse among the families with checklist scores of 2 or less. Thereafter, the higher the checklist score, the higher the rate of child abuse. A third of the children from families with a score of 10 or more were abused.

The new findings are those represented by the other two lines in Figure 13.5. The line marked by threes gives the percentage of parents who used physical punishment three or more times during the year but who did *not* engage in any of the acts included in the measure of child abuse. It can be seen that the Child Abuse Checklist is as highly associated with this measure of ordinary violence as is child abuse itself. That is, the same factors which (at least in the statistical sense) explain child abuse also explain the normal violence employed in child rearing.

On the other hand, the middle line in Figure 13.5, which gives the rate of using physical punishment once or twice, can be interpreted as showing either a curvilinear relationship or essentially no relationship between the checklist score and the rate of using physical punishment once or twice. This can be taken as evidence against the theory that physical punishment and child abuse share a similar etiology. An alternative interpretation, however, is that in the context of a society where the use of physical punishment is both typical and frequent, parents who have done so only once or twice during an entire year are likely to be parents who are, in effect, committed to nonviolence in child rearing.

The Individual Items

Although the checklist provides a compact method of summarizing and estimating the combined effect of a large number of etiological factors, there are hazards in using this method. Perhaps the effects are really the

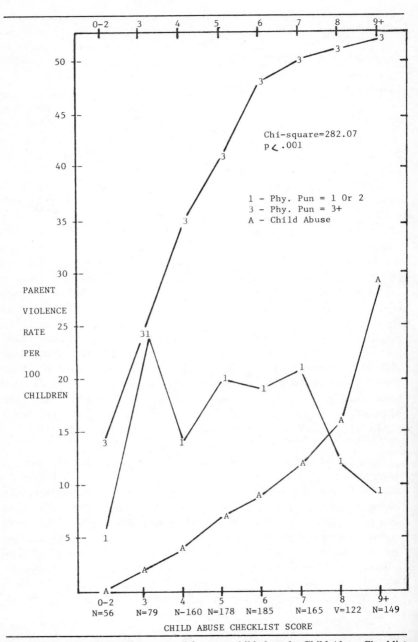

Figure 13.5 Physical punishment and frequent child abuse by Child Abuse Checklist score group.

result of only some of the items included in the checklist. Or it could be that one subset of items is related to abuse and another subset is related to use of ordinary physical punishment. To check this possibility, the cross-tabulations were repeated separately for each of the 16 items in the Child Abuse Checklist. All but three of the individual items were found to be associated with ordinary physical punishment as well as with child abuse. The three that are associated with child abuse but not with ordinary physical punishment are husband dissatisfied with his standard of living, blue-collar occupation, and two or more children.

Controls For Age of Child and Sex of Parent

The checklist analysis findings were replicated with controls for the source of the data (fathers reporting on their own behavior toward the child and on the mother's behavior; mothers reporting on their own a behavior and that of the father). Essentially the same relationship was found within each of the four categories. However, the link between the cheklist score and both child abuse and physical punishment is somewhat greater for mothers than for fathers. Two possible reasons for this come to mind. First, mothers are the primary caretakers (often the almost exclusive caretakers); therefore, the impact of factors associated with child abuse may show up more clearly for mothers. Second, when the items included in the checklist are examined (see note 4), they include variables which can be taken as indicators of the extent to which wives are victimized—for example, a husband who verbally and/or physically abused the wife. Since previous research indicates that victims of violence tend to victimize others more than do nonvictims (Owens & Straus, 1975), this might account for the closer correlation of the index with violence by mothers.

Frequency of Punishment

Before leaving the issue of the common ties between ordinary physical punishment and child abuse, one additional set of findings may help round out the picture. This is the average number of times parents reported using physical punishment (Figure 13.6). Since child-abusing families also engage in less severe violence, Figure 13.6 is restricted to families in which the parents did *not* engage in any of the acts in the child abuse measure. It can be seen that irrespective of the age of the child, the higher the Child Abuse Checklist score, the more often parents use ordinary physical punishment.[6]

FACTORS ASSOCIATED WITH WIFE-BEATING

The same questions that were examined in relation to child abuse will be examined in this section in relation to wife-beating, specifically: Do husbands who experienced physical punishment as a teenager have a higher

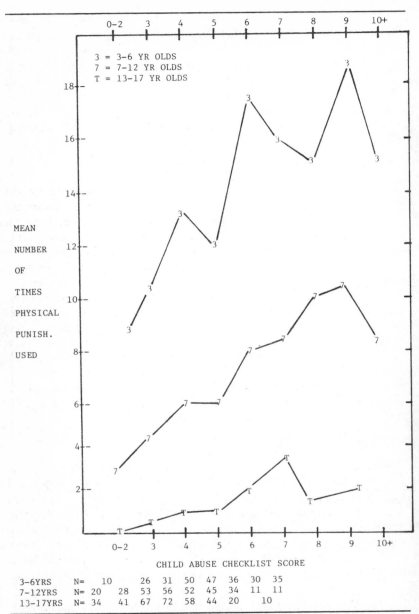

Figure 13.6 Mean number of times nonabusing parents used physical punishment.

rate of wife-beating than other husbands? Are the other factors that previous research indicated are associated with wife-beating also associated with minor violence by husbands?

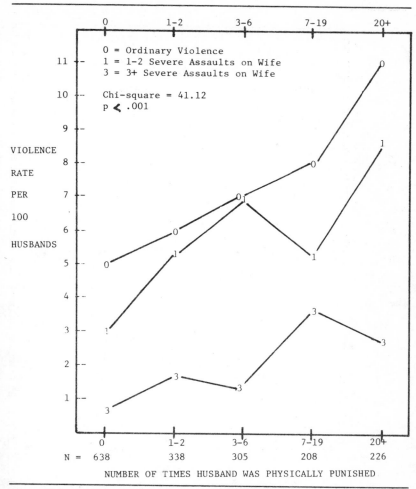

Figure 13.7 Husband-to-wife violence by physical punishment experienced by husband at about age 13.

Physical Punishment and Marital Violence

Figure 13.7 shows that the more physical punishment was experienced by the husbands in this sample, the higher was the rate of violence against wives. Moreover, this applies not only to frequent and severe attacks (the line of threes) but also to relatively infrequent severe attacks, and to the ordinary violence that is so frequent in American marriages.[7] Finally, Figure 13.8 shows the same results for violence by wives. That is, the more the wives in this sample were physically punished, the greater was the rate

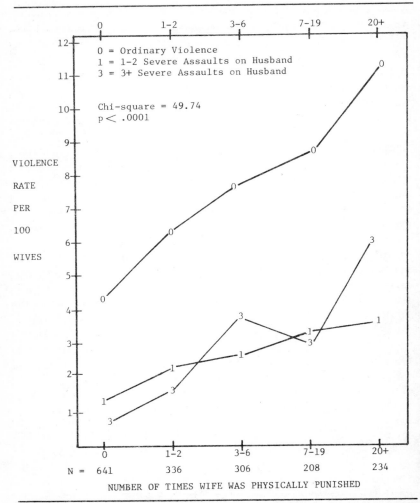

Figure 13.8 Wife-to-husband violence by physical punishment experienced by wife at about age 13.

at which they attacked their husbands, and this applies to measures of all three levels of severity of attack.

Other Factors Associated With Wife-Beating

Space limitations again rule out presenting the findings on each of the other variables found to be associated with wife-beating. Instead, the variables associated with wife-beating will be summarized using a Wife Beating Checklist. This consists of 26 items and is similar to the Child

Abuse Checklist. Indeed, the two indexes share a number of variables. Among the characteristics which were scored in this index are a male-dominant balance of power in the family and a high score on an index to measure stresses experienced during the survey year (see note 6).

Examination of Figure 13.9 leads to roughly the same conclusions as emerged from the other analyses. It shows that the rate of frequent wife-beating (the line of threes) starts at zero for those with checklist scores of 4 or under, then climbs gradually, and finally jumps to one out of five among the husbands with checklist scores of 20 or higher. Thus, the findings reported previously (Straus et al., 1980, chap. 9) for *any* severe assault on wives also apply when the more stringent criterion of frequent assaults is used. For purposes of this chapter, however, the most relevant data plotted in Figure 13.9 is the line of zeros. This shows that the rate for the ordinary minor violence of American marriages also increases as the checklist score increases.

Since the checklist is a composite of 26 variables, the similar association of the checklist score with both minor violence and severe violence might not reflect a real similarity in etiological factors. It could be that one subset of the 26 is associated with minor violence and another subset is associated with wife-beating. To check whether this is the case, each of the 26 items in the checklist was examined separately. This revealed that 24 of the 26 items were related to ordinary violence as well as to wife-beating.[8] Thus, the same factors that are associated with frequent and severe assaults on wives also explain such minor violence as pushing, slapping, and throwing things.

SUMMARY AND CONCLUSIONS

This analysis of 2143 American families shows how pervasive and interconnected violence is in the lives of these families.

(1) Over 97% of American children experience physical punishment. The data presented in this chapter show that the rate of physical punishment decreases rapidly as the child matures. However, data from another study indicate that for half of all American children, it does not end until the child leaves the parental home (Straus, 1971). Here I argue that such widespread use of ordinary physical punishment is one of the factors accounting for the high rate of child abuse and wife-beating.

(2) The more parents are violent toward their children, the more violent these children are to their siblings. This relationship applies to parents' use of ordinary physical punishment as well as to child abuse. The relationship is particularly dramatic for the 100 children in this sample who were frequently abused by their parents. Seventy-six percent of them repeatedly and severely assaulted a sibling during the year studied.

(3) The more violent husbands are twoard their wife, the more violent the wife is toward her children. Wives who were victims of violence that is

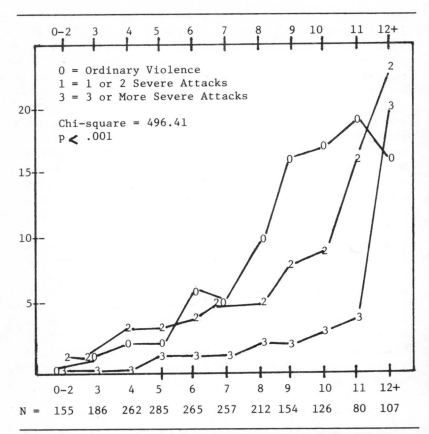

Figure 13.9   Ordinary violence and wife-beating by Spouse Abuse Checklist score.

sufficiently severe to meet the popular conception of wife-beating had the highest rate of child abuse. Even those who were subjected to minor violence such as pushes and slaps had more than double the rate of frequent severe assaults on their children than did wives whose husbands did not hit them.

(4) The experience of violence as a child in the form of presumably benign physical punishment shows up a generation later in the form of equally benign physical punishment of the respondents own childred *and also* in the form of elevated rates of child abuse and spouse abuse. In general, the more the parents in this study were physically punished, the higher was the rate of both ordinary physical punishment and child abuse.

These findings are consistent with other research in showing that being a victim of violence is strongly related to engaging in violence oneself. This does mean that everyone who has been a victim is violent. That probably depends in part on the intensity and length of victimization. To the extent that this is the case, the unintended training in violence that takes place in the family is particularly effective. Victimization in the family starts in infancy and, for half of all American children, continues until they leave home. Moreover, for one out of every seven children the violence is severe enough to be classified as child abuse. In addition, millions of American children have the opportunity to observe violent role models in the form of violence between their parents.

(5) Important as intrafamily experience with violence may be, one can overstate the case. Far from all husbands who experienced violence at the hands of their parents grow up to hit their wives. Not all abused children or abused wives abuse others. Conversely, there are violent people among those who grew up in nonviolent families. Clearly, many other variables are needed to fully account for both individual differences in violence and for the high overall incidence rate.

A number of these other variables were investigated as part of the larger study. Because of space limitations, two summary measures were used in this chapter to study the link between these variables and violence by parents and spouses. A Child Abuse Checklist was used to summarize the combined effect of 16 variables that previous analysis had shown to have a statistically significant and nonoverlapping relationship to child abuse. Similarly, a Spouse Abuse Checklist was used to summarize the combined effect of 26 variables known to be related to wife-beating.

Previous reports show that these checklist scores are highly related to the incidence of child abuse and wife-beating. The issue under study here is whether these same factors are also related to ordinary physical punishment and the minor violence which occurs between so many couples.

The results show that the same factors which explain child abuse and wife-beating also explain ordinary physical punishment and minor violence between spouses. Thus, in respect to at least the etiological variables investigated in this study, it seems that violence is violence—irrespective of the severity of the attack and irrespective of whether the violence is normatively legitimate (as in the case of physical punishment) or illegitimate (as in the case of child abuse and wife-beating). These findings have a number of implications and also raise questions which cannot be answered with these data.

One of the most important of these questions concerns the process which accounts for the link between ordinary violence and "abuse." The explanation which is implicit throughout this chapter is that even though ordinary violence provides a role model that limits the severity of violence, for a considerable number of people the limits are not learned as well as is the principle that violence can and should be used when necessary, when under stress, when frustrated, and so on.

Another, and probably complementary, interventing process hinges on the distinction between "expressive" or "hostile" aggression versus instrumental aggression (Gelles & Straus, 1978). Physical punishment is a clear example of instrumental aggression—that is, where the primary goal is not to hurt the other person but to use hurting to achieve some other end. However, cases of pure instrumental aggression are probably rare. Parents are usually also frustrated and angry when they physically punish. Consequently, they are modeling both instrumental and expressive aggression. It is likely that some children who experience physical punishment attend to the instrumental part of the parents' behavior and others attend more to the expressive or hostile part. It is the latter group which may account for the link between physical punishment and child abuse and wife-beating. These and other processes that might account for the link between ordinary violence and abuse need to be investigated. But even the findings reported here have important theoretical and practical implications.

The theoretical implication is that some reconsideration must be given to conceptual distinctions between different types or aspects of violence, such as instrumental versus expressive violence, minor versus severe violence, or socially approved versus illegitimate violence. Each of these has different antecedents, intervening processes, and reinforcers. At the same time, the findings I report suggest that each of these types of violence may also have more in common than is generally thought to be the case.

The practical implication of these findings concerns primary prevention (as contrasted with intervention to help victims of child abuse and wife-beating). To the extent that ordinary violence is linked to child abuse and wife-beating, efforts to reduce the incidence of child abuse and wife-beating must include attention to the ordinary violence typical of American families, including (and perhaps especially) ordinary physical punishment.

NOTES

1. This does not deny that there are also important differences between various acts of violence. These are discussed and classified in Gelles and Straus (1978).

2. Physical punishment was measured by four questions which asked "How often would you say that (your mother, stepmother, father, stepfather, you, your husband, your wife) used physical punishment, like slapping or hitting." The response categories were for the number of times during a one-year period, as follows: never, once or twice, 3-5 times, 6-10 times, 11-20 times, more than 20 times.

3. For purposes of this study, child abuse was measured by whether the parent did any of the following during the year: punching, kicking, biting, hitting with an object, beating up, threatening with a knife or gun, or actually using a knife or gun.

4. The items included are: belong to no organization; 2 or more children; respondent physically punished 2+ times by mother; respondent physically punished 2+ times by father, respondent age 30 or under; husband slightly or not satisfied with standard of living; respondent's mother hit father; married less than 10 years; lived in neighborhood 0-1 years; above average conflict with spouse; verbal aggression to child; verbal aggression to wife; husband violent to wife; blue-collar husband; blue-collar wife; wife not employed outside the home. Further information on the

checklist is given in Straus et al. (1980, chap. 9). The special questions from which these items were scored is available in the codebook for this study (Straus & Gelles, 1980).

5. The line for abuse of teenagers appears to indicate a less pronounced relationship. This is a function of the fact that teenagers are physically punished much less often than younger children. To adequately portray the findings for teenagers, the vertical axis scale would have to be set to a scale that would run the much higher figures for the younger children off the graph. For all three age groups, parents in families with checklist scores of 7 or more use physical punishment at least twice as often as is the case in families with scores of 0 to 2.

6. The items included in this index are: 2 or more children; respondent physically punished 2+ times by father; respondent age 30 or under; respondent nonwhite; family income under $6000; agreed about children never or only sometimes; part-time employed husband; unemployed husband; husband quite or extremely worried about economic future; respondent's father hit mother; respondent's mother hit father; wife slightly or not at all satisfied with standard of living; wife extremely worried about economic future; married less than 10 years; lived in neighborhood 0-1 years; above-average conflict with spouse; stress index 70 or more; verbal aggression to wife; wife verbally aggressive to husband; blue-collar husband; blue-collar wife; wife not employed outside home; no religious participation; couple gets drunk rarely or more often; wife-dominant couple; husband-dominant couple.

7. The prevalence of violence in American marriages is much greater than one might surmize from Figure 13.7. This is partly because the data in that figure are annual incidence rates—that is, whether these events occurred during the year of the survey. The prevalence rates—whether an assault had ever occurred—are much higher. For this survey sample, the prevalence rate is 28%. But for reasons stated elsewhere (Straus et al., 1980, pp. 34-36), the probable true prevalence rate is well over 50%; in other words, more than half of all American couples have engaged in physical violence at some point in the marriage.

8. The two items found to be related to wife-beating, but not to ordinary marital violence, are a wife who is not employed outside the home and respondents who are nonwhite.

REFERENCES

Bronfenbrenner, U. Socialization and social class through time and space. In E. E. Maccoby, T. M. Newcomb, & E. L. Hartly (Eds.), *Readings in social psychology.* New York: Holt, Rinehart & Winston, 1958.

Frude, N., & Goss, A. Parental anger: A general population survey. *Child Abuse and Neglect, 1979, 3*(1), 331-333.

Gelles, R., & Straus, M. A. Determinants of violence in the family: Towards a theoretical integration. In W. R. Burr, R. Hill, F. I. Nye, & I. L. Reiss (Eds.), *Contemporary theories about the family* (Vol. 1). New York: Free Press, 1978.

Kalmuss, D. S., & Straus, M. A. Wives' marital dependency and wife abuse. *Journal of Marriage and the Family, 1982, 44.*

Miller, D. R., & Swanson, G. E. *The changing American parent: A study in the Detroit area.* New York: John Wiley, 1958.

Owens, D. M., & Straus, M. A. The social structure of violence in childhood and approval of violence as an adult. *Aggressive Behavior, 1975, 1,* 193-211. (Also in I. H. Hyman & J. H. Wise, Eds., *Corporal punishment in American education:*

Readings in history, practice, and alternatives. Philadelphia: Temple University Press, 1979.)

Straus, M. A. Some social antecedents of physical punishment: A linkage theory interpretation. *Journal of Marriage and the Family,* 1971, *33,* 658-663.

Straus, M. A. Family patterns and child abuse in a nationally representative American sample. *Child Abuse and Neglect,* 1979, *3,* 213-225. (a)

Straus, M. A. Measuring intrafamily conflict and violence: The Conflict Tactics (CT) scales. *Journal of Marriage and the Family,* 1979, *41,* 75-88. (b)

Straus, M. A. Victims and aggressors in marital violence. *American Behavioral Scientist,* 1980, *23,* 681-704.

Straus, M. A., & Gelles, R. J. *Physical violence in American families.* Interuniversity Consortium for Political and Social Research, Codebook 7733. Ann Arbor: Institute for Social Research, University of Michigan, 1980.

Straus, M. A., Gelles, R. J., & Steinmetz, S. K. *Behind closed doors: Violence in the American family.* Garden City, NY: Doubleday, 1980.

14

A Hit Is a Hit Is a Hit . . .
Or Is It?

Approval and Tolerance of
The Use of Physical Force
By Spouses

CATHY STEIN GREENBLAT

I. INTRODUCTION

Cultural Norms and Family Violence

In any society there are "rules" of different sorts. *Prescriptive* (and *proscriptive*) rules define what one should do (and should not do); in other words, they are directions for action. *Interpretive* rules, on the other hand, tell societal members how to interpret and make sense of what someone (oneself or another) has done. While these can be conceptually distinguished, they are not independent. As Marsh, Rosser, and Harre explain:

> Indeed, before one can decide what action is appropriate one requires an understanding of the social context in which one is acting and an interpretation of the actions occurring in that context. Rules of interpretation, in attaching meaning to situations and their constituents, determine which prescriptive rules are applicable. Action on the basis of such prescription, however, can subsequently lead to changing definitions of the situation which in turn will alter the directions of conduct. Prescriptions presuppose interpretations, but actions on the basis of such prescriptions become themselves the subject of interpretation. (1978, pp. 16-17)

There are few forms of behavior for which there are constant rules of either sort; rather, the rules vary by context and by actor. In the case of violence, for example, murder of an enemy soldier is mandated in the war zone and applauded by one's countrymen, while murder of a neighbor is prohibited by law and responded to with horror. So, too, if one looks at milder forms of violence, such as hitting or beating up, one finds variable rules. Some cultural norms call for these aggressive acts if, for example, there has been sufficient provocation. Then rules of retributive justice ("an eye for an eye") can be invoked. Other norms urge a more pacifist stance, even in the face of the other's provocation ("turn the other cheek") (Blumenthal, Kahn, Andrews, & Head, 1972).

Interpretive rules also vary depending upon the domain and the relationship between the victim and assaulter. As part of an investigation of normative structure relating to the seriousness of criminal acts, Rossi et al. investigated the differential "seriousness" ratings assigned to a set of 140 crimes by a household sample of respondents. They found a tendency for crimes involving persons known to the offender to be viewed as less serious than crimes committed against strangers. This is manifested in the finding that forcible rape after breaking into a home was rated 4th, while forcible rape of a former spouse rated 62nd; beating up a stranger rated 64th, while beating up a spouse rated 91st (Rossi, Waite, Bose, & Berk, 1974, pp. 228-229).

In a similar vein, Murray Straus has argued that minor forms of violence, such as pushing and shoving, which are considered "ordinary" between family members, would not be tolerated in most work contexts. Testifying before the Subcommittee on Science and Technology of the House of Representatives, he stated, "I think, that when it refers to families, the public thinks of violence as things that go beyond that [slapping] : severe kicking, punching, beating up, stabbing, and so forth. So there is an implicit toleration or implicit permission for family members to use milder forms of violence on each other. But for members of university departments or a House committee no one says that 'just' pushing or slapping isn't violence" (Straus, 1979, p. 15).

Western tradition until the 19th century contained strong prescriptive rules concerning husbands' use of physical force, including beatings and sometimes murder, to keep their wives in line. Dobash and Dobash, in extremely thorough analyses, have traced the continuing presence in literature, law and ethical treatises of statements of a husband's right and even duty to punish his wife's transgressions from her marital responsibilities with physical force (1977-78, 1980). Wifebeating was not simply deviant behavior that was tolerated, but rather for centuries was considered to be a desirable part of a patriarchal family system. Late in the 19th century, reform movements began which eventuated in laws against wife beating being passed in Britain and the United States, though these are only mildly condemned in legal and judicial institutions in most jurisdictions (see Dobash & Dobash, 1981; Freeman, 1979; Center for Women's Policy Studies, 1980.) It would appear, then, that much *interpretation* of wife-beating historically has been based on ideas of the wife's precipitating actions and the husband's rule-following response.

Since the 19th century there have been challenges to these prescriptive rules. Surely for some persons, hitting one's wife is now *proscribed* behavior. These persons would concur with the court ruling in the 1891 case of Reg v. Jackson that "the moral sense of the community revolts at the idea that the husband may inflict personal chastisement upon his wife, even for the most outrageous conduct" (Eisenberg & Micklow, 1974, pp. 4-5). For other persons, it is proscribed except under certain circumstances (e.g., she won't listen to reason) or is proscribed beyond a point (i.e., it is alright so long as no physical injury results). There are others, however, who continue to believe that hitting one's spouse is sometimes tolerable, and is even desirable under certain circumstances.

Whatever the confusion about prescriptions, violence *does* take place between spouses. The incidence rates found and projected by researchers are very variable, partially as a result of different definitions of "violence" and partly as a result of different methodological approaches, but all agree that the rates are shockingly high.

Since spouses use physical force upon one another, there must be interpretations of the meaning of the behavior. Aggressors, victims, neighbors, friends, family, children, police, social workers, judges, newspaper and other media persons, the general public and social scientists are officially or unofficially called upon to interpret the meaning of incidents of family violence.

How is such violence interpreted? The social scientists who have done research on the topic have generally rejected the popular notions of "mental illness" and uncontrollable drives that predominate in lay theories of family violence. They are also uniformly condemnatory of family violence. On the other hand, the failure of the social services and legal system to seriously respond to violence between spouses seems to indicate that some persons not only consider family privacy inviolate, but that they hold to older beliefs that domestic violence, so long as it does not create injury, is not to be seriously deplored. Others seem to applaud such behavior.

On the whole, researchers seem to believe that support is more prevalent than condemnation, for the literature on family violence contains regular references to "cultural norms supporting family violence." Gelles, for example, states that ". . . violence between spouses is often viewed as normative and in fact, mandated in family relations" (1974, pp. 59-61). This position is maintained in particularly strong form with reference to interpretations of husband to wife violence. It is often argued that many men grow up thinking they have the right to the final say in family matters and that they thus believe they are justified in engaging in violent behavior if such rights are challenged (see Straus, all publications referenced; Walker, 1979). Dobash and Dobash, referring to the contemporary scene, state that " . . . men who assault their wives are actually living up to cultural prescriptions that are cherished in Western society—aggressiveness, male dominance, and female subordination—and they are using physical force as a means to enforce that dominance." (Dobash & Dobash, 1980, p. 24)

Straus extends the argument to wives hitting husbands. In almost all of his numerous publications he develops a version of the argument that "the marriage license is a hitting license." Because this argument has influenced many others and has been adopted by them, it warrants lengthy citation here:

> One very simple, but nonetheless important, factor is that the family has different rules about violence than do other groups. In an academic department, an office, or a factory, the basic rule is that no one can hit anyone else, no matter what they do wrong. A person can be a pest, an intolerable bore, negligent, incompetent, selfish, or unwilling to listen to reason. But that still does not give anyone the right to hit such a person. In the family the situation is different. There, the basic rule is that if someone does wrong and won't listen to reason, violence is permissible and sometimes even required.
>
> This is clearly the case in respect to the rights and obligations of parents; but it also applies to spouses. (Straus, 1980, p. 232)

What are the "rules" governing the occurrence of violence within the family, and which forms are "legitimate" or acceptable? In many families the norm seems to be that if someone is doing wrong, and "won't listen to reason" it is all right to hit. In the case of parents in relation to children, it is more than just all right; many American parents see physical punishment to "teach" the child as their obligation. As we have tried to show elsewhere (Gelles, 1974; Straus 1976; Straus and Hotaling, 1979) this norm often carries over to the relationship between husbands and wives. In identifying a husband who beats up his wife as violent, we used the phrase "for no good reason." The implication of this phrase is that there can be situations in which there IS "a good reason" for a husband to hit his wife, or vice versa. In fact, about one out of four Americans explicitly take that view. (Stark and McEvoy, 1970)

> What is a "good reason" varies from couple to couple and from subculture to subculture. But in our culture in general the marriage license is also a license to hit. To be sure, there are certain normative restrictions. One cannot inflict "excessive" injury even with a marriage partner.
>
> Just how much violence is "excessive" in marriage or to discipline children, also varies with the individual couple and their subculture. (Gelles & Straus, 1979, p. 35)

Empirical and Conceptual Problems

While the historical record surely supports the argument that cultural norms endorsing husband to wife violence abound, the contemporary picture is not so clear. In fact, there are several problems with the arguments just presented, however persuasive they may appear.

The first and most serious problem is that there is almost *no* empirical evidence that can be brought to bear, pro or con. One can, of course, argue as Straus does, that the existence of such norms is almost impossible to document because the very existence of the rule is not generally realized—it is taken-for-granted and therefore largely unrecognized (Straus, 1980a, p. 9). But the search for data cannot so readily be abandoned, nor would Straus himself like to see it abandoned.

The data that *are* used to support the argument are clearly deficient. The only data cited regularly are figures from a 1970 article by Stark and McEvoy. These figures derive from two questions included in a larger study of attitudes toward violence (see section II of this paper for details). Occasional reference is made to limited data gathered by Parnas, who found some wives believe it is acceptable for a husband to beat his wife "every once and a while" (Parnas, 1967, p. 952) and to a small set of attitudinal data gathered by Straus (1980).

A second type of data used in these arguments derives from interviews with persons who have been involved directly in incidents of family violence, usually as victims (e.g., Gelles, 1974, pp. 57-90). On the basis of their statements about why they committed the acts of violence or why their spouses did so, general ideas of "acceptable conditions" are sometimes inferred. But however accurate these attributions may be, they are nonetheless *accounts* (Lyman & Scott, 1970)—that is, they represent interpretations offered to explain one's own behavior (why I hit her; why I stayed with him despite the fact that he beat me) in terms that will be acceptable to the audience. Giving good accounts is a skill that is developed, one that depends upon the individual's stock of social knowledge (Marsh et al., 1978, p. 15). Persons learn to utilize those arguments that will be most acceptable and will gain the greatest understanding. Thus it is not legitimate to infer what norms exist in the general public from the accounts of these actors. (We will return to the utility of accounts data).

The third type of data are jokes and everyday expressions that can be found in folk culture, such as the ditty:

"A woman, a horse and a hickory tree
The more you beat 'em the better they be."

While this kind of data can be very illuminating to social scientists (see Rothbell, 1981), it hardly provides solid *evidence* of a contemporary cultural norm.

The second problem in the argument is that there is no criterion given for how one decides when a position is taken consistently enough that one can argue that it represents a *norm*. For example, Stark and McEvoy found that approximately one of four respondents approved of spouses slapping one another under certain conditions. Is that enough support to argue for a generally accepted cultural norm? It is not if one accepts that "a high degree of consensus concerning the rule is expected among members of the group or sub-culture in which the rule applies. Social conventions would clearly be of little use if only a small proportion of members was aware of them, and the same holds for the interpretative rules which guide the manner in which meanings are attached to objects and situations" (Marsh et al., 1978, p. 18). This position appears to be one adopted by Rossi et al., who state:

> The seriousness of a criminal act may be viewed as a normative evaluation . . . To be of theoretical or practical use, a measure of crime "seriousness" requires that a society show consensus about the order of seriousness of specific criminal acts. (Rossi et al., 1974, p. 224)

Even if good data on the degree of approval of family violence existed, then, we would have to ask if the extent of approval were great enough to warrant the argument that a *norm* of approval exists.

The third problem in the available literature is that norms of *approval* and norms of *tolerance* are lumped together. We are told that violence is normative, but that sometimes it is mandated and other times tolerated. Thus we find sentences referring to "violent acts which are legitimate (i.e., which are tolerated, permitted, or required"). Norms which demand and urge violence and norms stressing understanding of the use of violence are important subjects for investigation, but they are very *different* and such differences must be documented if we are to have a full understanding of the normative climate of family violence.

The purpose of this paper, then, is to add to the data base that might be employed to understand contemporary attitudes and norms concerning the use of physical force between spouses, including such questions as: How much approval is there? Under what conditions? How much tolerance or understanding is there? For what reasons? Are these different for husband to wife and wife to husband force? Are there gender differences in approval? Finally, we will examine the ways in which tolerance and understanding are used in accounts. Reflecting the author's concerns about application of the term "violence" to all use of physical force (Greenblat, 1981), this term will be avoided, but the present paper is meant to be a contribution to the literature on "family violence."

II. METHODS

The data presented in this paper represent the preliminary stages of analysis of sections of an exploratory study of emotional relationships in the early years of marriage. In the most general terms, the study was aimed at such questions as: What is meant by 'love' by contemporary Americans? How do they recognize it in themselves? How do they judge it in others? How do perceptions of what love is, how it is manifested, and how important it is, change over the early years of marriage? What do people mean by a "change from romantic to conjugal love"? Is this change felt by people, or is it an interpretive scheme developed by psychiatrists and social scientists? How do the expressive dimensions of marriage change? How do incidents of inter-spousal violence effect the expressive dimension of the marriage? Is the effect different for those who feel different degrees of 'love'? What is the relative impact of these violent interactions vs. other factors such as work roles, allocation of household tasks, fertility plans and events, economic concerns, other family crises, etc.? Respondents were asked about what they believed should take place between spouses as well as what actually took place in their relationships, and about the meaning they would attribute to various actions (including interspouse violence) that they might not have experienced.

A sub-contract was let to Opinion Research Corporation of Princeton, New Jersey for random digit dialing (see Dillman, 1978) of telephone numbers in the telephone area of New Brunswick, New Jersey. (This includes 8 communities: New Brunswick, North Brunswick, East Brunswick, Edison, Highland Park, Milltown, Piscataway, and Somerset.) With this procedure, names, addresses, and telephone numbers for 97 persons (41 males and 56 females) who were married 5 years or less were obtained. Attempts to locate these persons revealed that 5 of the males and 4 of the females had moved or changed their telephone numbers to unlisted numbers in the time between ORC's call (January 15-February 5) and our contact. Although it proved more difficult to attain the cooperation of the males than the females, we were more successful than had originally been anticipated, especially considering the time commitment that was required of respondents. Only six men and two women refused, yielding success rates of 83% for the men and 96% for the women. (See Greenblat, 1981 for greater detail.) The final sample was very heterogenous in terms of a number of characteristics, as seen in Table 14.1.

Interviews were done by the Principal Investigator and by Larry Baron with 30 males and 50 females. The interviews ranged from 2 hours to 5 hours in length, averaging about 2 hours and 45 minutes, and were tape-recorded while skeletal notes were written on the interview guide.

While some data concerning attitudes toward the use of physical force by husbands and wives is contained in the responses to questions about the character of the marriage, and other notions can be gleaned from examination of the analysis of reports of the *experience* of violence (Greenblat, 1981), most of the attitudinal data comes from later phases of the

TABLE 14.1 Demographic Characteristics, by Gender (percentages)*

	Male	Female		Male	Female
Age:			Marital Status:		
18-24	13	18	First marriage		
25-29	50	58	for both	80	76
30-44	37	18	Remarriage for		
45+	0	6	one or both	20	24
	—	—		—	—
Total	100	100	Total	100	100
	(30)	(50)		(30)	(50)
Time Married			Education:		
(months) :			High school grad		
1-11	30	10	or less	10	24
12-23	20	12	Some post-high		
24-35	17	26	school educ.	20	32
36-47	7	12	College grad or		
48-59	17	26	more	70	44
60-71	10	14		—	—
	—	—	Total	100	100
Total	101	100		(30)	(50)
	(30)	(50)			
			Couple income:		
Children:			Less than $19,999	23	32
None	80	62	$20,000-34,999	40	38
One	13	22	$35,000 or more	37	30
Two	7	16		—	—
	—	—	Total	100	100
Total	100	100		(27)	(46)
	(30)	(50)	Husband's Occupation:		
			Blue collar	23	26
			White collar	27	28
			Manager/prof'l	37	46
			Full-time student	13	0
				—	—
			Total	100	100
				(30)	(50)

*Ns are in parentheses.

interview material. Following the questions of personal experiences was a section prefaced by the statement:

What I would like to do now is to shift from talking about your own experience to some of your ideas about what love and marriage are like or should be like. I'd like to find out how you think people *should* act towards their spouses and how they might interpret the behavior of their spouses. You will have had experience with some of these issues, but may not have experienced others.

Then respondents were asked about showing affection, hitting one's spouse, sexual relations, conflict or disagreement, and time spent together. In each case, they were asked what they thought should be done. Then they were offered examples of what people might do, and were asked if they thought these actions said anything about how much the actor loved his or her spouse. The questions about hitting were worded as follows:

49. Can you think of any circumstances in which a husband might hit his wife? What do you think of his hitting her under those circumstances?

Are there some circumstances in which you think it is appropriate or reasonable for a husband to hit his wife?

If a man DOES hit his wife, do you think his hitting her says anything about how much he loves her? (If yes) What?

What do you think a wife should do if her husband hits her?

Question 50 contained identical questions concerning a wife hitting her husband.

When the interview was completed, except for a few background questions, respondents were given a self-administered four-page set of 45 Likert-type statements about love and marriage, each to be answered "strongly agree," "agree," "disagree," or "strongly disagree." Two items were included to tap attitudes toward hitting a spouse. In addition to slightly different wording, these differed from the prior questions in that responses did not have to be given aloud to the interviewer, and that the respondents had already answered a similar question in more detail. The items were as follows:

GG. "There are some conditions under which it is acceptable for a husband to slap his wife."

MM: "There are some conditions under which it is acceptable for a wife to slap her husband."

These statements were so worded to conform with the statements utilized by Stark and McEvoy (1970).

Let us begin with the questions of appropriate circumstances.

III. APPROPRIATE AND ACCEPTABLE CIRCUMSTANCES FOR THE USE OF PHYSICAL FORCE BY SPOUSES

Appropriate Circumstances

A number of respondents appear to have interpreted the questions of any circumstances in which a husband or wife MIGHT hit as referring to

LEGITIMATE circumstances. Thus only 66% of the men and 50% of the women offered a circumstance a husband might hit his wife, and only 48% of the men and 54% of the women offered a condition for a wife hitting her husband. These figures are low, considering most people have heard of such cases and should have been able to generate some circumstances. While a lower proportion of women gave a circumstance, the list they generated was more diverse.

There appear to be several themes in the lists of circumstances mentioned. If we begin with circumstances a husband might hit his wife (omitting "medical" ones), of the 24 reasons offered by the men, 4 (17%) refer to self-defense or defense of a child; 12 (50%) refer to the wife's behavior as the reason for his hitting; 3 (13%) refer to the influence of drugs or alcohol; four (17%) refer to his feelings; and one (4%) refers to an argument between them. If we exclude "by accident" there are 40 reasons offered by 24 women. Three (8%) entail self-defense or defense of a child; 14 (35%) use the wife's behavior as explanation of the husband's hitting; 6 (15%) offer his insanity or drunkenness as a circumstance; 9 (23%) refer to his feelings; and the other 19% includes a heterogeneous assortment of circumstances.

When the hitter is a husband, then, drunkenness, drug use or insanity is offered as a reason by some respondents. Other researchers have demonstrated that drunkenness in general provides a "time-out" period during which one can somewhat disregard norms of appropriate behavior, as alcohol provides an excuse for socially unacceptable behavior. In the particular case of family violence, drunkenness divests the aggressor of much of the responsibility for his abusive actions (Gelles, 1974; Coleman & Straus, 1981). Richardson and Campbell had subjects read accounts of wife abuse and found that when husbands were described as intoxicated they received less blame for their actions (1980, p. 55).

The victim's behavior, however, is the major reason listed by both the male and female respondents here, though the men are more likely than the women to have pointed to her precipitating actions as the basis of his hitting. Such victim-blaming is not uncommon. Although some people would probably agree with those who construe violence as fully or almost fully assailant-precipitated (cf. Walker, 1979; Pagelow, 1978a, 1978b; Pizzey, 1977), or that it is an emergent property of interaction (Ball-Rokeach, 1973), it appears that what Ryan (1971) considers the "generic problem of Blaming the Victim" is the most frequent interpretation of spouse abuse. It can be found not only in lay explanations, but is embedded in many of the social service and legal institutions nominally dedicated to assistance to victims:

Truninger (1971) reports that the courts are often mired in mythology about family violence (e.g., 'violence fulfills the masochistic need of women victims' and consequently the justice system is ineffective in dealing with marital violence. Field and Field (1973:225) echo these sentiments and state that unless the victim dies, the chances that the court system will deal seriously with the offender are slight. Women who are abused by their husbands must suffer grave injury in order to press legal charges. (Gelles, 1976, p. 666)

Others, such as Pagelow, add that family violence researchers, too, sometimes subscribe to this approach, while Wardell, Gillespie, and Leffler (1981) extend the argument, saying that victim-blaming is rampant, if often subtle and not deliberate, in social science studies of wife abuse.

Examining the two lists of categories of circumstances a wife might hit her husband, we again see some tendency to attribute the cause of hitting to the victim's behavior, but the figures for this are lower than when the topic was men hitting their wives. Drinking, drugs, and insanity are rarely mentioned. But now, for both male and female respondents, the modal explanation is the *hitter's feelings,* rather than the victim's provocative behavior. In other words, when women ARE HIT, they are often described as responsible; when women HIT, again they are responsible. THUS IT IS NOT A SIMPLE CASE OF BLAMING THE VICTIM, BUT OF BLAMING THE FEMALE.

When asked about circumstances under which it is APPROPRIATE for a husband to hit his wife, higher proportions of both men and women say "none" or offer life-saving, medical reasons ("snap her out of a coma"). Forty-one percent of the males' and 16% of the females offered a circumstance under which they consider hitting appropriate by husbands; for wives' hitting the proportions of men and women naming a circumstance were 38% and 20%. By this numerical measure it could be argued that the men show more support for use of hitting in the family. Again, however, it is fruitful to examine the nature of the circumstances that *were* offered.

Twelve men and 8 women indicated circumstances under which they felt a man's hitting his wife was reasonable or appropriate. The men's 17 responses are as follows (numbers in parentheses indicate number of responses):

    self-defense or defense of a child (2)
    she hit him first (2)
    she says something wrong (1)
    she does something major (wrong) (1)
    she's hysterical (1)
    he sees her with another man (1)
    she had an affair, was unfaithful (4)
    he catches her in bed with another man (2)
    it makes them happy.

The nine women who said "yes" mentioned a total of 10 circumstances, including:

"their thing" in sex (1)
self-defense or defense of a child (2)
she's hysterical (3)
she's out with another man (1)
she's caught in bed with another man (2)
she's been unfaithful (1)

When the question dealt with appropriate circumstances for a wife to hit, 62% of the men and 80% of the women said there were no circumstances. The 11 men who did respond gave these 12 responses:

self-defense or defense of a child (4)
she's very angry (1)
she's frustrated, tense or upset (1)
she can't get his attention (1)
he's flirting with another woman (1)
he's been unfaithful (2)
he's out with another woman (1)
"it's meaningful to them, it works, and it makes them happy" (1)

and the 10 women gave these 13 responses:

self-defense or defense of a child (5)
she's very angry (1)
she's frustrated, tense or upset (1)
he's hysterical (2)
he won't listen to her (1)
he calls her a whore and she's not (1)
he's been unfaithful (1)
he's caught in bed with another woman (1)

Two things are noticeable in these lists. First, in the case of appropriate circumstances for husbands to hit wives, there is again a tendency to blame the victim—that is, the reasons are now almost all given in terms of her precipitating provocations. This is also the case when we look at appropriate circumstances for wives to hit husbands.

Second, the reasons tend to be heavily *sexual* in character. Forty-one percent of the men's responses and 50% of the women's responses concerning husbands hitting their wives refer to sexual causes; for wives hitting their husbands, the percentages drop to a still-high 33% for the men and 23% for the women. Thus the sexual realm appears to have continuing importance as a domain in which the "rules of relationships" developed by couples to safeguard identities and avoid or minimize embarrassment (Denzin, 1970, p. 131) remain crucial.

Both men and women who transgress against the monogamous norms are seen by some respondents as appropriate recipients of physical force by their spouses. But, as wives in general have historically been more "appropriate" victims of marital violence (Dobash & Dobash, 1977-78), they continue to be excused less than husbands from violations of sexual norms. If Cato the Censor's fifth century B.C. injunction that "If you catch your wife in adultery, you could put her to death with impunity . . ." (Hecker, 1910, p. 23) is too strong for many contemporary tastes, wives' violation of rules of sexual exclusivity nonetheless seems the most legitimate ground for using physical force to these respondents.

Acceptable Conditions for Slapping a Spouse

Approval or endorsement of the use of physical force between spouses can also be examined in terms of the responses to the statements included in the battery of Likert items at the end of the interview. The top half of Table 14.2 shows that when asked in this way, different figures emerge. About one of six men and one of ten women agree with the statement that there are conditions that it is acceptable for a husband to slap his wife, and more than half of each group strongly disagree. The bottom half of Table 14.2 shows somewhat MORE agreement by men than women on the acceptability of a wife slapping her husband: 26% of the men and 16% of the women. Putting these together, one finds that twice as many women and almost twice as many men approve of women slapping husbands as approve of husbands slapping wives. (Nobody strongly agreed with either statement.) Higher proportions of men than of women agree with the statements.

These figures are fairly similar to those obtained by Stark and McEvoy (1970) and by Straus (1980a, 1980b), employing slightly different questions. As shown in Table 14.3, in all 3 studies, women show less approval of slapping or hitting than do the men (though the differences are not statistically significant). Stark and McEvoy report equal support for husbands slapping wives and wives slapping husbands, while the present data show more acceptance of wives slapping husbands than the reverse. As will be seen in Section IV, this seems to be related to the beliefs by these respondents—beliefs which are supported by national victimization studies and other research—(Berk, Berk, Loseke, & Rauma, 1981) that female aggressors are far less likely to do physical harm than are male aggressors.

For the women, there was no relationship between attitudes toward a husband hitting his wife, and any of the background variables. That is, about equal proportions of women who differed in husband's occupation, couple income, education, marital status, age, children, and time married, agreed with the statement. For the women there was also no relationship between attitude toward a wife slapping her husband and any of the background variables.

TABLE 14.2   Attitudes Toward Husbands' and Wives' Slapping, by Gender (percentages)

	Male	Female
Agreement with statement "There are some conditions under which it is acceptable for a husband to slap his wife."		
Strongly agree	0	0
Agree	14	8
Disagree	32	20
Strongly Disagree	54	71
Total	100	100
	(28)	(49)
Agreement with statement "There are some conditions under which it is acceptable for a wife to slap her husband."		
Strongly agree	0	0
Agree	26	16
Disagree	33	24
Strongly disagree	41	59
Total	100	100
	(28)	(49)

*Ns are in parentheses.

For the men, only age was related to agreement with the statement about husbands slapping: men under 30 were more likely to agree, while men over 30 were more likely to strongly disagree (P=.06). For the men, marital status, age, and time married were all related to agreement with the statement concerning wives slapping (p= .15, .04, and .03 respectively). Approximately 40% of men in first marriages, men under 30, and men married less than 2 years agreed with the statement, while 0-10% of their counterparts agreed.

Stark and McEvoy do not report differences related to marital status or time married, but report that agreement with both statements is inversely related to age (Stark & McEvoy, 1970, p. 45). Since these age findings are not reported separately for men and women, and levels of significance are not reported, however, full comparisons with these data cannot be made.

IV. TOLERANCE AND UNDERSTANDING

Tolerance of Husbands Hitting Wives

Straus has suggested that unless circumstances are specified, almost everyone will say "no" to the question of whether violence is legitimate

TABLE 14.3 Attitudes Toward Husbands' and Wives' Slapping

	Male	Female
Greenblat: Percentage who agree that "There are some conditions under which it is acceptable for a husband to slap his wife."	14	8
Stark-McEvoy*: Percentage who "could approve of a husbnad's slapping his wife's face."	25	16
Straus**: Percentage who could see some justification in hitting a spouse	31	25
Greenblat: Percentage who agree that "There are some conditions under which it is acceptable for a wife to slap her husband."	26	16
Stark-McEvoy: Percentage who "could approve of a wife's slapping her husband's face."	26	19

*Stark and McEvoy (1970).
**Straus (1980, p.694).

(1980a, p. 9). These respondents not only say "no," they say it with considerable adamance. In addition to indicating very few circumstances they consider hitting one's spouse to be appropriate or reasonable, the respondents' discussions of the topic are filled with strong statements to the effect that hitting is absolutely inappropriate, unjustifiable behavior. Many state with conviction that they personally would not tolerate it; women especially often indicate they would permanently sever the relationship, if not after the first incident, after a subsequent one, no matter how much they love their spouses. Studies of battered wives, of course, indicate it is far easier to plan such action than to take it when the situation arises (cf. Gelles, 1976; Walker, 1979; Pizzey, 1977; Pagelow, 1978a, 1978b). In all these ways, the respondents show disapproval of hitting, particularly by husbands, often stating it shows a lack of respect and failure to confer adult or even human status. Some, for example, say it involves treating the wife like a child or worse, an animal.

When one examines the way respondents interpret hitting by a hypothetical husband, however, many of the statements imply that however abominable the act, the man may not be fully responsible for his behavior, and thus some understanding must be shown him. Dobash and Dobash (1980, pp. 438-439) and other social scientists suggest that husbands utilize violence to demonstrate their authority and control over wives whom they consider to be their subordinates. These respondents, however, rarely indicate that they believe husbands hit because they believe hitting is a legitimate right or in order to show their dominance or superiority, or to demonstrate who is "boss." Indeed, only two respondents directly indicated this. In a few other cases, as the foregoing summary of circumstances indicated, reference was made to his *right* to hit her if her behavior, usually sexual, was wrong:

> 013 Female: "Well, I can only answer for my own situation. If he ever found out I was cheating on him, he'd *kill* me. If he found out that I was fooling around, he would hospitalize me, *for sure*. I think if I ever cheated on him and he found out I'd never come back to the house, *never,* because that would be the death of me, for sure."

> 025 Female: "He might hit her if she hit him first. Maybe if she says something, the wrong thing, something she shouldn't say. I wouldn't like it, but I can understand it."

> 038 Male: "Yeah—if she was making love to the milkman. If she was unfaithful, I'd say yeah, give her a good shot. I'd think he'd have every right in the world to do it. Although I don't think that I could ever do that, I could accept someone else doing it."

> 105 Male: "If she had an affair, he has a right to do it. He put his love in her and she's throwing it away. He's committed himself and he's like being slapped in the face."

In contrast, most of the respondents' explanations rest heavily on the idea that the man is "sick" or "crazy" or does not have control over his temper when he is angry or frustrated. That is, the attributions refer not to the aggressors' logical or rule-following behavior, but to primitive, sometimes animal-like impulses and drives. Marsh et al. (1978) has shown that such attributions are commonly made by the media and by the lay public when attempting to explain violence by sports fans, though social scientific analysis reveals the actors act with reasoning and motives. Athens (1980) shows the same for violent criminals.

In the present case, then, accompanying the strong expressions of disapproval of hitting are many statements that indicate that the respondents UNDERSTAND how a man might hit his wife—that is, statements of explicit or implicit tolerance and legitimacy.

Some persons referred to the hitting husband as being "sick," "mentally ill," pathological, or the "kind of person who can't help doing that." For example:

> 017 Female: "I think it says something about his emotional make-up and stability."

> 020 Female: "There are all kinds of circumstances I can think of. I mean, you can have a *nut* who blows up at the slightest thing—I mean dinner is a little cold on the table and he hits her. I don't think there should be any kind of physical violence at all in a marriage, but

for some men, they think that's how to show their love. I don't think so—I think that shows the lack of respect if a husband goes around hitting. Like a little child . . ."

053 Female: "I think he'd have to be sick to hit her. To deliberately hurt someone else . . . I don't think it's normal."

098 Male: "I think it just shows that the person that is doing the hitting has a pretty sick mind. There are some things that I think are weird with people. I think that it's amazing that some women stick with men who beat them. They wouldn't stay unless they enjoy it. I think it's one of the weirdest and sickest things, and yet it's true."

By far the most frequent mention, however, was to anger and frustration and bad tempers. In some cases, reference was made to the husband being very angry or frustrated, but there was no explicit statement that he *couldn't* control his temper to avoid hitting her. In other words, another action might have been possible, and hence there is limited tolerance, as in the following:

045 Female: "I think it's not a lack of love, but some other problem. I think someone who hits still could love the person, but just not know how to show his anger in a healthy way."

052 Female: "He might hit her out of frustration, maybe with his job, or maybe frustration at not having accomplished anything is built up. I don't think he should hit her under any circumstances and I don't think she should put up with it, but I can imagine why he might do it."

057 Female: "It could be frustration. Sometimes he comes home in a terrible mood and he just complains about everything. I say I know something bad happened at work today, I know something. Sometimes when you have to take so much guff at work it has to come out someplace and somewhere. And some men, maybe they hit . . ."

In other instances, however, the interpretations stress that emotions carried the person away—that his temper "got out of control." Here, the person is *understood* at the same time that his actions are condemned. He, like the victim of the aggressive act, was a victim—this time of his lack of control. Such understanding may be considered implied tolerance.

004 Female: "He may still love her, but he just can't help it if he has a bad temper—but that is really uncalled for."

015 Female: "He could still love her a lot and hit her. He might have just got pushed to the limit. He lost a job, he did this, he did that, he came home and the house was a mess and they got into a big fight and it was something that he just couldn't blow off. O.K.—if

it's only once. But if he does it again, there'd be no question in my mind about putting up with it again."

064 Female: "I don't know. Probably it doesn't mean he loves her any less, but that he has a lack of self-control."

066 Female: "It doesn't say anything about love, but about his lack of control. Maybe there is some situation if it's a common occurrence, but if it's a once in a blue moon thing maybe there is a tension there that he didn't talk about and she didn't know about and she just coaxed him until he lost control."

072 Female: "He might hit her if he caught her in bed with somebody or with another man, say in a bar or a dancehall. That would be anger, and I don't think that he would know what he was doing and he wouldn't have any control. I'm not saying that I feel sorry for him."

095 Female: "I realize that there are some people who can deeply love another person and still hit them. I mean there are times when I just feel like hitting him. It doesn't mean that I don't love him. It does mean that I am so upset with him at that point . . . So if they can't control themselves that's too bad—that's their problem and their wife's problem, but it doesn't mean there isn't love for her."

073 Male: "I can imagine people losing their temper and becoming so crazy with the lack of response or the lack of a particular response. I can imagine getting mad doing that. It's not appropriate or reasonable to hit for that, it's not reasonable at all, but it's understandable."

091 Male: "I think under the influence of drugs, in a fit of anger, uncontrollable anger, or insanity, for whatever reason, a man might hit his wife. Not that I would tolerate or agree with it, but I can understand that happening . . . I think that just like child abuse it's a crime, a personal violation."

092 Male: ". . . In a fit of anger, of really deep emotion, you could really belt somebody and not have it have anything to do with your love for them."

Tolerance of Wives Hitting Husbands

What about women hitting their husbands? Two males strongly asserted it was a woman's *right* to hit her husband if he had been unfaithful; otherwise, as we have seen, there was not much support for women hitting husbands in terms of considerations that this was *appropriate* behavior. Once again, however, there is considerable *tolerance* alongside the lack of positive support or endorsement. By and large, just as the justifications offered for men hitting their wives rest on the "kind of person they are"— i.e., one who is "sick" or a "nut" or can't control his temper—these attributions also serve, to some degree, to permit the respondents to

Cathy Stein Greenblat   253

interpret the actions of wives who hit their husbands, but to a lesser degree. Only two respondents, both female, suggested that a woman who hits her husband is "sick" (clearly referring to mental illness.) Though a number of references were made to her being out of control, there was more emphasis on women using hitting to express their anger or frustration (i.e., it is a behavioral style she adopts) and less on her being carried away, as seen in the following:

009 Female: "I just think it says that she is overwrought about something. She has to be overwrought."

020 Female: "She's angry and she's just letting it out that way."

021 Female: "It doesn't show anything about love, it just shows she can't control her temper."

052 Female: "Well if she works it could be frustration with her job or maybe she's home and has kids all day long with screaming and then he'll come home and say "Oh what wonderful kids . . .""

055 Female: "Well, I guess the same as the husband—if she had a short temper control it doesn't necessarily mean that she doesn't love him. It's more like an immature thing to just reach out and smack somebody when you don't get your own way."

068 Female: "I think it says something about the situation she is in at the moment, about the pressures she's under. I don't think it says anything about love at all."

022 Male: "Well, I can see when a wife gets kind of mad and she may not realize what she's doing and slap her husband or something like that. I can see that situation. I guess some people when they get mad they don't know what they are doing. That's the only case I could see of somebody hitting her husband. I don't think that's appropriate at all."

028 Male: "I think it's a sense of frustration, that's what I feel, not a sign of love or lack of it."

By far more numerous, however, are explanations that partially "excuse" women from hitting their husbands which rest on the perceived (and probably actual) lower probability of her hurting him. These statements regarding the lower probability of hurt far outnumber and outweigh the statements about her lack of control or about her feelings of anger or frustration:

010 Female: "She might hit if she found him in bed with another girl, but I don't think a woman could hurt a man anyway . . ."

057 Female: "I guess she might hit him out of frustration or if she found him cheating. I hate to say this, but I guess I would do it. I don't think it's so terrible. She wouldn't hurt him as much. That's

why I think that it isn't so terrible. I don't mean beat him with a bat or something, I just mean slap him or something like that."

072 Female: "She might hit him like me, when I get mad at him, but I only really hit him when it doesn't hurt him at all. If I caught my husband in bed with another woman I would just slam the door and never see him again, I wouldn't hit him. Maybe I'd hit the girl or kill her. But hitting him wouldn't do anything except show him I'm angry, while leaving him would hurt him. I don't think a woman should hit a man because he shouldn't hit her, but I think a man would understand more than a woman getting hit by him because it wouldn't hurt him."

029 Male: "I'd say that it doesn't matter that much to him [if she hits him] because it's rare that a wife can hurt her husband, just hurt his emotions. I wouldn't feel that bad as a husband, because I would say she's angry and it doesn't hurt me at all, so let her get her anger out."

033 Male: "With an attempt to hurt, I would say no, there are no good circumstances. If it's just really on an arm or something like that a lot of times it's more comic than anything else. If it's in a vital area then I definitely can see no reason why she should. It's more or less the same thing; I respect you and I'm not going to hit you and you should do the same thing. But I don't think he can react in the same manner that she would be able to react. There is definitely a difference of physical strength there."

090 Male: "It happens. I imagine there are husband beaters. A wife can find any excuse for hitting her husband because she's smaller and she can get away with it. I don't think it's appropriate, though."

098 Male: "I suppose there are circumstances, though none that are reasonable. I sort of feel that it isn't as bad as the man hitting the wife. Most women I think can go ahead and hit their husbands without hurting them. I'd have to say that there isn't any reason for doing that. I think that any time she hits him, she is honestly trying to promote a problem."

This belief that women are more likely to be hurt than to inflict hurt is also reflected in responses to the questions of what a wife should do if she is hit and what a husband should do if he is hit. The responses varied widely, from "I don't know," "laugh," "ignore it," "leave temporarily," "discuss what is wrong," to "throw him (her) out," "hit back," "get a divorce," to "call the police." These have not been tabulated, as many respondents gave several answers. The two answers given by each respondent, however, were examined, and each case was coded in terms of whether the actions prescribed were the same for both, more serious for the husband, or more serious for the wife. As Table 14.4 shows, once again there are data to support the notion that for these respondents, a woman

TABLE 14.4 Responses Suggested for Husbands and Wives to Being Hit, by Gender of Respondent (percentages)*

	Men	Women
What should a wife do if hit?		
What should a husband do if hit?		
Action advocated for him is stronger	4	7
Same action advocated for both	38	56
Action advocated for her is stronger	58	37
Total	100	100
	(24)	(43)

*Ns are in parentheses.

hitting her husband is a much less serious matter than a man hitting his wife.

V. CONCLUSION: MORAL ENVIRONMENTS AND THE USE OF PHYSICAL FORCE

Let us begin this concluding section with a review of what has been found thus far.

First, we have found little evidence of approval of hitting one's spouse or slapping one's spouse. Asked in two different ways, less than one quarter of the respondents indicated there were circumstances it was appropriate to hit one's spouse or that there were conditions it was acceptable to slap one's spouse. Men were somewhat more accepting of the use of physical force than were women, and both were more accepting of wives hitting husbands than the reverse. The degree of support for use of physical force was somewhat lower than had been found a decade ago in the only study regularly cited.

Second, when the use of physical force was seen as appropriate it was most often in circumstances involving self-defense or in response to the victim's "transgressions," particularly known or suspected sexual infidelity.

Third, despite the low level of approval evidenced, there is considerable understanding or tolerance that is at least *implicit* in their comments. While many said use of physical force was unacceptable to them, the explanations they gave of why a man might hit his wife made heavy reference to factors which reduce or eliminate responsibility. Social scientists have largely rejected explanations of wife-beating that rely on mental illness (Gelles, 1981) or alcohol (Coleman & Straus, 1981; Berk et al., 1981) or overbearing stress, as in the following statements:

> In other words, once in a while a man may attack his family as a direct result of some severe mental disturbance or sickness, but in most cases of marital violence there is no evidence of what would be clinically defined by a psychiatrist as mental illness.

> . . . Leaving aside the comparatively rare occasions when unbearable stress provokes an otherwise controlled and peaceful man to an outburst of physical violence, there seems no doubt that the majority of battering husbands suffer from a constellation of problems, some of which are psychological but none of which classify him as mentally ill. (Renvoize, 1978, pp. 30-31)

> . . . most of the couples in this sample who were subject to a high degree of stress were not violent. (Straus, 1980, p. 24)

But these respondents continue to accept such explanations. Moreover, they frequently describe men as being "out-of-control" when they hit their wives; the action then is deplorable, but the hitter cannot be held accountable for his behavior. When it is women who hit, their actions tend to be tolerated on the grounds that after all they are not likely to create physical injury.

Why is this tolerance important? The answer appears to me to be complex but critical. Wife-beating, which for most of Western history, was prescribed, has in the last century in this country moved to the realm of officially proscribed behavior. Nonetheless, it continues in frightening numbers of cases, most of which escape both official and informal sanction and punishment. The data here relate primarily to the lack of the latter form of sanctions. The queries in this research were not about severe forms of use of physical force, but "only" about hitting and slapping. It might be argued that far more adamant objection would have been found to the more extreme forms, and I think this is surely the case. But by asking about the milder, more "normal" use it was possible to unearth some of the assumptions these respondents make about the bases of use of force.

The tolerance of milder forms helps to create a moral domain and definitions of responsibility. These explanations or excuses are employed by violent persons in creating their verbal self-defense and also by victims to excuse their assailants (see Greenblat, 1981; Gelles, 1974). Does the tolerance of small acts, we might ask, make it more likely that larger ones will follow when the issue is more serious or the strain greater, since the costs have been defined as low?

The argument that the hit "wouldn't hurt," so the act of hitting was tolerable is used not only by those who give light taps, but by those who have been victims or assaulters in cases involving far more severe force. This appears in a number of the accounts collected in this project including a report by a woman who was choked by her husband several times but says "it wasn't serious because he didn't really want to hurt me."

The "out-of-control" theory is a controversial one, for there is considerable dispute among social scientists about it. Some argue that much violence does stem from people going "out of control" (see Berkowitz, 1981), so the respondents can find some company in the scientific community. But others have argued that this is not the case most of the time. Gelles, for example, suggests that this is a *convenient* explanation:

> In situations where status can be lost by being violent, individuals employ accepted vocabularies of motive (Mills, 1940) or "accounts" (Lyman and Scott, 1970) to explain their untoward behavior. Thus, a violent father or mother might explain their actions by saying they were drunk or lost control. Parents who shared the same desire to batter their children might nod in agreement without realizing that a real loss of control would have produced a much more grievous injury or even death. (Gelles, 1981, p. 15)

Marsden supports the position that most persons who act violently have first reflected about the costs or likely costs of their acts. Actors tend to be deterred, he suggests, from violent actions to the extent they believe they will be unsuccessful. If there is no critical audience and if the costs of failure are low (police and courts are unlikely to respond with serious sanctions, wives have no place to go and obtain little sympathy from others), the violent outburst is more likely. Then it may be neutralized with an "out-of-control" explanation. One way a physically violent act may fail to be defined as illegitimate violence is that "the act itself may be admitted to have taken place, but the aggressor may claim not to have been fully responsible for it, because of some extraneous factor such as stress at work ('things got on top of me'), alcohol ('I didn't know what I was doing'), or some kind of 'uncharacteristic' mental lapse" (Marsden, 1978, p. 119).

Further rejection of the legitimacy of the out-of-control explanation comes from Athens' study of violent criminal acts and actors. Analyzing interview data, Athens found a high incidence of *near* violent situations—situations in which violence did not emerge because "restraining judgments" were made:

> This occurs when the actor breaks out of a fixed line of indication and decides that he should not carry out his violent plan of action into overt conduct. He *redefines* the situation and on the basis of his new definition of it *now* judges that he should not act violently. Thus, in forming a restraining judgment, the actor completely drops or shelves the violent plan of action which he had built up and his

violent interpretation of the situation subsides. The study of these near situations suggests several types of reasons why actors form restraining judgments.

First, an actor may form a restraining judgment in the situation because he fears that he will be unsuccessful. By taking the role of the person whom he had planned to assault, the actor implicitly or explicitly indicates to himself that the other person will retaliate if the actor assaults him ... Second, an actor may form a restraining judgment in the situation because the other person has suddenly changed his line of action ... Third, an actor may form a restraining judgment because he fears that he will seriously damage the social relationship such as friendship or marriage that exists between him and the other person ... Fourth, an actor may form a restraining judgment out of deference to another person ... And fifth, an actor may form a restraining judgement because he fears possible legal sanction. (Athens, 1980, pp. 31-35)

Those sociologists who likewise reject the "drive" theories of violence tend to include in their explanations of the high prevailing rates of violence, factors which make it "easy" for spouses to get away with using violence. They, too, point to continuing beliefs that when there is a disagreement husbands presume they have the right to the final say, and when they are thwarted, they believe they have the right as well as the power to use physical force. This latter is reinforced to the extent that they believe the police and courts will not seriously intervene, their wives will not leave, and they will not be condemned by the community at large.

It is in this context that the data reported herein must be viewed. As we ask what the moral environment is within which such "calculations" may be made by potentially violent spouses, the question of the potential deterrent power of negative attitudes must be raised. We have seen that there is at present considerable disapproval of hitting one's spouse. But so long as there is tolerance based upon "drive" theories of persons' inability to control themselves, violent actions are easier and more likely as there is a ready-made excuse for them.

REFERENCES

Athens, L. *Violent criminal acts and actors: A symbolic interactionist study*. Boston: Routledge & Kegan Paul, 1980.

Ball-Rokeach, S. Values and violence: A test of the subculture of violence thesis. *American Sociological Review*, 1973, *38,* 736-749.

Berk, R., Berk, S. F., Loseke, D. R., & Rauma, D. *Mutual combat and other family violence myths*. Paper presented at the National Conference for Family Violence Researchers, Durham, New Hampshire, July 1981.

Berkowitz, L. *The goals of aggression: Implications for family violence research*. Paper delivered at the National Conference for Family Violence Researchers, Durham, New Hampshire, July 1981.

Blumenthal, M., Kahn, R., Andrews, F., & Head, K. *Justifying violence: Attitudes of American men.* Ann Arbor: Institute for Social Research, University of Michigan, 1972.

Browne, S. In sickness and in health. Mimeograph, 1980.

Cazenave, N., & Straus, M. A. Race, class, network embeddedness and family violence: A search for potent support systems. *Journal of Comparative Family Studies,* 1979, *10*(3), 281-299.

Center for Women's Policy Studies. State legislation on domestic violence. *RESPONSE,* August/September 1980.

Coleman, D., & Straus, M. A. *Alcohol abuse and family violence.* Family Violence Research Center, University of New Hampshire, February 1981, mimeograph.

Denzin, N. Rules of conduct and the study of deviant behavior: Some notes on the social relationship. In J. Douglas (Ed.), *Deviance and respectability.* New York: Basic Books, 1970.

Dillman, D. A. *Mail and telephone surveys: Total design method.* New York: John Wiley, 1978.

Dobash, R. E., & Dobash, R. P. Wives: The "appropriate" victims of marital violence. *Victimology,* 1977-78, *2*(3-4), 426-442.

Dobash, R. E., & Dobash, R. P. *Violence against wives.* New York: Free Press, 1980.

Eisenberg, S., & Micklow, P. *The assaulted wife: Catch 22 revisted. (An exploratory legal study of wifebeating in Michigan).* Ann Arbor: University of Michigan Law School, 1974, mimeograph.

Field, M., & Field, H. F. Marital violence and the criminal process: Neither justice nor peace. *Social Service Review,* 1973, *47,* 221-240.

Freeman, M.D.A. *Violence in the home.* Westmead, England: Saxon House, 1979.

Gelles, R. *The violent home.* Beverly Hills, CA: Sage, 1974.

Gelles, R. Abused wives: Why do they stay? *Journal of Marriage and the Family,* 1976, *38,* 659-668.

Gelles, R. *Family violence.* Beverly Hills, CA: Sage, 1979.

Gelles, R. *An exchange/social control theory of intrafamily violence.* Paper presented at the National Conference for Family Violence Researchers, Durham, New Hampshire, July 1981.

Gelles, R., & Straus, M. A. Violence in the American family. *Journal of Social Issues,* 1979, *35*(2), 15-39.

Giles-Sims, J., & Price, M. *Till death do us part?* Durham: University of New Hampshire, 1978, mimeograph.

Greenblat, C. S. *Physical force by any other name . . .: Quantitative data, qualitative data, and the politics of family violence research.* Paper delivered at the National Conference for Family Violence Researchers, Durham, New Hampshire, July 1981.

Hecker, E. A. *A short history of women's rights: From the days of Augustus to the present time.* London: Putnam, 1910.

Hepburn, J. R. Violent behavior in interpersonal relationships. *Sociological Quarterly,* 1973, *14,* 419-429.

Lyman, S. M., & Scott, M. B. *A sociology of the absurd.* New York: Appleton-Century-Crofts, 1970.

Marsden, D. Sociological perspectives on family violence. In J. P. Martin (Ed.), *Violence and the family.* New York: John Wiley, 1978.

Marsh, P., Rosser, E., & Harre, R. *The rules of disorder.* London: Routledge & Kegan Paul, 1978.

Melville, J. Some violent families. In J. P. Martin (Ed.), *Violence and the family.* New York: John Wiley, 1978.

Pagelow, M. D. *Social learning theory and sex roles: Violence begins in the home.* Paper presented at the annual meetings of the Society for the Study of Social Problems, September 1978. (a)

Pagelow, M. D. *Secondary battering: Alternatives of female victims to domestic violence.* Paper presented at the annual meetings of the American Sociological Association, September 1978. (b)

Parnas, R. The police response to domestic disturbance. *Wisconsin Law Review,* 1967, *914,* 914-960.

Pizzey, E. *Scream quietly or the neighbors will hear.* Harmondsworth, England: Penguin, 1977.

Renvoize, J. *Web of violence: A study of family violence.* London: Routledge & Kegan Paul, 1978.

Richardson, D., & Campbell, J. Alcohol and wife abuse: The effect of alcohol on attributions of blame for wife abuse. *Personality and Social Psychology Bulletin,* 1980, *6*(1), 51-56.

Rossi, P. H., Waite, E., Bose, C. E., & Berk, R. E. The seriousness of crimes: Normative structure and individual differences. *American Sociological Review,* 1974, *39,* 224-237.

Rothbell, G. W. *The Jewish mother: Social construction of a popular idea.* Paper presented at the annual meetings of the American Sociological Association, Toronto, September 1981.

Ryan, W. *Blaming the victim.* New York: Vintage, 1971.

Stark, R., & McEvoy, J. M. III. Middle class violence. *Psychology Today,* 1970, *4,* 52-65.

Straus, M. A. Leveling, civility, and violence in the family. *Journal of Marriage and the Family,* 1974, *36,* 13-30.

Straus, M. A. *Cultural approval and structural necessity or intrafamily assaults in sexist societies.* Paper presented at the International Institute of Victimology, Bellagio, Italy, July 1975.

Straus, M. A. Societal morphogenesis and intrafamily violence in cross-cultural perspective. *Annals of the New York Academy of Sciences,* 1977, *285,* 717-730.

Straus, M. A. A sociological perspective on the prevention and treatment of wife beating. In M. Roy (Ed.), *Battered women.* New York: Von Nostrand Reinhold, 1979.

Straus, M. A. *Husbands and wives as victims and aggressors in marital violence.* Paper delivered at the annual meetings of the American Association for the Advancement of Science, San Francisco, 1980. (a)

Straus, M. A. Wife-beating: How common and why? *Victimology,* 1980, *2,* 443-458. (b)

Truninger, E. Marital violence: The legal solutions. *Hastings Law Journal,* 1971, *23,* 259-276.

U.S. Department of Justice, Bureau of Justice Statistics. *Intimate victims: A study of violence among friends and relatives.* Washington, DC: Government Printing Office, 1980.

Walker, L. *The battered woman.* New York: Harper & Row, 1979.

Wardell, L., Gillespie, D., & Leffler, A. *Science and violence against wives.* Paper delivered at the National Conference for Family Violence Researchers, Durham, New Hampshire, July 1981.

15

The Context-Specific Approach

RUSSELL P. DOBASH and R. EMERSON DOBASH

In contrast to most social science, our "research program" on violence against wives has not been an attempt to answer abstract theoretical questions or to provide narrow and circumscribed empirical descriptions (Lakatos, 1970).[1] Nor has it been oriented simply to gathering information relating to minor reforms in existing attitudes, social practices, and policies. Instead, we have adopted a concrete research strategy meant to provide a thoroughgoing explanation of the problem of wife-beating that might serve as a foundation for meaningful social action. We did not begin, however, with what we now call the context-specific method. Our training in a logical positivist tradition was very apparent when we began our research in 1973. As such, we began to work on developing a "model" of the processes involved in "marital violence" (Dobash & Dobash, 1974). We had borrowed the concept "marital violence" from the existing literature — which we now see as a gross, relatively useless and erroneous abstraction — and presented a research proposal and prepared a theoretical paper which emphasized the importance of subcultural factors and deviant background characteristics in the explanation of marital violence. We argued for the importance of a context-specific method, but the background of the proposal and the paper reflected our training in a sophisticated logical positivism.

As part of this preliminary we proposed to conduct a pilot study, a usual aspect of a positivistic programmatic. The initial objective of the pilot study was to develop a meaningful and comprehensive interview schedule. However, the pilot study turned out to be a great deal more than we had originally planned. The year spent on the pilot was not just devoted to developing an interviewing technique. We also spent a great deal of time learning about the nature of the problem from women who lived and worked in Women's Aid refuges and from social workers, police, and others involved in working with the problem. This enlightened us enormously about the issues and complexities relating to the problem and the institutional responses to it and its victims. We began to learn far more than we had gleaned from the meager literature available at the time, and expanded and altered our conceptions of the domain and parameters relating to the problem. This led us to see how the perspectives and procedures associated with the generally positivist approach we originally proposed were simply inadequate and too narrow to capture the dynamics and the complexity of what we were being told by those involved. This, in turn, led us to question our methodology and to seek an approach that would be sensitive to the complexities of the problem and reflect it in greater depth and detail.

The research methodology we eventually adopted for researching violence against wives constitutes a radical alternative to the arid procedures and false posturings of positivistic research. We have used various research strategies and adopted a critical, holistic, and contextual approach that includes historical, institutional and interactional analysis. Examination of the contemporary aspects of the problem included a thorough analysis of its concrete manifestations in the daily lives of men and women and of the institutional supports and responses both to battered women and to the general problem of wife-beating. We employed diverse research strategies, including our background knowledge of the problem, the research findings of others, and, most important, historical analysis, in-depth interviews with battered women, and police and court records.

In this chapter we will reconstruct our general methodology that is concrete and embedded in the social context and compare it to the work based on a generally positivist stance that is abstracted from the social world. Before presenting the context-specific method, we will examine the tenets of logical positivism that are usually accepted uncritically and consider the more recent criticisms and developments in the philosophy of science that have challenged its validity.

LOGICAL POSITIVISM, SOCIOLOGY, AND AN ALTERNATIVE PHILOSOPHY OF SCIENCE

At the moment the sociological enterprise is in a state of considerable turmoil and self-criticism. Of course, this has always been the case, but at other times there has been greater consensus and more agreement on theoretical imagery, methodological assumptions, and research strategies.

At present we are told that we suffer from a crisis and are then presented with a multitude of pathways and "new rules" that are proposed as *the* route to sociological purity and enlightenment. Those seeking security and a simple way out of the seeming confusion adopt simple answers, embrace one of these pathways, and attempt to conform rigidly to a strict and unbending programmatic without realizing that such entrenchment is just the opposite of scientific activity. Indeed, if we are suffering from a crisis, it arises from decades of rigid adherence to doctrines that promised methodological tickets to scientific respectability but delivered intellectual blinkers and mindless adherence to a sterile sophistication. It is the doctrine of logical positivism, that emerged from the Vienna Circle of philosophers in the 1920s and 1930s, that forms the foundation of our present predicament. Although a great deal has been written about "positivism" and "empiricism," most of this work has not provided us with a clear conception of the philosophical background to sociological research, because it is not the tenets of these orientations that have dominated recent research but rather those of "logical positivism."

The philosophical tenets of logical positivism (sometimes called logical empiricism) were meant to supersede or replace all other philosophies. This was to be achieved by combining the doctrines of seventeenth- and eighteenth-century English empiricism, expounded by Hume, Locke, and Bacon, with the new rationalist/mathematical procedures established in the early part of this century (Ayer, 1959; Richenback, 1951; Feigl, 1969; Achinstein & Barker, 1969). These hard-headed thinkers were radically opposed to metaphysics of any kind and sought to create "a philosophy to end all philosophies" (Feigl, 1969, p. 4). Inspired by the extraordinary advances in physics, they sought to reconstruct logically the procedures of conducting good science and to provide evaluative criteria for assessing ongoing research. For them, good science was epitomized by the experimentation and mathematical calculus of physics. There has always been considerable diversity in these doctrines (Nagel, 1961; Pap, 1961; Scheffler, 1963; Hempel, 1966, 1969; Ackerman, 1970), but a general emphasis on the strict separation between ideas (theory) and observations (methods), inordinate emphasis on the experimental design, demands for extreme clarity and precision in concepts, and the concomitant emphasis on measurement and statistical analysis have had significant consequences for the social sciences.

When surveying the course of the sociological enterprise throughout this century, we can see the extraordinary impact that the translated, often misinterpreted, proposals of the logical positivists have had on the social sciences. While psychologists embraced the potential benefits and constrictions of the experimental method, sociologists relied on survey methods, abstracted measuring devices and statistical manipulations to give their discipline a "scientific" appearance. C. Wright Mills (1971), while not interested in the roots of this enterprise, nevertheless eloquently and rightly criticized the results of the adoption of logical positivism by sociologists—that is, grand theory and abstracted empiricism. Within this tradition, the abstract empiricists, exemplified by Lundberg (1964) and Lazarsfeld and Barton (1964), championed operationalism, explicit and stipulative definitions, abstracted measurement, and statistical manipulations as sure routes to "scientific" sophistication. The theoreticians, most notably Parsons (1951), sought to create abstract ahistorical theories of society in general and to develop schema devoid of empirical content in the belief that this would make them applicable to diverse social settings and societies. Some sociologists offered various logical rules of axiomatizing, building, or perfecting these abstract theoretical schemes (Zetterberg, 1965; Stinchcombe, 1968; Dubin, 1969). Others, most notably Blalock (1970), emphasized mere technical solutions to problems of meaning and explanation. He argued that establishing cause is "a difficult and technical task" (p. 64) that can be solved primarily through the use of multiple regression techniques and path analysis (see also Blalock, 1968, 1969, 1971, 1979).

There has always been, and continues to be, a great deal of grumbling about the division between theory and methods that characterizes the logical positivist approach, and disquiet about the resulting aberrations, including the slums of studies based solely on statistics and the rarefied metaphysics of grand theory. Yet, sociologists have much to gain from maintaining a rigid distinction between these two arenas, not the least of which are careers for academic technicians able to manipulate abstract theoretical languages and abstruse methods that confer status but obscure knowledge about the social world. As such, a rigid distinction between theory and methods continues, and many social scientists cling both to the idea that research methods are unaffected by theoretical presuppositions and ideologies and to the assumption that intellectual work can warrant the label "theory" only if it has the appearance of the abstract and "free-floating calculi" proposed by logical positivists (Feigl, 1970).

Within the philosophy of science, such views are no longer in ascendency. Kuhn (1962, 1970) challenged the foundations of logical positivism directly and devastatingly and sought to redirect the philosophy of science by proposing that science was not guided solely by rational and logical principles and that theory and methods could not and should not be separated.[2] His analysis of shifts or revolutions in "normal science" demonstrate that they do not occur entirely because of logical arguments, improved experimentation, better data, crucial tests, or more elegant and parsimonious theories, but also because of psychological, social, and institutional factors, including beliefs, intuition, accidents, and social factors that impinge on theory and observation. In contrast to the rigid separation of theory and methods, Kuhn argues that theoretical paradigms determine the methods, problem field, and standards of solution and that these change according to the reigning paradigm.

Feyerabend (1965a, 1965b, 1970, 1975) has also argued that the practices and progress of science bear little resemblance to the abstract models presented by logical positivists. Using historical materials, especially the case of Galileo's defense and promulgation of the Copernican view of the universe, he constructs an account of how science actually operates. From this analysis and other historical examples, he concludes that logical positivists constructed a mythical view of science. Science, he argues, is not advanced solely by logical principles but also by other epistemologies and sometimes even by emotion, ad hoc arguments, propaganda, "power struggles," and "sordid personal" controversies. His fundamental point, however, is that the blueprints provided by the logical positivists' view of scientific activity are wrong. The rigid distinction between theoretical discourse, observational language, and observation itself is a myth. Instead, the entire scientific enterprise is *context-dependent:*

> The meaning of every term we use depends upon the theoretical context in which it occurs. Words do not 'mean' something in isolation; they obtain their meanings by being part of a theoretical system. (Feyerabend, 1965a, p. 180)

> If you want universal standards, I say, if you cannot live without principles that hold independently of situation, shape of the world, exigencies of research, then I can give you such a principle. But it will be empty, useless and pretty ridiculous. (Feyerabend, 1978, p. 41)

Social scientists can draw important conclusions from the work of historians and philosophers of science such as Kuhn (1962), Toulmin (1969), Lakatos (1970), and Feyerabend (1975). First, if we wish to understand the overall scientific enterprise, we must conduct research on our own research, including a careful consideration of personal, social, institutional, and political contexts in order to establish the actual manner by which certain perspectives and evidence come to be accepted over others. Second, to the extent that they are ahistorical or use abstracted and substantively impoverished concepts, schemes, and classificatory systems, we must reject as uninformative the abstracted theoretical work of logical positivism and some forms of Marxism. This should be replaced with works that are concrete, historical, and specific to the phenomenon under investigation and to the contexts in which it occurs. Third, we must recognize that there can be no distinct "observation language" of a neutral nature and that the type of observation used in a research program and the evidence emanating from it is partly if not entirely dependent on theory and ideologies. Because evidence is theory-dependent, this negates the assumption that we can settle our disputes about competing theories by simply assessing the empirical evidence relative to them. Instead, it is the overall research program, including theory, methodology, methods, and findings, that must be evaluated and compared.

For us the most significant implication that might be drawn from this body of work is that theory and methods are both interrelated and context-dependent. Furthermore, no necessary or rigid separation exists between scientific activity and political, personal, and social action (Touraine, 1981; Dobash & Dobash, 1981a). This integration of theory, research, and action forms a strong aspect of the realist perspective (Keat & Urry, 1975; Wartofsky, 1976) and is fundamental to the approach we have adopted. Given the continuing debate about what constitutes a genuine realist method, we describe our methodology as a "context-dependent" or "context-specific" form of analysis.

A CONTEXT-SPECIFIC APPROACH

In order to elucidate the context-specific approach we will provide a reconstruction of some of the general methodology and empirical strategy used in our research program on violence against wives or cohabitants. These will be compared with examples of research based on a logical positivist approach. Although the reconstruction of a research program should include a wide range of logical, social, and political issues, we will concentrate in this chapter on the empirical strategy, historical analysis, and theoretical explanation. Admittedly, any reconstruction is a wide-ranging task, and this study can only be a partial and unfinished effort, but it should serve to open discourse and thus enhance the development of this area of study.

Empirical Strategies

Our overall research program was oriented to providing a description, explanation, and understanding of the phenomenon of wife-beating. The empirical strategy formed a crucial component of this, and, as stated earlier, it included an analysis of historical materials (which will be discussed later), police and court records, and in-depth interviews with women who had experienced violence from their husbands or cohabitants. For the sake of brevity and because it is the more important of the two, we will concentrate on the construction and execution of the interviews. One of the crucial aspects of the interview was to gain a thorough description and understanding of the violence itself, the contexts in which it occurred, its development over time, and its meaning, particularly for the victim. To do this, we spent one year developing an interview schedule that was systematic and in-depth and could be conducted in a style that allowed maximum participation of the respondent without loss of systematic content (Dobash, Dobash, Cavanagh, & Wilson, 1977-78, Dobash & Dobash, 1979, 1980).

While diverging in many important respects, the style and content of our interviews have much in common with the techniques employed by other researchers, particularly those using naturalistic, subjective, and ethnographic forms of fieldwork. Researchers adopting these methods think that human actions, beliefs, and intentions cannot be explained and understood without careful attention to the interactional contexts in which they occur. Cicourel has argued persistently for this orientation. His research is devoted to the assessment of how institutional contexts, such as probation departments, affect taken-for-granted assumptions and modes of response (Cicourel, 1964, 1968, 1974, 1979). Other researchers have argued for the importance of considering the characteristics of interactive settings, such as ice hockey matches and police arrests, in the genesis of violent events (Toch, 1969; Westley, 1970; Faulkner, 1973). They reject, as we do, the reductionist methods that attempt to establish only the psychological or social characteristics of violent individuals and/or their victims (Moran, 1971; Faulk, 1974; Gayford, 1975, 1976; Kolb & Straus, 1974; Gelles, 1974; Walker, 1979). Instead, they embed their analysis of violent events in the everyday settings in which they occur.

The interviewing technique we employed followed the general dictates of this contextual strategy by embedding violent events in the day-to-day activities of men and women. However, we went further than other naturalistic researchers and considered it necessary to examine the wider history and background of the relationship. We began the interview by asking each woman about her personal background, the beginning of the relationship, and her perceptions and evaluations of the initial relationship with the man who eventually became her husband. This discussion progressed to a consideration of the beginning of their married life. Through this approach we sought to establish the manner in which the daily lives of men and especially women are altered as they become husbands and wives and as violence enters the relationship. We encouraged women to tell us about their perceptions of marriage relative to their own concrete experiences, not as responses to a series of abstract questions derived from a priori specified hypothetical relationships. The interview then progressed to a close examination of the violence itself (Dobash et al., 1977-78; Dobash & Dobash, 1982). We asked the women numerous questions about three specific violent events: the first, the worst (as they evaluated it), and the last one they experienced before going to a refuge for battered women. The exploration of these specific violent events would begin by asking the woman a somewhat general question: "Could you tell me what happened the first time your husband used violence against you?" Such an approach allowed the woman to develop and recount the violence in her own terms and relative to her feelings and emotions relating to that specific event.

Many women gave elaborate and detailed accounts of the violence they had experienced and in doing so answered a whole series of subsequent questions we had about the event. Some women gave less detailed accounts and it was necessary to ask the additional questions and/or probe a bit further in order to obtain information that would be comparable throughout the sample and enable us to assess the recurring and persistent elements of these violent events. Using this technique, we gathered an enormous amount of systematic and detailed information regarding the exact nature of the violence, the resulting physical and emotional injuries, the intentions and meaning associated with the violence, the response of bystanders, the subsequent response and evaluations of the man and woman, the kinds of help sought, and responses received from outsiders, such as relatives, friends, social workers, doctors, and the police. After exploring these three separate events in a detailed and elaborate manner, we asked the women to describe a usual violent event relative to the same aspects. The final sections of the interview related to the nonviolent nature of the relationship. The entire interview was oriented toward determining in a systematic manner the concrete nature of the violence and its relationship to other aspects of the marriage.

The interviews lasted from 2 to 12 hours and were tape-recorded and transcribed. This technique allowed for a more conversational style of interviewing and enabled the interviewer to pursue issues relative to the woman's frame of reference and experiences. It also enabled the interviewer to achieve a better understanding of the woman's experiences and evaluations because they could be assessed relative to her overall background and experiences, rather than relative to some abstracted scales.

In using this approach to interviewing we followed many of the tenets of a naturalistic and subjectivist perspective, but we found this approach to be limited and used it only as a partial method. We certainly think that explanations of social phenomena must include a consideration of the accounts and assessments of the participants in violent events and of the interactional contexts in which action occurs, but for us this is only a necessary basis for explanation and not a necessary and sufficient condition. It is also crucial to include a consideration of the wider history of relationships between men and women, along with the social, cultural, and economic background of the institution of marriage. Only this wider analysis makes an interpretation of the accounts possible and meaningful. Our work also differs from many subjective approaches which often sacrifice the rich substance of the events of everyday life by placing an extreme emphasis on their meaning.

We also think it is appropriate and important to provide quantitative data based on the qualitative information. As such, we do not reject quantification and have used it throughout our research program (Dobash & Dobash, 1977-78, 1979, 1982; Dobash, Dobash, & Cavanagh, 1982).

However, statistics have a specific and contained role in our overall methodology and never become a substitute for everything else. They are used in describing the violence and elucidating the *processes* involved in it, but never in a reductionist manner to specify the characteristics of individuals.

Another aspect of our empirical strategy involved the use of a reflexive technique in the preparation and analysis of the quantitative and qualitative information. For example, in coding the responses to open-ended questions for computer analysis, we read the verbatum accounts, developed preliminary response categories, and then reread the accounts to add additional categories or modify the initial ones. Thus, a process of successive approximation was used. Obviously, this was a time-consuming process but one which was fundamental in order to retain the maximum amount of information and, more important, to retain its concrete nature. The reflexive technique was also important in the development of concepts and theoretical explanations and in the presentation of findings. One pragmatic example of this involved the construction of a file of verbatum accounts that was used in developing concepts and employed in illustrating recurring and predominant patterns. Finally, the reflexive technique can be seen in the style we use to present our findings; one that uses both qualitative and quantitative information to reveal the recurring patterns and sequence of events composing the violence and the violent relationship and the meanings and evaluations attached to them.

HISTORICAL AND THEORETICAL ANALYSIS

Sociologists have discovered history, and it is seen by some as a way out of our epistemological confusions; others seem to have decided that it is politically, and sometimes professionally, safer to work on history; and still others think that a simple statement demonstrating that a particular problem, such as violence against wives, existed in the past is a sufficient preliminary to a consideration of its present manifestations. Historical *analysis* for us is a necessary aspect of a holistic approach to the study of violence against wives. However, simplistic citing of examples from the past does not constitute a historical analysis, is rarely very informative, and can often lead to erroneous conclusions and unfortunate exaggerations. Steinmetz (1977-78), for example, cites a single example from Shorter's *The Making of the Modern Family* (1977) to support her claim that husbands were often subjected to beatings by their wives. Shorter's example of charavaris and misrules (ritualized rebuking) directed at women who used violence against husbands is taken out of context in order to support the fallacious conclusion that the "battered husband syndrome" was, and still is, a widespread and significant problem. This conclusion emanated from a superficial historiography and resulted in the failure to recognize the paradoxical and ironic nature of these rituals, which is evident to those who have done a thorough historical analysis (Davis, 1971; Thompson, 1972; Shorter, 1977). The evidence actually indicates that the use of the term "beating" or "battering" when applied to husbands was as inappropriate in the past as it is today (Dobash & Dobash, 1981a). Historical evidence demonstrates overwhelmingly that it is women in their positions as wives who have been subjected to severe and persistent violence (O'Faolain & Martinez, 1974; Castan, 1976; May, 1978; Tomes, 1978; Dobash & Dobash, 1977-78), and that ritual rebuking, such as misrules, are more accurately interpreted as direct and symbolic supports for patriarchal relationships (Dobash & Dobash, 1981b).

Sociologists trained in the generally reductionist procedures of the hypothetico-deductive method and other forms of positivism find it difficult, if not impossible, to deal with historical materials (see Lukacs, 1971, for an early and insightful analysis of this limitation). In contrast, the form of historical analysis we adopted was contextual and holistic and sought to establish the interrelated nature of social phenomena. This methodology emphasizes the crucial importance of establishing the necessary linkages between contemporary problems and patterns and the historical processes that aid in their explanation and understanding. In using this methodological principle we have drawn considerable inspiration from certain tenets of Marx and Weber. For all their important and significant differences, they had at least one important principle in common: a rejection of ahistorical, timeless, and universal laws of societies in general (Weber, 1949; Marx, 1970, 1973, pp. 100-108). They both argued for the importance of thorough and far-reaching historical analysis as an aspect of a wider and in many other respects divergent methodological programmatic. Adopting this approach, the historical analysis we undertook was oriented to revealing the manner in which economic, religious, and legal institutions and processes affected the status of women and wives and directly or indirectly affected the problem of violence used against them (Dobash & Dobash, 1977-78, 1979, pp. 31-74, 1980, 1981b). For example, we explored the way religious ideology, promulgated from the pulpit beginning in the early seventeenth century, emphasized the inferior and subordinate position of women, especially wives, and supported patriarchal domination in general and the power of husbands in particular. Contradictorily, religious leaders and Christian tenets often expressly forbid the use of physical chastisement of wives while emphasizing strict obedience of subordinates. Thus, they directly supported male domination and indirectly supported the use of various means (such as violence) to achieve and maintain rightful control. This analysis was developed in considerable detail and enabled us to establish the significance of various processes and institutions in the maintenance of violence against wives. A similar approach was adopted for the economic and legal legacies that relate to wife-beating (Dobash & Dobash, 1979).

In seeking to integrate history, empirical examples, and theoretical discourse, we have followed the examples of E. P. Thompson and Michel Foucault. Foucault and Thompson have only recently attempted to articulate and formulate their methodological principles (Thompson, 1979; Foucault, 1977, 1979). Yet their work has offered examples of a form of historical analysis that integrates the concrete and the analytical. In somewhat different guises, they both adopt a context-dependent method. Foucault argues that all knowledge and knowledge of knowledges is contextually determined and limited by specific historical conditions. For Thompson, arguments and concepts cannot be divorced from the substance to which they apply. He argues that historical concepts must emerge from "empirical engagements" and be utilized relative to specific historical sites (1979, p. 391; see also Zaret, 1978). Foucault relies on polemic and dramatic empirical examples to emphasize and punctuate his analysis, whereas Thompson's empirical materials are more detailed and accentuated by a more direct and concrete analysis. Interpretation, theory, empirical materials, and political issues and concerns are all part of the context in which they both work and are components of the historical analyses they produce.

Social scientists who attempt to adhere to the epistemological principles associated with logical positivism usually reject or neglect historical analysis and seek instead to follow the dictates of the hypothetico-deductive model of theory that is both ahistorical and acontextual. Researchers following this tradition in the sociology of violence have attempted to develop abstract concepts and propositions such as "clarity demands that we separate the behavior [violence] from its social meanings which exist in society or across societies" (Gelles & Straus, 1979b), from which it is thought to be possible to deduce generalized hypotheses such as "persons who vary in their participation in violent behavior should also vary in attitudes toward violence . . . [and] persons who vary in participation in violence should also vary in underlying patterns" (Ball-Rokeach, 1973, p. 737; see also Hepburn, 1973). When attempts are made to apply such general, abstract, ahistorical, and acontextual propositions and hypotheses to specific social contexts and research domains, one of two things happens: If the original character is retained, they are meaningless, inapplicable, and relatively useless in the specific research domain; if made to apply to the particular research domain, they are transformed beyond recognition and cease to be general propositions. Failing to recognize this problem, researchers investigating "domestic" violence and "spouse" abuse have constructed abstract scales such as the Conflict Tactic Scale (Straus, 1979) meant to apply to several specific types of violence occurring between a variety of family members.

Perhaps the most generalized and abstract approach representing the logical positivist tradition is the general systems perspective (Straus, 1973;

Gelles & Straus, 1979b). This perspective is usually devoid of any substantive content and has little or no informative value when applied to a specific research domain. A positivistic programmatic of this nature leads to a poor fit between theoretical discourse and empirical research, often resulting in arid conceptual schemes and charts derived more from current sociological convention than from the particular substantive problem under scrutiny. Social scientists have often abused various theoretical perspectives in studying the family. At best, we have seen structural functionalism, exchange theory, conflict theory, and now general systems theory borrowed and simply laid over the various phenomena under scrutiny. At worst, the conceptual framework is simply reiterated alongside a set of empirical data in hopes the reader will make some connection between them. If this tradition continues, we would expect to see the latest approach, sociobiology, emerging as the "new" perspective and to be treated in a similar fashion with little consideration of its epistemological weaknesses and political implications. Explanation and understanding are of little importance in this enterprise. Rather than being paramount, such concerns are omitted by this sociological convention and by the demand for technological routes to knowledge.

By contrast, using a context-specific (realist) approach leads the researcher to attempt to develop thorough explanations of social phenomena through a substantively informed theoretical discourse in which concepts, propositions, and assertions are rooted in specific, delimited empirical contexts (Black, 1956; Shapere, 1969; Putnam, 1973; Feyerabend, 1975). As with the historical analysis outlined above, theoretical discourse is meaningful only when it is related to cultural, social, institutional, interactional, and political contexts. Thus, theoretical discourse and empirical analysis and evidence cannot be isolated and separated from one another but must be interrelated. This form of analysis will result in informative and meaningful explanations of the social world and provide direction for social action.

NOTES

1. In order to evaluate competing explanations of any phenomenon, Lakatos (1970) proposed that researchers should compare their overall research programs rather than comparing only their competing theories. More generally, this would include a comparison of the entire research enterprise from which the explanation was finally derived, rather than simply a comparison either of the theoretical frameworks from which they began or of the specific methods or measurements they eventually adopted.

2. Sociologists, ignoring Kuhn's explicit statement that the social sciences were preparadigmatic, seized on the concept "paradigm" as a means of describing and comparing various sociological theories and perspectives (Heyl, 1975).

REFERENCES

Achinstein, P. & Barker, S. F. (Eds.). *The legacy of logical positivism.* Baltimore: John Hopkins University Press, 1969.

Ackerman, R. *The philosophy of science.* New York: Pegasus, 1970.

Ayer, A. J. (Ed.). Editor's introduction. In A. J. Ayer (Ed.), *Logical Positivism.* New York: Free Press, 1959.

Ball-Rokeach, S. Values and violence: A test of the subculture of violence thesis. *American Sociological Review,* 1973, *38,* 736-49.

Black, M. Definition, presupposition and assertion. In S. Hook (Ed.), *American philosophers at work.* New York: Criterion Books, 1956.

Blalock, H. M. The measurement problem: A gap between the languages of theory and research. In H. M. Blalock & A. B. Blalock (Eds.), *Methodology in social research.* New York: McGraw-Hill, 1968.

Blalock, H. M. *Theory construction: From verbal to mathematical formulations.* Englewood Cliffs, NJ: Prentice-Hall, 1969.

Blalock, H. M. *An introduction to social research.* Englewood-Cliffs, NJ: Prentice-Hall, 1970.

Blalock, H. M. *Causal models in the social sciences.* Chicago: Aldine, 1971.

Blalock, H. M. Dilemmas and strategies of theory construction. In W. E. Snizek, E. R. Fuhrman, & M. K. Miller (Eds.), *Contemporary issues in theory and research.* London: Aldwych, 1979.

Castan, N. *Divers aspects de la constrainte maritale, d'apres les documents judiciaries due XVIII siède* (Documents of eighteenth-century France). Paper presented at the annual meeting of the American Sociological Association, New York, August 1976.

Cicourel, A. *Method and measurement in sociology.* New York: Free Press, 1964.

Cicourel, A. *The social organization of juvenile justice.* New York: John Wiley, 1968.

Cicourel, A. *Theory and method in a study of Argentine fertility.* New York: Wiley Interscience, 1974.

Cicourel, A. Field research: The need for stronger theory and more control of the data base. In W. E. Snizek, E. K. Fuhrmen, & M. K. Miller (Eds.), *Contemporary issues in theory and research.* London: Aldwych, 1979.

Davis, N. Z. The reasons of misrule: Youth groups and charivaris in sixteenth century France. *Past and Present,* 1971, *51,* 51-75.

Dobash, R. E. & Dobash, R. P. *Violence between men and women within the family setting.* Paper presented at the VIII World Congress of Sociology, Toronto, Canada, August 1974.

Dobash, R. E., & Dobash, R. P. Wives: The appropriate victims of marital violence. *Victimology,* 1977-78, *2*(3-4), 426-442.

Dobash, R. E., & Dobash, R. P. *Violence against wives: A case against the patriarchy.* New York: Free Press, 1979.

Dobash, R. E., & Dobash, R. P. Wife beating: Patriarchy and violence against wives. In Open University (Eds.), *Conflict in the family.* Milton Keynes: Open University, 1980. (a)

Dobash, R. E., & Dobash, R. P. Explanations of wife beating that blame the victim. Open University (Eds.), *Conflict in the family.* Milton Keynes: Open University, 1980. (b)

Dobash, R. E., & Dobash, R. P. Community response to violence against wives: Charivari, abstract justice and patriarchy. *Social Problems,* 1981, *28*(5), 563-581. (a)

Dobash, R. E., & Dobash, R. P. Social science and social action: The case of wife beating. *Journal of Family Issues,* 1981, *2*(4), 439-470. (b)

Dobash, R. E., & Dobash, R. P. *The antecedents and nature of violent episodes.* Paper presented at the annual meetings of the American Sociological Association, San Francisco, August 1982.

Dobash, R. E., Dobash, R. P., & Cavanagh, K. *The professions construct the problems of women: Medical and social work responses to battered wives.* Paper presented at the 31st Annual Meeting of the Society for the Study of Social Problems, San Francisco, August 1982.

Dobash, R. E., Dobash, R. P., Cavanagh, K., & Wilson, M. Wifebeating: The victims speak. *Victimology,* 1977-78, *2*(3-4), 608-622.

Faulk, M. Men who assault their wives. *Medicine, Science and the Law,* 1974, *14,* 180-183.

Faulkner, R. On respect and retribution: Toward an ethnography of violence. *Sociological Symposium,* 1973, *9,* 17-35.

Feigl, H. The origin and spirit of logical positivism. In P. Achinstein & S. F. Barker (Eds.), *The legacy of logical positivism.* Baltimore: John Hopkins University Press, 1969.

Feyerabend, P. K. Problems of empiricism. In R. Colodny (Ed.), *Beyond the edge of certainty.* Englewood Cliffs, NJ: Prentice-Hall, 1965. (a)

Feyerabend, P. K. Reply to criticism: Comments on Smart, Sellers and Putnam. In R. S. Cohen & M. W. Wartofsky (Eds.), *Boston studies in the philosophy of science* (Vol. II). New York: Humanities Press, 1965. (b)

Feyerabend, P. K. Against Method: Outline of an anarchistic theory of knowledge. In M. Radner & S. Winokur (Eds.), *Minnesota studies in the philosophy of science* (Vol. IV). *Analyses of theories and methods of physics and psychology.* Minneapolis: University of Minnesota Press, 1970.

Feyerabend, P. K. *Against Method: Outline of an anarchistic theory of knowledge.* London: New Left Books, 1975.

Feyerabend, P. K. On the critique of scientific reason. In R. S. Cohen, P. K. Feyerabend, & M. W. Wartofsky (Eds.), *Essays in memory of Imre Lakatos.* Dordrecht, Holland: D. Reidel, 1976.

Feyerabend, P. K. From incompetent professionalism to professionalized incompetence: The rise of a new breed of intellectuals. *Philosphy of the Social Sciences,* 1978, *8,* 37-53.

Foucault, M. *Discipline and punish: The birth of the prison.* London: Allen Lane, 1977.

Foucault, M. *The history of sexuality* (Vol. I) (R. Hurley, trans.). London: Allen Lane, 1979.

Gayford, J. J. Wife battering: A preliminary survey of 100 cases. *British Medical Journal,* January 15, 1975, pp. 194-197.

Gayford, J. J. Ten types of battered wives. *The Welfare Officer,* 1976, *1,* 5-9.

Gelles, R. J. *The violent home.* Beverly Hills, CA: Sage, 1974.

Gelles, R. J., & Straus, M. A. Violence in the American family. *Journal of Social Issues,* 1979, *35*(2), 15-39. (b)

Gelles, R. J., & Straus, M. A. Determinants of violence in the family: Toward a theoretical integration. In W. R. Burr et al. (Eds.), *Contemporary theories of the family: Research based theories* (Vol. 1). New York: Free Press, 1979. (b)

Hempel, C. G. *Philosophy of the natural sciences.* Englewood Cliffs, NJ: Prentice-Hall, 1966.

Hempel, C. G. Logical positivism and the social sciences. In P. Achinstein & S. F. Barker (Eds.), *The legacy of logical positivism.* Baltimore: John Hopkins University Press, 1969.

Hepburn, J. R. Violence behavior in interpersonal relationships. *Sociological Quarterly,* 1973, *14,* 419-429.

Heyl, J. Paradigms in social science. *Society,* 1975, July/August, 61-67.

Keat, R., & Urry, J. *Social theory as science.* London: Routledge & Kegan Paul, 1975.

Kolb, T. M., & Straus, M. A. Marital power and marital happiness in relation to problem-solving ability. *Journal of Marriage and the Family,* 1974, *36,* 756-766.

Kuhn, T. *The structure of scientific revolutions.* Chicago: University of Chicago Press, 1962.

Kuhn, T. Reflections on my critics. In I. Lakatos & A. Musgrave (Eds.), *Criticism and the growth of knowledge.* London: Cambridge University Press, 1970.

Lakatos, I. Falsification and the methodology of scientific research programmes. In I. Lakatos & A. Musgrave (Eds.), *Criticism and the growth of knowledge.* Cambridge: Cambridge University Press, 1970.

Lazarsfeld, P. F., & Barton, A. H. Qualitative measurement in the social sciences: Classification, typologies and indices. In R. D. Lerner & H. D. Laswell (Eds.), *The policy sciences.* Stanford: Stanford University Press, 1964.

Lukács, G. What is orthodox Marxism? In *History and class consciousness* (R. Livingstone, trans.). London: Merlin Press, 1971.

Lunberg, G. A. *Foundations of sociology.* New York: David McKay, 1964.

Marx, K. *A contribution to the critique of political economy* (M. Dobb, Ed.). Moscow: Progress Publishers, 1970. (Originally published, 1859.)

Marx, K. *Grundrisse: Foundations of the critique of political economy.* (M. Nicolaus, trans.). Harmondsworth, England: Penguin, 1973. (Originally published, 1939.)

May, M. Violence in the family: An historical perspective. In J. P. Martin (Ed.), *Violence in the family.* London: John Wiley, 1978.

Mills, C. W. *The sociological imagination* Harmondsworth, England: Penguin, 1971.

Moran, R. Criminal homicide: External restraint and subculture of violence. *Criminology,* 1971, *8*(4), 357-374.

Nagel, E. *The structure of science.* New York: Harcourt Brace Jovanovich, 1961.

O'Faolain, J., & Martinez, L. *Not in God's image.* Glasgow: Fontana Collins, 1974. (Reissued in 1979 by Virago.)

Pap, A. *The structure of science.* New York: Harcourt Brace Jovanovich, 1961.

Parsons, T. *Toward a general theory of action.* New York: Harper & Row, 1951.

Putnam, H. Explanation and reference. In G. Pearce & P. Maynard (Eds.), *Conceptual change.* Dordrecht, Holland: D. Reidel, 1973.

Richenback, H. *The rise of scientific philosphy.* Berkeley: University of California Press, 1951.

Scheffler, I. *The anatomy of inquiry: Philosophical studies in the theory of science.* New York: Bobbs-Merrill, 1963.

Shapere, D. Notes toward a post-positivistic interpretation of science. In P. Achinstein & S. F. Barker (Eds.), *The legacy of logical positivism.* Baltimore: John Hopkins University Press, 1969.

Shorter, E. *The making of the modern family.* Glasgow: Fontana/Collins, 1977.

Steinmetz, S. K. The battered husband syndrome. *Victimology,* 1977-78, *2*(3-4), 499-509.

Stinchcombe, A. L. *Constructing social theories.* New York: Harcourt Brace Jovanovich, 1968.

Straus, M. A. A general systems approach to a theory of violence between family members. *Social Science Information,* 1973, *12*(3), 105-125.

Straus, M. A. Measuring conflict and violence: The conflict tactics (CT) scales. *Journal of Marriage and the Family,* 1979, *40*(1), 75-88.

Thompson, E. P. Frontieres Nouvelles ≪Rough Mosic≫: Le charivari anglais. *Annals (Economies, Societies, Civilisations),* 1972, *27*(2), 285-312.

Toch, H. *Violent men: An inquiry into the psychology of violence.* Chicago: Aldine, 1969.

Tomes, N. A "torrent of abuse": Crimes of violence between working-class men and women in London, 1840-1875. *Journal of Social History,* 1978, *11*(3), 329-345.

Toulmin, S. E. From logical analysis to conceptual history. In P. Achinstein & S. F. Barker (Eds.), *The legacy of logical positivism.* Baltimore, MD: Johns Hopkins University Press, 1969.

Touraine, A. *The voice and the eye: An analysis of social movements* Maison des Science de l'Homme and U.U.P., trans.). Cambridge: Cambridge University Press, 1981.

Walker, L. *Battered women.* New York: Harper & Row, 1979.

Wartofsky, M. W. The relation between philosophy of science and history of science. In R. S. Cohen, P. K. Feyerabend, and M. W. Wartofsky (Eds.), *Essays in memory of Imre Lakatos* (Vol. 39). Dordrecht, Holland: D. Reidel, 1976.

Weber, M. *The methodology of the social sciences* (E. Shils & H. A. Finch, Eds. and trans.). New York: Free Press, 1949.

Westley, W. A. *Violence and the police: A sociological study of law custom and morality.* Cambridge: MIT Press, 1970.

Zaret, D. Sociological theory and historical scholarship. *American Sociologist,* 1978, *13,* 114-121.

Zetterberg, H. *On theory and verification in sociology* (3rd ed.). New York: Bedminster Press, 1965.

16

Using a Feminist Approach in Quantitative Research
A Case Study

KERSTI YLLÖ

Over the last decade our awareness of the relationship between wife-beating and patriarchy has grown enormously. Studies of this relationship can be grouped into two broad categories. Feminists have used historical and case study data to analyze the link between patriarchy as a social system and wife abuse (Dobash & Dobash, 1980; Martin, 1976). Other researchers have assessed the relationship between the balance of power within marriages and spousal violence (Allen & Straus, 1980; Straus, Gelles, & Steinmetz, 1980). While both approaches have made important contributions to understanding violence against wives, each is also limited. The feminist expositions generally lack empirical evidence regarding the impact of sexual inequality. In particular, quantitative data have not been brought to bear on this issue. The interpersonal power researchers, on the other hand, have been myopic in their perspective. Husband dominance has been studied empirically, but in isolation from the patriarchal system of which it is a part. The purpose of this chapter is to begin to bridge the gap between these two approaches. In the following sections, a quantitative methodology for investigating feminist issues is outlined.

PATRIARCHY AND WIFE-BEATING:
THE FEMINIST ANALYSIS

The feminist analysis of wife-beating is, at heart, a critique of patriarchy. The central argument is that the brutalization of an individual wife by an individual husband is not an individual or "family" problem. It is simply one manifestation of the system of male domination of women

Author's Note: *This chapter is a revised version of a paper presented at the Feminism and the Critique of Capitalism Symposium at Johns Hopkins University, March 1980.*

which has existed historically and cross-culturally. Societal tolerance of wife-beating is a reflection of patriarchal norms which, more generally, support male-dominance in marriage. Traditional marriage, in turn, is a central element of patriarchal society.

Del Martin, a noted feminist analyst of wife-beating, writes in *Battered Wives* (1976):

> The historical roots of our patriarchal family models are ancient and deep. . . . New norms for marriage and family must be created, since the battering of wives grows naturally out of ancient and time-honored traditions. (p. 26)

A more scholarly volume on wife-beating which follows along the lines of Martin's work is the Dobashes' *Violence Against Wives* (1980). The authors set wife abuse in historical and social context through comprehensive analysis of its legacy in the past and its perpetuation in the present. Using a wealth of international data and their own interviews with battered women, they illustrate how being a wife makes a woman an "appropriate victim" of assault. They assert that

> men who assault their wives are actually living up to cultural prescriptions that are cherished in Western society—aggressiveness, male dominance, and female subordination—and they are using physical force as a means to enforce that dominance. (p. 24)

Their book concludes with the statement that "the problem lies in the domination of women. The answer lies in the struggle against it" (p. 243).

The works of Martin and the Dobashes (emphasized here because they are two of the best and best-known feminist analyses of this issue) are powerful. They, and other explicitly feminist analyses, reveal the connection between societal patriarchy and the abuse of individual wives by building a strong case from many historical examples and contemporary illustrations.

What the feminist approach has not included is any quantitative analysis. In part, this may be because reliable statistics on violence against wives have generally been unavailable. But it is also a consequence of a distrust of quantitative methodology as a whole. The Dobashes, for example, maintain that in such analysis "the goal of understanding society is forgotten and ignored: the major preoccupation . . . is the development of standardized measuring techniques to test hypothetical statements, an activity unlikely to lead to an understanding and explanation of social problems" (1980, p. 25). This sweeping indictment of quantitative sociology is neither justified nor necessary for their purposes, one of which is to show the value of a "context-specific" approach.

The feminist focus on the social context of violence against wives, which emphasizes that wife abuse is neither deviant nor pathological, is not *inherently* linked to a particular type of methodology. More important than the particular research tool are the theoretical questions asked. The questions raised by feminist theory can be answered most fully through the use of a range of research designs by many researchers working in a cooperative atmosphere. Any single research method has its limitations. Feminist analyses of wife-beating that rely on qualitative data have been rich in detail regarding particular incidents and cases. However, they have lacked generalizability. The issue of how the current context of patriarchy affects the level of violence against wives throughout American society has not yet been adequately addressed.

MARITAL POWER AND WIFE-BEATING:
THE INTERPERSONAL POWER RESEARCH

Researchers studying marital power and violence against wives came to the issue because of an academic interest in marital relationships and interaction. While some have feminist sympathies, they regard their purpose as doing research to explain social behavior rather than to formulate a critique of patriarchy.

This body of research has focused not on structured inequality on the societal level, but on inequality and the balance of power within the family. In *Behind Closed Doors* (1980), Straus et al. report the level of violence against wives is lowest among couples who followed a pattern of egalitarian decision-making. Fewer than 3% of these wives had suffered a severe violent attack within the previous year. In contrast, more than double that percentage (7.1%) of wife-dominant couples reported such violence. The rate of wife-beating in couples where the husband dominates is 10.7%: that is, 50% higher than for wife-dominant couples and more than 300% greater than for egalitarian couples.

Clearly, husband violence is associated with nonegalitarian decision-making. It may be that among couples where the wife tends to make the final decisions, for whatever reasons, some husbands lash out violently because their masculinity is threatened. In male-dominant relationships, a sizable number of husbands may turn to violence to maintain the subordination of their wives.

While this empirical research provides valuable evidence on the relationship between husband dominance and violence, it is too narrowly focused. Its major shortcoming is common to all analyses which consider male-female power and inequality within the confines of the family unit. The patriarchal social and cultural context, within which the family is enmeshed and marital power relations are played out, is overlooked. The notion that patriarchal norms have largely been replaced by egalitarian ones is accepted too readily. The inequitable social structure from which husbands derive legitimizing resources is not taken into account.

Research concentrating on the interpersonal relationship between spouses is too restricted. However, this limitation is more a consequence of the theoretical orientation of the researchers than the quantitative methodology they use. The patriarchal social context can be examined using a quantitative methodology. The remainder of this chapter focuses specifically on this methodology.

States as Social Context Units

This methodology, with its emphasis on macrosociological context, focuses on American states as the contextual unit of analysis for a number of reasons. First, the states are theoretically appropriate units for the comparative study of the status of women. Despite the sense that America is becoming increasingly "nationalized" through centrally controlled media, corporations, and the federal government, states are still more than different colored areas on the map. Not only were states founded by peoples of diverse national backgrounds and values, but the timing of their settlement and development have influenced their individual characteristics and the position of women within them. Further, states are often the initiators of legislation and programs and are frequently the unit of implementation of federal policies, all of which can affect women.

The second reason that this research focuses on states is a practical one. Many of the variables of interest here are gathered by the Census Bureau on a state-by-state basis. In addition, a number of other agencies gather state-level data (for example, NOW's information on women and education). The uniformity of data from state to state makes them most useful for comparative purposes. Variables from different sources can easily be related to one another.

Violence Against Wives

The term "violence," as used here, refers to *physical* aggression. The data on rates of violence were obtained from a major national survey entitled "Physical Violence in American Families." In 1976, a nationally representative area probability sample of 2143 husbands and wives were interviewed by a specially trained staff. Black interviewers were used in areas where the majority of the population was Black and Spanish-speaking interviewers (and Spanish questionnaires) were utilized in Hispanic areas. The interviews lasted approximately one hour and were completely anonymous and confidential.

The data on family violence based on this survey are the best national figures currently available. The clear advantage of wife-beating rates drawn from this survey is that they are based on a representative sample of the general public. In contrast, police, hospital, and shelter records of abuse are limited because they provide information only on those cases that come to the attention of the authorities. These cases are not representative of all abuse cases in the same sense that imprisoned criminals are not representative of all persons who committed crimes.

Nevertheless, the figures on violence from the survey are almost certainly underestimates of the true rate of wife abuse. It is likely that respondents did not "tell all" in the interviews, although many were quite candid (e.g., a number admitted to using a knife or gun). Also, the survey sample included only those couples who were cohabiting at the time of the interview. It is likely that a number of the most violent relationships were terminated and were therefore excluded from the study. Despite the possibility that the actual rate of wife-beating may be double the survey estimates (see Straus et al., 1980, for additional details), these estimates remain superior to any others available.

Although the violence rates are based on data gathered from a national area probability sample, only 36 states were included in this sample. In addition, since only certain areas of states were included after the first stage of sampling, these areas might not be representative of the whole state, particularly in those states in which only one or two areas were selected.

Rather than proceed on the assumption that the state samples are representative, we investigated this by comparing key variables from the survey data with parallel variables from census data, which we know to be representative. The variables considered were men's/husband's income, men's/husband's employment rate, men's/husband's education, and women's/wives' education.

Generally, the sets of variables paralleled in value. States with high income, education, and employment levels according to the Census Bureau ranked similarly on the survey data, in most cases. However, all but two of the states (Oregon with 14 cases and Mississippi with 13) having sample sizes of 20 or fewer cases appeared to be unrepresentative. These six states were dropped from the analysis, leaving a final sample size of 30 states.

In most of the analyses it is useful to group states into quartiles or quintiles by degree of patriarchal structure or norms. The mean violence rate for a group of states is more reliable than individual state rates because it is based on a larger number of cases.

Measurement of Wife-Beating

The rate of wife-beating was determined through the use of the Conflict Tactics Scale (discussed in detail in Straus, 1979, and presented in full in Appendix A).

The rate of wife-beating is the proportion of couples who indicated that the husband had used any of the following tactics against his wife in the year prior to the interview: kicked, bit, or hit with a fist; hit or tried to hit with something; beat up; threatened with a knife or gun; used a knife or gun. A state violence rate of 10%, for example, indicates that 10% of the husbands perpetrated serious acts of violence against their wives within the past year. Note that more "minor" forms of violence, such as pushing, shoving, or slapping, are not included in the calculation of the rate. This is not because such acts are condoned here, but because they are so common an element of family conflict that they would weaken the discriminating power of the index.

PATRIARCHAL STRUCTURE

Patriarchal structure is seen here as the status of women as a group, compared with the status of men as a group, in key societal institutions. The status of women relative to men in these institution spheres is assessed through a Status of Women Index (Yllö, 1980). Each sphere is considered a distinct dimension of women's status and makes up a separate part of the index. The specific dimensions that are included are the economic, educational, political, and legal. The particular items making up each dimension are listed below. The sources for the data are listed in Appendix B.

ECONOMIC DIMENSION
EC1 = % of women in the labor force
EC2 = % female in professional and technical occupations
EC3 = % female in managerial, administrative occupations
EC4 = Unemployment: male rate as % of female rate
EC5 = Median income: female as % of male, for full-time workers
ECX = Economic status of women index

EDUCATIONAL DIMENSION
ED1 = High school graduation: female rate as % of male rate
ED2 = Postsecondary enrollment: % female
ED3 = High school interscholastic athletes: % female
ED4 = High school administrators: % female
EDX = Educational status of women index

POLITICAL DIMENSION
POL1 = Members in U.S. Congress: % female
POL2 = Members of state senate: % female
POL3 = Members of state house: % female
POL4 = Judges on major appelate and trial courts: % female
POLX = Political status of women index

LEGAL DIMENSION
L1   = No occupations barred to women
L2   = Equal pay laws
L3   = Fair employment practices act
L4   = No maximum hours restrictions for females
L5   = Proof of resistance not required for rape conviction

L6 = Corroborating testimony not required for rape conviction
L7 = Husband and wife jointly responsible for family support
L8 = Husband and wife have equal right to sue for personal injury
L9 = Hus. and wife have equal right to sue for loss of consortium
L10 = Wife's property rights unrestricted
L11 = Wife's right to use maiden name unrestricted
L12 = Wife's right to maintain separate domicile unrestricted
L13 = Ratified federal Equal Rights Amendment
L14 = Passed a state Equal Rights Amendment
LEGX = Legal status of women index

The individual items were standardized so that they could be combined into indexes for each of the four dimensions and a total index. Table 16.1 gives the rank order of the state from most to least egalitarian. Clearly, this is a just relative ranking, since no state was truly egalitarian on any index.

FEMINIST ISSUES AND
QUANTITATIVE METHODS

The discussion above illustrates how a quantitative methodological approach does not preclude the exploration of concepts central to feminist analysis—such as violence against wives and the status of women. A contextual analysis, in which variance in rates of violence is examined according to state status of women, is the approach I have taken in data analysis (see Yllö, in press). The impact of institutional sexual inequality on levels of wife-beating (holding constant other state factors such as income levels, urbanization, and overall rate of violent crime) can thus be studied quantitatively.

It is not suggested here that this method is the only way to operationalize either violence against wives or the status of women. Rather, the purpose of this chapter is to present the case study of one possible approach which illustrates a different method for examining the connection between patriarchy and wife-beating. It is hoped that this approach is just one of many brought to bear on this crucial issue.

The triangulation of research methods is central to the development of a better understanding of any research issue, and feminist issues are no exception. Since each method has particular strengths and weaknesses, there is always a danger that a finding will reflect, in part, the method of inquiry. This approach provides a balance to the qualitative analyses which have been predominant in feminist research. In doing so, it provides an additional approach to understanding the relationship between patriarchal society and the violence that individual wives endure.

TABLE 16.1 State Rankings on the Dimensions and on the Overall Status of Women Index

Economic Status of Women	Educational Status of Women	Political Status of Women	Legal Status of Women	Status of Women Index (SWX)
89. D.C.	77. *VT*	79. ARIZ	100. ALAS	70. ALAS
68. N.C.	74. ALAS	71. MD	89. N.J.	62. CONN
67. *VT*	67. WASH	69. N.H.	78. DEL	61. MD
64. ALAS	66. CONN	67. WASH	78. WIS	61. *VT*
64. ARK	64. MINN	66. COLO	78. CONN	61. COLO
63. HAWA	63. MICH	66. CONN	66. COLO	60. N.J.
63. S.C.	62. ICWA	65. OREG.	66. WASH	60. N.H.
63. N.Y.	62. MD	61. R.I.	66. N.H.	59. WASH
60. TENN	61. KANS	60. N.J.	66. CAL	57. WIS
58. MD	60. N.D.	58. N.C.	66. S.D.	57. NEBR
58. NEBR	59. MONT	56. HAWA	66. HAWA	55. HAWA
57. NEV	58. WYO	55. FLA	66. INDI	55. OREG
57. GA	57. S.D.	53. DEL	66. MASS	55. ARIZ
56. CAL	57. COLO	52. NEBR	66. NEBR	55. MASS
55. COLO	56. ME	52. MASS	62. WYO	55. N.Y.
54. MISS	55. OREG	52. KANS	55. N.Y.	55. D.C.
54. WIS	54. N.M.	52. NEV	55. MD	54. CAL
53. N.H.	53. N.Y.	52. *VT*	5.5 ARIZ	54. S.D.
52. KY	52. N.H.	51. ME	55. IOWA	53. IOWA
52. MINN	51. VA	50. IOWA	55. MINN	53. MINN
52. FLA	51. NEBR	50. N.D.	55. OREG	53. KANS
51. MASS	50. WIS	49. D.C.	55. PA	53. FLA
51. PA	50. MASS	49. ILL	555. FLA	52. MICH
50. MC	49. FLA	49. S.D.	55. KANS	51. WYO

284

49. VA	49. KY	48. TENN	55. R.I.	50. DEL
49. MICH	48. CAL	48. ARK	50. MICH	50. ME
48. ME	48. D.C.	48. INDI	50. *VT*	49. TENN
48. N.J.	48. IDA	48. N.Y.	44. ARK	49. R.I.
47. ALA	47. TEX	48. OHIO	44. KY	49. ARK
46. IOWA	47. MISS	47. CAL	44. TENN	49. INDI
45. OREG	47. NEV	46. WIS	44. N.D.	49. PA
44. KANS	45. N.C.	46. IDA	44. IDA	48. N.D.
43. R.I.	45. TENN	46. PA	44. OHIO	48. N.C.
43. TEX	45. OKLA	45. MICH	44. GA	47. MONT
43. S.D.	44. N.J.	44. MONT	44. MONT	46. KY
43. N.M.	44. ILL	43. MO	44. MO	45. GA
42. WYO	44. ARIZ	42. TEX	44. TEX	45. MO
41. ARIZ	43. OHIO	42. MINN	44. ME	44. NEV
41. CONN	43. PA	41. WYO	33. UTAH	44. TEX
40. OKLA	42. INDI	41. ALAS	33. ILL	44. OHIO
40. N.D.	42. GA	41. LA	33. MISS	43. IDA
39. OHIO	42. MO	41. KY	33. D.C.	43. MISS
39. ILL	39. ARK	40. OKLA	33. VA	42. VA
39. MONT	39. DEL	40. W.VA	33. N.M.	41. N.M.
39. W.VA	38. W.VA	39. UTAH	21. NEV	41. ILL
38. INDI	37 R.I.	39. GA	21. N.C.	39. S.C.
36. WASH	36. UTAH	37. VA	21. OKLA	36. OKLA
36. IDA	36. HAWA	37. N.M.	21. W.VA	34. W.VA
32. DEL	34. LA	36. S.C.	21. S.C.	34. UTAH
29. UTAH	34. S.C.	36. MISS	10. LA	28. ALA
27. LA	24. ALA	33. ALA	10. ALA	28. LA

APPENDIX A: CONFLICT TACTICS SCALE

HAND RESPONDENT CARD A

87. No matter how well a couple gets along, there are times when they disagree on major decisions, get annoyed about something the other person does, or just have spats or fights because they're in a bad mood or tired or for some other reason. They also use many different ways of trying to settle their differences. I'm going to read a list of some things that you or your (husband/partner) might have done when you had a dispute, and would first like you to tell me how often you did it in the past year.

	Q. 78 RESPONDENT – IN PAST YEAR								Q. 79 HUSBAND/PARTNER – IN PAST YEAR								Q. 80 EVER HAPPENED		
a. Discussed the issue calmly	0	1	2	3	4	5	6	X	0	1	2	3	4	5	6	X	1	2	X
b. Got information to back up (your/his) side of things	0	1	2	3	4	5	6	X	0	1	2	3	4	5	6	X	1	2	X
c. Brought in or tried to bring in someone to help settle things	0	1	2	3	4	5	6	X	0	1	2	3	4	5	6	X	1	2	X
d. Insulted or swore at the other one	0	1	2	3	4	5	6	X	0	1	2	3	4	5	6	X	1	2	X
e. Sulked and/or refused to talk about it	0	1	2	3	4	5	6	X	0	1	2	3	4	5	6	X	1	2	X
f. Stomped out of the room or house (or yard)	0	1	2	3	4	5	6	X	0	1	2	3	4	5	6	X	1	2	X
g. Cried	0	1	2	3	4	5	6	X	0	1	2	3	4	5	6	X	1	2	X
h. Did or said something to spite the other one	0	1	2	3	4	5	6	X	0	1	2	3	4	5	6	X	1	2	X

i. Threatened to hit or throw something at the other one	0	1	2	3	4	5	6	X	0	1	2	3	4	5	6	X
j. Threw or smashed or hit or kicked something	0	1	2	3	4	5	6	X	0	1	2	3	4	5	6	X
k. Threw something at the other one	0	1	2	3	4	5	6	X	0	1	2	3	4	5	6	X
l. Pushed, grabbed, or shoved the other one	0	1	2	3	4	5	6	X	0	1	2	3	4	5	6	X
m. Slapped the other one	0	1	2	3	4	5	6	X	0	1	2	3	4	5	6	X
n. Kicked, bit, or hit with a fist	0	1	2	3	4	5	6	X	0	1	2	3	4	5	6	X
o. Hit or tried to hit with something	0	1	2	3	4	5	6	X	0	1	2	3	4	5	6	X
p. Beat up the other one	0	1	2	3	4	5	6	X	0	1	2	3	4	5	6	X
q. Threatened with a knife or gun	0	1	2	3	4	5	6	X	0	1	2	3	4	5	6	X
r. Used a knife or gun	0	1	2	3	4	5	6	X	0	1	2	3	4	5	6	X
s. Other (PROBE): _____	0	1	2	3	4	5	6	X	0	1	2	3	4	5	6	X

79. And what about your (husband/partner)? Tell me how often he (ITEM) in the past year.

FOR EACH ITEM CIRCLED EITHER "NEVER" OR "DON'T KNOW" FOR BOTH RESPONDENT AND PARTNER, ASK:

80. Did you or your (husband/partner) *ever* (ITEM)?

IF *ANY* BRACKETED ITEMS HAPPENED IN PAST YEAR; GO TO NEXT PAGE. IF *NO* BRACKETED ITEMS IN PAST YEAR, SKIP TO Q. 82.

TAKE BACK CARD A

APPENDIX B:
SOURCES OF DATA FOR THE STATUS OF WOMEN INDEX

Items from Source are listed in parentheses.

Alexander, S. *Women's legal rights.* Los Angeles: Wollenstonecraft, 1975. (L1-LL14)

Council of State Governments. *Book of the states.* Lexington, KY: Council of State Governments, 1975. (POL1-POL4)

Johnson, M., & Stanwick, K. *Profile of women holding office.* New Brunswick, NJ: Eagleton Institute of Politics, 1978. (POL1-POL4)

Project on Equal Education Rights. *Back to school line-up: Where girls and women stand in education today.* Washington, DC: National Organization for Women, 1979. (ED3-ED4)

U.S. Bureau of the Census. *Statistical abstract of the U.S.* Washington, DC: Government Printing Office, 1977. (ED1-ED2)

U.S. Department of Labor. *Survey of income and education, Spring, 1976.* Washington, DC: Bureau of Labor Statistics, Report 536, 1978. (EC1-EC5)

REFERENCES

Allen, C., & Straus, M. A. Resources, power, and husband-wife violence. In M. A. Straus & G. T. Hotaling (Eds.), *The social causes of husband-wife violence.* Minneapolis: University of Minnesota Press, 1980.

Dobash, R. E., & Dobash, R. P. *Violence against wives.* New York: Free Press, 1980.

Martin, D. *Battered wives.* San Francisco: Glide Publications, 1976.

Straus, M. A. Measuring intrafamily conflict and violence: The Conflict Tactics (CT) scales. *Journal of Marriage and the Family,* 1979, *41,* 75-88.

Straus, M. A., Gelles, R. J., & Steinmetz, S. K. *Behind closed doors: Violence in the American family.* Garden City, NY: Doubleday, 1980.

Yllö, K. A. *The status of women and wife-beating in the U.S.: A multi-level analysis.* Unpublished Ph.D. dissertation, University of New Hampshire, 1980.

Yllö, K. Sexual equality and violence against wives in American states. *Journal of Comparative Family Studies,* in press.

17

A Feminist Analysis of
Child Abuse and Neglect

CAROLYN KOTT WASHBURNE

Since child abuse and neglect are problems which affect families, especially women and children, it is puzzling and disturbing that very little has been written on the subject from a feminist perspective, in either the professional or feminist literature. There are several obvious reasons for this and perhaps others that are not yet apparent. Since 1962, when child abuse was "discovered" and publicized by C. Henry Kempe in his article on the battered child syndrome, organized efforts on behalf of maltreated children have primarily been the province of the established social service system—social work, medicine, law—with the general public becoming more involved in recent years. Since professional literature in general has little feminist content, it is not surprising that virtually nothing in the literature on child abuse and neglect is written from a feminist perspective.

The absence of material on child abuse and neglect in feminist literature, however, is more surprising. The feminist movement began and continues to be primarily a grass-roots movement, challenging established systems and working to create new ones. There has been considerable focus in feminist literature, in particular the literature on battered women and family violence, on the nuclear family as a major contributor to the oppression of women and children. While in recent years there has been emphasis on the devastating effects of violence in the home on women and, to a lesser extent, on children, most of what has been written has focused on male-initiated violence. There is little about violence by women except in situations where abused women retaliate.

It is unfortunate that there is no well-developed and widely disseminated feminist analysis of child abuse and neglect. The need for such an analysis goes beyond professional and political turf-fighting to the basic issue of how to stop violence and protect children. Proverbially speaking, child welfare professionals have been barking up the wrong tree. Since 1962 considerable time, energy, and money have been spent on the problem of child abuse and neglect with less than spectacular results. Interventions with parents who abuse their children have been based on the stated assumption that the family should be preserved if possible and the unstated assumption that the kind of family most worth preserving is the traditional one. Treatment goals, especially for abusive mothers, often reinforce traditional female roles and behavior. A woman who wants her children returned from placement, for example, is often required to clean up her home and improve her appearance. Even self-help groups, which tend to have greater success than treatment programs in working with abusive parents, are more likely to focus on helping women become better wives, mothers, and girlfriends than on helping them develop their own strengths and interests. While some practitioners have developed innovative approaches, such as using assertiveness training, the field as a whole has not moved much beyond the traditional ways of working with women.

Prevention efforts in the field of child abuse and neglect have tended to focus on reducing general societal violence and eliminating corporal punishment. There has been little discussion of how rigid sex roles within families and stereotyped sex-role conditioning of children contribute to violence. Other prevention efforts have concerned promoting public awareness about the difficulty of parenting and the importance of support systems for parents. Missing from that emphasis is a discussion of how strongly women are programmed into motherhood and how the general lack of support for parenting affects mothers more dramatically than fathers. For child welfare professionals to be more effective in their work with abusive families, it is critical for them to understand the role of women in the family. Since women are the primary nurturers of children in this society, the welfare of children is inextricably bound up with the welfare of women. Until efforts are aimed at promoting women's equality, professionals will not make a dent in the problem of child abuse and neglect.

Feminists have a better understanding than child welfare professionals of the causes and consequences of violence in families. Feminist analysis recognizes abuse as rooted in unequal power relationships in the family and speaks to how women and children are victims of those relationships. This analysis has been translated into treatment programs in women's shelters and other counseling programs where women are encouraged to develop their own power and autonomy.

The literature on battered women points out that children are often the accidental, and sometimes nonaccidental, victims of violence between their parents, and that even children who are not physically harmed are emotionally scarred by being in the presence of their parents' violence. As it became obvious that the children of battered women have special needs of their own, many shelters and counseling programs developed children's components. Child welfare professionals have commonly failed to recognize that there is often violence against women in families where children are abused. Finally, feminists are also looking creatively at preventing violence in families, based on their analysis of how sex-role conditioning creates aggressive men and passive women who are locked into destructive patterns of interaction.

But feminists have not gone far enough. Mothers abuse children, too, even more than fathers, according to some research, and not always when they are battered themselves. Violence by women toward their children is glossed over by feminists, perhaps because of their discomfort with the idea of women as victimizers and perhaps for fear of discrediting a movement which is already politically controversial. Yet feminists have recognized that women are on occasion violent toward men and understand *that* violence as the result of societal and interpersonal pressures on women. Women's violence toward children needs to be recognized and discussed in the same context. Women's abuse of children stems directly from their own oppression in society and within the family. Women are expected to be the major caretakers of children, yet have few supports for that task; women are more invested in their children's behavior and accomplishments since they have primary responsibility for maintaining the family; women have fewer options than men for self-fulfillment and self-definition outside the family. It is not surprising, then, that some women displace their frustration and anger on their children, the family members who are less powerful than they.

A feminist analysis of child abuse and neglect needs to be developed and integrated into the literature if the field is to advance and the problem of child abuse to be dealt with effectively. There needs to be thoughtful research into the differences between women and men who abuse and into how and why girls and boys are abused differently. Such research should take into account the effect of changing societal conditions, in particular the effect increasing economic stress has on rates of woman abuse and child abuse. Researchers need to share their information with practitioners so that effective models of intervention and treatment can be designed, implemented, and evaluated. These models should be based on the assumption that helping women develop themselves is essential, even though this means that some families cannot be "preserved." This approach will not result in the destruction of the American family, as some have charged, but is the key to strengthening families, protecting children, and ensuring a less violent future. Until men and women learn to relate in mutually supportive ways, and until children are viewed not as the property of adults but as individuals with rights, violence in families will continue.

Everyone concerned about children needs to begin discussing how alternatives to the traditional family, alternatives which stress equality among all family members, can reduce child abuse. This is particularly important in light of growing right-wing and fundamentalist influences in our society. If men played a more central role in child-rearing, would their nurturing capacities be more pronounced and their tendencies toward violence reduced? Would women, given the opportunity to develop themselves outside of home and family and provided with more support for the job of parenting, stop displacing anger onto their children? Would women be better able to intervene when men become violent with children? Would women be better able to intervene when men become violent with them? Are there special coping skills demonstrated by nontraditional families (single parent, blended, lesbian/gay) which could be helpful to other families? Can any of these questions be answered through research? Developing and promoting a feminist analysis of child abuse and neglect is crucial; the needs of our most vulnerable children are too important not to do so.

18

Maternal and Paternal Abuse of Children
Theoretical and Research Perspectives

JUDITH MARTIN

In its examination of violent activity within the family, current literature depicts an interesting division of labor. Adult males are usually described as the primary maltreaters of spouses, while adult females are considered mainly responsible for physically abusive behavior toward children. Violent activity appears to follow a "pecking order" in which larger and stronger family members attack those who are smaller and weaker. As a result of use of this model, study of male abusive parents has been neglected. This chapter explores available information concerning mothers and fathers who maltreat their offspring and points to specific areas in which more detailed knowledge of abusive fathers should be developed.

In actuality, physical child abuse differs from other types of severe dysfunction in parent/child relationships in the degree to which parents of both genders become involved. In the study of sexual abuse, the vast majority of reported cases and published studies focus on male perpetrators; in neglect cases most published works suggest overreporting of homes in which very poor women are single heads of household. In the physical abuse area, in contrast, the contributions made by each parent are substantial.

Large sample, representative surveys, such as that published by the American Humane Association (1978, p. 21), find that in 55% of the physically abusive cases perpetrators are male. (See also Kadushin & Martin, 1981.) In the well-known, classic study conducted by David Gil (1970), mothers or mother substitutes were abusive in 47.6% of the cases and fathers in 39.2%. Gil goes on to say:

> Though in absolute numbers slightly more children in the sample were abused by mothers than by fathers, one must remember that

29.5% of the children were living in fatherless homes. Fathers or substitutes were involved as perpetrators in nearly two-thirds of the incidents occurring in homes that did have fathers or father substitutes, and mothers or substitutes were involved in slightly fewer than one-half of the incidents occurring at homes that did have a mother or mother substitute. Thus, the involvement rate of fathers was actually higher than of mothers. (p. 116)

Research conducted on a much smaller scale and studies conducted with hospital or treatment populations provide more variable results. The proportion of mothers in these publications range from 50% (Justice & Justice, 1978; Creighton, 1979) to 75% (Baher, et al., 1976). Overrepresentation of abusive females is frequently ensured by the development of treatment programs specifically designed for mothers (Gabinet, 1979a) and the structuring of programs that operate during the daylight hours only, so that working fathers are much less likely to attend.

Because fathers are primary contributors in physical abuse events, questions concerning similarities and differences between their actions and those of abusive mothers are both relevant and pertinent. In one research effort (Martin, 1978) it was found that mothers and fathers are equally likely to abuse infants, but three out of four adolescents were mistreated by their fathers. Different etiological factors and varying interactive dynamics may be operative in paternal as distinct from maternal maltreatment cases. This study documents the relative over-emphasis on the role of maternal figures as perpetrators in physical child abuse cases and explores some consistent differences in research efforts undertaken to study the etiology of maternal and paternal violence toward children.

METHODOLOGY

Data were collected using studies of abusive parents published since 1976. Research efforts examining the etiology and epidemiology of adult abusive behavior were included, as were those testing the effectiveness of treatment efforts with parents. Publications were discovered through a computer search of the literature, from a review of recent research (Kalisch, 1978), and from other available sources. When multiple works were published by the same author using the same data, only the most comprehensive study was included, unless substantially different analyses of the data were performed in each work. Publications used in this literature review are listed in the bibliography.

The bibliography represents a thorough, albeit incomplete, listing of recent efforts in the abuse area. Due to the nature of the resources used, dissertations and books are probably underutilized while well-known journal offerings are better represented. The list contains no other known sources of consistent bias.

STUDIES OF ABUSIVE MOTHERS AND FATHERS

Research examining abusive mothers, fathers, and both parents published in the last six years was analyzed. Those dealing exclusively with males make up 2 of the 76 works reviewed. One of these discusses use of systematic desensitization with one father who maltreated his young daughter. The second work, entitled "Aggression Against Cats, Dogs, People," describes the childhood of violent male psychiatric patients (Felthous, 1980). Studies of mothers, in contrast, total 41% of the group and are highly variable in terms of the substantive issues covered. Very few of the two-parent studies attempt to differentiate between maternal and paternal characteristics in data analysis, and an even smaller number use gender of the parent as a control factor when examining results.

In the course of classifying these publications, three quite distinct approaches to the question of male abuse emerged. A number of reports systematically exclude fathers and fail to explain why. In an attempt to develop reliable diagnostic categories or evidence of treatment effectiveness for "child abusers," these authors simply assume that mothers alone needed to be studied. Others appear to have some commitment to consideration of male and female maltreaters. They carefully use terms such as "the abusing parent" in place of the "maltreating mother" to emphasize the existence of paternal abuse. However, they express no concern about differential evaluation of the qualities of each type of parent. In reviewing their research, it frequently proves difficult to determine they have actually studied both parent types.

Still other works reflect concern for perpetrators of both genders and awareness of potential differences between them, but the role of the female parent is still considered primary. Diagnostic categories in these studies contain references to "mothering" but pay no attention to "fathering." Some writers in this category use a data collection approach commonly found in child development research; while data are sought describing both parents, mothers alone are used as informational resources. No effort is made to assess the degree of congruence in perceptions and attitudes between parents (see, for example, Oates et al., 1979).

Overall, this review points to a chronic overemphasis on the importance of maternal qualities and deemphasis of the contributions made by fathers. Greater sensitivity to the potential significance of gender differences and greater attention to the special qualities of abusive males are required.

Review of this recently published research afforded an opportunity to explore some potential differences in data that focus on maternal as compared with paternal contributions to abuse. Because the number of father-only studies was so small, comparisons were made between those involving both parents and those exclusively examining mothers. In a preliminary and relatively "rough" estimate of the extent mothers are considered more "responsible" for child maltreatment, the following questions were explored.

(1) Are mothers more likely to be studied when cases are drawn from younger, more seriously injured hospitalized populations?

(2) Are mothers more likely to be studied in small-sample "intensive" studies than in large-scale research?

(3) Are mothers more likely to be studied when the focus of the research involves intrapsychic rather than environmental factors significant in the etiology of abuse?

Literature describing reported abuse cases (American Humane Association, 1978; Gil, 1970) finds that most abused children sustain minor injuries. In a study of confirmed cases occurring in 1974-1975 in Wisconsin, children sustained only bruises or welts in 79% of the incidents. Eighty-six percent required no medical attention, and only 6% were hospitalized (Kadushin & Martin, 1981, p. 108). Children receiving medical attention in hospitals tend to be younger and more susceptible to severe injury. Researchers focusing on these atypical cases are therefore more attuned to the life-threatening aspects of maltreatment. Although fathers are as likely as mothers to abuse young children (Martin, 1978), we may find research focusing more specifically on maternal abuse in these specialized cases. Table 18.1 reflects results of the survey in response to this issue.

The data suggest no differences in the proportion of maternal studies (24%) conducted in hospital settings. Maternal studies, however, are twice as likely to be drawn from outpatient treatment populations. Two-parent studies are more often drawn from large-scale probability samples or reporting populations. These differences are not statistically significant.

It is also possible that maternal studies are overrepresented in small, intensive examinations of abuser attributes, while fathers would be more likely to be included in large-scale research efforts. Table 18.2 contains data on this issue. When the table was collapsed so that small-scale efforts (1-20 cases) were compared with more extensive samples, differences are significant. Almost half of the maternal reports but only one in four two-parent reports described 20 or fewer parents (chi-square = 3.896, d.f. = 1).

Finally, it is possible that studies focusing primarily on intrapsychic characteristics of abusers tend to examine women, while those stressing environmental factors in abuse are more likely to study men. In part, this may develop out of the long-standing practice, evident in the developmental literature, of publishing intensive analyses of the multifaceted pathological tendencies of mothers (Ehrenreich & English, 1978). An intrapsychic focus also suggests a greater degree of individual responsibility for correcting one's behavior than do interpersonal or environmentally

TABLE 18.1   Sample Sources of Mother-Only and Two-Parent Abuse Studies

Sample Source	Type of Study	
	Mother Only	Both Parents
Hospital cases	24% (4)	24% (8)
Parents anonymous Outpatient treatment	47% (8)	24% (8)
Probability samples, Reported cases	29% (5)	53% (18)
Total	100% (17)	100% (34)
Insufficient evidence to classify	14	9

Chi-square = 3.93, d.f.=2, N.S.

TABLE 18.2   Sample Sizes of Mother-Only and Two-Parent Abuse Studies

Sample Size	Type of Study	
	Mother Only	Both Parents
Small (1-10)	18% (5)	10% (4)
Moderately small (11-20)	29% (8)	14% (6)
Moderate (21-30)	18% (5)	17% (7)
Moderately large (31-60)	7% (2)	26% (11)
Large (61+)	29% (8)	33% (14)
Total	100% (28)	100% (42)
Insufficient evidence to classify	3	1

based explanations for problematic family conditions. Difficulties that arise out of social group membership are least amenable to personal control, since their cause lies outside the individual, while responsibility for interpersonal problems is shared with an intimate other with whom one interacts. Table 18.3 contains results of analyses dealing with this

TABLE 18.3   Etiological Factors Studied in Mother-Only and Two-Parent Abuse Research

Etiological Factors	Type of Study	
	Mother Only	Both Parents
Intrapsychic	19%	19%
	(3)	(5)
Intrapsychic & Interpersonal	13%	19%
	(2)	(5)
Interpersonal	25%	15%
	(4)	(4)
Intrapsychic & Environmental	0	7%
		(2)
Interpersonal & Environmental	6%	11%
	(1)	(3)
Environmental	19%	19%
	(3)	(5)
Intrapsychic, Interactional, & Environmental	19%	11%
	(3)	(3)
Total	100%	100%
	(16)	(27)
Insufficient evidence to classify	11	10
Study purpose inappropriate for this analysis	4	6

issue. Treatment studies and dissertations were omitted from this analysis. The focus of the former was not on etiology, while information was insufficient to adequately classify the latter.

Results indicate a similar distribution of mother and two-parent studies. In classifying this research, it proved exceptionally difficult to identify "pure" cases of each specific type. To a considerable extent, current research is multivariate. In part this approach reflects recent emphasis in the field on the use of multicausal models (Burgess, 1979; Parke & Collmer, 1975; Seaberg, 1980). Further, more carefully designed efforts are required to deal adequately with this particular study question.

SUMMARY AND IMPLICATIONS

Review of recently published research efforts has documented the need for greater emphasis on paternal abusive behavior and on comparisons between male and female abusive parents. Preliminary attempts to differentiate between those studies incorporating data from both parents and those focusing only on mothers pointed to the use of larger samples in studying the former group. Efforts to identify differential use of sampling sources and differential theories concerning the etiology of abusive behavior were less successful and require further research. More information is needed concerning virtually every quality of paternal abuse. The only detailed information readily available concerning male perpetrators describe their fairly substantial tendency to maltreat their children in family settings.

We can only speculate on possible reasons for this neglect of fathers. Baher et al. (1976) discuss one factor of possible importance. In intensive treatment work with 25 abusive families, they were able to clearly identify the abusive parent in only 12 instances. In 9 of these it was determined that the mother abused the child, while in 3 others the father was labeled the abuser. It is possible that the lack of definitive information available to most investigators in the field leads them to guess that the mother's role in the incident is more significant. Her activities as a parent, therefore, tend to get studied.

Perhaps of even greater importance are the impact of powerful cultural expectations and social attitudes concerning the role of each parent in child-rearing. In the developmental literature itself, maternal characteristics receive the bulk of the attention, while the father's role is clearly undervalued. Recent studies exemplify this attitude. Within the last few years Harvard University Press has published a series of manuscripts discussing key aspects of early parent-child relations and summarizing the available research literature. One of these, authored by Rudolph Schaffer, is entitled *Mothering* (1977); the other, by Daniel Stern, is called *The First Relationship: Mother and Infant* (1977). Both profess to adequately survey major aspects of development affecting the young child. Authors writing about fathers frequently find themselves in a defensive position, having to assure the reader that fathers are significant figures in the child's life who should not be ignored (Lamb, 1976).

Fowler and Stockford (1979), in a review of reported cases in England, stress this point. Fathers who mistreat their offspring are not studied. The authors state:

> There is an underlying assumption in much of the literature on non-accidental injury that the person who is responsible for the child's injuries, even if she has not actually inflicted them, is the child's mother. This assumption is often disguised by apparently neutral references to 'the battering parent' or 'the family', but careful reading will usually reveal the underlying assumption that the person who is actually responsible, and in particular the one for whom therapeutic techniques are designed, is female. (p. 855)

Fowler and Stockford suggest that a primary reason for the situation involves assumptions about responsibility for child care. It is their contention that the mother is not only expected to be most deeply and intimately concerned with child-rearing; she is also at fault should any mischance occur in that process. No matter who actually harms the child, mother has failed in her duty to create a safe environment for her young. In some published reports, mothers have been criticized for failing to be present when the child comes home from school and for allowing other adults (father, neighbors, relatives) to care of the child when ill (Garbarino & Sherman, 1980). In a study of 49 abusive parents with hospitalized children in South Africa, Robertson and Juritz (1979, p. 861) claim:

> The large proportion of male batterers is possibly related to the high rate of male unemployment and the preponderance of *working mothers* in the coloured population. *Unsatisfactory care arrangements made by working mothers* for their children may contribute to the relatively high percentage of children abused by persons other than parent figures. (italics added)

In a survey of reported abuse cases in London, Moore and Day (1979) clearly suggest that some mothers are at fault when fathers mistreat their offspring:

> [T]he 20 cases where the father or step-father had hit the child, the following pattern emerged.... In 7 of these cases the mother's behavior acted as a trigger for the assault. Either she had provoked her husband in some way and then made sure—perhaps by going out—that the child got the full weight of the anger produced, or she had complained to her husband about the child's behavior (sometimes, perhaps, to take the spotlight off herself in an explosive situation). For instance, in one family the 6-year-old daughter was very close to her father. Her mother resented this and used an opportunity when her husband was in an aggressive mood to complain about the daughter's behavior. The father responded to this by bruising the daughter's eye, neck and arm. (p. 392)

Because the outcome of child-rearing is such a significant concern of any culture, attitudes concerning appropriate and inappropriate approaches to this task will always be powerful and deeply ingrained. When these views are uncritically accepted and applied to analysis of data in research studies, however, they become sources of potential bias that distort knowledge and unnecessarily restrict therapeutic efforts. Based on this review, it is clear that more attention must be paid to frequently unstated, untested assumptions concerning the role and responsibilities of mothers and fathers in abusive families.

REFERENCES

American Humane Association. *National analysis of official child neglect and abuse reporting.* Denver: AHA, 1978.

Baher, E. et al. *At risk: An account of the work of the Battered Child Research Department, NSPCC.* Boston: Routledge & Kegan Paul, 1976.

Burgess, R. Project interact: A study of patterns of interaction in abusive, neglectful, and control families. *Child Abuse and Neglect, 1979, 3,* 781-791.

Creighton, S. J. An epidemiological study of child abuse. *Child Abuse and Neglect, 1979, 3,* 601-605.

Ehrenreich, B., & English, D. *For her own good: 150 years of the experts' advice to women.* Garden City, NY: Doubleday, 1978.

Felthous, A. R. Aggression against cats, dogs, and people. *Child Psychiatry & Human Development, 1980, 10(3),* 169-177.

Fowler, J., & Stockford, D. Leaving it to the wife: A study of abused children and their parents in Norfolk. *Child Abuse and Neglect, 1979, 3,* 851-856.

Gabinet, L. MMPI profiles of high-risk and outpatient mothers. *Child Abuse and Neglect, 1979, 3,* 373-379. (a)

Garbarino, J., & Sherman, D. High-risk neighborhoods and high-risk families: The human ecology of child maltreatment. *Child Development, 1980, 51(1),* 188-198.

Gil, D. *Violence against children: Physical child abuse in the United States.* Cambridge: Harvard University Press, 1970.

Justice, B., & Justice, R. Evaluating outcome of group therapy for abusing parents. *Corrective Social Psychiatry Journal of Behavior Technology, 1978, 24(1),* 45-49.

Kadushin, A., & Martin, J. *Child abuse: An interactional event.* New York: Columbia University Press, 1981.

Kalisch, B. *Child abuse and neglect: An annotated bibliography.* Westport, CT: Greenwood Press, 1978.

Lamb, M. (Ed.). *The role of the father in child development.* New York: John Wiley, 1976.

Martin, J. *Gender-related behaviors of children in abusive situations.* Unpublished doctoral dissertation, University of Wisconsin, 1978.

Moore, J., & Day, B. Family interaction associated with abuse of children over five years of age. *Child Abuse and Neglect, 1979, 3,* 391-399.

Oates, R. K. et al. Risk factors associated with child abuse. *Child Abuse and Neglect, 1979, 3,* 547-553.

Parke, R., & Collmer, C. *Child abuse: An interdisciplinary analysis.* Chicago: University of Chicago Press, 1975.

Robertson, B. A., & Juritz, J. M. Characteristics of the families of abused children. *Child Abuse and Neglect, 1979, 3,* 857-861.

Schaffer, R. *Mothering.* Cambridge: Harvard University Press, 1977.

Seaberg, J. R. *Physical child abuse: An expanded analysis.* Saratoga, CA: Century Twenty-One Publishing, 1980.

Stern, D. *The first relationship: Mother and infant.* Cambridge: Harvard University Press, 1977.

BIBLIOGRAPHY

Baher, E. et al. *At risk: An account of the work of the Battered Child Research Department, NSPCC.* Boston: Routledge & Kegan Paul, 1976.

Bavolek, S. et al. Primary prevention of child abuse and neglect: Identification of high-risk adolescents. *Child Abuse and Neglect, 1979, 3,* 1071-1080.

Billing, L. et al. Occurrence of abuse and neglect of children born to amphetamine addicted mothers. *Child Abuse and Neglect, 1979, 3,* 205-212.

Bolton, F. G. et al. Child maltreatment risk among adolescent mothers: a study of reported cases. *American Journal of Orthopsychiatry*, 1980, *50*(3), 489-504.

Burgess, R. Project Interact: A study of patterns of interaction in abusive, neglectful, and control families. *Child Abuse and Neglect*, 1979, *3*, 781-791.

Buriel, R. et al. Child abuse and neglect referral patterns of Anglo and Mexican Americans. *Hispanic Journal of Behavioral Sciences*, 1979, *50*(3), 215-227.

Ceresnie, S. J. Child abuse: A controlled study of social and family factors. *Dissertation Abstracts International*, 1977, *37b*(11), 5826.

Clark, K. N. Knowledge of child development and behavior interaction patterns of mothers who abuse their children. *Dissertation Abstracts International*, 1976, *36b*(11), 5784.

Cohn, A. H. Essential elements of successful child abuse and neglect treatment. *Child Abuse and Neglect*, 1979, *3*, 491-496.

Cohn, M. S. Assessment of risk in child abusing and neglecting parents. *Dissertation Abstracts International*, 1979, *39*(10-B), 5059.

Collins, M. *Child abuse: A study of child abusers in self-help group therapy.* Littleton, MA: PSG Publishing, 1978.

Conger, R. D. et al. Child abuse related to life change and perceptions of illness: Some preliminary findings. *The Family Coordinator*, 1979, *28*(1), 73-78.

Creighton, S. J. An epidemiological study of child abuse. *Child Abuse and Neglect*, 1979, *3*, 601-605.

Dean, J. G. et al. Health visitor's role in prediction of early childhood injuries and failure to thrive. *Child Abuse and Neglect*, 1978, *2*(1), 1-17.

Denicola, J., & Sandler, J. Training abusive parents in child management and self-control skills. *Behavior Therapy*, 1980, *11*(2).

Dibble, U., & Straus, M. A. Some social structure determinants of inconsistency between attitudes and behavior: The case of family violence. *Journal of Marriage and the Family*, 1980, *42*(1), 71-80.

Egeland, B. et al. Prospective study of the significance of life stress in the etiology of child abuse. *Journal of Consulting and Clinical Psychology*, 1980, *48*(2), 195-205.

Elmer, E. *Fragile families, troubled children.* Pittsburgh: University of Pittsburgh Press, 1977.

Evans, A. L. An Eriksonian measure of personality development in child-abusing mothers. *Psychological Reports*, 1979, *44*(3), 963-966.

Felthous, A. R. Aggression against cats, dogs and people. *Child Psychiatry Human Development*, 1980, *10*(3), 169-177.

Floyd, L. M. Personality characteristics of abusing and neglecting mothers. *Dissertation Abstracts International*, 1976, *36b*(7), 3600.

Fowler, J., & Stockford, D. Leaving it to the wife: A study of abused children and their parents in Norfolk. *Child Abuse and Neglect*, 1979, *3*, 851-856.

Frodi, A. M., & Lamb, M. E. Child abusers' responses to infant smiles and cries. *Child Development*, 1980, *51*(1), 238-241.

Gabinet, L. MMPI Profiles of high-risk and outpatient mothers. *Child Abuse and Neglect*, 1979, *3*, 373-379. (a)

Gabinet, L. Prevention of child abuse and neglect in an inner-city population: II. The program and the results. *Child Abuse and Neglect*, 1979, *3*, 809-817. (b)

Gaines, R. et al. Etiological factors in child maltreatment: A multivariate study of abusing, neglecting, and normal mothers. *Journal of Abnormal Psychology*, 1978, *87*(5), 531-540.

Garbarino, J. A preliminary study of some ecological correlates of child abuse: The impact of socioeconomic stress on mothers. *Child Development*, 1976, *47*, 178-185.

Garbarino, J., & Sherman, D. High risk neighborhoods and high-risk families: The human ecology of child maltreatment. *Child Development,* 1980, *51*(1), 188-198.

Geddis, D. C. et al. Early prediction in the maternity hospital—The Queen Mary Child Care Unit. *Child Abuse and Neglect,* 1979, *3,* 757-766.

Gelles, R. *A profile of violence towards children in the United States.* Paper presented at the Annenberg School of Communications Conference on "Child Abuse: Cultural Roots and Policy Options," Philadelphia, November 1978.

Gray, C. L. Empathy and stress as mediators in child abuse: Theory, research, and practice implications. *Dissertation Abstracts International,* 1979, *39*(9-A), 5731-5732.

Gray, J. D. et al. Prediction and prevention of child abuse and neglect. *Journal of Social Issues,* 1979, *35*(2), 127-139.

Green, A. H. A psychodynamic approach to the study and treatment of child-abusing parents. *Journal of the American Academy of Child Psychiatry,* 1976, *15*(3), 414-429.

Herrenkohl, R. C. et al. The repetition of child abuse: How frequently does it occur? *Child Abuse and Neglect,* 1979, *3,* 67-72.

Hett, E. J., & Fish, J. E. Some descriptive characteristics of abusive families evaluated at Kansas University Medical Center. *Journal of Clinical Child Psychology,* 1979, *8*(1), 7-9.

Hyman, C. A. Some characteristics of abusing families referred to the NSPCC. *British Journal of Social Work,* 1978, *8*(2), 171-179.

Hyman, C. A. et al. An observational study of mother-infant interaction in abusing families. *Child Abuse and Neglect,* 1979, *3,* 241-246.

Jacobson, R. S., & Straker, G. A research project on abusing parents and their spouses. *Child Abuse and Neglect,* 1979, *3,* 381-390.

Justice, B., & Justice, R. Evaluating outcome of group therapy for abusing parents. *Corrective Social Psychiatry Journal of Behavior Technology,* 1978, *24*(1), 45-49.

Justice, B., & Justice, R. *The abusing family.* New York: Human Sciences Press, 1976.

Kadushin, A., & Martin, J. *Child abuse: An interactional event.* New York: Columbia University Press, 1981.

Katz, M. L. A comparison of ego functioning in filicidal and physically child-abusing mothers. *Dissertation Abstracts International,* 1976, *36B*(11), 5798.

Kertzman, D. Dependency, frustration tolerance, and impulse control in child abusers. *Dissertation Abstracts International,* 1978, *39*(3-B), 1484.

Kirkpatrick, F. K. Patterns of role dominance—Submission and conflict in parents of abused children. *Dissertation Abstracts International,* 1976, *36B*(11), 5800.

Lourie, I. Family dynamics and the abuse of adolescents: A case for a developmental phase specific model of child abuse. *Child Abuse and Neglect,* 1979, *3,* 967-974.

Martin, M. J. Familial correlates of child abuse and neglect. *Dissertation Abstracts International,* 1979, *40*(4—B), 1653-1654.

Mastria, E. O. et al. Treatment of child abuse by behavioral intervention: A case report. *Child Welfare,* 1979, *58*(4), 253-262.

Mayfield, R. M. Child abuse and parental locus of control. *Dissertation Abstracts International,* 1979, *39*(7-B), 3529.

Milner, J. S., & Wimberly, R. C. An inventory for the identification of child abusers. *Journal of Clinical Psychology,* 1979, *35*(1), 95-100.

Moore, J., & Day, B. Family interaction associated with abuse of children over five years of age. *Child Abuse and Neglect,* 1979, *3,* 391-399.

Mulhern, R. K., & Passman, R. H. The child's behavioral pattern as a determinant of maternal punitiveness. *Child Development,* 1979, *50*(3), 815-820.

Murphy, A., & Davis, S. Modification of a mother's verbal abuse. *Child Abuse and Neglect,* 1979, *3,*1087-1092.

Neufeld, K. Child-rearing, religion, and abusive parents. *Religious Education,* 1979, *74*(3), 234-244.

Oates, R. K. et al. Risk factors associated with child abuse. *Child Abuse and Neglect,* 1979, *3,* 547-553.

Paulson, M. J. et al. Clinical application of the PD, MA and (OH) Experimental MMPI scales to further understanding of abusive parents. *Journal of Clinical Psychology,* 1976, *32*(3), 558-564.

Pierce, R. L. Child abuse: A stress frustration aggression paradigm. *Dissertation Abstracts International,* 1979, *40*(2-A), 1078.

Robertson, B. A., & Juritz, J. M. Characteristics of the families of abused children. *Child Abuse and Neglect,* 1979, *3,* 857-861.

Rosen, B. Self-concept incongruence and interpersonal values among child abusive mothers. *Dissertation Abstracts International,* 1979, *39*(11-B), 5581-5582.

Rosenblatt, G. C. Parental expectations and attitudes about child rearing in high-risk vs. low-risk child-abusing families. *Dissertation Abstracts International,* 1979, *39*(7-B), 3537.

Rosenblatt, S. et al. Effects of diphenylhydantoin on child-abusing parents: A preliminary report. *Current Theories in Research,* 1976, *19*(3), 332-336.

Sanders, R. W. Systematic desensitization in the treatment of child abuse. *American Journal of Psychiatry,* 1978, *135*(4), 483-484.

Sandler, J. V. et al. Training child abusers in the use of positive reinforcement practices. *Behavior Research Therapy,* 1978, *16*(3), 169-175.

Sartin, R. A. The identification of factors related to potential child abusiveness in adults. *Dissertation Abstracts International,* 1979, *39*(7-A), 4128.

Seaberg, J. R. *Physical child abuse: An expanded analysis.* Saratoga, CA: Century Twenty-One Publishing, 1980.

Shapiro, D. *Parents and protectors.* New York: Child Welfare League of America, 1979.

Spinetta, J. J. Parental personality factors in child abuse. *Journal of Consulting and Clinical Psychology,* 1978, *46*(6), 1409-1414.

Starr, R. H., Jr. The controlled study of the ecology of child abuse and drug abuse. *Child Abuse and Neglect,* 1978, *2*(1), 19-28.

Stultz, S. L. Childrearing attitudes of abusive mothers: A controlled study. Dissertation Abstracts International, 1976, *37*(3-B), 1419.

Thoburn, J. "Good enough care?" A study of children who went home "on trial." *Child Abuse and Neglect,* 1979, *3,* 73-80.

Thompson, J. W. Frustration tolerance, parenting attitudes and perceptions of parenting behavior as factors in the incidence of child abuse. *Dissertation Abstracts International,* 1978, *38*(11-B), 5598.

Unruh, D. K. Abusive and nonabusive family relationships and parental behaviors: Children's perceptions versus parents' predictions. *Dissertation Abstracts International,* 1978, *39*(6-B), 3011.

Walker, L. M. Patterns of affective communication in abusive and non-abusive mothers. *Dissertation Abstracts International,* 1978, *38*(10-B), 5049-5050.

Wells, M. G. Some causes of child abuse. *Dissertation Abstracts International,* 1979, *39*(9-A), 5732-5733.

West, J., & West, E. Child abuse treated in a psychiatric day hospital. *Child Abuse and Neglect,* 1979, *3,* 699-707.

Wood, A. G. Differences in child management among court-identified abusive mothers, self-identified abusive mothers, and other mothers. *Dissertation Abstracts International,* 1979, *39*(7-B), 3546.

Wright, L. The "sick but slick" syndrome as a personality component of parents of battered children. *Journal of Clinical Psychology,* 1976, *32*(1), 41-45.

19

Perspectives on the
Intergenerational Transmission
of Abuse

ELLEN C. HERRENKOHL, ROY C. HERRENKOHL,
and LORI J. TOEDTER

A significant number of clinicians and researchers have described an intergenerational pattern of abuse in which harsh treatment of children by parents is perpetrated across three (Silvers, 1969; Oliver & Cox, 1973), four (Freedman, 1975), or as many as five generations (Oliver & Taylor, 1971). The dynamics that have been hypothesized to explain such intergenerational transmission of violence are diverse. A social learning theory approach would stress the long-range influence of imitation of behavior of powerful adults by their less powerful children. Or children may be emotionally associated in the parent's mind with grandparents who demanded a great deal and could never be pleased (Morris, 1963), leading to the displacement of repressed anger toward the parents on the child (Ostrow, 1970). According to a third perspective, the parents' internal conflict between impulse expression and repression may be projected on the child: the impulses which were suppressed as a child due to fear of

Authors' Note: *Portions of the research reported here were supported by the National Center on Child Abuse and Neglect Grant Nos. 90-C-428 and 90-C-1831 and by the National Institute of Mental Health Grant No. 1-RO1-MH-26291. We are grateful to the Lehigh County (PA) Office of Children and Youth Services and to the Northampton County (PA) Children and Youth Division for their cooperation in the study. We also wish to thank Monica Newman for her assistance in conducting the study.*

their parents' abusive response are at first encouraged by the parent and enjoyed vicariously through the child's expression, but are then punished through harsh rules and treatment in a repetition of their childhood experiences (Zilboorg, 1932). Finally, stress and abuse have been found to be linked in many studies of child abuse (e.g., Elmer, 1975; Garbarino, 1976; Herrenkohl & Herrenkohl, 1981). Thus it is possible that many stresses on the family of origin may have elicited violent reactions in response to the frustrations generated, with violence then being incorporated by the children as a "coping strategy" for responding to stress in their current lives.

While the cases of intergenerational transmission of violence are dramatic, by no means is this an unvarying pattern. Surveys of studies find more deviations from the pattern than they do conformity (Jayaratne, 1977). One of the problems in the case studies usually cited in support of this phenomenon is the absence of control groups, making conclusions about the importance of a history of abuse difficult. Furthermore, emotional deprivation rather than physical abuse may be the salient factor in a high-risk childhood. An abusive parent may have suffered damaged self-esteem as a child due to lack of parental respect, affection, or pride. Parents who have been emotionally deprived as children are often consumed with their own needs, turn to their children to fulfill these needs, and become abusive when frustrated in these excessive expectations (Steele, 1970).

While many abused parents may indeed be the product of abusive homes, it is of interest to know how many are not, how many victims of abusive parenting do not themselves behave in an abusive fashion toward their own children, and the extent to which other factors in the individual's childhood history which affect emotional development are related to the severity of discipline used in parenting. This chapter will examine these issues.

HYPOTHESES

Several hypotheses about the relationship between an adult's experiences as a child and that adult's own child-rearing practices were tested in the present study.

Severity of discipline. The parent who as a child was abused will in turn use abusive methods of discipline with his or her own children.

Stress. Adults whose families, when they were children, were subjected to high levels of stress are more likely to use severe discipline methods with their own children.

Nurturance. Adults who, in their own perception, received little nurturance as children will be more likely to severely discipline their children than will adults who as children experienced more nurturance.

METHOD

Overview

The present results are based on two related studies; one, a follow-up of all families cited for abuse over a 10-year period in a two-county area of eastern Pennsylvania; the other, a controlled study of families cited for abuse and families selected because there was no reason to believe they were abusive. In both studies, one or both parents were extensively interviewed using the same interview instrument. A portion of the interview focused on the parent's experiences as a child and another portion focused on the type and severity of discipline practices used by the respondent. The interviews were done in the home of the participants. The results presented below are from these interviews.

Participants

The participants were 399 female heads of household and 130 male heads of household, a total of 529. Child welfare participants included 251 from families which had been charged with abuse and 89 from families served for neglect only. The remainder were heads of families with preschool-age children served by various community programs: 61 from families served by Head Start, 59 from families served by day care programs, and 69 from families served by private preschool programs.

Measurement

The interview instrument was designed to examine issues relevant to different explanations for the occurrence of abuse. Of the two portions of the interview relevant here, one pertained to the discipline practices used by respondents with their own children. The other examined the respondent's experiences as a child.

Discipline Practices

Questions regarding parents' discipline practices with their own children were asked in each of three ways: (1) discipline practices used in the "last three months," (2) discipline practices used prior to the "last three months," and (3) acts of discipline about which the respondent was particularly pleased, acts of discipline about which the respondent was particularly sorry, and those which were considered to be particularly effective. The respondent was asked to indicate whether or not he or she had used any of 35 specific practices. The specific behaviors ranged from mild practices such as making a child sit in a chair, taking away desserts, or explaining to a child, to very severe practices, such as hitting a child with a hard object so as to bruise or burning a child so as to leave a mark.

The responses were then coded as abusive, severe, or mild. Putting pepper in a child's mouth, hitting or slapping so as to bruise, biting, or burning were considered to be physically abusive discipline. Physically severe but possibly not abusive discipline included hitting with a belt or other object. These operational definitions followed, as closely as possible, the types of incidents considered abusive according to formal citations. Each participant's responses on the discipline section were then scored to identify the number of abusive and the number of severe methods used by each respondent in disciplining any of their children. Based on these scores an index of severity of discipline with three levels was developed: 0 = never reported using abusive or severe discipline, 1 = reported using severe but not abusive discipline, and 2 = reported using abusive discipline.

Control Variables

Three control variables were used in the present analyses. These are scores on a social desirability index, number of children living with the respondent, and income level.

Social Desirability

In designing the discipline practices assessment measure, the investigators were aware of the possibility that parents might underreport the extent of harsh discipline used because of a need to give socially desirable answers. To provide some means for assessing this issue, a 6-item social desirability measure was included. The strategy used in designing this measure was to ask about feelings or behavior most parents would be likely to admit if they were honest. A strong tendency to respond in the socially desirable direction would cause the respondent to deny such behavior or feelings (see Wright, 1976). One item, for example, was "Do you ever feel uncomfortable disciplining your children in front of other people?" The index used consisted of the number of questions answered in the socially desirable direction with a possible range of 0 to 6.

Number of Children

There was the possibility that the more children a respondent reported disciplining, the greater were the chances of abuse occurring. To control for this possibility, the number of children disciplined was included as a control variable.

Income Level

As part of the interview, respondents were asked their current income level. This index was used as an additional control variable, since income level has been found by many (Gil, 1969; Pelton, 1981) to be negatively related to abusive practices.

Independent Variables

The independent variables of relevance here were based on the section of the interview dealing with the respondent's experiences as a child.

Discipline

Respondents were asked about their experiences of being disciplined as children. The same list of discipline practices was used in this section of the interview as was used in the section inquiring about respondents' disciplining of their own children. The respondent was asked whether or not each practice was used on him or her during childhood by mother (natural or surrogate), by father (natural or surrogate), or by other caretakers. The practices cited were categorized as abusive or severe and an index score reflecting the use of severe and abusive discipline was developed for each of the respondent's caretakers.

Each respondent was given several scores. Dichotomous scoring indexed whether or not the respondent was abused by his or her mother, father, both parents, or by any caretaker. Another score was a count of the number of caretakers who abused the respondent.

Stress

Respondents were asked to indicate which of 39 types of stress they remember their families experiencing during their childhood. A count of all stresses cited by a respondent was tabulated.

Nurturance

Respondents were asked whether they felt they had been mistreated or neglected as children by their caregivers. Answers were represented as dichotomous variables (yes = 1, no = 0). They were also asked several questions which reflect the quality of the caregiver's relationship to the respondent. These included questions about the extent to which each caregiver expressed pride in him or her as well as criticism, the degree to which he or she had felt free to discuss important issues or to disagree with each caregiver, and the degree to which each caregiver expressed affection to the respondent. An index reflecting the climate of "nurturance," based on these variables, was then developed. Scores for all caregivers were summed and divided by the number of caregivers, providing an "average" nurturance index.

Statistical Analyses

Initially, cross-tabulations were done using SPSS. Multiple regression analyses were then done.

The control variables (the social desirability index, the number of children disciplined, and the level of current income) were first entered

TABLE 19.1   Cross-Tabulation of Parent's Discipline with Way Parent Was Disciplined

| Number of Abusive Care-takers | Discipline of Children | | Total |
	Nonabusive	Abusive	
None	206	88	294
1 or more	124	111	235
Total	330	199	529

$$X^2 = 15.93 \qquad df = 1 \qquad p < .001$$

into the equation. As a second step, scores on variables related to the three hypotheses described above were entered into separate equations. With 529 respondents included in the present analyses, the degrees of freedom range from 1 and 527 to 525 for the control variables and 1 and 524 for each of the independent variables.

RESULTS

A general overview of the relationship between a respondent's childhood experience of discipline and his or her discipline techniques is given in Table 19.1, which is a cross-tabulation of number of caretakers who abused the respondent and severity of discipline used by the respondent. The relationship between these two variables is statistically significant, although 53% of those individuals who were abused do not abuse their children. Fifty-six percent of those who admit to using abusive techniques were themselves abused, as compared to 38% of those denying use of abusive techniques. Furthermore, the proportion of those who harshly discipline or abuse their children increases as the number of abusive caretakers in their own lives increases.

Control Variables

The cross-tabulation results do not control for the social desirability effect, the number of the respondent's children, or the respondent's income level. These control variables are all significantly related to the dependent variable, as is indicated in Table 19.2. They were entered into the regression equation before each of the independent variables was entered.

Discipline

The use of abusive techniques by the respondent's mother alone and mother and father together, and the number of caretaking situations in

TABLE 19.2 Multiple Regression Analyses of Control Variables and Independent Variables with Discipline Index

Control Variables	Discipline Index			
	F	% Var.	p	r
Social desirability	11.59	2.1	=.001	−.13
Number of children	14.62	2.7	<.001	.16
Income level	11.50	2.0	=.001	−.15
Independent Variables				
Number of caretakers	2.32	0.4	ns	.06
Number of stresses	10.11	1.7	<.01	.16
Perception of neglect	3.26	0.5	ns	.11
Perception of mistreatment	1.42	0.2	ns	.08
Abuse by father	1.51	0.2	ns	.05
Abuse by mother	15.22	2.6	<.001	.18
Abuse by both parents	7.46	1.3	<.01	.11
Nurturance	4.07	0.7	<.05	−.09
Number of abusive caretakers	15.14	2.6	<.001	.17

which the respondent had lived and had been subjected to physical abuse were significantly related to the discipline index.

Nurturance

The respondent's perception of having been neglected as a child was not significantly related to his or her discipline index, nor was the perception of having been mistreated. However, the nurturance index was negatively related to the discipline index; the less positive the climate, the more severe the discipline used by the respondent.

Stress

Finally, the greater the number of stresses on the family as the respondent grew up (as reported by the respondent), the more severe the discipline index. Six of the 39 stresses in the list were individually related to the discipline index: lack of home conveniences, dissatisfaction of the respondent's parents with their own marital relationship, difficult children in the family, chronic school problems of any of the children, responsibilities of parenthood, and loneliness of a family member (which could include the respondent).

Further Analyses

Further analyses were carried out in an effort to explain the differences between those individuals whose scores on "abuse in childhood" and abusive disciplining as parents were in the opposite direction from the prediction. Respondents were coded as belonging to one of four groups: (1) not abused-not abusive; (2) abused-not abusive; (3) not abused-abusive; (4) abused-abusive. Groups 1 and 4 were in line with the predictions; groups 2 and 3 were contrary to the predictions. One-way analyses of variance of the means of the four groups on the perception of mistreatment as a child, perception of neglect as a child, stresses on the family of origin, number of caretakers as a child, average nurturance index as a child, current number of children, and current income level were carried out. The between-groups F levels were significant for four variables (perception of mistreatment and of neglect, number of stresses, and nurturance index). The groups did not differ on the number of caretakers, current number of children, and income level. These results are given in Table 19.3.

A further analysis was done to compare the means of pairs of groups on each variable on the four statistically significant variables. Using t-tests (see Table 19.4), the analyses indicate that as a group, respondents who were abused as children report more negative perceptions of their childhood on each of the four significant variables than do respondents who were not abused. Among respondents who were not abused as children, those who have abused their own children report significantly more neglect, more stresses, and less nurturance than do those who have not abused their own children. The abused respondents who do not abuse their own children report fewer stresses on their family of origin than do those who have abused their children, but they do not differ from the latter on perceptions of being neglected, mistreated, or nurtured.

DISCUSSION

The social desirability dimension was included in the interview as a means of controlling for a tendency to minimize the severity of discipline in the self-report by a respondent. An assumption was made that respondents who score high on the social desirability dimension may underreport harshness of discipline used. The significant, negative relationship between this dimension and the severity of discipline reported by the respondent confirmed the need to maintain this variable in the analyses as a control variable.

The positive relationship between family size and severity of discipline and the negative relationship between income level and severity of discipline, in the view of the authors, reflect the tendency to use increasingly harsh discipline practices with increased parenting responsibilities and reduced availability of alternative coping strategies in response to stress due to low income levels.

The findings of a positive relationship between abusive discipline used by the respondent's mother and father, and by other caretakers, and abusive techniques used by the respondent support the hypothesis that

TABLE 19.3 Means for Groups on Variables Related to Parents' Experiences as a Child

	Not Abused-Not Abusive	Abused-Not Abusive	Not Abused-Abusive	Abused-Abusive	F	p
Number of children	2.48	2.55	2.71	2.84	2.05	ns
Number of caretakers	4.15	4.21	4.18	4.31	1.07	ns
Current monthly income	839	787	726	709	2.34	ns
Perceived neglect	.17	.50	.28	.51	20.97	<.001
Perceived mistreatment	.12	.56	.17	.56	46.13	<.001
Number of stresses	4.43	7.15	5.48	8.58	23.97	<.001
Nurturance	31.12	28.49	30.31	28.61	20.00	<.001

TABLE 19.4 Comparison of Groups on Variables Related to Parents' Experiences as a Child

Groups* Compared	Perceived Neglect		Perceived Mistreatment		Number of Stresses		Nurturance Index	
	t	p	t	p	t	p	t	p
1 with 2	6.82	<.001	9.75	<.010	5.80	<.001	6.55	<.001
1 with 3	2.13	<.05	1.12	ns	2.19	<.05	1.99	<.05
1 with 4	6.74	<.001	9.59	<.001	8.56	<.001	6.41	<.001
2 with 3	3.33	<.001	6.25	<.001	2.43	<.05	3.41	<.001
2 with 4	<1	ns	<1	ns	2.12	<.05	<1	ns
3 with 4	3.34	<.001	6.20	<.001	4.37	<.001	3.36	<.001

*Groups are:
1. Not abused-not abusive
2. Abused-not abusive
3. Not abused-abusive
4. Abused-abusive

exposure to abusive discipline as a child increases the risk for reliance on severe discipline techniques as a parent. Interestingly, while exposure to abusive discipline as a child was related to the discipline index, the perception by the parent that he or she was mistreated as a child was not. This may be a result of the very specific way in which the discipline practices were asked, in contrast to the judgment implied in the use of the labels "mistreat" and "neglect."

Support was also found for the hypotheses that stressed family life or emotional rejection during childhood are related to abusive disciplining as a parent. The less supportive the atmosphere in which an individual was raised, the more severe the discipline used by the individual as a parent. These findings seem to provide support for those who suggest that a contributing condition for abusive behavior is the inner deficit resulting from rejection and lack of nurturance as a child. Not only the negative model provided by harsh discipline, but also the lack of a positive parenting model and lack of positive support for the growth of self-esteem contribute to problems of parenting. Furthermore, physical abuse and emotional deprivation appear to be positively related in an individual's history.

However, these results also suggest that while abuse and physical and emotional neglect in childhood significantly increase the risk that a parent will mistreat his or her own children, other past and current life stresses or supports can be highly influential in tipping the balance and positively or negatively affecting parenting behavior.

These results recalled for the authors the life story of a nonabusive participant who was interviewed in the course of the study, which is suggestive of some of the dimensions that influence an individual's parenting in addition to a childhood history of abuse and neglect. A mother of three, she had been physically and emotionally abused by her mother, who had also abandoned her and her brother for a period of time when she was six. In addition, she had been sexually molested by a stepfather when she was a teenager. A variety of factors appeared to have helped her avoid reliance on abusive discipline techniques and progressively improve in her ability to express affection toward her own husband and children: (1) a highly supportive and patient husband; (2) membership in a supportive religious group, which, in the ritualization of hugging and kissing, helped her to overcome her inhibitions in this regard; and (3) her own intelligence, which had attracted the encouragement and support of teachers in childhood and opened up new avenues of knowledge through her readings.

Future analyses of the study data may shed more light on the factors that either reinforce or counterbalance the effects of an abusive or deprived childhood.

REFERENCES

Elmer, E. A social worker's assessment of medico-social stress in child abuse cases. In *Collected papers of the 4th National Symposium on Child Abuse, Charleston, South Carolina, 1973.* Denver, CO: American Humane Association, Children's Division, 1975.

Freedman, D. A. The battering parent and his child: A study in early object relations. *International Review of Psychoanalysis,* 1975, *2*(2), 189-198.

Garbarino, J. A preliminary study of some ecological correlates of child abuse: The impact of socioeconomic stress on mothers. *Child Development,* 1976, *47*(1), 178-185.

Gil, D. G. Physical abuse of children: Findings and implications of a nationwide survey. *Pediatrics,* 1969, *44*(5, Part II), 857-864.

Green, A. H., Gaines, R. W., & Sandgrund, A. Child abuse: Pathological syndrome of family interaction. *American Journal of Psychiatry,* 1974, *131*(8), 882-886.

Herrenkohl, R. C., & Herrenkohl, E. C. Some antecedents and developmental consequences of child maltreatment. *New Directions for Child Development,* 1981, *11*, 57-76.

Jayaratne, S. Child abusers as parents and children: A review. *Social Work,* January 1977, 5-9.

Morris, M. G., & Gould, R. W. Role reversal: A necessary concept in dealing with the "battered child syndrome." *American Journal of Orthopsychiatry,* 1963, *33*(2), 298-299.

Oliver, J. E., & Cox, J. A family kindred with ill-used children: The burden on the community. *British Journal of Psychiatry,* 1973, *123*(572), 81-90.

Oliver, J. E., & Taylor, A. Five generations of ill-treated children in one family pedigree. *British Journal of Psychiatry,* 1971, *119*(552), 473-480.

Ostrow, M. Parents' hostility to their children. *Israeli Annals of Psychiatry,* 1970, *8*(1), 3-21.

Pelton, L. H. Child abuse and neglect: The myth of classlessness. In L. H. Pelton (Ed.), *The social context of child abuse and neglect.* New York: Human Sciences Press, 1981.

Silvers, L., Dublin, C., & Lourie, R. S. Does violence breed violence? Contributions from a study of the child abuse syndrome. *American Journal of Psychiatry,* 1969, *126*(3), 404-407.

Steele, B. F. Parental abuse of infants and small children. In A. E. James & T. Benedek (Eds.), *Parenthood: Its psychology and psychopathology.* Boston: Little, Brown, 1970.

Wright, L. The "sick but slick" syndrome as a personality component of parents of battered children. *Journal of Clinical Psychology,* 1976, *32*(1), 41-45.

Zilboorg, G. Sidelights on parent-child antagonism. *American Journal of Orthopsychiatry,* 1932, *2*(1), 35-43.

20

Social Cognition and the Transmission of Abuse

SHARON D. HERZBERGER

The last few years have seen a new beginning in efforts to understand the transmission of abuse from one generation of a family to the next. In 1972, Spinetta and Rigler reported that "one basic factor in the etiology of child abuse draws unanimity: abusing parents were themselves abused or neglected physically or emotionally as children" (p. 298). Spinetta and Rigler were not alone in their confidence and support for the "cyclical hypothesis." Few discussions of child abuse failed to cite agreement with the hypothesis in one form or another (e.g., Kempe, Silverman, Steele, Droegemueller, & Silver, 1962; Parke & Collmer, 1975).

Two recent developments, however, have altered our initial acceptance of this view. First, investigators began to question the evidence used to support the cyclical hypothesis (Jayaratne, 1977; Potts, Herzberger, & Holland, 1979). Potts et al. (1979), for example, reviewed citations which claimed support for the hypothesis and found that the evidence was based primarily on selected case studies which lacked comparisons with appropriate control groups. Furthermore, some of the studies cited by others as providing supportive evidence actually presented no evidence whatsoever. Thus, the citations were a result of faulty referencing procedures. Second, Straus and his colleagues (Straus, 1978) conducted a controlled investigation of intergenerational family violence. Their results revealed that among individuals who had been physically punished by their parents twice or more a year as a teenager, 17.6% had abused a child. Among individuals who had been physically punished less often, 12.5% had abused a child. This study was important for two reasons: It confirmed that there is a relationship between parental treatment and the treatment of one's own children, but it also suggested that a small proportion of children who have

Author's Note: *Preparation of this manuscript was supported by a Faculty Research Grant from Trinity College. The author's address is: Sharon D. Herzberger, Department of Psychology, Trinity College, Hartford, CT 06106*

been physically disciplined become child abusers and not all child abusers were physically disciplined as children.[1]

The result of these new developments has been an increased awareness of limitations to the cyclical pattern and the need for sound research on the phenomenon. If abuse does not inevitably lead to abuse, under what conditions will the intergenerational transmission most likely take place? This chapter will begin to address this question by examining the possible role of social cognitive or attributional factors. Although the role of social cognition has received little attention in previous research or writings on family violence (for an exception see Hotaling, 1980), it has contributed to our understanding of a wide range of psychological phenomena (e.g., Dienstbier, Hillman, Lehnhoff, Hillman, & Valkenaar, 1975; Dweck, 1975).

A researcher interested in pursuing the problem of the transmission of abuse from a social cognitive perspective might begin by studying how children gather information and form judgments about the treatment they receive and how these judgments relate to subsequent disciplinary encounters with their own children. Implicit in this viewpoint is the recognition that the child is an active, thinking, interpreting being. Therefore, an identical set of circumstances may affect various children differently, depending on which pieces of information each attends to, how the information is combined with prior knowledge, and the connections the individual makes between this set of information and future events. In other words, it is likely that the child's response to parental abuse, as with any other parental behavior, is a function of how he or she perceives and interprets the particular treatment received (Herzberger, Potts, & Dillon, 1981).

I will discuss the role of social cognition as an influence on aggressive behavior and moral development in general. I will also provide suggestions about directions for future research on the influence of social cognitive factors on the cross-generational transmission of abuse.

THE DEVELOPMENT OF THE MOTIVATION TO AGGRESS

One theoretical perspective from which to study aggression is offered by Seymour Feshbach (1974, 1980). In accordance with social learning theory (e.g., Bandura, 1977), Feshbach proposes that children learn how to aggress by observing aggression in their families and in the surrounding society. Learning the mechanics of aggression, however, entails developing a set of rules about when and under what conditions the individual should use aggression. To a young child the conceptual ambiguities involved in attempts to distinguish proper from improper aggressiveness may seem overwhelming, particularly if the child's parents utilize physical forms of discipline. Consider a familiar example: a child hits the child next door and receives a spanking from his or her parent in return. As Feshbach (1974) notes, "aggression and punishment are often formally indistinguishable" (p. 179). Both acts could be termed aggressive and indeed may appear the same to a young child. Thus, a parent, whose goal is to inhibit the child's violent behavior, may only serve to reinforce it by adding to the child's confusion about the conditions under which aggressive behavior is proper.

Feshbach (1974, 1980) suggests that children who are exposed to aggressive models eventually learn "retaliatory norms" or social rules for the expression of aggression. Learning that it is proper to retaliate for perceived or actual harmdoing is consistent with other beliefs the child may have. For example, Piaget (1932) demonstrated that young children believe in the concept of "immanent justice"; that is, the belief that wrongdoing should and will be punished. This "eye for an eye" philosophy pervades the child's moral judgments throughout middle childhood and forms a strong basis for retaliation. Furthermore, cognitive balance theorists (e.g., Heider, 1958) have long noted the human desire to seek balance in affective relationships. If an individual is harmed or humiliated by another, he or she will be motivated to retaliate and thus correct the imbalance. The degree of retribution warranted is, of course, an individual decision based on the perceived strength of the initial wrongdoing and its cause (see Tedeschi, Smith, & Brown, 1974).[2] The development of retaliatory norms marks the beginning of "aggressive motivation" and provides the moral basis for violence against others (Feshbach, 1974, 1980).

Feshbach (1974) believes that as the child grows older he or she presumably learns nonaggressive retribution strategies that may complement the earlier aggressive ones. However, vestiges of aggressive motivation are likely to remain, and continued exposure to familial and cultural norms to engage in aggression will reinforce this style of response. In addition, the individual learns stategies to justify violence. One may justify aggression by focusing on the other's intention to harm or the other's imagined or real negative characteristics. Furthermore, rationalization may also occur by denying the severity of the aggressive act or by invoking socially acceptable norms. Feshbach notes that the amount of aggression in society could be reduced substantially if we limited our acceptance of justifications for violence.

Feshbach presents a cogent analysis of how cognition may operate to encourage the use of violence in society. Although more theoretical development is necessary to outline the conditions under which individuals learn rules for the use of aggression and to specify factors that encourage rationalization, the analysis exemplifies a means by which cognition affects the display of aggression.

Application to Abusive Interactions

Some of the ideas expressed in the preceding discussion should seem familiar to researchers in child abuse. Although to my knowledge there has been no coherent attempt to map the role of cognition in abusive interactions, individual investigations have uncovered relationships between various rationalization tendencies and the incidence of abuse.[3] For example, Steele and Pollock (1968) note that abusive parents often view physical discipline as essential to proper child-rearing, a means of ensuring that the child remains on a correct course of development. Hence, some forms of abuse may be rationalized as being for the child's own good. Furthermore, Bishop (1978) and Young (1964) report that abusive parents derogate their child, labeling the child with undesirable characteristics that may or may not be perceptible to others. In this way, abuse may also be justified. Finally, abusive parents often have unreasonably high expectations for their child's development and behavior (Steele & Pollock, 1968) and may lack the ability to empathize with a victim's feelings (Spinetta & Rigler, 1972). These characteristics render it likely that parents will misjudge their child's actions and intentions. A parent who misunderstands the child's developmental abilities and who lacks the empathic skill to discern what his or her child is thinking or feeling may interpret the child's failure to perform some activity as deliberate or willful, perhaps done to spite the parent. The effect of such an interpretation may be the incitement of retaliatory motivation and subsequent aggression. Therefore, rationalizations of aggressive behavior may act as cognitive mediators of the punitive discipline exhibited by abusive parents.

Relevance to the Cyclical Pattern

How might Feshbach's (1974, 1980) analysis be used to understand the cyclical pattern? Under what conditions is it likely that a child will adopt his or her parent's abusive mode of discipline? We might hypothesize that parents are more likely to use abusive discipline techniques if, as victims of abuse as children, they developed the impression that such treatment was appropriate under certain circumstances (see Gelles, 1973). Clinical interviews (Kempe & Kempe, 1976) reveal that some children do regard their abusive treatment as proper, blaming themselves for incurring parental wrath or perceiving that such treatment is common. Furthermore, Herzberger and Tennen (1982) asked college students to judge the abusive treatment received by children as described in presented case histories. Students who had been physically abused regarded the treatment received by the child as less severe, more appropriate, and more reflective of the child's responsibility than did students who had not received comparable treatment. In addition, students who had received severe physical discipline were less likely to label such treatment as "abuse" than their nonabused counterparts. It is evident, however, that not all abused individuals develop such convictions. Interviews with abused children who had been placed in foster care (although the foster placement was not directly related to the abusive treatment) revealed that abusive treatment was rarely regarded as appropriate (Herzberger et al., 1981).

Since research and clinical interviews demonstrate differential perceptions of abusive treatment, a productive area for investigation would be the conditions under which individuals develop the belief that abusive treatment is appropriate or legitimate. Let me suggest the following as hypotheses for investigation: An individual will be more likely to believe that abusive treatment is appropriate (a) to the extent that parental behavior is perceived as normative, (b) when the circumstances under which abuse occurs are generally considered proper, and (c) when the abuse is accompanied by compelling verbal communication that substantiates parental actions. I will now examine each hypothesis in more detail.

Normative Parental Treatment

Physical violence toward children is more likely to be seen as illegitimate to the extent that it is uncommon or prohibited within a given society. In some societies, including the United States, violence toward children is not only permitted, it is condoned and even encouraged (see Garbarino, 1977; Gil, 1970; Parke & Collmer, 1975). To the extent that neighborhood and cultural norms support the use of physical punishment, we would expect children to learn that parents have a legitimate right to harm children to achieve certain ends. Such learning is particularly likely if the child perceives consensual validation for his or her parents' treatment (Kelley, 1967). Consensual validation may be derived from several sources. First, if the child observed that he or she is not the only family member treated in this fashion, the child may recognize that his or her parents are not responding to him or her alone, but that there are behaviors which prompt the need for this type of punishment. This recognition may lead the child to discover rules for the application of violent discipline techniques. Second, validation of parental practices should ensue from observing the use of violence in other families. Third, to the extent that the use of harsh discipline is jointly supported, if not jointly engaged in, by all adults in the household, the violence is seen as more legitimate. When one parent's abuse is questioned by the other, the child may be more likely to perceive the treatment as inappropriate.

Proper Disciplinary Circumstances

Abusive treatment also may be perceived as more legitimate when it occurs during efforts to discipline the child following an actual wrongdoing rather than occurring noncontingently. Consider the following example: A child is asked repeatedly to drink juice in the kitchen, not in the livingroom. When the child spills grape juice on the livingroom rug, the parent grabs the child and bangs him or her against the wall. Or consider the parent who returns home from work, sees the child, and grabs him or her, banging the child against the wall. When the child provokes parental discipline, the child's action is observed as part of the causal chain of events, and punishment—even severe punishment—is therefore likely to be regarded as somewhat deserved. In contrast, punishment applied noncontingently focuses attention on the parent and the parent's action rather than the child and is more likely to be perceived as harsh and undeserved.

Support for this hypothesis is derived from laboratory studies on retaliation (see Tedeschi et al., 1974). Fishman (1965), for example, found that when individuals believed they deserved the harm-doing of others, they were less likely to retaliate than when they felt that the harm-doing was undeserved. Thus, they were more accepting of the punitive behavior of others. Furthermore, in the investigation described previously, Herzberger and Tennen (1982) provided some subjects with a description of the child's moderately provocative act along with a description of the parent's abusive or nonabusive response. Those who were apprised of the child's behavior judged that the child was more responsible for parental discipline and tended to rate the discipline as less severe. The perception that harsh parental treatment results from the child's own actions provides the observer with a rationale for the use of such treatment in future interactions.

The characteristics of the treatment may also moderate the degree to which the abuse is perceived as improper. Data presented by Giovannoni and Becerra (1979) demonstrate that professionals who handle child abuse cases (lawyers, pediatricians, social workers, and the police) rate some forms of violence more severely than others. As Table 20.1 shows, burning a child with a cigarette or immersing a child in hot water was regarded as more harsh than striking the child in the face with a fist or banging the child against the wall.

Why would certain types of abusive behavior be regarded as more violent than other types, irrespective of the physical consequences incurred? First, abusive treatment may be perceived as less severe if it takes the form of common physical punishment that went too far (e.g., bruises resulting from a spanking) as opposed to unusual violence (e.g., burning a child). The judgment that the punishment is commonly utilized may lead the observer to regard it as more appropriate and less a function of the unique characteristics of the punishing agent (Kelley, 1967). Second, some forms of punishment (e.g., burning) permit the agent to foresee the harmful consequences. In these cases, the hurt to the child may be regarded as intentional, and the agent is thus more likely to be viewed as acting improperly (see Tedeschi et al., 1974). Third, some types of abuse, such as forcing a child to drink a noxious substance, involve planning, whereas other types resemble impetuous behaviors. To the

TABLE 20.1 Ratings of the Seriousness of Parental Physical Abuse*

Vignette	Overall Rating	Lawyers	Pediatricians	Social Workers	Police
		Group Ratings			
1. Parent burned child on buttocks and chest with cigarette	8.34	7.71	8.57	8.45	8.76
2. Parent immersed child in tub of hot water	7.56	6.08	8.00	7.67	8.65
3. Parent hit child in face, striking with fist	7.25	6.37	7.69	7.05	7.94
4. Parent banged child against wall while shaking by shoulders	6.39	5.21	6.96	7.31	5.60
5. Parent struck child with wooden stick	4.59	4.47	5.06	4.21	5.00
6. Parents spanked child with leather strap	4.07	3.19	4.04	4.91	3.75

*Seriousness ratings range from 1, least serious, to 9, most serious.

The table is adapted from Table 3-2 in Giovannoni & Becerra (1979).

extent that the perception of impetuosity lessens the individual's responsibility for the act, the treatment may be deemed less serious.

Accompanying Communications

When abuse is accompanied by compelling verbal communications that substantiate the parent's action, the child is likely to be more accepting of the treatment. A parent who derogates the child or justifies the act in some way provides a rationale for performing the act and makes it seem more reasonable. The provision of a rationale complements the child's belief in a "just world," in which events are perceived as orderly and deserved (Lerner & Miller, 1978; Piaget, 1932). Furthermore, research on victims of accidents (Bulman & Wortman, 1977) and illness (Tennen, Allen, Affleck, McGrade, & Ratzan, 1981) has shown that victims who blame themselves for their plight often cope more effectively and maintain a better sense of control over their lives than those who blame external forces. To the extent that this research finding is applicable to child abuse victims, the parent's verbal support for his or her action may reinforce the child's own reasoning generated by the need to maintain control over environmental circumstances.

In summary, abusive behavior that is supported by cultural norms and rationalizations and is perceived as stemming from the child's actions in a sense calls less attention to the irregularity of the treatment. These conditions render it less likely that the victim will develop cognitive rules rejecting the treatment as inappropriate. Consequently, the aggressive behavior modeled by the parent may have a greater chance of being adopted by the child.

THE ADVANTAGES OF INDUCTION

A second approach to the implication of abusive treatment for future parenting styles is to investigate what training the child lacks by not being exposed to other forms of discipline (Aronfreed, 1961; Hoffman, 1977; Hoffman & Saltzstein, 1967). The socialization literature often characterizes parents according to their "sensitization" and "induction" discipline techniques. Sensitization techniques include yelling and corporal punishment. Induction techniques include asking the child to explain his or her actions, making the child recognize the consequences of the action, and refraining from punishment when the child demonstrates remorse. While sensitization is believed to control the child's behavior, it does so by encouraging the child to consider the possible consequences of misbehavior to himself or herself. Induction procedures, on the other hand, are hypothesized to encourage the development of internalized moral standards and empathy (see also Staub, 1971). Thus, children who have been exposed to inductive punishment are more likely to experience regret and guilt on committing a transgression and to consider their actions in light of moral norms and the consequences for others.

Hoffman and Saltzstein (1967) tested these assumptions by interviewing mothers about their discipline techniques and about whether the child confessed following misbehaviors. They also assessed, by use of a projective task, the child's tendency to feel guilty. As predicted, the use of sensitization or "power assertive" techniques was associated with weak moral development in the child, while the use of induction techniques was associated with strong moral internalization and social responsibility. Similar results were obtained in an experimental study by Dienstbier and his colleagues (1975). Children in this study were asked to monitor a slot car and to use a braking device if the car began to travel too fast. When the child was distracted momentarily, the experimenter caused the car to jump the track. The experimenter punished the child for the "transgression" in one of two ways: by communicating either that children should feel guilty for not doing what they are supposed to do or that children should feel shame for being caught not doing what they are supposed to do. Afterwards, the children were again asked to monitor the slot car but were informed that no one would be able to detect whether or not the car jumped the track. Children who were trained to feel guilty were more careful about monitoring the car during the session than children who were trained to feel shame. Thus, methods of discipline that induce guilt are more likely to promote responsible future behavior.

The above research suggests a drawback to the use of physical punishment and abuse: To the extent that parents employ sensitization rather than inductive discipline, the parents do not encourage the development in their child of a tendency to reflect on his or her actions. Therefore, not only does an abusive parent provide a model for aggressive behavior, but the parent may fail to provide the child with the cognitive ability to evaluate the morality of his or her own aggressive and nonaggressive behavior. Herein lies another mechanism by which abusive treatment by a parent may be adopted by the child.

THE TRANSMISSION OF A PERSPECTIVE

It is also possible that a perspective from which to view human behavior is transmitted from parent to child and that the perspective increases the likelihood of aggression in both generations of parents. Let me briefly outline two ways in which perspective may influence the tendency to aggress.

First, recent research (Messé, Stollak, Larson, & Michaels, 1979) has shown that adults differ in terms of "interpersonal perceptual style" (IPS). Some individuals tend to "see" more positive qualities and behavior in others, some "see" more negative qualities and behavior, and others "see" an equivalent proportion of each. Interpersonal perceptual style relates to social behavior, with negatively biased individuals acting in a more authoritarian manner with a child. Other research (Cohen, 1981) has shown that individuals attend to and organize information about others in a manner consistent with the goal of the observation. Goals, such as information-seeking and judgment, may be experimentally induced or may represent longer-term individual differences in observational strategies. Again, observational goals affect the way individuals approach tasks and social interaction.

While neither of these studies was conducted with abusive parents in mind, the results may be applicable. As mentioned previously, abusive parents tend to derogate their children and to evaluate critically their behaviors. It is possible that abusive parents are more likely than others to judge their child's actions rather than merely observing them and to judge them with a negative interpersonal bias. This perceptual style may prime the parent for aggression by providing the appropriate justification. Since cognitive or perceptual styles of adults are often imitated by children (e.g., Denney, 1972) it is possible that the parent's negative and evaluative biases may be adopted by the abused child, thus increasing the likelihood of abuse to another generation.

Second, Tedeschi, Gaes, and Rivera (1977) suggest that individuals with low self-esteem and a lack of self-confidence may feel powerless. In turn, feelings of powerlessness increase the likelihood of engaging in coercion to affect change. Descriptions of abusive parents emphasize their low self-regard (Kempe & Kempe, 1978; Schneider, Hoffmeister, & Helfer, 1976) and suggest that the parent's self-esteem is further threatened when the child misbehaves (see Feshbach, 1980). Consequently, the parent may resort to forceful attempts to control the child's actions. Interview studies reveal that, similar to their parents, abused children also develop low self-esteem (Martin & Beezley, 1977) and experience a sense that their environment is unpredictable and uncontrollable (Martin & Rodeheffer, 1976). These findings appear pertinent to the cyclical pattern: The parent's abusive behavior may result to some extent from a derogatory self-regard; the abusive treatment may produce similar feelings in the child; and the likelihood of transmission of a pattern of behavior from one generation to the next is thereby increased.

CONCLUDING REMARKS

In this chapter I have suggested three mechanisms by which abuse may be transmitted from generation to generation: by teaching children that aggressive behavior is appropriate, by failing to teach children an internalized morality, and by transferring a particular self or interpersonal perspective from parent to child. It is important to stress several cautions at this point. First, much of the discussion here is speculative. Although the ideas are drawn from related research areas, few of the ideas have been tested for their relevance to abuse. They are presented in order to stimulate empirical investigation into the role of social cognitive correlates of abuse. Second, in designing research projects to examine these hypotheses, we must recall that the abused individual will be exposed to other styles of discipline, alternative views on morality, and varied interpersonal treatment as he or she grows up and moves out into the world. While the importance of early experience as a mold for adult personality is not denied, the effects of early experience are not immutable. Therefore, we need to study the circumstances that reinforce or alter the learning experiences of the home environment. Third, as Straus (1978) has indicated, the cross-generational transmission of abuse accounts for a small proportion of abuse cases. Given that many factors are probably responsible for the cross-generational tendency, we would thus expect to observe the influence of any given factor in only a small percentage of cases. Therefore, it would be wise to test the contributions of various factors in analog studies, in addition to investigations with victims and perpetrators of abuse.

Finally, none of the foregoing discussion is meant to suggest that social cognitive factors are the sole or primary determinants of abusive behavior or the intergenerational transmission of abuse. Zigler (1979) had called on researchers to expand their horizons—to cease examining abuse as an isolated behavioral phenomenon and instead to consider it in relation to other well-established literatures, such as aggression and attachment. The social cognitive perspective is merely one approach and should be supplemented with investigations from, among others, social learning, biological, and sociological points of view.

NOTES

1. The reader should note that a broad definition of abuse was used in this study, one that includes "hitting with an object." In addition, the investigators sought evidence of "physical punishment" and not specifically "abuse" in the childhood histories of respondents and inquired about physical punishment during the teenage years. Therefore, the study does not directly test the hypothesis that childhood abuse leads to abusive behavior as a parent.

2. Tedeschi, Gaes, and Rivera (1977), in fact, urge that we distinguish between "the use of coercive power" and "aggression." Aggression, they insist, is a label attached by an observer to coercion that is judged to be illegitimate or nonretaliatory.

3. Of course, we do not yet know whether rationalizations and misinterpretations of children's behavior precede or follow the abusive acts. Although cognitions may precede and thus permit abuse to occur, it is likely that in some instances the justifications will be created post hoc to explain prior abuse. Regardless of when during the abusive interaction the cognitive justifications were developed, however, it is likely that once in place, they will serve as rationalizations for future abusive behavior.

REFERENCES

Aronfreed, J. The nature, variety, and social patterning of moral responses to transgression. *Journal of Abnormal and Social Psychology,* 1961, *3,* 223-241.

Bandura, A. *Social learning theory.* Englewood Cliffs, NJ: Prentice-Hall, 1977.

Bishop, F. I. The abusing parent: Perceptions, memories, and pathological identifications as precipitants in the attack. In E. J. Anthony, C. Koupernik, & C. Chiland (Eds.), *The child in his family: Vulnerable children* (Vol. 4). New York, John Wiley, 1978.

Bulman, R. J., & Wortman, C. B. Attributions of blame and coping in the "real world": Severe accident victims react to their lot. *Journal of Personality and Social Psychology,* 1977, *35,* 351-363.

Cohen, C. Goals and schemata in person perception: Making sense from the stream of behavior. In N. Cantor & J. Kihlstrom (Eds.), *Personality, cognition and social interaction.* Hillsdale, NJ: Lawrence Erlbaum, 1981.

Denney, D. R. Modeling effects upon conceptual style and cognitive tempo. *Child Development,* 1972, *43,* 105-119.

Dienstbier, R. A., Hillman, D., Lehnhoff, J., Hillman, J., & Valkenaar, M. C. An emotion-attribution approach to moral behavior: Interfacing cognitive and avoidance theories of moral development. *Psychological Review,* 1975, *82,* 299-315.

Dweck, C. S. The role of expectations and attributions in the alleviation of learned helplessness. *Journal of Personality and Social Psychology,* 1975, *31,* 109-116.

Feshbach, S. The development and regulation of aggression: Some research gaps and a proposed cognitive analysis. In J. De Wit & W. W. Hartup (Eds.), *Determinants and origins of aggressive behavior.* Paris: Mouton, 1974.

Feshbach, S. Child abuse and the dynamics of human aggression and violence. In J.

Gerbner, C. J. Ross, & E. Zigler (Eds.), *Child abuse: An agenda for action.* New York: Oxford University Press, 1980.

Fishman, C. G. Need for approval and the expression of aggression under varying conditions of frustration. *Journal of Personality and Social Psychology,* 1965, *2,* 809-816.

Garbarino, J. The human ecology of child maltreatment: A conceptual model for research. *Journal of Marriage and the Family,* 1977, *39,* 721-735.

Gelles, R. J. *The violent home.* Beverly Hills, CA: Sage, 1973.

Gil, D. C. *Violence against children: Physical child abuse in the United States.* Cambridge: Harvard University Press, 1970.

Giovannoni, J. M., & Becerra, R. M. *Defining child abuse.* New York: Free Press, 1979.

Heider, F. *The psychology of interpersonal relations.* New York: John Wiley, 1958.

Herzberger, S. D., Potts, D. A., & Dillon, M. Abusive and nonabusive parental treatment from the child's perspective. *Journal of Consulting and Clinical Psychology,* 1981, *49,* 81-90.

Herzberger, S. D., & Tennen, H. *The social definition of child abuse.* Paper presented at the annual meetings of the American Psychological Association, Washington, D.C., August 1982.

Hoffman, M. L. Moral internalization: Current theory and research. In L. Berkowitz (Ed.), *Advances in experimental social psychology* (Vol. 10). New York: Academic Press, 1977.

Hoffman, M. L., & Saltzstein, H. D. Parent discipline and the child's moral development. *Journal of Personality and Social Psychology,* 1967, *5,* 45-57.

Hotaling, J. T. Attribution processes in husband-wife violence. In M. A. Straus & G. T. Hotaling (Eds.), *The social causes of husband-wife violence.* Minneapolis: University of Minnesota Press, 1980.

Jayaratne, S. Child abusers as parents and children: A review. *Social Work,* 1977, *22,* 5-9.

Kelley, H. H. Attribution theory in social psychology. In D. Levine (Ed.), *Nebraska Symposium on Motivation.* Lincoln: University of Nebraska Press, 1967.

Kempe, R., & Kempe, C. H. Assessing family pathology. In R. E. Helfer & C. H. Kempe (Eds.), *Child abuse and neglect: The family and the community.* Cambridge, MA: Ballinger, 1976.

Kempe, R. S., & Kempe, C. H. *Child abuse.* Cambridge: Harvard University Press, 1978.

Kempe, C. H., Silverman, F., Steele, B., Droegemueller, W., & Silver, H. The battered child syndrome. *Journal of the American Medical Association,* 1962, *181,* 17-24.

Lerner, M. J., & Miller, D. T. Just world research and the attribution process: Looking back and ahead. *Psychological Bulletin,* 1978, *85,* 1030-1051.

Martin, H. P., & Beezley, P. Behavioral observations of abused children. *Developmental Medicine and Child Neurology,* 1977, *19,* 373-387.

Martin, H. P., & Rodeheffer, M. A. The psychological impact of abuse on children. *Journal of Pediatric Psychology,* 1976, *1,* 12-16.

Messé, L. A., Stollak, G. E., Larson, R. W., & Michaels, G. Y. Interpersonal consequences of person perception processes in two social contexts. *Journal of Personality and Social Psychology,* 1979, *37,* 369-379.

Parke, R. D., & Collmer, C. W. *Child abuse: An interdisciplinary analysis.* Chicago: University of Chicago Press, 1975.

Piaget, J. *The moral judgment of the child.* New York: Harcourt Brace Jovanovich, 1932.

Potts, D. A., Herzberger, S. D., & Holland, A. E. *Child abuse: A cross-generational pattern of child rearing?* Paper presented at the annual meetings of the Midwestern Psychological Association, Chicago, May 1979.

Schneider, C. W., Hoffmeister, J., & Helfer, R. E. A predictive screening questionnaire for potential problems in mother-child interaction. In R. E. Helfer & C. H. Kempe (Eds.), *Child abuse and neglect: The family and the community.* Cambridge, MA: Ballinger, 1976.

Spinetta, J. J., & Rigler, D. The child-abusing parent: A psychological review. *Psychological Bulletin,* 1972, *77,* 296-304.

Staub, E. The learning and unlearning of aggression: The role of anxiety, empathy, efficacy, and prosocial values. In J. L. Singer (Ed.), *The control of aggression and violence: Cognitive and physiological factors.* New York: Academic Press, 1971.

Steele, B. F., & Pollock, D. A psychiatric study of parents who abuse infants and small children. In R. E. Helfer & C. H. Kempe (Eds.), *The battered child.* Chicago: University of Chicago Press, 1968.

Straus, M. A. *Family patterns and child abuse in a nationally representative American sample.* Paper presented at the Second International Congress on Child Abuse and Neglect, London, 1978.

Tedeschi, J. T., Gaes, G. G., & Rivera, A. N. Aggression and the use of coercive power. *Journal of Social Issues,* 1977, *33,* 102-125.

Tedeschi, J. T., Smith, R. B., & Brown, R. C. A reinterpretation of research on aggression. *Psychological Bulletin,* 1974, *81,* 540-562.

Tennen, H., Allen, D., Affleck, G., McGrade, B. J., & Ratzan, S. *Coping and compliance in juvenile diabetes: The role of perceived control.* Paper presented at the Eastern Psychological Association Convention, New York, April 1981.

Young, L. *Wednesday's children: A study of child abuse and neglect.* New York: McGraw-Hill, 1964.

Zigler, E. Controlling child abuse in America: An effort doomed to failure? In R. Bourne & E. H. Newberger (Eds.), *Critical perspectives on child abuse.* Lexington, MA: D. C. Heath, 1979.

21

Social Knowledge, Social Policy, and the Abuse of Women
The Case Against Patriarchal Benevolence

EVAN STARK and ANNE FLITCRAFT

THE CYCLE OF CONCERN

Over a century ago, British feminist Frances Power Cobbe (1878) wrote a startling exposé of "Wife Torture in England." Noting that wife-beating occurred in "respectable" London homes as well as in the "kicking districts" of Liverpool, she touched on its links to alcohol, job frustration, and male character. But, she argued, whatever its immediate cause in any given home, since domestic "torture" was rooted in the subordination of women, nothing short of full political and economic equality could reduce its incidence. A student of the literature on abuse current today would be hard-pressed to show a significant advance in knowledge.

Virtually every 20 years since Cobbe wrote, the popular press has joined women's groups and charitable organizations to denounce wife-beating, child abuse, and related forms of family violence in the strongest terms. Public anger quickly reaches a peak, but then it recedes, leaving only the most modest legal reforms in its wake. The political status of women has dramatically improved since Cobbe's article appeared. But the enforced subordination of women in private life remains a major—perhaps *the* major—source of female suffering and personal injury.

Authors' Note: *Support for this research was provided by a grant from the National Institute of Mental Health, "Medical Contexts and Sequelae of Domestic Violence" (MH-30868-01A1), as well as by the Department of Sociology, University of Essex and the Office of Domestic Violence (HEW).*

As we write, it looks like we are passing through yet another cycle of concern about violence against women. Abuse became central on a number of public agendas in the late 1970s. But in the last months of the Carter administration, the Office of Domestic Violence closed, federal legislation to support shelters died in the House, and a number of community-based programs on abuse sponsored by the Law Enforcement Assistance Agency were defunded. Having lost funds from the Comprehensive Employment Training Act (CETA) so crucial to local groups, with the women's movement defending itself from the New Right on a number of other fronts, with private and state agencies fighting for jurisdictional control over a diminishing pool of public resources, shelters throughout the country are either closing or becoming indistinguishable administratively from the traditional service and charity bureaucracy. However, things are not totally bleak. Several state coalitions for battered women have proved remarkably viable. Where shelters have fallen back on the communities from which they originally emerged a new vitality and stability has been gained. And the traditional helping services are still being pressured to become "more sensitive." But current efforts seem to be rationalizing the transformation of wife-beating from an explicit focus of grass-roots politics into another seemingly inevitable "tragedy" facing poor and black women primarily.

There is a crucial difference, however, between this and previous cycles of concern. For the first time, social science and the helping professions have lent their weight to smashing the closed doors of family life. Following the campaign against rape and battering in the early 1970s, hundreds of original research monographs described marital rape, wife-beating, husband-battering, "multiple family victimization," child abuse, incest, "granny-bashing," and "mutual combat." A new social knowledge of family life has been produced. We now "know" that thousands, perhaps millions, of women and children are being assaulted in their homes on a regular basis, primarily by adult males with whom they are presumed to be intimate. What was new in the 1970s was not an obvious increase in domestic violence but its selection as a vantage from which to interpret and respond to family life more generally, the fact that intellectuals of every persuasion employed photojournalism, surveys, complex statistical maneuvers, and myriad techniques for direct observation to construct one of the most disturbing headlines in social history: THE HOME IS A BATTLEGROUND.

What lies behind this announcement? From what frame of reference should the new social knowledge be evaluated? How will the intervention of social science and the helping professions affect the cycle of concern? To what social reality does the new social knowledge of family life correspond? Which social reality does it evoke? In other words, to what extent does the new imagery—and the forms of state intervention this imagery supports—actually bring into being the reality it claims merely to describe?

A certain opportunism undoubtedly explains part of the sudden social science concern with family violence. And it is easy to sense in current work the same self-righteous puritanism that reappears in every upper-class campaign to abolish "sin" (prostitution, alcoholism, "dirty homes" and wife-beating) among the working classes. But earlier campaigners offered relatively simply panaceas for the vices they exposed—prohibition, for example, or stiff prison terms. And even the most single-minded moral fanatic believed that when sinners saw the error in their ways, things might return to normal. By contrast, current accounts in the United States and Britain suggest that violence is endemic in certain forms of culture, personal history, or even in family life itself, either a tragic but necessary dimension of "social stratification" or else a chronic situation requiring what French sociologist Jacques Donzelot (1977) terms constant "policing." If the family is the "cradle of violence" as American researchers like Straus, Gelles, and Steinmetz now contend, then we should either "abolish the family"—hardly a popular position at the moment—or invest heavily in its public restraint, a process that would ultimately transform medicine, psychiatry, and other social services from institutions to "treat" the sick or deviant into forms of categorical political discipline.

This sets the theme—namely, that just behind the cycle of concern about abuse lies a new ideological affinity between those who document the evils at the heart of family life, those who "treat" these evils, and those who, like the ideologues supporting the current Family Protection Act, would unhesitatingly restore traditional patriarchal authority whatever the costs in individual freedom, an alliance between those who locate the principles of violence in "private" life and those who would leave violence against women to private solutions.

In earlier papers (Stark and Flitcraft, 1979, 1981) we focused on the role of service providers in this alliance. Drawing on our research into the medical records of abused and nonabused women who use a major medical complex, we argue that the medical response to abuse, on an aggregate basis and over time, is a key situational determinant of the emerging "battering syndrome." Interestingly, the logic which appears to guide the medical response to abuse is shaped around the same images that are current in social science research. In addition to suffering acute physical injury, battered women disproportionately suffer a range of psychosocial problems such as rape, suicide attempts, alcoholism, depression and fear of child abuse. These problems significantly differentiate battered women only *after* the first reported incident of abuse and are therefore its sequelae, not its context. Despite this, medicine typically identifies these secondary problems as the focus for intervention, attributes the abuse to these secondary problems, and treats the "multiproblem complex" by reconstituting and maintaining families in which ongoing violence—and escalating psychosocial problems—are virtually inevitable. This strategy is rationalized by re-cognizing the problems the woman has as a result of her abuse as a problem the woman *is* for herself, her family, and her helpers. The clinical failure to identify the emergent social context from which abusive injuries arise is projected onto the woman and read back through the medium of psychiatric labels which justify her "management." Finally, the chain of problems—amid which the violence easily disappears—is rooted in the personality, history, or culture which allegedly predisposes "this sort of woman" to a sociopathic complex.

In this chapter we examine the intellectual basis for this intriguing process of intervention and the political context within which the new knowledge of battering is produced in the United States and Britain. We by no means think of the alliances among social science, social therapy, and the New Right as conspiratorial. To the contrary, social science presents its new knowledge as the next logical step in the progress of research, a claim to which all parties to the family violence debate accede. There is no discussion—and no sense—that the images projected about women and families are forms of intellectual promotion or, worse, as much means to discipline women as the old images of domestic bliss now debunked as "romantic." Unlike anthropologists who maintain a certain self-conscious humility in the face of alien experience, sociologists, psychologists, and social service providers refuse to recognize how their image of abuse affects it and shapes it, highlighting or repressing certain details and certain principles, all the while establishing a certain command over the subjects they claim merely to be studying or helping. Just as clinical intervention helps stabilize an irrational situation—"the violent family"—so too does the sociologist approach the abused woman as incapable of interpolating herself politically (hence requiring "interpretation" from outside) and yet as subsisting in a situation that is stable enough to constitute a legitimate object of research. The result is the intellectual portrayal of domestic violence as an apparently self-constituting form of irrationality, a type of family behavior whose stability derives from its inherent contradictoriness. By locating the "cause" of the subject's "silence," her lack of rational purposiveness, *in* the social situation (though not in its subjects), the sociologist creates the illusion of distance from domestic violence, absolving self and colleagues from the process through which silence is imposed.

In Britain, battering is traced to the "cycle of deprivation" whereby the poverty and attendant immaturity of one generation presumably evoke this behavior in the next. In the United States, despite a wider variety of approaches, the most influential also assume that persons who hit or are hit as adults have learned this behavior from their parents or culture (Walker, 1979; Straus, 1977-78). The battered woman is pictured as a pathetic victim of circumstances doomed by the fact that one set of social tragedies leads automatically to another, what we term "social genetics." And the deadening of her experience only begins here.

Social science methods and the images drawn on by social scientists to describe abuse function as fetishes which conceal paradigmatic biases. Researchers think about abuse amid a complex of other social problems—alcoholism, the "culture of violence," parental abuse or female immaturity, for instance—and pose specific questions about these problems to the battered woman. As we shall see, the questions are structured so as to enforce a genetic logic which transfers the rationality of abusive situations from the participating subjects (including researchers and helpers) to social factors devoid of political intentionality or historical specificity. Regardless of how battered women respond to the questions they are asked, they help generate rates, correlations, no matter how pitiable, which they quickly come to represent, to carry. The intellectual constructs through which abused women are seen now take on the life the women suddenly appear unable to control. Thus, just as medicine and psychiatry expand by inventing diagnoses and interventions for fragments, symptoms of social ailments (Stark, 1982), so too does social science develop through a distinct and negative correspondence to the subjectivity of its objects. The images constructed help fix the priorities for the social services and even provide the abused woman with a prism through which to re-cognize herself. The method is also adapted. In social work practice, for instance, social genetics is the heart of "overcontextualization," a process of case description in which an emphasis on myriad historical and secondary problems either makes the abuse seem trivial or the inevitable consequence of private troubles rooted in an overwhelming (and inpenetrable) "environment." In medical practice, meanwhile, the image of a victim silenced by the overbearing weight of her history frames a literal process of silencing that includes inappropriate referrals, tranquilizing medication, mental hospitalization, and the removal of children presumed to be at risk in "the violent home." Ultimately, however, social knowledge and social therapy are linked by their mutual ties to social policy and the broad institutional effort to discipline and subordinate the social imagination of women and youth to an expanding "private" economy.

ENGLAND: MUGGING, BATTERING, AND THE "CYCLE OF DEPRIVATION"

In August 1972, the British media borrowed the term "mugging" from America and began applying it regularly to robberies committed by young adults where force was threatened or used. The concrete phenomenon was neither new nor rising, but its public redefinition—the importation of the label from America—elicited and legitimated a specific social knowledge and political response. The label moved speedily through what Stuart Hall et al. (1978) call its "career," changing from an image on American media to an image of America in Britain to a widely accepted image—and forecast—of British society. The context imported with the label recast council estates as "slums" and "ghettoes" where "lawlessness" created a need for "law and order." As sociologists studied "the minority problem" and government statisticians divided crime figures by race for the first time, the notorious "SUS laws" were introduced and used to stop and search young blacks in Brixton and elsewhere. In the midst of sharply rising unemployment, the image of "the mugger" provided a ready scapegoat for workaday fear and anger. By conceptualizing its future in racial images adapted from the American media, Britain justified expanding political control over black immigrants, school-leavers, and other "riotous" segments of the working class.

Neither the career nor the political role of domestic violence is as clear. Hall thinks the media's inherent interest in violence made mugging an excellent source of legitimation for expanded state repression. But a distinct absence of public attention has always legitimated violence against women. The mugger, rapist, and child-beater are held in contempt. But not the wife-beater. Until very recently, wife-beating ranked with banditry as a widely accepted "social crime." If its meaning has changed, it is because the balance of power has shifted between the victims of violence and those who benefit from it, a shift reflected at the center of knowledge and service.

Whatever the differences between mugging and battering, the discovery of domestic violence has elicited images that are in every way as mystifying as those elicited by mugging. Thus, while nineteenth-century references to wife-beating suggest its legitimate use to discipline lower-class viragos, the current term "battering" simultaneously recognizes the seriousness of the act and transforms it into an anonymous, almost irrational process with no clear social location, an act requiring professional interpretation and management, not simply punishment. Muggers are no more recognizable than assassins. But the newspapers picture them nevertheless, head lowered, young and black, handcuffed in front, their particularity a caricature of the fear of attack rooted deep in our collective unconscious. But the batterer is known, both by his victim and those to whom she turns for help. He is accessible and within limits, completely predictable. Yet his remains a crime apparently without authorship; he is rarely or never seen by the services and never pictured in the press. The state invests the mugger with interest, using his crime and punishment to link our fear of personal safety to the protection of "private property." But we attend to battering only reflexively, because its victims demand our attention and it is their story that makes news. Battered women are not just "hit." They need *more* than simple protection or shelter. Indeed, the damage to their selves that researchers uncover is so fundamental that only a basic reconstruction of the person will suffice.

Mugging is publicized in ways that conceal the normative violence of the status quo—racial discrimination or malnutrition, for example—behind isolated acts of estranged aggression and which call forth precisely that extension of state intervention that underlies normative violence. To this degree, the images of mugging and rape are analogous. Both instill a sense of vulnerability-in-public and a corresponding dependence on authority in the case of mugging and a "strong man" in the case of rape. By contrast, the image of battering in Britain—and to a lesser degree also in the United States—is constructed to do two things. First, by portraying family problems apart from their political context, the new imagery ideologically separates the subordination of particular homemakers to "bad" husbands from welfare state policies that reinforce female subordination along a broad front. Even as families become the stage where failings of state "benevolence" are expressed in escalating fights, the conceptualization of this hostility is designed to evoke ever higher levels of state protectionism. From the standpoint of working-class women, domestic battering, mugging, rape, and the omnipresent dependence structured by welfare policies often feel like mere variations on a unitary theme of estrangement in a world "haunted by men." Second, the social knowledge of battering in Britain separates working and minority women from normal others and separates the family as the good and proper source of personal discipline in the community and political solidarity in the state from pathological households apparently incapable of sustaining appropriate domestic standards. The genealogy of abuse is held to lie deep within the body or personality of its participants or in their culture, and there is no suggestion at all—as there is in the American image of abuse, for example—that violence results from the politics of family life as such.

The evolution of the British image begins with the well-known story of Erin Pizzey, the "courageous" founder of Chiswick House, the first battered woman's shelter. Pizzey (1974) describes how the neighborhood house she opened was immediately filled by battered women. By now it seems so natural to define abuse as the single distinguishing characteristic of the women who enter Chiswick that we forget the political context in which the demand for emergency shelter arose or its early and continued links to the expanded intervention of the welfare bureaucracy in the lives of the poor. The demand for shelter must be framed by the chronic housing shortage in postwar London, the increasingly marginal status of immigrant families thrown aside by massive disinvestment in jobs, and by the subjective expression of these conditions, the fact that more than 100,000 persons were already squatting in London when Chiswick opened. What was new was not the "solution" (free housing for poor families), but the emergence within the free housing movement of resistance to male domination and the identification of male power with physical abuse.

Chiswick evolved as part of a broad public dialogue about how to define the problem of the poor. At issue was whether political change or a mere transfer of resources would suffice to contain militancy. Pizzey fails to explain why Chiswick was funded by Bovis, the building conglomerate owned by Sir Keith Joseph, then Conservative Secretary of State for Social Services (Marsden, 1978). More than any other figure, Joseph promoted the view that "inadequate people tend to be inadequate parents and that inadequate parents tend to rear inadequate children" (Townsend, 1975). This proposition exemplifies what we term "social genetics" because it is constructed as if one social affliction leads inevitably, almost organically, to another presumably less primary affliction, and in a virtually unmediated way.[1]

More than 100 refuges have been opened in Britain since Chiswick, united primarily by Women's Aid, a feminist coalition which, despite its provision of service, believes that battering requires a political solution. But Pizzey's account of abuse remains the source of "authentic" knowledge on the British media. Like Joseph, she argues that domestic violence is transmitted intergenerationally and that battered women may have a hormonal need for violence (Pizzey & Shapiro, 1981). Welfare and medicine, not law or politics, therefore, are the appropriate realms within which abuse must be resolved. Obviously, this view appeals to the Tory press. But the authority for these views derives not simply from their getting apparent life in media melodrama, but also from "data."

Invited by Pizzey to interview Chiswick residents, psychiatrist J. J. Gayford presented them with a catalogue of problems such as divorce, drug abuse, alcoholism, illegitimacy, and child abuse. Since he lacked a control group or any other comparative source of information about the prevalence of these problems in the general population, the mere posing of the various questions guaranteed that he would produce rates of psychiatric pathology *however the women replied.* The juxtaposition of the fact that these were battered women with the produced rates appeared to establish a causal chain and to validate the psychiatric image of abuse. Gayford (1975a, 1975b) portrayed battered women as pathetic, almost childlike individuals on whom social inheritance had imposed tragic, yet somehow inevitable, choices. "Such women," he concluded, "need protection against their own stimulus-seeking activities. Though they flinch from violence like other people, they have the ability to seek violent men or by their behavior provoke attack from the opposite sex." Gayford's ambiguous reference to "other people" evokes a general image of health and normalcy, of persons who can presumably control their stimulus-seeking activities and who lack "the ability" (sic!) to provoke attack.

Thus, a policy imperative (Joseph's) led to a certain political practice (Chiswick), which in turn generated rates of pathology to support it (Gayford). But when, in 1975, the Select Committee on Violence in Marriage concluded its "open" hearings, it cited Gayford's data as the source of its image of the battered woman as someone who had "been inadequately prepared for adult life" (Wilson, 1970). Apparently it was her upbringing in violent or disordered homes (i.e., the homes of the poor) that "disposed" her to violence in her adult life. A virtual consensus emerged among policymakers that battering signified deprivation. At the same time, deprivation had been reduced to a multiplicity of afflictions among which battering was prominent, an instance of overcontextualization. The Joseph-Pizzey-Gayford image of the battered woman has provided support for stepped-up intervention in the daily lives of the poor by caseworkers, home visitors, and the like. The social construction of battering as the consequence of multiple deprivations evoked social service in place of radical change as the vehicle for attacking (managing) poverty.

AMERICA: THE SOCIAL CONSTRUCTION OF "THE VIOLENT FAMILY"

In Britain, the cycle of deprivation approach to wife abuse helps the welfare state integrate the militancy of the working poor into a broad effort to manage a major industrial crisis. The American crisis is less explicit and expresses itself most directly at the level of family recomposition and "individual rights" rather than in terms of "class militancy." It is at the level of the family, therefore, that the conception of abuse has developed.

The relatively greater power of individual women in the United States compared to Britain, particularly in the labor market, is reflected by a certain feminist bent among American researchers studying abuse. Despite this, when we turn to the actual substance of research and writing in the United States, we find little attention to male power. Instead, wife-battering is described as merely one dimension of a multiproblem profile to which families are somehow predisposed by their peculiar history or culture. This view has been developed most explicitly in the work of family sociologists Straus, Gelles, and Steinmetz, whose considerable output significantly influences social service thinking about abuse in the United States.

The sociological situation of the American family is relatively complex. On one side, at least since the early 1940s and probably earlier, Keynesian policies have taken the family-Ford-factory connection as the key to economic growth—that is, family demand mediated by the factory wage was organized to stimulate industrial growth. On the other side, this connection is being destructured from within by the abandonment of women and teenage children and from without by the dissolution of its material basis. The rapid disintegration of consumer and labor discipline evokes massive social expenditures and a corresponding qualitative increase in the degree to which family maintenance, particularly among the working poor, falls increasingly to the social services. This poses a quandary for family sociologists. Required by their livelihood to conceptualize the family as "a sphere apart" with a distinct moral economy, they must nevertheless appear to document and explain the obvious and increasing interdependence of family life with welfare, counseling, the police, and other helping institutions. It is to the credit of Straus, Gelles, and Steinmetz that they have assumed the thankless task of providing an ideological ground to fulfill this contradictory project. By arguing that the moral distinctiveness of the family lies precisely in the rates of pathology it spontaneously produces, and particularly in the various forms of violence it apparently hosts, these researchers propose a reconceptualization of family life to which service intervention is intrinsic. In other words, if social service intervention is required by the inherent weakness (pathology) of the family as such, it cannot be read—or confronted—as a political response to the historically specific struggles of women and children to "get out from under." The evolution of this standpoint is interesting.

Until the 1950s, family sociologists typically argued that family harmony was an essential component and reflection of family stability (Safilios-Rothschild, 1969). Women's distinctive role was managing the family's economic and psychic resources in peaceful competition with other families. By urging women to interpolate the "real needs" of their husbands and children through the medium of consumer durables, sociology joined mass advertising in reconstituting "the home" as a fetish toward which family relations were now mere means. Family sociology gave product loyalty a moral reading and translated family dynamics into economic terms by accumulating data on "attachments," emotional "investments," "exchange," and "values." The fact that women increasingly chose to imaginatively develop their individuality against traditional family conventions created both the opportunity and challenge for Keynesian demand theory. Perhaps the convergence of family sociology with a Keynesian interest in disciplining female aggressivity (translated, "consumer demand") is best exemplified by the reading of challenges to traditional dynamics as problems in "task allocation,", "leadership," and "decision-making" and by a failure even to ask who in the final instance decided who decided what. The image of the woman as chief family manager/consumer re-cognized female aggressivity as a positive aspect of economic growth and attempted to contain the new individuality that developed as a consequence of women's increasing use of family wages for personal mobility and changes in lifestyle. Even the most conservative family theory rests on the subversive egalitarianism implicit in female aggressivity.

As Ewen (1976) argues, modern women were joined by modern firms in viewing the virtues of traditional domesticity as obstacles to the free alienation of their labor power for consumption and wage work. *Craig's Wife* is portrayed as "sick" in the 1920s play when she puts family success before virtue. But the women and children the Lynds met in *Middletown* willingly sacrificed for "the Ford" and other consumer delights what earlier generations thought basic. Except for the brief resurgence of domestic imagery after World War II—associated with the aggressive construction of consumer fortresses in the suburbs—female assertiveness is increasingly acknowledged from the 1920s on, until in '50s films like *Diary of a Mad Housewife* or fringe sociology texts like Reisman's *Lonely Crowd* or Whyte's *Organization Man,* we find overconformity with traditional mores defined as explicitly pathological. For millions of women, rising real wages and job opportunities have meant an escape from conventional households. However, the majority continue to constitute their individuality through as well as against the family as such. In the late 1950s, family theorists—including Freidan in the United States and Laing and his colleagues in Britain—portrayed the conflict between individual assertiveness and family stability as the essence of domestic life and constructed an image of femininity around the internal and psychosocial dynamics of "conflict management." Now "marital success" is equated with "effective control" of conflict, not the absence of fights.

The new conflict model evoked studies of family fights as a cause of divorce, "victim-precipitated homicide," and "acquaintance rape" (Levinger, 1977; O'Brien, 1971; Wolfgang, 1956). While it may seem strange to consider studies of such grizzly topics optimistic, in fact they approached these problems not as instances of a common domestic malaise but as exceptions that revealed the boundaries of otherwise effective processes of tension management among the middle classes, as signposts of an amorphous space where family life ended but where help (and interpretation) had yet to enter.

A similar model was applied to the poor, whom studies now showed to lack "impulse control," a lack revealed by displays of "inadequate socialization" such as delinquency, drunkenness, and street crime. The social worker's version of the conflict paradigm was "the multiproblem family," a household network apparently joined by mutual deviance. In reality, the image of the multiproblem family reflected nothing so much as the projected inability of multiple agencies competing for dominance over the family terrain to reach any long-term compromise about how territory should be allocated. Although this general failure might be temporarily resolved at periodic case conferences, the interest in preserving the family as an open plane onto which the changing power relations in the services could be projected mitigated efforts to identify any single source of pathology inherent in or acting on family life.

The riots, Vietnam, and the undisciplined aggressivity of women and youth in the 1960s and '70s changed all this. The immediate response to the riots and the antiwar movement, the introduction of "full employment" policies, and a dramatic increase in social expenditures during the first years of the "Great Society" was premised on the belief that a certain amount of social conflict could provide the incentive to economic growth if it was institutionally contained through "maximum feasible participation" in limited programs of categorical aid. Transferred from the general demand for more to the arena of intragroup competition for a share of the social service pie, social aggressivity would turn inward, producing an interpersonal calculus adapted to tradeoffs and appropriate to Keynesian demand management. But the material ground for the attempt to use "reasonable" demands to stimulate economic expansion quickly eroded, and so did the optimistic view of patriarchal benevolence. Real wages continued to rise. And within the context of an unpopular war, it was impossible to curtail social consumption (e.g., welfare or health costs) or restrain individual activity in the shop, community, or market. With the notorious "Green Amendment" to the Poverty Act, Congress turned the Great Society programs over to the entrenched, racialist city bureaucrats they had been designed to supplant. No longer could political violence—or undisciplined social imagination—be accepted simply as "social conflict by other means." Instead, to paraphrase C. Wright Mills, public issues were read back into the family as "private troubles" and the household—and women's behavior in it—were targeted as arenas for first-line observation and management.

Moynihan's work is paradigmatic of post-Johnson Keynesianism. From a formal standpoint, the Moynihan Report (1965) used shoddy data from family sociology to bemoan the "disintegration" of black families and spearhead a racist campaign to resurrect traditional patriarchal authority via the destruction of municipal day care, the elimination of abortion, and the like. However, the real importance of Moynihan's work (1973) lies in his recognizing the specific initiatives of women and youth. For example, he read the riots as a demand for *more* money and consumer goods (not for jobs and welfare, as radicals claimed), advocated a guaranteed national income, and selected the household as the site through which income redistribution (Nixon's Family Assistance Program) could help actualize the new and creative sources of labor power women represented. The alleged absence of the black male from homes was the specific image Moynihan used to evoke "the family crisis" as an object of policy debate. This fiction legitimated a larger decision-making process designed to integrate family dynamics and economic growth in a far more immediate way than the Great Society planners imagined, using categorical dependence on state support as a way of capturing the new households women and youth created through their mobility out of traditional families and neighborhoods. The problem was—and remains—to produce a family ideology to support comprehensive dependence, a "scientific" image which formally acknowledges the integrity of traditional values while at the same time emptying them of all content, an image of the family as a world apart which "reveals" an inherent need for outside management. What Moynihan tried to provide was a public reading of uncontrolled female independence as illegitimate, a reading that transformed what business and government perceived as a frontal assault by blacks, women, and youth into a legitimate object of repression—and, if necessary, of private force— for all those who oppose the breakdown of the family. In short, women's revolt against patriarchal conventions could be profitably harnessed only if the public was convinced that unrestrained individuality—like other forms of violence—so threatened the fabric of family and social life that the broad use of institutional authority to quash female subjectivity in the home was justified.

It was this problem which Straus, Gelles, and Steinmetz addressed (1980). Again, the limitations of the data from which they built their model are far less important than their use of earlier research to "recognize" the family, to know it in a new way which made it susceptible to new forms of therapeutic control.

Like conflict theorists, Straus et al. begin simply by seeing "violence-prone families" as a deviant subtype. Setting aside the qualitative distinction so important during the Johnson years between "conflict" and "violence," they proceed to reconceptualize conflict and violence as different only in degree. Thus, where violence appears as a strictly marginal phenomenon in the conflict model of the late 1950s and '60s, some violence can now be identified in all families brought there, Straus et al. add, by "social heredity." The implication is clear. Since conflict is different from more severe violence only in degree, the latter can be prevented only if the former is suppressed. Thus, argue the researchers in an early paper, "violence in the home" deserves as much attention as "Crime in the Streets" (Straus & Steinmetz, 1975). Like Moynihan and the Nixon White House, moreover, they also imply it deserves the same kind—that is, careful policing. The repressive and ameliorative functions of the services now become inextricably linked. Set in the context of the collapse of Keynesian optimism, the invention of the violent family as the prototype mediates the routinized management of political conflict by the helping services at the level of interpersonal relations.

How were data produced to support the conclusion that "some form of violence will occur in almost every family"? Or, more exactly, how was the question posed so that conflict in the family suddenly appeared as "violence"? First, "violence" was completely abstracted from any juridical or historical framework and given a moral reading. Any implied or direct use of force, no matter how harmless in intent or consequence and no matter by whom, was violent and therefore bad. Thus, sibling rivalry (most common among children under eight!) and parental threats to discipline their children were placed on a continuum of violence with brutal homicides to prove "violence is as common as love" (Straus & Steinmetz, 1975). The continuum was rooted by social genetics, for example, in the claim that "violence begets violence" and this same theory suggested that the continuum could be extended to include public violence, even war (Owen & Straus, 1975). Appreciation of the violent family was deepened by our presumed "knowledge" that "America is a violent society." By now, the family had lost all specificity. No longer a hierarchical structure of unequal authority materially based in work performed primarily by women, it was simply a space where rates of relative pathology were generated, a depoliticized terrain where human purposiveness in general and female subjectivity in particular were replaced by statistical probabilities of behavior fragments. Not surprisingly, the measurement instruments used to assess "family violence" such as the Conflict Tactics Scale (CTS) incorporated the assumptions of the image—for instance, combining threats with actual hitting, determining consequence on the basis of "probable risk," rating "arguments" on the same scale as "shooting," and so on (Straus et al., 1980). By turning female aggressiveness (arguments over money, child care, and sex, for example) into simply another statistical point on a seemingly naturalistic continuum of violence with patriarchal force, Straus and his colleagues contribute to the invisibility of the very phenomenon they are credited with exposing.

Thus the "knowledge" that the family is "violent" is less a discovery than a manipulation of definitions. And the knowledge is a form of re-cognition in another sense as well. The image of the violent family invokes its opposite as an ideal, the peaceful, harmonious, *and* repressed family of yore. But whereas in the traditional picture, harmony and stability require withdrawal from the market (that "jungle filled with wilde beasties" in Jonathan Edward's phrase) to the home, in the current oversocialized account family members can be protected from their inherited tendency to explode only by constant external vigilance and restraint. Nor is such policing in any sense neutral. Since the unequal authority between family members is a source of chronic tension, particularly where women enjoy relative equality in the juridical and economic spheres, to eliminate the threat family violence poses to society, the relations between men and women (and between parents and children) must be either completely revolutionized or contained and reconstituted so as to stabilize the inheritance of violence. Not surprisingly, the services opt for the latter alternative.

Wife-battering is far and away the most common, volatile, and long-term form of serious violence in family life, and along with child abuse, its persistence and political visibility lend the image of "the violent family" whatever popular saliency it now has. In therapeutic practice as well, the images of the multiproblem woman predisposed to violence and of the violent family take shape primarily in response to the persistence with which abused women present their injuries and related psychosocial problems, another instance of women's refusal to suffer in silence from traditional family mores. Oddly, however, it is precisely the political logic from which wife-battering arises that dissolves beneath the conception of family life as a multifaceted battleground. Instead of revealing female subjectivity as intensely purposive and rational, it is shown to be irrational and to draw its purposes genetically from a pathological environment. This is the legacy we inherit from social science research.

CONCLUSION

In previous work, we examined the medical response to abuse, showing that health personnel consistently mistake abusive injuries and their sequelae for something else and intervene in ways that actually increase the probability that abuse will escalate into the socioclinical syndrome we identify as "battering" (Stark & Flitcraft, 1979, 1981). This process could not be adequately explained simply by analyzing the helping services as such. The dominant images used in helping encounters to construct battering from abuse arise outside of medicine, on the broader intellectual and political terrain where domestic violence itself is constituted.

Sociologists often call ideas and theories that are not immediately drawn from data "abstract." But the real meaning of abstract is to take away from, to think apart from the material reality through which a phenomenon takes shape. In this more orthodox sense, the new knowledge social scientists have produced about domestic violence is abstract, a fact which functions to conceal the political basis of this knowledge and to help shape the material reality of abused women by dislocating, even silencing, their subjectivity. Constructs such as "the battered woman" and "the violent family" are ideological fetishes, but not merely. They are also "cognitive practices," forms of intervention which assume the subjectivity, the life, they claim to represent. The dichotomy alleged to exist between research, therapy, and policy on one side and "the private event" of battering on the other turns out to be a fiction required by the peculiar terms on which abused women meet their interpreters and helpers.

In Britain, the prevailing view is that abuse results from an individual history of multiple pathologies, including a predisposition to violence, carried by immature personalities from one generation of poor to the next. This "knowledge" is constructed from three elements primarily, the "cycle of deprivation" theory developed by Sir Keith Joseph; the experience of Chiswick House, whose founder, Erin Pizzey, is a popular expert on abuse; and the findings of Dr. John Gayford. Since Gayford studied only Chiswick (i.e., no other shelter and no controls) and Joseph both funded Chiswick and saw Gayford's findings used by the Select Committee on Violence in Marriage to support his deprivation thesis, it is hardly farfetched to see theory, research, social therapy, and policy joined by a single political thread. In Britain, this thread is the legitimation of expanded therapeutic intervention on an individual basis as a means of containing the militancy of the poor. By organizing the facts about domestic violence into a problem (the cycle of deprivation) whose solution seems to lie in an expanded caretaking role for the welfare state, science helps conceal the contradictory nature of that state and, more immediately, the ways in which its patriarchal benevolence converges with client/female dependence. This convergence became particularly apparent when, after the Brixton riots in April 1981, the image of dependent subjects needing protection against their own violent impulses was extended from social science to police science and from a deprived minority to the entire immigrant population.

In America, despite the influence of feminism on the rhetoric of social research, the view dominating treatment is constructed in response to two contradictory pressures: the need to identify the family as a distinct sphere of private life where social problems originate, and the need to combat the apparently self-directed (i.e., "unrestrained") individuality (or aggressivity) of women by ideologically (and therapeutically) reconstituting the family's inner life. By reading women's struggle for individuality — their "fight"—as formally identical to the use of force to stifle individuality and by interpreting wife-abuse as a chronic aspect of the multi-problem character of the family as such, researchers reconcile these seemingly contradictory pressures, suggesting that what is distinct about the family is its dependence for stability (and rationality) on interpretation, aid, and management. The image of the violent family whose inner tendencies toward fragmentation must be constantly monitored and repressed legitimates a larger policy initiative directed at policing and integrating the unfolding subjectivity and labor power of women and youth.

Both the British and the American theories produce causal links between primal afflictions (parental abuse, for example) and battering through "genetic" modes of inquiry. On the one hand, ordinary behaviors such as spanking or fighting are set on a continuum with extreme behaviors such as battering so that pathology appears to be a normative dimension rooted in the nature of the family as such. On the other hand, by juxtaposing rates of these behaviors and then reading them into individual and family biographies, a self-generating and expanding cycle appears whereby spanking in one generation leads naturally to battering and homicide in the next. In these accounts, to paraphrase Marx's description of commodity fetishism, rates of pathology take on the life that people lack, and all sense is lost of the social specificity of violence against women or of the historical and political context in which this violence is constructed. Although Pizzey, Gayford, Straus, Gelles, and others frequently appeal to biology directly, the essence of the genetic explanation is the reduction of "environment," "culture," "deprivation," "violence," even "family" from social to natural categories without reference to political relationships or determinacy. The ideological character of this work is reflected in its reliance for saliency on the very phenomenon it mystifies— domestic violence—and by the already noted tendency to reduce public issues to private troubles. The loss of familial boundaries required for us to think of the family as a cradle for war (Owen & Straus, 1975) converges with a capacity to accept therapeutic command as a chronic constraint on private life.

The relation between the new social knowledge of abuse and the actual constitution of battering as a social event of epidemic proportions is neither simple nor mechanical. Dominant imagery is adapted to the situational requirements of the clinical encounter by a process Weber termed "elective affinity." Indeed, the relative prestige of genetic explanations in clinical settings derives from their capacity to rationalize the clinical projection of failure through a variety of therapeutic strategies. The clinical transfer of blame requires the relative silence of the patient, while, according to the genetic view, the abused woman is a passive medium through which pathology reproduces itself. Thus the same basic imagery underlies medical fragmentation, psychiatric individuation, and the over-contextualization of abuse by social work and sociology. In each case, the most narrow interests are at work. At the same time, however, these various responses are organized into a descending hierarchy of degradation and in specific response to the evolution of the battering syndrome which they also evoke. What appears from a superficial standpoint to be the mutual validation of social research and clinical experience (or the experience at Chiswick House) appears, from the vantage of the subject/object of domestic violence, as a common disciplinary project. Ultimately, it is only the success of this project, only the process by which power struggles are driven inward and reflected in personal or familial pathology, that makes the new social knowledge of abuse produced by science anything more than pure fancy.

The body of the battered woman receives the bruises. But it is her femininity that is being attacked, re-cognized, disciplined. Here lies the quintescence of domestic violence that genetic explanations fail to grasp.

Like battering, femininity is a single social practice rooted in continuous historical activity, in concrete material and imaginative struggles to earn a living, to reproduce a community of loved ones, and to gain and sustain sexual pleasure. Like battering as well, femininity is constructed from a complex of social relations through which the personal is joined with the political and conceptual. However, while battering destructures the claims of a female subject to autonomy, the dynamic of femininity lies in the unfolding of this subjectivity on a broad front that obviously extends far beyond the grip of social science or social therapy.

The responses of social researchers to abuse parallel the initiatives of an abuser facing female resistance to his authority. Beyond this, the new knowledge makers help reconcile patriarchal authority to the external support it now requires, given the material erosion of its base in family property and its loss of direct command over women and children. It is not the prestige of science that determines the political misappropriation of findings for political ends. To the contrary, it is the convergence of research with political authority that makes otherwise transparent ideological invention appear as "an objective portrayal of a serious social issue" such as abuse.

The aura of inevitability which the new social knowledge lends wife abuse dissolves only when we recognize that the organizing principles of both the new knowledge and domestic violence are social-historical, not genetic. Indeed, few things more clearly illustrate the contingent nature of battering, the fact that it can now be eliminated once and for all, than the growing interdependence of violence in the home and social science, social therapy, social policy, and the police.

NOTE

1. The thrust of the genetic view is to separate the realm of social problems from politics and economics. This reflects a larger tendency within capitalist societies to view social dislocations occasioned by contradictions in the productive sphere (joblessness, for instance, or overcrowded housing conditions) as "a realm apart" with their own developmental laws. These laws are typically formulated by sociology (or, in Britain, by a strange field called "social administration") with little reference to their materialist basis.

REFERENCES

Cobbe, F. P. *Wife torture in England.* London: Contemporary Review, 1878.

Donzelot, J. *La Police des Familles.* Paris: Editions de Minuit, 1977.

Ewen, S. *Captains of consciousness.* New York: McGraw-Hill, 1976.

Gayford, J. Battered wives, *Medicine, Science and Law,* 1975, *15*(4), 237-245. (a)

Gayford, J. Wife battering: a preliminary survey of 100 cases. *British Medical Journal,* 1975, *25,* 194-197. (b)

Hall, S. et al. *Policing the crisis: Mugging, the state and law and order.* London: Macmillan, 1978.

Levinger, G. Sources of marital dissatisfaction among applicants for divorce. *American Journal of Orthopsychiatry*, 1977, 883-897.

Marsden, D. Sociological perspectives on family violence. In J. M. Martin (Ed.), *Violence and the family*. New York: John Wiley, 1978.

Moynihan, D. P. *The politics of a guaranteed income*. New York: Vintage Books, 1973.

O'Brien, J. Violence in divorce prone families. *Journal of Marriage and the Family*, November 1971, 692-698.

Owen, D. J., & Straus, M. A. The social structure of violence in childhood and approval of violence as an adult. *Aggressive Behavior*, 1975, *1*, 193-211.

Pizzey, E. *Scream quietly or the neighbors will hear*. Harmondsworth, England: Penguin, 1974.

Pizzey, E., & Shapiro, J. Choosing a violent relationship. *New Society*, April 1981, 23.

Safilios-Rothschild, C. The study of family power structure: A review, 1960-1969. *Journal of Marriage and the Family*, November 1969, 539-552.

Stark, E. Doctors in spite of themselves: The limits of radical health criticism. *International Journal of Health Services*, 1982, *12*(3), 419-457.

Stark, E., Flitcraft, A., Frazier, W. Medicine and patriarchal violence: The social construction of a "private" event. *International Journal of Health Services*, 1979, *9*(3), 461-493.

Stark, E., & Flitcraft, A. Psychiatric perspectives on the abuse of women: A critical approach. In A. Lurie & E. B. Quitkin (Eds.), *Identification and treatment of spouse abuse*. New York: Long Island Jewish-Hillside Hospital, 1981.

Straus, M. A. Wife beating: How common and why? *Victimology*, 1977-78, *2*(3-4), 443-458.

Straus, M. A., Gelles, R., Steinmetz, S. *Behind closed doors*. Garden City, NY: Doubleday, 1980.

Straus, M. A., & Steinmetz, S. The family as a cradle of violence. In M. Straus & S. Steinmetz (Eds.), *Violence in the family*. New York: Dodd, Mead, 1975.

Townsend, P. *The cycle of deprivation—The history of a confused thesis*. Unpublished paper, 1975.

Walker, L. *The battered woman*. New York: Harper & Row, 1979.

Wilson, E. *The research into battered women*. London: National Women's Aid Federation (374 Gray's Inn Road, London, WC1), 1970.

Wolfgang, M. E. Husband and wife homicides. *Corrective Psychiatry and Journal of Social Therapy*, 1956, 263-271.

22

Theories, Professional Knowledge, and Diagnosis of Child Abuse

RICHARD O'TOOLE, PATRICK TURBETT,
and CLAIRE NALEPKA

Understanding of the social process through which child abuse is labeled by professionals is basic to the study and treatment of child abuse. As Gelles (1975, 1980) has pointed out, there is a circular relationship between diagnostic labels of child abuse, the production of official statistics, theoretical and clinical knowledge, and the treatment of child abuse.

In this analysis we use a societal reaction or labeling approach in an attempt to explain how "signs" and "causes" are linked in judgments of possible child abuse. To explore this problem we consider (1) the relationship between theories of family violence and professional knowledge of child abuse; (2) how professional knowledge, as well as other sources of information, are used in diagnostic behavior; and (3) how diagnostic behavior affects diagnosis of child abuse. Nurses and physicians are compared.

Hawkins and Tiedeman (1975) present a seven-step model of the process by which behavior is labeled deviant. Their formulation will help us understand how theory, professional knowledge, and general ideas of violence are employed by professionals in the process of diagnosing or labeling child abuse. 1. *Observation.* "The act [or attribute] is monitored in some way so that its occurrence is known" (p. 64). The question here is when and under what circumstances child abuse is "visible" to be observed. For example, who takes their children to emergency rooms? 2. *Recognition.* "The act is seen as a rule violation—i.e., a violation of the rules-in-use" (p. 64). Child abuse is rarely observed by social control agents such as physicians and nurses. Injuries to the child, the child's behavior, and so on are observed which are "possibly" the result of child abuse or which may serve as clues to possible abuse. 3. *Imputed Cause.* The act or attribute is categorized "accidental, not really intended, or intentional" (p. 64). This determination is a key factor in all definitions of child abuse, as well as the application of definitions we describe. 4. *Motive*. The observer considers the motive or intention of the parent. The parent may offer "accounts" (Scott & Lyman, 1968) as evidence of motive. During steps 3 and 4 typifications are used to assess cause and motive. "Typifications are descriptions drawn from a common stock of knowledge which serve as short-hand notation for various phenomena." They "are thus simplified, standardized categories or labels" (p. 82). 5. *Potential Reactions*. The observer "rehearses possible reactions to the act and actor based on situational factors, normalization and denial attempts, typifications of role suggested by motive imputation, rules in use, and other factors" (p. 65). 6. *Reaction is Chosen*. A reaction is chosen among available alternatives. Important factors include the background and training of the observer, organizational categories, existing precedents, and societal expectations. 7. *Impact of Reactions*. "What is the potential influence of reactions on the actor's future behavior, on perceptions of opportunities to conform or deviate, and on personal identity?" (p. 65). This is such a weighty issue that for some persons it has come to stand as the major concern of labeling theory. As important as this question is, we must also research the source of labels, their content, and how they are selectively applied in order to fully understand their impact on the deviant.

As noted, child abuse is not directly observed. Therefore, the nurse or physician must infer what happened to cause the child's condition. Outside of what Gelles (1975) called "outrageous" cases, much possible abuse is fairly ambiguous. According to the labeling model (Hawkins & Tiedeman, 1975), typifications of child abuse will play a major role in the diagnostic process. We explore the thesis that by focusing on certain theoretical explanations of child abuse, typifications are created in professional knowledge concerning the "types of people" and "types of situations" which characterize child abuse. Research which investigated the influence of socioeconomic status, ethnic status, and level of injury on recognition and reporting of abuse by physicians and nurses is discussed. We then report results of surveys of nurses' and physicians' diagnostic behavior, (i.e., how they link signs and causes of abuse).

THEORIES OF FAMILY VIOLENCE

We use the inventory provided by Gelles and Straus (1979, pp. 560-561) as a basic conceptualization of types of theories in order to analyze which theories have influenced practice. These authors divide theories into three basic levels of analysis as follows: (1) Intraindividual—psychopathology, alcohol and drugs; (2) Social Psychological—frustration-aggression, social learning, self-attitude, "Clockwork Orange," symbolic interaction, exchange theory, attribution theory; (3) Sociocultural-Functional, culture of violence, structural, general systems, conflict, resource. The list of theories has been updated by Gelles (1980) and is in this volume. However, these theories were not published in time to affect the professional writings we analyzed.

Medical and Nursing Conceptions of Child Abuse

We surveyed recent pediatric texts for physicians and for nurses, along with influential articles in each professional field, to research which of the above theories have influenced professional knowledge of child abuse. The analysis is based on the assumption that these materials reflect the current state of knowledge in a profession. They are used to train new professionals and are referred to by physicians and nurses to update their knowledge.

Medical Conceptions of Child Abuse

The sections on child abuse in three leading pediatric texts were analyzed (Kempe, Silver, & O'Brien, 1978; Einhorn, 1977; Schmitt & Kempe, 1979). Since the landmark article by Kempe et al. (1962), medical etiological theories have remained heavily reliant on psychopathology as an explanation of child abuse. Abusive parents "are often lonely, immature, isolated, unloved, depressed and angry people" or "have poor impulse control" (Kempe et al., 1978). Cohen (1966) termed these formulations "kinds of people theories." Deviance is explained by concepts which characterize something about the actor, often some underlying psychological characteristic. The question such theories attempt to answer is, "What kind of person would do this sort of thing?" (p. 43). The answer, in medical texts, is a disturbed, although not psychotic, person (except in murder, where psychosis is often involved). Cohen (1966) explains that once characteristics of the deviant have been identified, the next logical question concerns "how they got to be that way." The medical authors we surveyed answered the question largely in terms of a developmental notion or learning theory, often calling attention to the "cycle of violence." Subsequent additions to the basic idea of parental psychopathology have resulted in what Cohen terms a "conjunctive" theory (1966). Theories of this type describe a chemical mixture of factors which "set off" the deviance. Thus characteristics of the child, the parent-child relationship, and environmental sources act as stressors to trigger abusive tendencies present in the parent. The authors point out that while some social categories may experience more stress, child abuse is found in all sectors of the community.

In terms of diagnostic indicators, physical injury is the most important signal of abuse. Other data sources, such as X-rays, are to be used to confirm the diagnosis and include observation of the child's behavior and past history of similar problems. Kempe et al. (1978) call for a family assessment to be conducted by a specialist which would identify certain psychosocial factors usually found in abusive families.

Perhaps reflecting methodological and sampling procedures, etiological notions are largely confined to intraindividual theories of psychopathology. There were few even indirect references to the social psychological theories with the exception of "cycle of violence," or sociocultural theories listed above. Medical text authors do not reference the writings of social and behavioral researchers whose names are connected with these theories. In a survey of family violence research, Gelles (1980) noted that the majority of writings in the 1960s were done by and for health professionals. Our survey shows that by the late 1970s, while a great deal of social and behavioral science research was available, very little had been incorporated into standard pediatric texts. To the extent that medical knowledge, as measured here, influences practice, we can conclude that physicians at this time were predominantly using theories of child abuse based on psychopathology and "conjunctive" theories which added stressors that led to the release of abusive tendencies.

Nursing Conceptions of Child Abuse

Two leading pediatric nursing texts were consulted (Whaley & Wong, 1979; Marlow, 1977) and an article on recognizing child abuse in the widely circulated *American Journal of Nursing* (Olson, 1976). In general, these authors describe a more eclectic group of signs of abuse and etiological formulations. The texts we surveyed reflect differences in the nursing profession regarding reliance on the medical model. The text by Marlow (1977) employs the medical psychopathology orientation, but there is a clear-cut notion of frustration-aggression theory with the child as scapegoat. According to the text, "the etiologic factor is that parents or caretakers have a defect in character structure which allows aggressive impulses to be expressed too freely when they are under tension" (p. 481). Whaley and Wong (1979) develop a model which encompasses (1) the parent who has the potential for abuse (e.g., through the cycle of violence); (2) the characteristics of the child (e.g., temperament, family position or "special child"); and (3) environmental stressors (e.g., financial or marital crisis coupled with inadequate support systems).

There is a greater concern for family dynamics here than in the medical literature surveyed, but the eclectic approach adds up to a conjunctive theory (1966, p. 44), although it considers a larger number of factors. Combinations of the factors produce child abuse in an unspecified chemical-type reaction. An implicit conjunctive theory also seems to lie behind Olson's (1976) "index of suspicion," in which various behaviors and characteristics of parent, child, and family receive different weights which add to a risk score. There is no explicit theory to explain the interrelationships of factors. Although specific theories are not noted or referenced, from his clinical experience Olson touches on a wide variety of social factors as potential indicators of abuse including family structure, ethnicity, family problems, and strength of religious affiliation.

In nursing works there is not the same degree of reliance on physical signs of abuse, and the child's and parent's behaviors are important indicators. There is somewhat wider referencing of research and practice literature (e.g., to social work), but there is a noticeable absence of sociological sources. Nursing text authors also inform readers that child abuse is not limited to lower-class groups.

Diagnostic Behavior of Nurses and Physicians

Experimental Studies Using Vignettes

Using an experimental design we investigated the influence of socioeconomic status, race, and level of injury on physicians' recognition and reporting of child abuse (Turbett & O'Toole, 1980a, 1980b) and then replicated the method with nurses (Nalepka, O'Toole, & Turbett, 1981). Respondents judged vignettes (emergency room forms) in which these variables were experimentally manipulated. Physicians' (N = 76) judgments were affected by socioeconomic status, race, and level of injury. Nurses' (N = 178) judgments were affected by level of injury, but their recognition was not influenced by socioeconomic status or race. In a vignette which presented a child with a serious injury, 70% of the physicians judged child abuse when the parent was of low socioeconomic status, as indicated by occupation, whereas only 51% judged abuse on the form where the parents' socioeconomic status was high. Similarly, in a low injury case, 43% recognized child abuse when the parent was black as compared to 23% when the parent was white. In both studies, virtually all nurses and physicians judged that an obvious case, where the child had old cigarette burns on his back, was in fact child abuse. It is in the gray areas (Silver, Dublin, & Lourie, 1969) that the factors we researched become operative.

Surveys of Physicians' Diagnostic Behavior

Signs. Exploratory interviews with emergency room, general practice, and pediatric physicians (N = 30) revealed that physical injuries lead other categories of signs used to diagnose abuse. Smaller numbers had interviewed the family, observed the child in the diagnostic situation, or had used family history or dress as indicators. Replies which were particularly informative in this phase of the research included: "I don't see child abuse in my private practice. It doesn't happen in middle-class neighborhoods"; "It was a large poor family; the child was dirty and complaining—a *typical* case of abuse" (italics added). Others stated that dress and demeanor, with reference to socioeconomic status, were major indicators. Following a pretest of emergency room forms with small groups of physicians (N = 20) which were to be used in the experimental study, one physician somewhat sheepishly remarked, "I always looked at race first. That's an important indicator." Several others then remarked that race entered their judgments.

We also asked what signs physicians should use to be alert for abuse to tap their general beliefs about diagnostic indicators. Physical injuries were again predominant, and uncleanliness or some type of family characteristic (e.g., family trauma) were each mentioned by a third of the respondents. These are the variables which appear to be used to screen in or screen out possible cases of abuse.

In relation to this judgmental process, one of the most interesting responses was "you have to smell out abuse, use your intuition." This and other replies suggested that in many cases no definite signals exist for detecting abuse. Another respondent said that in comparison to the criteria provided in medical training, actual cases were "very difficult to detect."

Causes. Physician responses about causes of child abuse reveal a very interesting relationship between signs and causes. While using physical injuries as their major indicators, along with inferences about current and past psychological and social status of the child and family, they listed the following as causes: poverty (17), alcohol and drugs (12), family trauma or parental stress (9), parental ignorance or lack of education (9), psychological disease (8), parental background (6), unwanted children (3), and broken homes (3). Analysis of causes shows there is hardly a well-integrated etiological model which specifies events leading to child abuse.

Requests for Additional Information. In the experimental study after the physicians had rated each vignette concerning the possibility of child abuse, they were asked, "What additional information would aid you in this determination?" On the average the physician requested only 1.5 additional information items after each judgment (N = 570 requests). Approximately 20% of physician requests can be categorized as "physical" (e.g., more tests) followed by 16%, related to emotional or social situation of the family; 10%, hospital records or child's medical history; 10%, interview with child; 6%, interview with parent. In contrast, only a small number of requests (4% in each case) involved interviewing witnesses to the injury or securing information from school records. For the most part, data collection is limited to the diagnostic situation, and, with the exception of where other professions might chart data on medical records and the 4% of requests for school records, the physician makes the diagnosis by himself in the diagnostic situation.

Surveys of Nurses' Diagnostic Behavior

Signs. In an exploratory study we asked 31 pediatric and emergency room nurses who were employed in the hospitals "what signs, or clues, should nurses use or be alert for to recognize child abuse." Nurses, like physicians, place the greatest emphasis on what could be termed a suspicious injury, which would vary from the obvious cigarette burns to an injury that could have been received in an accident but does not fit well with their own logic. Quite often they compare the accounts given by the parents and then that of the child. They are concerned with observing the child's behavior and parent-child interaction. The parent's attitude, appearance of the child, and repeated admissions were the signs mentioned next most often. Only one nurse listed getting information from relatives or neighbors. (It should be pointed out that we did not interview public health nurses.) Indicators of social class were not listed.

Causes. We asked the 31 emergency room and pediatric nurses what they thought caused child abuse. The nurses' conceptions of the causes of child abuse are not only instructive for the relationship between theory and practice but are suggestive as to how signs of child abuse are linked with its causes. A total of 24 of 31 nurses listed the cycle of violence notion; in fact, it was often one of the first mentioned. The stress or frustration theme is seen as a major cause by nurses. Specific conditions which augment stress were noted. The mentally ill or psychologically flawed parent and alcohol and drugs were each listed by several nurses. Thus, while a number of nurses mentioned the same "causes," there would appear to be no integrated theoretical scheme which explains how causes are interrelated or how signs are related to causes.

Nurses' Requests for Additional Information. After judging each of the five vignettes, the 179 nurses requested 2306 new types of information. The average number of requests for additional data was 2.6, as compared to 1.5 for physicians. Nurses were much more eclectic in their requests and emphasized a different type of data. The single largest category of information requested had to do with "accounts" of the incident, with a larger portion (16%) wanting the child's account, while 6% would seek the parent's rendition. A larger number were widely scattered into many specific requests concerning the psychological characteristics of the child and parent-child interaction. A smaller proportion requested physical data, 13%, as compared to 20% for physicians. Again, data collection is restricted to the diagnostic situation, with only 2% requesting reports from a combined category of resources: welfare, police, school, and other hospitals. Thus, while nurses request a much wider variety of types of data, there does not appear to be an underlying theoretical scheme which guides their judgment. Their search, like physicians, is limited situationally and in terms of possible interorganizational dimensions.

Nurses' Background Differences. Thus far we have attempted to relate professional knowledge to diagnostic behavior. Our theoretical guidelines (Hawkins & Tiedemen, 1975) would point to other background differences, in addition to professional socialization, which would account for how professionals recognize deviance. Attempts to partial out how different backgrounds of professionals might affect their diagnostic behavior have met with only limited success thus far due to sample homogeneity and size. Our small sample of physicians is very homogenous as to race and socioeconomic status. We cannot distinguish sex-role socialization and professional socialization because all physicians sampled were male and all nurses female. We were, however, able to analyze the nurses' judgments in the vignette study (N = 179) according to background differences. Following are the results of this analysis.

1. When the nurses judged vignettes with a high injury condition (not the evident case but a serious injury) none of the background characteristics has an effect on the judgment of child abuse.

2. Race of the parent had an effect on recognition of abuse for nurses of low socioeconomic status (SES) background, but not for nurses of high SES background.

3. The SES of the family is related to child abuse recognition for young nurses but not for older nurses. This may also reflect experience.

4. Data analysis suggests that nurses with no children are affected in their recognition of child abuse by the parent's SES, while nurses with children are not affected by this factor.

5. The following variables appear to have no effect on the relationship between SES of the parent and child abuse recognition: SES background, marital status, community of origin, current work setting, education in child abuse, or amount of contact with child abuse.

6. For the nurses sampled, the following variables appear to have no effect on the relation between parent's race and child abuse recognition: age (experience), number of children, marital status, community of origin, current work setting, education in child abuse, and amount of contact with child abuse.

DISCUSSION

Before turning to theoretical and practical implications of the research, methodological limitations should be discussed. First, both the vignette experimental studies and the surveys raise problems of external validity. Our results should be tested in carefully controlled observations in clinical settings. Second, there are the questions of representativeness and small sample size in each of the substudies and in the sampling of texts to represent professional knowledge.

Theory, Professional Knowledge, and Practice

Of the available theories of family violence (Gelles & Straus, 1979), few have been incorporated into professional literature in medicine or nursing. In turn, diagnostic behavior of physicians and nurses appears to be guided by a limited number of theoretical notions of child abuse, as well as commonly held cultural beliefs in the case of physician judgments. Medical models for diagnosis rely heavily on conceptions of individual psychopathology. While nursing models have adopted a more eclectic view which includes more emphasis on environmental factors, there is still the theme that child abuse is caused by "special kinds of people" who abuse children when the right mix of environmental stressors is present. Neither model up to the time of our analysis has incorporated sociological theories. However, there is some evidence of the integration of sociological perspectives (e.g., Millor, 1981) which may be incorporated into standard diagnostic conceptions.

We are concerned about the effect of the pathological view on public policy and the treatment of child abuse. There appears to be a circular relationship between diagnostic typifications, clinical samples, the production of clinical knowledge, tabulation of official statistics interpreted for epidemiological theory, and the treatment of child abuse. Treatment and social policy may be misguided to the extent to which they are based on limited theoretical conceptions of child abuse. The specific treatment ideology of psychopathology, for example, individualizes a social problem and focuses attention on treatment modalities and social control agents with those diagnostic and treatment skills. Social structure and process are neglected. If social psychological and sociological theories are incorporated so that family violence is seen, in additional to individual and social pathology, as a *normal* part of family life (Gelles & Straus, 1979), then practice and policy should benefit.

Implications for the Labeling of Child Abuse

We feel that the labeling approach has a number of implications for theory and research on child abuse. A first major factor in the Hawkins and Tiedeman (1975) model is the "visibility" of the act. Visibility can be defined as "the probability that an event will be encountered either directly (observed by a witness) or indirectly (written or verbal reports by others)" (p. 76). Child abuse occurs most often "behind closed doors" and therefore is less visible than those types of deviance which occur in public. However, there is a tendency for certain groups (e.g., the poor) to secure health care in public places such as emergency rooms (Roth, 1972), which should make their abuse more visible. Also, there is a greater distribution of agencies, programs, and professional workers in areas in which lower socioeconomic groups live. There may be more agency and interagency record-keeping on these persons, so that a record to justify the diagnosis may be more easily compiled. We could also speculate that the parent suffering some type of psychopathology may be more visible in these clinical settings, thus reinforcing the typification.

Once potential child abuse becomes visible, what happens then so that some parents are judged abusers while others are not? We speculate that physicians and nurses have conceptions of "normal injuries" and that when these are violated, conceptions of "abnormal injuries" or abuse are entertained (Sudnow, 1965). At one end of a continuum we would find what Gelles (1975) called outrageous cases (e.g., those reported in exposé tabloids). Our research showed that "obvious" child abuse, old cigarette burns, was diagnosed by virtually all nurses and physicians. Yet, as we travel along the continuum, evidence of child abuse becomes increasingly more ambiguous, and it is here that the social process of labeling we describe should explain differential responses. Following Hawkins and Tiedeman (1975), we suggest that typifications are employed to direct this perceptual judgmental process based on the judges' general background, professional socialization, on-the-job training, and organizational roles, for example.

Cause and *motive* assignment is incorporated as part of the typification and is particularly important in diagnosing child abuse. There is an explicit attempt in much of the medical literature to make physicians realize that parents can abuse their children. Silver et al. (1969) interviewed physicians concerning the gray areas in diagnosing child abuse and found that three diagnostic problems centered on the attribution of cause and motive: differentiating punishment from child abuse, unwillingness to accept the fact that parents could abuse their children, and problems in establishing the "responsibility" of the parent. The medicalization of child abuse, particularly creating a sick role for the abuser, should help take this responsibility away by making the parent a psychologically disturbed person (Freidson, 1970). However, child abuse is a type of deviance which is both a crime and a medical problem. The question is, could the parent have caused the injury? Einhorn's (1977) section on child abuse in a pediatric textbook is titled, in part, "intentional accidents."

Motive assignment and moral character is often incorporated, we speculate, as part of the typification, for example, through the cycle of violence or flawed character explanation. In this manner the labeler may be led to substitute routine psychological backgrounds and common stress-related events for what actually happened. Child abuse may be seen as evidence for psychopathology which is then viewed as a cause of psychopathology. Selective questioning of the parent may confirm dependent feelings and attempts at "role reversal when overwhelmed with economic or marital stress." Both nurses' and physicians' diagnoses were confined to the here and now of the diagnostic situation, and there were few attempts to get additional information from other sources concerning family, community, and school. Thus, through what Hawkins and Tiedeman (1975) call "biography building," a case history is constructed around the typification. The typification guides the inquiry rather than being its product. Of course, other typifications protect some persons from the label "child abuser."

Our experimental research leads to this question: How do physicians incorporate race and socioeconomic status into their typification of child abuse? (It would appear that these variables are not part of the typifications which nurses employ.) First, many commonsense views and scientific theory and research support the association between class and family violence, crime, and mental illness, among other social problems. Scheff (1966) has shown how class is related to physician's diagnosis of mental illness. In the scientific literature class has been a controversial topic, but much theory and research supports the association between class and crime (Pope, 1979) and abuse (Straus, Gelles, & Steinmetz, 1980). Our research supports the finding by Newberger et al. (1977) that lower-class and minority children are more likely to be labeled as abused when seen with injuries in a hospital. Second, specific professional socialization experiences may support the typification. While medical textbooks say that child abuse occurs in all social classes, they point to sources of stress which are class-related. A residency with experience in an emergency room of an inner-city teaching hospital may confirm the notion. Thus, there is a good deal of thought to support the association between class and abuse. Race may become a part of the typification through its association with class or, in addition, through coupling race with violence, crime, or mental illness. Epidemiological associations are employed through typifications to link individual characteristics such as dress and other indicators of social class to child abuse. Also, it may be easier to apply the label when the deviant is socially distant from the labeler and powerless. All these factors combine to support the typification through selective perception, which provides further evidence for its validity.

Differences Between Nurses and Physicians

At this stage of the research program we are not able to identify what factors account for the differences between nurses and physicians in recognizing and reporting abuse. Nursing theories are more eclectic and nurses use more signs of abuse and conduct a more extensive investigation of clues to child abuse in their diagnoses. Unlike physicians, nurses' judgments were not affected by socioeconomic status and race. The differences may be due to professional educational experiences, sex-role socialization, or perhaps to the fact that nurses are recruited from more varied socioeconomic backgrounds. Physicians sampled were all males from fairly homogeneous backgrounds, while all nurse respondents were female. It has been suggested that nurses have more training in child abuse than physicians. Or it could be that nurses are not sure of their role in judging child abuse and therefore hedge on their judgments in less overt cases. Analysis of background differences among nurses are suggestive but await further research and analysis.

The Diagnostic Situation—
Roles and Organization

Our analysis suggests further study of professional roles and organizational settings concerning judgment and reporting of child abuse. There is some concern in both the medical and the nursing literature regarding their respective roles in diagnosis. As noted above, an underlying theme in several medical sources is to overcome physician resistance to diagnosing and reporting abuse. Part of the solution offered is to restrict the physician role to identification. In identification the physician role is to *suspect* and then turn the case over to other professionals for confirmation and treatment. The message is clear. Children are being severely injured and killed. When in doubt, make the identification. If successful, this theme should result in more recognition and reporting. The role of the nurse in diagnosing child abuse reflects controversy concerning the role of professional nursing. Text authors provide different roles; Whaley and Wong (1979) advocate an independent vigorous role for nurses, while Marlow (1977) calls for a data collection role for nursing, reserving diagnosis for the physician. Our nursing respondents, however, appear to have resolved the problem by viewing diagnosis as part of their role. However, we need to know how these roles are played in the various settings where child abuse is diagnosed. Our findings suggest that physicians and nurses would differ in their diagnosis of child abuse. This leads to the logical and highly important question of how such differences are resolved. A role analysis also specifies questions concerning the parts other professionals play in the diagnostic setting. According to our data, the answer would be "not much." We noted a tendency, and this was particularly true for physicians, to be self-reliant and not to seek information from other professionals or agencies. Diagnosis seems to take place on a here and now basis.

The spatial and temporal limitations in the search for diagnostic signs of abuse led us to speculate concerning organizational variables, particularly in the manner in which patients are processed. Suggestive leads are provided in the work of Rosengren and Lefton (1969) on the *lateral* and *longitudinal* orientations of organizations toward their clients, by Roth (1972) on the moral evaluation of patients in the emergency room, and by Hawkins and Tiedeman (1975), who offer several hypotheses which specify when typifications will be used (e.g., independent variables are ambiguity of diagnosis, volume of cases, interchangeability of agency personnel). The emergency room, according to Rosengren and Lefton, is oriented to only a very limited view of the patient's total characteristics and for a very brief time span. This orientation would seem to lead to diagnosis of child abuse in only outrageous cases or those which fit the typifications of those empowered to make the diagnosis. In particular, this orientation would not seem to mesh well with theories of child abuse that would require extensive investigation of etiological notions that consider interaction of complex individual, family, and societal factors. Thus, a number of factors may lead to different outcomes in the labeling process through which child abuse is recognized and reported. Understanding of this process is essential to research, theory, treatment, and policy concerning child abuse.

REFERENCES

Cohen, A. K. *Deviance and control.* Englewood Cliffs, NJ: Prentice-Hall, 1966.

Einhorn, A. H. Intentional accidents (maltreatment of children, child abuse, child battering, non-accidental injuries). *Pediatrics,* 1977, *16,* 827-831.

Freidson, E. *Profession of medicine.* New York: Harper & Row, 1970.

Gelles, R. J. The social construction of child abuse. *American Journal of Orthopsychiatry,* 1975, *43,* 611-621.

Gelles, R. J. Violence in the family: A review of research in the seventies. *Journal of Marriage and the Family,* 1980, *42*(4), 873-885.

Gelles, R. J., & Straus, M. A. Determinants of violence in the family: Toward a theoretical integration. In W. R. Burr, R. Hill, F. I. Nye, & I. L. Reiss (Eds.), *Contemporary theories about the family* (Vol. 1). New York: Free Press, 1979.

Hawkins, R., & Tiedeman, G. *The creation of deviance.* Columbus, OH: Charles E. Merrill, 1975.

Kempe, C. H., Silverman, F. N., Steele, B. R., Droegmueller, N., & Silver, H. K. The battered child syndrome. *Journal of the American Medical Association,* July 7, 1962, *181,* 17-24.

Kempe, C. H., Silver, H., & O'Brien, D. *Current pediatric diagnosis and treatment.* Los Altos, CA: Lange Medical Publications, 1978.

Marlow, D. R. *Textbook of pediatric nursing.* Philadelphia: W. B. Saunders, 1977.

Millor, G. K. A theoretical framework for nursing research in child abuse and neglect. *Nursing Research,* 1981, *30,* 78-83.

Nalepka, C., O'Toole, R., & Turbett, J. P. Nurses' and physicians' recognition and reporting of child abuse. *Issues in Comprehensive Pediatric Nursing,* 1981, *5,* 33-44.

Newberger, E. H., Reed, R. B., Daniel, J. H., Hyde, J. N., Jr., & Kotelchuck, M. Pediatric social illness: An etiologic classification. *Pediatrics,* 1977, *60,* 178-185.

Olson, R. J. Index of suspicion: Screening for child abuse. *American Journal of Nursing,* 1976, *76,* 108-110.

Pope, C. E. Race and crime revisited. *Crime and Delinquency,* 1979, *25,* 347-357.

Rosengren, W. R., & Lefton, M. *Hospitals and patients.* New York: Atherton, 1969.

Roth, J. A. Some contingencies of the moral evaluation and control of clientele: The case of the hospital emergency service. *American Journal of Sociology,* 1972, *77,* 839-856.

Scott, M. B., & Lyman, S. M. Accounts. *American Sociological Review,* 1968, *33,* 46-62.

Scheff, T. J. *Being mentally: A sociological theory.* Chicago: Aldine, 1966.

Schmitt, B. D., & Kempe, C. H. Abuse and neglect of children. In V. Vaugh, J. R. McKay, & R. Behrman (Eds.), *Nelson textbook of pediatrics.* Philadelphia: W. B. Saunders, 1979.

Silver, B., Dublin, C. D., & Lourie, R. S. Child abuse syndrome: The "gray areas" in establishing a diagnosis. *Pediatrics,* 1969, *44,* 594-600.

Straus, M. A., Gelles, R. J., & Steinmetz, S. K. *Behind closed doors: Violence in the American family.* Garden City, NY: Doubleday, 1980.

Sudnow, D. Normal crimes: Sociological features of the penal code in a public defender office. *Social Problems,* 1965, *12*(3), 255-276.

Turbett, J. P. & O'Toole, R. *Physician labeling of child abuse.* Paper presented at the annual meetings of the North Central Sociological Association, Dayton, Ohio, May 1980. (a)

Turbett, J. P., & O'Toole, R. *Physician's recognition of child abuse.* Paper presented at the annual meetings of the American Sociological Association, New York, August 1980. (b)

Whaley, L. F., & Wong, D. L. *Nursing care of infants and children.* St. Louis: C. B. Mosby, 1979.

23

Feminist, Political, and Economic Determinants of Wife Abuse Services

DEBRA S. KALMUSS and MURRAY A. STRAUS

Wife-beating is an age-old pattern that recently has gained recognition as a pressing social problem. This transition from private trouble to public problem is reflected in policy and programmatic responses, including domestic violence legislation, shelters and other services for battered women, funds for research on and direct services to victims of abuse, and special agencies and commissions to generate and disseminate information, educational resources, and technical assistance to wife abuse programs and to the general public.

Official responses to social problems are not inevitable consequences of problem recognition. In the last decade social problem theorists have moved from a view of social problems as objective conditions that are harmful to the social unit to a view of social problems as conditions that are collectively recognized and defined as harmful (Becker, 1963; Blumer, 1971; Spector & Kitsuse 1973, 1977; Mauss, 1975, Ross & Staines, 1972). This new approach focuses on the processes by which issues are identified, legitimated, and responded to as social problems. Because resistance may be mobilized to prevent the emergence of a particular problem, each stage of the emergence process is problematic and requires explanation. In short, problem identification does not ensure legitimation, nor does legitimation ensure policy and programmatic responses to the problem.

Sociologists have focused empirical attention on the determinants of social problem identification, definition, and legitimation and largely have ignored the response-resolution stage. This study addresses this empirical gap and examines the determinants of programmatic responses to wife abuse. While some states have developed responses to wife-beating, others have not (Daniels, 1980). Moreover, there are large differences among "responders" in the extent and comprehensiveness of their efforts. This study explores these state-level differences in responses. Specifically, it investigates the determinants of between-state differences in the number of programs for battered women.

TYPES OF RESPONSE

Legislation

State-level responses to wife abuse generally have involved the enactment of legislation. As of 1980, 47 states passed some form of domestic violence legislation, assigning civil and/or criminal remedies for victims of domestic abuse.[1] Such legislation increasingly has created economic ties between states and wife abuse programs. Twenty-one states have passed legislation with appropriations for services, and six states have passed legislation imposing a surcharge on the marriage license, the funds from which are distributed to domestic violence programs.

While such legislation has created links between individual states and wife abuse programs, the nature of legislative appropriations makes such linkages tenuous at best. First, legislative appropriations generally involve relatively small amounts of money that provide only partial support for selected services. Second, such monies often are targeted for specific services (e.g., shelters, counseling, legal advocacy) and thus do not provide support for the range of necessary programmatic responses. Finally, appropriations are made for a limited time period (one or two years) and thus do not represent stable and ongoing funding sources. In sum, although some state monies now are available, wife abuse programs continue to be initiated and supported by community-based organizations and interest groups.

Local Services

Programs for battered women are locally organized responses to wife abuse that have been developed by a range of organizations, including YWCAs, community services agencies, health or mental health centers, child and family service agencies, and women's groups (Back, Bradley, Benson, & Miller, 1980a). While these community-based responses occur in all states, they do not occur to the same extent in all states (see Appendix A). The number of wife abuse services ranges from 2 in Mississippi to 78 in New York. What factors account for these state-level variations in the provision of wife abuse programs?

DETERMINANTS OF RESPONSE

State Characteristics

Although efforts to create programs for battered women are locally initiated, they also occur within specific state contexts. These efforts may be affected by characteristics of the states in which they occur. For example, affluent states may provide an economic environment with sufficient discretionary resources to generate local monies for wife abuse programs. Similarly, politically liberal states might contain a larger pool of support for such programs than conservative states. To explore this issue, we examined the effects of various state-level characteristics on the number of wife abuse services within each state.

Political scientists have systematically investigated the effects of state-level characteristics on public policy outcomes. The current study falls within this research tradition, in the sense that public policies and programs both constitute official responses to social problems. The major point of departure is that this study focuses on diferentials in community-level programmatic responses, while political scientists consistently have examined differentials in state-level policy responses, such as the incidence of particular state laws, the speed of adoption of such laws, and expenditures for state programs (Broach, 1979; Daniels, 1980; Hofferbert, 1966; Weber & Shaffer, 1972; Welch & Gottheil, 1978). Nonetheless, it is possible that variables that have been found to be related to state-level policy outputs may also be related to community-level programmatic outputs.

Political scientists primarily have focused on economic and political characteristics of states to explain differentials in policy. While there is ongoing debate about the relative influences of economic and political factors (Dawson & Robinson, 1963; Dye, 1966; Lewis-Beck, 1977), we have included both sets of independent variables in the current analysis. Based on previous findings, we expect affluent, politically liberal states to have more wife abuse services than less affluent, more conservative states.

Interest Groups

In addition, we incorporated a set of interest group variables that typically have been ignored in studies of the determinants of state policy.[2] Interest groups are defined as formal or informal groups of organizations which seek to shape the development and implementation of governmental policy and programs in a direction they favor (Zeigler & Huelshoff, 1980). The sociological literature suggests that the emergence and framing of social problems occur within a political context that is influenced by interest group activity (Blumer, 1971; Pfohl, 1977; Ross & Staines, 1972; Spector & Kitsuse, 1973). Groups with vested interests in particular issues mobilize to place those issues on the public agenda. Such interest group activity should have equal bearing on the extent and nature of official responses to social problems.

Interest groups can have direct and indirect effects on responses to social problems. Although such groups cannot directly pass or implement public policy, they can indirectly affect policy through their influence on policymakers and relevant third parties (Lipsky, 1968). Similarly, interest groups can have an indirect effect on programmatic responses to social problems by lobbying policymakers, bureaucrats, and professional groups for desired programs. However, they also can have a direct effect by initiating their own programs at a grass-roots level. Examples of these effects of interest groups exist within the realm of women's policies and programs (Freeman, 1975). Systematic lobbying and organizational efforts by feminist groups clearly have accelerated and intensified official responses to sex discrimination. In addition, these groups have directly initiated various programs and services to help women identify and overcome the obstacles of discrimination (e.g., consciousness-raising and support groups, women's health centers, women's law collectives, the National Organization for Women's Legal and Educational Defense Fund).

In a similar fashion, we expect the level of feminist organization within a state to be an additional determinant of the number of wife abuse services within that state. Furthermore, we predict that the organizational component is critical in this process. Individual-level feminist sentiment is not expected, in and of itself, to be strongly related to public responses to wife abuse. The pooling and mobilization of that sentiment into organized women's groups is viewed as a prerequisite for influencing policy outcomes.

The hypotheses of this study can be summarized as follows:

(1) The affluence, political liberalism, and level of feminist organization within individual states are positively related to the number of wife abuse services within those states.
(2) The level of feminist organization is a better predictor of the number of wife abuse services within individual states than affluence and political liberalism.
(3) Individual-level feminist sentiment that does not have an organizational base is not as strongly related to the number of wife abuse services within a state as is the level of feminist organization.

DATA AND METHOD

Control for Population Size

Multiple regression was used to test these hypotheses. It was necessary to control for state population, since populous states, as a function of their size, tend to have more wife abuse services than less populous states. This is indicated by the .83 correlation between state population size and the number of wife abuse services.

One way of controlling for population size would have been to transform the wife abuse services variable (and any explanatory variables that were strongly related to population size) into ratios with state population as the denominator. However, several researchers have shown that regressions done with ratio variables sharing a common denominator (e.g., x/z, y/z) may produce misleading results. Specifically, the correlation between two ratios may be greater than zero even though Rxy = Ryz = Rxz = 0 (Pearson, 1897). The "spurious" correlation exists in part because of the common denominator in the ratios.

An alternative method of avoiding the confounding effects of population size, while at the same time avoiding the problems of ratio data, is "residualization" (Schuessler, 1974; Fuguitt & Lieberson, 1974; Vanderbok, 1977; Bollen & Ward, 1979). A residualized variable is obtained by regressing the confounded variable on population and using the residuals (the deviations from the regression line) as a new variable. This produces a set of scores which measure the variance that is not associated with state population size.

Measures

Wife Abuse Services

The score on wife abuse services is the number of such programs located in each state. The data are from the two major directories of programs for battered women (Back, Blun, Nakhnikian, & Stark, 1980b; Center For Women's Policy Studies, 1980). The programs included in the directories provided one or more of the following services: housing, legal aid, counseling, support and educational programs, referrals, crisis aid, and victim advocacy. As explained above, to avoid the problems of ratio data, we created a residualized version of this variable. This measures variation in the number of wife abuse services in a state that is not a function of the state's population size.[3]

Affluence

The measure of state-level affluence is the average per capita income in 1977 for each state. We used the ratio form of income because the correlation between the component variables (state population and raw score personal income) was so high ($r = 99$). Since this is the only ratio included in the analyses, spurious correlation is not a problem.

Political Liberalism

One of the obstacles to the formulation of policy and programs for wife abuse victims is the pervasive notion that the family is a private domain which should not be monitored or regulated by outside parties. Wife abuse legislation or services thus represent an illegitimate invasion of public actors in family affairs.

Elazar's (1966) concept of political culture assesses individual conceptions of the limits on political and governmental action and thus represents a critical aspect of political liberalism for the study of domestic violence policy. He defined political culture as an indicator of the particular "orientation to political action in which each political system is embedded" (p. 84). Two of the dimensions of a state's political culture are its orientation toward government intervention in the community and toward the initiation of new programs (Sharkansky, 1969). These dimensions of political culture clearly are related to policy and programs regarding family violence.

Elazar identified three principal political cultures: moralist, individualist, and traditionalist. The moralist culture is most accepting of governmental intervention and new programs: the traditionalist culture is the least accepting; and the individualistic culture falls in the middle. In a study of state-level domestic violence legislation, Daniels (1980) found that the more traditionalist the state, the more limited the scope or comprehensiveness of its legislation. We expect a similar relationship between political culture and programs for battered women. To measure this aspect of political culture, we used an index developed by Sharkansky (1969) which operationalizes Elazar's concept. The index is coded from 1 (moralistic) to 9 (traditionalistic), with individualistic cultures coded as 5.

Interest Group Variables

The women's movement has been the dominant interest group involved in advocating for policy and programmatic responses to wife abuse. We thus focused on the National Organization for Women (NOW) in our interest group variables. While NOW's predominantly white, well-educated, and middle- to upper-class membership is not representative of all women, the group is the largest, mass-based feminist organization in the country. As such, state-level data on NOW membership and NOW groups serves as an indicator of the strength of feminist organization in each state.

We used two measures of interest group strength: the number of people in the state who are members of national-level NOW, and the number of local NOW groups in the state. Since both variables were strongly related to population size ($r = .88$ and $.89$, respectively), we regressed each individually on state population and used the residuals as the "NOW membership" and "NOW groups" variables.

Individual Feminist Sentiment

Individual feminist sentiment refers to pro-feminist attitudes that are not organizationally tied to the women's movement. Our measure of individual feminist sentiment is the number of copies of *Ms.* magazine sold for the March 1979 issue in each state. Since *Ms.* is the best-known and most successful feminist periodical, its sales serve as an indicator of feminist sentiment within each state. Specifically, purchasers of *Ms.* are assumed to hold relatively pro-feminist attitudes and beliefs. While these pro-feminist sentiments are held by individual consumers of the magazine, there is no indication that they are channeled into organized women's movement activity. As such, *Ms.* sales represent an indicator of individual rather than collective feminist sentiment.

Domestic Violence Legislation

The final variable assessed whether or not a state had passed domestic violence legislation as of June 1979 and, if so, whether the legislation included appropriations for services. Since states whose legislatures have passed domestic violence bills with funds for services should have more money for and thus more programs than other states, we felt it was important to control for the presence of such legislation. The legislation was scored so that 0 equals no state legislation, 1 equals the presence of a state law that does not allocate monies for services for battered women, and 2 equals the presence of a law with monies for services.

ECONOMIC, POLITICAL, AND INTEREST GROUP EFFECTS

The first column of Table 23.1 shows that the combination of the economic, political, and two interest group variables explains over half (53%) of the variance between states in the number of programs for battered women. The standardized beta coefficients for Model 1 of Table 23.1 indicate that the individual relationships of political culture, NOW membership, and NOW groups to wife abuse services are in the predicted direction. The less traditional a state's political culture and the greater its level of feminist organization, the more wife abuse services it has. However, contrary to our expectations, per capita income has virtually no effect on programs for battered women once the political culture and interest group variables are controlled.

The beta coefficients also indicate that the interest group variables are stronger determinants of wife abuse services than either per capita income or political culture. Models 2 and 3 directly compare the explanatory power of the interest group variables to that of the economic and political variables. The former explain twice as much variance in the number of wife abuse services in each state as the latter (52% versus 25%). In fact, adding either per capita income, political culture, or both variables to the interest group set does not significantly increase the amount of variance explained in the dependent variable. In other words, Model 1 does not explain significantly more variance in wife abuse services than does Model 3.

Feminist Sentiment Versus Feminist Organization

What is it about the NOW membership and NOW groups that has such a major impact on wife abuse services? Two possibilities exist, one representing an individualistic approach to interest groups and the other representing an organizational approach. On one hand, the National Organization for Women may be viewed as a group of individuals with pro-feminist attitudes and beliefs. Therefore, the larger NOW's membership, or the greater the number of local NOW groups, the more individuals in a state

TABLE 23.1   Regression of Wife Abuse Services on State-Level
Economic, Political, and Interest Group Variables

	Standardized Beta Coefficients		
	Model 1	Model 2	Model 3
Per capita income	−.02	.11	−
Political culture[a]	−.10	−.44	−
NOW membership	.46	−	.49
NOW groups	.37	−	.41
R^2	.53[b]	.25[c]	.52[d]

a. Scores on the political culture variable were not available for Alaska, Hawaii, and Washington, D.C.

b. $F = 12.23$; df + 4,43; $p \leqslant .001$

c. $F = 7.32$;   df = 2,45; $p \leqslant .01$

d. $F = 26.58$; df = 2,48; $p \leqslant .001$

who are ideologically or attitudinally predisposed to support wife abuse services. This is similar to Weber and Shaffer's (1972) conception of interest groups representing the "policy preferences of special publics." In this view the number of NOW groups and members enables one to estimate the level of individual feminist sentiment in each state.

On the other hand, from an organizational perspective NOW is more than the accumulation and manifestation of individual feminist sentiment or policy preferences. It is an organized interest group that acts collectively on behalf of its constituency. In the area of wife abuse, NOW has acted to mobilize members and others to develop, lobby for, and support domestic violence programs and policies. The number of NOW groups and members thus represents the level of feminist organization in each state.

Discriminant Validity of the NOW Measures

Although it is plausible to assume that the NOW groups measure is an indicator of the level of feminist organization over and above indicating feminist sentiment, empirical evidence in support of that assumption is needed. This is even more true of the NOW membership measure. To examine this issue we essentially tested the "discriminant validity" (Campbell & Fisk, 1959) of the two NOW measures by correlating them with a third measure—one which has no organizational component: the number of copies of the March 1979 issue of *Ms.* magazine sold in each state.

State-level sales of *Ms.* indicate the level of feminist sentiment in each state. However, reading *Ms.* is a purely individual matter. It does not involve membership in an organization. Therefore, high correlations between *Ms.* circulation and the two NOW variables indicate a lack of discriminant validity because this suggests that NOW membership and NOW groups do not reflect anything very different from the individual feminist sentiment presumably measured by reading *Ms.* If, however, the correlations are *low* this can be taken as evidence for the discriminant validity of the NOW measures because not all of the variance is accounted for by individual pro-feminist attitudes and beliefs as measured by reading *Ms.*

The correlations of *Ms.* magazine circulation with NOW membership and NOW groups (in raw score form) are -.03 and -.08. The correlations of *Ms.* with the two NOW variables residualized to control for state population size are .12 and .01. Since all four of these correlations are close to zero, we can conclude that the NOW variables do have discriminant validity, in the sense that they measure more than individual feminist sentiment in each state. We suggest that these two variables represent the level of feminist organization in the states.

Test of the Organization Theory

We can now address the issue of whether the level of feminist organization or individual feminist sentiment is a better predictor of programmatic response to domestic violence as measured by wife abuse services. The beta coefficients presented in Table 23.2 show that the two interest group variables are far more important determinants of wife abuse services than is pro-feminist sentiment as measured by *Ms.* readership.[4] Our interpretation of the relatively weak association of feminist sentiment with spouse abuse services is based on the assumption that supportive attitudes do not themselves create new programs. Organized efforts are necessary to communicate a need for the program, justify why money should be used for it as opposed to other programs, and plan and develop the program. As stated previously, interest groups may influence programmatic responses to social problems indirectly through lobbying relevant public agencies and actors and directly by starting programs on their own. They possess or have easier access to necessary resources (e.g., money, time, skills, contacts, staff) that individuals without an organizational base lack. Consequently, the level of feminist organization bears a stronger relationship to wife abuse services than does individual feminist sentiment.

DOMESTIC VIOLENCE LEGISLATION VERSUS INTEREST GROUP EFFECTS

The last stage of analysis considers whether a state has passed domestic violence legislation which funds shelters. The presence of such legislation should increase the number of programs for battered women in a state. This raises the question of whether the interest group variables have a significant effect on wife abuse services, once we account for domestic violence legislation. Moreover, the relationship between the NOW variables

TABLE 23.2   Regression of Wife Abuse Services on Individual Feminist Sentiment and the Level of Feminist Organization in Each State

	Regression Coefficient	Standard Error	Beta Coefficient
#*Ms.* copies sold	.00001	.00001	.18[b]
NOW membership	.58[a]	.126	.47
NOW groups	.54[a]	.132	.41
Constant = −.102 R^2 = .56[b]			

a. Coefficient is significant at the .01 level.

b. F = 19.81; df = 3,47; p ⩽ .001

and wife abuse programs may operate through the effect of the level of feminist organization on the passage of wife abuse laws. States with a strong base of feminist organization may have a more effective lobby and thus be more likely to pass legislation that funds shelters, which in turn may increase the number of wife abuse programs. As such, the level of feminist organization may affect wife abuse services indirectly through its effect on state domestic violence laws.

The beta coefficients presented in Table 23.3 indicate that each of the NOW variables has a greater relative effect on the number of wife abuse services in a state than does the legislative variable. In fact, adding the legislative variable to the NOW variables only increases the explained variance in wife abuse services by 4% (52% to 56%), which is not a statistically significant increment (F = .35). Finally, the notion that the NOW variables affect wife abuse services indirectly through their affect on the likelihood that a state has passed domestic violence legislation assumes a strong relationship between the NOW and legislative variables. However, the correlations between the NOW groups and domestic violence legislation and NOW members and legislation are relatively weak (r = .14 and .29, respectively). In sum, the level of feminist organization in a state is directly related to wife abuse services whether or not the state has passed domestic violence legislation which funds shelters.

CONCLUSION

This analysis indicates that the level of feminist organization in a state is a significant determinant of the number of wife abuse services in that state. Moreover, the level of feminist organization is a more potent predictor of programs for battered women than is per capita income, political culture, individual feminist sentiment, or domestic violence legislation that allocates funds for services.

TABLE 23.3   Regression of Wife Abuse Services on State Domestic Violence Legislation which Funds for Shelters and the Level of Feminist Organization

	Regression Coefficient	Standard Error	Beta Coefficient
Domestic violence legislation	.12[a]	.068	.19
NOW membership	.59[b]	.125	.48
NOW groups	.46[b]	.138	.35
Constant = −.07	R^2 = .56[c]		

a. Coefficient is nonsignificant at the .05 level.
b. Coefficient is significant at the .001 level.
c. F = 19.72; df = 3,47; p ⩽ .001

This study illustrates the importance of extending investigations of public responses to social problems beyond the level of federal and state policy to include programs initiated by local community and interest groups. Responses by nongovernmental units will be increasingly important to the extent that federal and state government retreat from promoting and funding social policies and programs.

Interest group influences are particularly important in examining local responses to social problems. Interest groups can have only indirect effects on state policy. Since they cannot pass legislation themselves, they must rely on lobbying, persuading, and pressuring policymakers. Moreover, many interest groups are organized most effectively at the national and local levels and thus lack the state-level organizational base to engage in state legislative battles. On the other hand, their base in local communities facilitates direct involvement in grass-roots programs responding to social problems. Finally, interest group initiation of such local programs can lead, over time, to subsequent federal and state support and funding.

How do interest groups choose between initiating programs themselves or lobbying policymakers and professionals groups to do so? Do they tend to develop grass-roots programs only after they have been unsuccessful in lobbying efforts, or do they view the initiation of such programs as an indirect lobbying technique? In the area of wife abuse, women's organizations began by developing programs and shelters for battered women. There are several reasons why they might have initially adopted this direct strategy. First, they may have viewed the need for services as so pressing that they were not inclined to use the time-consuming strategy of lobbying policymakers. Second, while involvement by policymakers and professional groups might have increased the resource base of the services, it also would have reduced direct control over the programs by women's groups. Finally, the development of services for battered women may have been viewed, at least in part, as a means of documenting the need for and feasibility of programmatic responses to wife abuse. Thus, grass-roots program development might have served as a more effective strategy for inducing policymakers to respond to the problem of wife abuse than more direct lobbying efforts.

The results of this study suggest that public responses to social problems are not predominantly a function of the availability of economic resources, political liberalism, or attitudinal support for policy and programs related to the problem. Given the number and diversity of pressing social problems, response to a particular issue depends on the existence of an interest group or coalition of groups that exerts pressure for the solution of that problem or that initiate responses on their own. In terms of wife abuse, this analysis shows that programmatic responses have been contingent on the presence of feminist organizations that have pressured policymakers to fund programs and that have directly developed such programs themselves.

APPENDIX A   Ranking of the Number of Wife Abuse Services in Each State

Rank	State	# of Wife Abuse Services	Rank	State	# of Wife Abuse Services per 100,000 women
1	N.Y.	78	1	ALAS	7.6
2	CAL	60	2	N.D.	4.2
3	PA	50	3	MONT	3.1
4	WASH	37	4	WASH	2.7
5	N.C.	31	5	NEBR	2.6
6	N.J.	29	6	D.C.	2.4
7	MINN	29	7	S.D.	2.3
8	MASS	27	8	VT	2.2
9	MICH	24	9	WYO	2.1
10	TEX	24	10	OREG	1.9
11	MD	22	11	MINN	1.9
12	ILL	21	12	N.M.	1.8
13	OHIO	20	13	DEL	1.8
14	WIS	20	14	COLO	1.6
15	FLA	19	15	N.C.	1.4
16	OREG	18	16	ME	1.4
17	NEBR	16	17	MD	1.4
18	CONN	16	18	R.I.	1.3
19	COLO	16	19	CONN	1.3
20	TENN	16	20	IDA	1.3
21	MO	15	21	W. VA	1.2
22	VA	15	22	MASS	1.2
23	IOWA	11	23	WIS	1.1
24	N.D.	10	24	PA	1.0
25	W. VA	9	25	N.Y.	1.0
26	KY	9	26	ARIZ	1.0
27	MONT	9	27	N.J.	1.0
28	ARIZ	9	28	IOWA	1.0
29	ALAS	9	29	HAWA	1.0
30	KANS	8	30	TENN	0.9
31	INDI	8	31	N.H.	0.9

APPENDIX A Continued

Rank	State	# of Wife Abuse Services	Rank	State	# of Wife Abuse Services per 100,000 women
32	N.M.	8	32	UTAH	0.9
33	D.C.	8	33	KANS	0.9
34	ME	6	34	NEV	0.9
35	LA	6	35	MO	0.8
36	S.D.	6	36	VA	0.8
37	R.I.	5	37	CAL	0.7
38	ALA	5	38	KY	0.7
39	OKLA	5	39	MICH	0.7
40	GA	5	40	FLA	0.5
41	DEL	4	41	TEX	0.5
42	VT	4	42	ILL	0.5
43	UTAH	4	43	OHIO	0.5
44	IDA	4	44	OKLA	0.5
45	HAWA	3	45	LA	0.4
46	N.H.	3	46	INDI	0.4
47	WYO	3	47	ALA	0.3
48	S.C	3	48	S.C.	0.3
49	NEV	2	49	GA	0.3
50	ARK	2	50	ARK	0.2
51	MISS	2	51	MISS	0.2

NOTES

1. For the purposes of this analysis, Washington, D.C. is included as a state.

2. Two exceptions to political scientists' tendency to ignore interest group effects in studies of state policy are Weber and Shaffer (1972) and Broach (1979).

3. Since extreme outliers affect the placement of the regression line and thus the size of the regression coefficients, we used a modified Windsorization procedure to pull in extreme deviant scores. In a normal distribution 99% of the scores fall within two and a half standard deviations from the mean. Thus we assigned the score representing that point to all extreme outliers. The variables that were transformed in this manner were state population size, wife abuse services, NOW membership, and the number of *Ms.* copies sold. In all cases the outlying states were either California or New York.

4. Three different multiple regressions are presented in this chapter. If the number of cases were larger, these could have been combined into one regression using all the independent variables together. However, the N of 51 limits the number of independent variables which can be included in the equation. If a large number of independent variables are used relative to the number of cases, erroneous results are quite likely; for example, such equations can result in "accounting for" more than 100% of the variance in the dependent variable.

REFERENCES

Back, S., Bradley, P., Benson, K., & Miller, S. Results of a questionnaire survey. In *Monograph on services for battered women.* Washington, DC: U.S. Department of Health and Human Services, 1980. (a)

Back, S., Blun, J., Nakhnikian, E., & Stark, S. *Spouse abuse yellow pages.* Denver: University of Denver, 1980. (b)

Becker, H. S. *Outsiders: Studies in the sociology of deviance.* New York: Free Press, 1963.

Blumer, H. Social problems as collective behavior. *Social Problems*, 1971, *18*, 298-306.

Bollen, K., & Ward, S. Ratio variables in aggregate data analysis. *Sociological Methods and Research*, 1979, *7*, 431-450.

Broach, G. T. Political power and policy benefits: Voting rights and welfare policy in Mississippi. In M. Palley & M. Preston (Eds.), *Race, sex, and policy problems*. Lexington, MA: D. C. Heath, 1979.

Campbell, D., & Fisk, D. Convergent and discriminant validation by the multitrait-multimethod matrix. *Psychological Bulletin*, 1959, *6*, 85-105.

Center for Women's Policy Studies. *Programs providing services to battered women*. Rockville, MD: National Clearinghouse on Domestic Violence, 1980.

Daniels, M. *Wife abuse and public policy: An analysis of the variation and speed of formulation*. Unpublished paper, Oklahoma State University, Stillwater, 1980.

Dawson, R., & Robinson, I. Inter-party competition economic variables and welfare policies in the American states. *Journal of Politics*, 1963, *25*, 265-289.

Dye, T. *Politics, economics, and policy: Policy outcomes in the American states*. Chicago: Rand McNally, 1966.

Elazar, D. *American federalism: A view from the states*. New York: Thomas Y. Crowell, 1966.

Freeman, J. *The politics of women's liberation*. New York: David McKay, 1975.

Fuguitt, G., & Lieberson, S. Correlation of ratios on difference scores having common terms. In M. Costner (Ed.), *Sociological methodology 1973-1974*. San Francisco: Jossey-Bass, 1974.

Hofferbert, R. The relation between public policy and some structural and environmental variables in the American states. *American Political Science Review*, 1966, *60*, 73-82.

Lewis-Beck, M. S. The relative importance of socioeconomic and political variables for public policy. *American Political Science Review*, 1977, *71*, 559-566.

Lipsky, M. Portest as a political resource. *American Political Science Review*, 1968, *62*, 1144-1158.

Mauss, A. L. *Social problems as social movements*. Philadelphia: J. B. Lippincott, 1975.

Pearson, K. On a form of spurious correlation which may arise when indices are used in the measurement of organs. *Proceedings of the Royal Society of London*, 1897, *60*, 489-498.

Pfohl, S. The "discovery" of child abuse. *Social Problems*, 1977, *24*, 310-321.

Ross, R., & Staines, G. L. The politics of analyzing social problems. *Social Problems*, 1972, *20*, 18-40.

Schuessler, K. Analysis of ratio variables. *American Journal of Sociology*, 1974, *80*, 379-396.

Sharkansky, I. The utility of Elazar's political culture. *Polity*, 1969, *2*, 66-83.

Spector, M., & Kitsuse, J. I. Social problems: A reformulation. *Social Problems*, 1973, *21*, 145-159.

Spector, M., & Kitsuse, J. I. *Constructing social problems*. Cummings Series in Contemporary Sociology. Menlo Park, CA: Cummings, 1977.

Vanderbok, W. On improving the analysis of ratio data. *Political Methodology*, 1977, *4*, 171-184.

Weber, R., & Shaffer, W. Public opinion and American state policy making. *Midwest Journal of Political Science*, 1972, *16*, 683-699.

Welch, S., & Gottheil, D. L. Women and public policy: A comparative analysis. *Policy Studies Journal*, 1978, *7*, 258-264.

Zeigler, H., & Huelshoff, M. Interest groups and public policy. *Policy Studies Journal*, 1980, *9*, 439-448.

About the Editors and Authors

RICHARD A. BERK is Professor of Sociology at the University of California, Santa Barbara. He has published widely in a number of social science journals, including *American Sociological Review, Social Science Research, Sociological Methods and Research, Law and Society Review,* and *Law and Policy Quarterly.* He is co-editor of *Evaluation Review* (formerly *Evaluation Quarterly*). His most recent books include *Money, Work and Crime: Experimental Evidence,* written with Peter H. Rossi and Kenneth J. Lenihan (Academic Press, 1980), and *Water Shortage: Lessons in Conservation from the Great California Drought,* written by Thomas Cooley, C. J. LaCivita, and Katharine Sredl (Abt Books, 1981). He is currently involved in several research projects on the criminal justice system, where policy concerns are paramount.

SARAH FENSTERMAKER BERK is Associate Professor of Sociology at the University of California, Santa Barbara. Her work has appeared in *Law and Society Review, Sociology of Work and Occupations, Social Science Research* and *Sociological Methods and Research.* Dr. Berk has also written (with R. A. Berk), *Labor and Leisure at Home: Content and Organization of the Household Day.* More recently, she edited the fifth volume of the Sage Yearbooks in Women's Policy Studies, *Women and Household Labor.* Her current research focuses on the socioeconomic determinants of domestic violence.

LEONARD BERKOWITZ is Vilas Research Professor of Psychology at the University of Wisconsin. Dr. Berkowitz has published over 60 articles on aggressive behavior and is author of the influential book, Aggression: *A Social-Psychological Analysis* (McGraw-Hill, 1962). He is editor of the prestigious Advances in Social Psychology Series and is currently President of the International Society for Research on Aggression.

ROBERT L. BURGESS is Professor of Human Development at Pennsylvania State University. He is a recognized scholar in the area of child abuse and neglect. He has been awarded several grants to continue his studies in this area, most notably *Project Interat: A Study of Patterns of*

Interactions in Abusive, Neglectful, and Control Families (National Center on Child Abuse and Neglect, 1978). He has published several articles, book chapters, and books, including *Behavioral Sociology* (Columbia University Press, 1969) and *Social Exchange in Developing Relationships* with Ted L. Huston (Academic Press, 1979).

DAVID L. CORWIN, M.D., is Co-Director of the Family Support Program, a treatment program for sexually abused children and their families at the Neuropsychiatric Institute, University of California, Los Angeles. His contribution to this volume was supported in part by a two-year Fellowship in Child Psychiatry at U.C.L.A. Dr. Corwin completed training in General Psychiatry at the U.C.L.A.-Sepulveda Veterans Administration Medical Center and is board-certified in psychiatry. He received his M.D. from Michigan State University and his B.S. degree from the University of Michigan.

RUSSELL P. and REBECCA E. DOBASH are both tenured faculty at the University of Stirling, Scotland. They have served as consultants for the British Department of the Environment and for HEW. They have also been involved in an SSRC French-Anglo exchange focusing on violence against women. Since 1974, they have worked closely with the National Women's Aid Federation (England and Wales) and the Scottish Women's Aid Federation. The have published numerous papers on domestic violence, as well as their highly influential book *Violence Against Wives* (Free Press, 1979).

JEFFREY A. FAGAN, PH.D. is a policy researcher and Principal of the URSA Institute. He has conducted program evaluation and policy research in crime and delinquency, youth development services, drug and alcohol programs, and law and justice. He was Principal Investigator for the National Family Violence Evaluation, a study of 25 federally funded domestic violence intervention programs. He is also Principal Investigator of the Violent Juvenile Offender Research and Development Program, a national initiative testing treatment and prevention models for chronically violent youths. He is the author of several articles and reports on crime and delinquency, juvenile justice, and violent behavior. He received his doctorate in policy sciences from the State University of New York at Buffalo.

DAVID FINKELHOR is Assistant Director of the Family Violence Research Program at the University of New Hampshire. His second book, *Sexually Victimized Children* (Free Press, 1979), has been highly acclaimed in the *New York Times Book Review* and in professional journals. He has received grants from the National Center on Child Abuse and Neglect and the National Center for the Prevention of Rape and has published articles in the *American Journal of Orthopsychiatry, Archives of Sexual Behavior,* and the *Journal of Marriage and Family Counselling.* He is currently working on this third book, *License to Rape* (Holt, Reinhart & Winston, 1983), an analysis of marital rape with Kersti Yllö.

ANNE FLITCRAFT is Research Associate at Yale Medical School and the Institution for Social and Policy Studies at Yale. She is a founding member of the New Haven Project for Battered Women and since 1978 has co-directed a study funded by NIMH titled "The Medical Contexts and Sequelae of Domestic Violence."

JAMES GARBARINO received his B.A. from St. Lawrence University in 1968 and his Ph.D. from Cornell University in 1973 in human development and family studies. He is currently Associate Professor of Human Development at the Pennsylvania State University. He is the author of more than 40 articles or chapters dealing with social development, adolescence, child welfare, and education. In addition, he has authored four books: *Protecting Children from Abuse and Neglect* (Jossey-Bass, 1980); *Understanding Abusive Families* (Lexington, 1980); *Successful Schools and Competent Students* (Lexington, 1981); *Children and Families in the Social Environment* (Aldine, 1982). He is the recipient of awards for research and writing from the American Educational Research Association, the American Library Association, the Woodlands Conference on Growth Policy, International Television and Film Festival, and the Kellogg Foundation. He has served as a consultant on youth and family issues to organizations including NBC News, the National Academy of Sciences, the National Committee for the Prevention of Child Abuse, the National Institute for Mental Health, and the U.S. Senate Human Resources Sub-Committee.

RICHARD J. GELLES is a professor in the Department of Sociology and Anthropology at the University of Rhode Island. His book, *The Violent Home* (Sage, 1974), was the first systematic empirical investigation of family violence and continues to be highly influential. He is also author of *Family Violence* (Sage, 1979) and co-author of *Behind Closed Doors: Violence in the American Family* with Suzanne Steinmetz and Murray Straus (Doubleday, 1980). Dr. Gelles has authored numerous articles on family violence and book chapters and has presented innumerable lectures to policy-making groups, practitioners, and media groups on family violence research. In 1979, he was a Research Fellow in the Family Development Study at Children's Hospital Medical Center, Boston.

DAIR L. GILLESPIE received her M.A. from the University of Houston and her Ph.D. from U.C. Berkeley. She is currently Assistant Professor of Sociology at the University of Utah. Her publications include works on marital power, social movements, and nonverbal behavior. She is now working on a study of sexual harassment for the Division of Personnel Management, State of Utah.

CATHY STEIN GREENBLAT is Professor of Sociology at Douglas College, Rutgers University. She has published several books and monographs and her articles appear in a number of social science journals. She was postdoctoral fellow in the Family Violence Research Program at the University of New Hampshire in 1979-1980. She is currently involved in a study of emotional relationships in the early years of marriage.

CHRISTINE R. HANNEKE is a research associate at Policy Research and Planning Group, Inc., in St. Louis. Her areas of research interest include interpersonal violence, social psychology, and evaluation research.

KAREN V. HANSEN, M.A. is a research associate for the URSA Institute. She is currently involved in the OJJDP Violent Juvenile Research and Development Program. Past research projects include a national evaluation of LEAA-funded Family Violence Programs and historical analysis of household labor. She received a Master's degree in sociology from the University of California, Santa Barbara.

ELLEN C. HERRENKOHL, PH.D., received her doctorate in clinical psychology from New York University. She is a Research Scientist in the Center for Social Research, Lehigh University and is in the private practice of clinical psychology.

ROY C. HERRENKOHL, PH.D., received his doctorate in social psychology from New York University. He is Professor of Social Psychology in the Lehigh University Department of Social Relations and Director of the Center for Social Research.

SHARON D. HERZBERGER received her B.A. in psychology from the Pennsylvania State University and her M.S. and Ph.D. degrees from the University of Illinois in Urbana-Champaign. After teaching for five years at Northwestern University, she moved to Trinity College in Hartford, Connecticut. In an ongoing research program, Dr. Herzberger has combined her interest in the causes and consequences of child abuse and a more general interest in social cognitive processes. Current investigations include an interview study designed to investigate the interpersonal perceptions of abusing and nonabusing parents and their children. Previous research and writings have concentrated on the cyclical hypothesis (Midwestern Psychological Association Conference paper, 1979), the perceptions of abused and nonabused children toward their parents (*Journal of*

Clinical and Consulting Psychology, 1981), the primary prevention of child abuse (*Infant Mental Health,* 1980), and the social definition of abuse (American Psychological Association Conference paper, 1982).

DEBRA KALMUSS is postdoctoral fellow in the Department of Social Relations at Johns Hopkins University. She received her Ph.D. from the University of Michigan and MSW from Bryn Mawr College. In 1980-1981, she was a postdoctoral fellow in the Family Violence Research Program at the University of New Hampshire. Her research interests include family violence, law and social science, and social policy. Her research appears in several social science journals, including the *European Journal of Social Psychology, Victimology,* and the *Journal of Marriage and the Family.*

ANN LEFFLER received her Ph.D. from the University of California at Berkeley, and is currently Assistant Professor of Sociology at Utah State University. She has published in the areas of social movements, theories of gender stratification, and nonverbal behavior. She is currently working on a study of sexual harassment for the Division of Personnel Management, State of Utah.

DONILEEN R. LOSEKE is Assistant Professor of Sociology at the State University of New York at Geneseo. Her past work has appeared in *Social Science Research, Law and Society Review,* and *Sociology of Work and Occupations.* Her current research focuses further on violence against women, with a particular interest in social structural responses to battered women.

JUDITH MARTIN is an assistant professor at the University of Pittsburgh School of Social Work. She is Chair of the Children and Youth Cluster at the school, a division of the Master's program that focuses on social services to children and their families. She is the author of *Gender Related Behavior of Children in Abusive Situations* (1978). With Dr. Alfred Kadushin, she has also co-authored a research work on parent/child interaction in abuse situations entitled *Child Abuse: An Interactional Event* (1981).

CLAIRE D. NALEPKA received her B.S. in nursing from Kent State University (1971) and her M.S. in nursing from the University of Kentucky (1973). She is presently working on her doctorate in education administration in higher education at the University of Akron. She is licensed to practice nursing by the State Board of Nursing in Ohio. She is currently employed as Assistant Professor in Nursing at Kent State University, where she teaches maternity and pediatric nursing. Mrs. Nalepka is particularly interested in the premature and high-risk newborn and has authored two articles related to this subject. She is a member of the American Nurses Association and the Association for the Advancement of Nursing Practice.

RICHARD O'TOOLE is Professor of Sociology at Kent State University. He received his Ph.D. at the University of Oregon and has taught at the University of Oklahoma, Case Western Reserve University, the University of Oregon, and Akron University. He has served as Research Director of Vocational Guidance and Rehabilitation Services, Cleveland, Ohio. His principal areas of interest, in addition to family violence, are medical sociology and symbolic interaction. He has authored several papers and articles, as well as editing *The Organization, Management and Tactics of Social Research* (1971) and *Roles for Sociologists in Service Organizations* (1973, with James E. Trela).

DAVID RAUMA is a Ph.D. candidate in the Department of Sociology, University of California, Santa Barbara. His interests include research methods and statistics, evaluation research, and criminology, and his dissertation will focus on the impact of transfer payments on the immediate postprison experiences of released offenders. His work has appeared in the *American Sociological Review,* the *Journal of Criminal Law and Criminology,* and *Social Science Research.* He is currently working on several research projects, including a study of long-term trends in the use of imprisonment in California and two studies of domestic violence.

RICHARD J. SEBASTIAN received his Ph.D. from the University of Wisconsin-Madison in 1974 and has been Assistant Professor of Psychology at the University of Notre Dame and a postdoctoral research fellow in the Family Violence Research Program at the University of New Hampshire. He is currently Assistant Professor of Organizational Behavior in the Whittemore School of Business and Economics at the University of New Hampshire. He has published articles and chapters on a number of social psychological issues, including human aggression and speech style and social evaluation.

NANCY M. SHIELDS is a research associate at Policy Research and Planning Group, Inc., in St. Louis. Her areas of research interest include interpersonal violence, social psychology, and research methodology.

EVAN STARK is Research Associate at Yale Medical School and the Institution for Social and Policy Studies at Yale. He is a founding member of the New Haven Project for Battered Women and since 1978 has co-directed a study funded by NIMH: "The Medical Contexts and Sequelae of Domestic Violence." He is also involved in research on the impact of job stress on families and children of working people.

DOUGLAS K. STEWART is Group Leader/Analysis at the URSA Institute. He holds a Ph.D. in sociology from the University of Pittsburgh and held an Office of Education postdoctoral fellowship in multivariate statistics. In addition to ongoing work in criminal justice related areas (violent juveniles, public defenders, juvenile criminal careers), he has a continuing interest in science and technology policy, including the evaluation of research programs and research portfolios. Journal articles have appeared in *Psychological Bulletin, Behavioral Science, American Behavioral Scientist, Social Science Information,* and *Western Political Quarterly.*

MURRAY A. STRAUS is Professor of Sociology and Director of the Family Research Laboratory at the University of New Hampshire. In addition to authoring over 100 articles on the sociology of the family, Dr. Straus has received numerous grant awards from the National Institute of Mental Health to conduct family violence research. He is co-editor, with Suzanne Steinmetz, of *Violence in the Family* (Harper & Row, 1974), and with Gerald Hotaling of *The Social Causes of Husband-Wife Violence* (University of Minnesota Press, 1980). He has also co-authored the results of the first national study of the incidence and causes of family violence in *Behind Closed Doors: Violence in the American Family* (Doubleday, 1980). Dr. Straus is past president of the National Council on Family Relations (1972-1973) and a recipient of the Ernest W. Burgess Award of the National Council of Family Relations for outstanding research on the family (1977).

KATHLEEN J. TIERNEY, Ph. D., teaches in the Department of Sociology at the University of California, Los Angeles. Formerly, she held a two-year postdoctoral traineeship in Mental Health Evaluation Research, funded by the National Institute of Mental Health, in the U.C.L.A. Department of Sociology. She received her Ph.D. in sociology from the Ohio State University in 1979. Her research interests include social movements, wife abuse, the sociology of health and mental health, and social responses to disasters.

LORI J. TOEDTER, Ph.D., received her doctorate in clinical psychology from the University of Connecticut. She is a research scientist in the Lehigh University Center for Social Research.

PATRICK TURBETT serves as an assistant professor in the Department of Sociology at the College of Arts and Sciences, State University of New

York at Potsdam. He received his B.A. from West Chester State College in 1973 and his Ph.D. from Kent State University in 1979. His interest in family violence began while working as a parent surrogate in a group cottage with abused and neglected children. He has additional experience and interest in the areas of mental health and social welfare. He serves as consultant for planning for the St. Lawrence County Community Services Board.

LENORE E. WALKER is a licensed psychologist and President of Walker and Associates, a consulting firm in Denver, Colorado. She is Associate Professor of Psychology at Colorado Women's College. She is also Founder and Director of Domestic Violence Institute, a nonprofit private institute which conducts research on family violence. As a recognized authority in the area of family violence, she has given numerous lectures, testified before Congress, published various articles and book chapters, and written a book on interviews with battered women, *The Battered Woman* (Harper & Row, 1979). She was awarded the 1979 Distinguished Media Award for this work by the Association for Women in Psychology.

LAURIE WARDELL graduated in philosophy from Lawrence University and is currently underemployed.

CAROLYN KOTT WASHBURNE, MSW, is an associate in Family Development at the Region V Child Abuse and Neglect Resource Center at the School of Social Welfare, University of Wisconsin-Milwaukee. She was a co-founder of Women in Transition, Inc., a women's counseling program in Philadelphia, and a founding board member of the Sojourner Truth House shelter for battered women in Milwaukee. She is the co-author of *Women in Transition: A Feminist Handbook on Separation and Divorce* (Scribners, 1975) and *For Better, For Worse: A Feminist Handbook on Marriage and Other Options* (Scribners, 1977).

KERSTI YLLÖ is Assistant Professor of Sociology at Wheaton College. In 1980-1981, she was a postdoctoral fellow in the Family Violence Research Program at the University of New Hampshire. She has published articles on interpersonal violence among cohabitors, marital rape, and family power. She is currently involved in the publication of the book, *License to Rape* (Holt, Rinehart & Winston, 1983) with David Finkelhor.

DATE DUE

Cat. No. 23-221

BRODART